The Scripture on the Ten Kings
and the Making of Purgatory
in Medieval Chinese Buddhism

Kuroda Institute
Studies in East Asian Buddhism

STUDIES IN EAST ASIAN BUDDHISM 9

The Scripture on the Ten Kings

and the Making of Purgatory in Medieval Chinese Buddhism

Stephen F. Teiser

A KURODA INSTITUTE BOOK
University of Hawaii Press
Honolulu

03 04 05 06 07 08   5 4 3 2 1

Library of Congress Cataloging-in-Publication Data
Teiser, Stephen F.
The scripture on the ten kings and the making of purgatory in
medieval Chinese Buddhism / Stephen F. Teiser.
p.   cm. — (Studies in East Asian Buddhism ; 9)
"A Kuroda Institute Book"
Includes bibliographical references and index.
ISBN 0–8248–1587–4
ISBN 0–8248–2776–7 (pbk.)
1. Eschatology, Buddhist.   2. Shih wang ching—Criticism,
interpretation, etc.   3. Hell—Buddhism.   4. Buddhism—China—
Doctrines.   I. Shih wang ching. English.   II. Title.
III. Series.
BQ4485.T45   1994
294.3'423—dc20   94-2531
CIP

The Kuroda Institute for the Study of Buddhism and Human Values is
a nonprofit, educational corporation founded in 1976. One of its primary
objectives is to promote scholarship on the historical, philosophical,
and cultural ramifications of Buddhism. In association with the University
of Hawai'i Press, the Institute also publishes Classics in East Asian
Buddhism, a series devoted to the translation of significant texts
in the East Asian Buddhist tradition.

University of Hawai'i Press books are printed on acid-free
paper and meet the guidelines for permanence and durability
of the Council on Library Resources.

Publication of this book has been assisted by a
grant from the Chiang Ching-kuo Foundation
for International Scholarly Exchange.

Designed by Kenneth Miyamoto

In memoriam
Anna K. Seidel

Contents

Contents

List of Illustrations

Plates 1a–14c follow page 179

Preface

MY FIRST GLIMPSE of the materials studied in this book was not terribly auspicious. My passport was stolen while I traveled on a train by hard berth (i.e., second class, in a country where third class does not in principle exist) in India in February 1981. Returning home after spending a few years in Asia, I had decided to make a quasi-scholarly pilgrimage to holy places in South and Southeast Asia. I was en route from Gayā, the nearest railhead to Bodhgayā, where the historical Buddha achieved enlightenment, to New Delhi, a convenient jumping-off point for visiting Buddhist sites in the Northwest. When I readied my backpack to disembark at Delhi, I discovered I had no passport, travelers' checks, or camera. After filling out a police report, I proceeded by bus not to the Sunny Guest House, where I had originally planned to stay in a dormitory room for one dollar a night, but to the opulent Ashok Hotel, where the manager took pity on me and accepted my sole remaining valuable (a VISA credit card) for a room with hot running water, meals, and some spending money. I spent the next day at the U.S. Consulate, initiating the paperwork to receive a new passport.

The next three days in New Delhi provided my first, unplanned introduction to the medieval treasures unearthed in the Grottoes of the Thousand Buddhas (Ch'ien-fo-tung) or the Caves of Unsurpassed Height (Mo-kao-k'u) near the town of Tun-huang in modern Kansu Province in China. A large cache of paintings and manuscripts, the latter consisting mostly of Buddhist scriptures, had been deposited in the Museum for Central Asian Antiquities (now called the Central Asian Department of the National Museum of India) in New Delhi by Marc Aurel Stein (1862–1943). Like many Jewish families in Budapest, Stein's parents had their son (but not their daughter) baptized in the Lutheran church. That Protestantization allowed him access to higher education in Vienna, Leipzig, Tübingen, and London in the area of Indo-Iranian philology. For over ten years he held academic and archaeological positions in India, but, styling himself an explorer, he sought to chart the ancient Silk Road between China and the West. Permission from Her Majesty's government finally came in 1899, and in the following year Stein embarked on the first of three expeditions across Chinese Turkestan. On the second expedition (1906–1907) he was able to bribe Wang Yüan-lu, a local priest at the Tun-huang caves, to part with over 15,000 texts, paintings, and artifacts that had been sealed behind an unused shrine room in the eleventh century. The Sinologist Paul Pelliot (1878–1945) arrived late in 1907 to collect a batch for the French government, and over the next several years teams from Prussia, Japan, Russia, and Sweden crisscrossed Central Asia, nominally under the control of a strife-torn China, and sent booty back home. Stein's cache resided in the basement of the British Museum, where none other than Arthur Waley compiled a catalogue of paintings (published in 1931) and Lionel Giles began work on a catalogue of the manuscripts (published in 1957). Stein, who had already become a British subject, was knighted in 1912. Stein's "discoveries" were divided between England and India. In accord with its three-fifths share in funding Stein's reconnaissances, the government of India received about three hundred of the original five hundred paintings plus some manuscripts, mostly in Indian languages, housed where I saw them in the National Museum in New Delhi. Most of the written texts, including manuscripts and early printed editions, were assigned to the British Library.

The discovery of the Tun-huang manuscripts and the development of the field of Tun-huang studies have fundamentally changed the modern understanding of Chinese Buddhism and medieval Chinese society. The Tun-huang corpus contains unprecedented sources on Chinese economy (land contracts, loan agreements, purchase receipts, tax documents), folk life (divination books, almanacs, marriage etiquettes, funeral invitations), and literature (primers, copybooks, commentaries on the classics, vernacular entertainments), to name but a few of the fields revolutionized by the finds at Tun-huang. Historians of Chinese art have only begun to study in detail the overwhelming number of statues and wall paintings in the nearly five hundred surviving caves. The largest portion of the written corpus is related to Chinese Buddhism. The manuscripts walled up behind what is now cave number seventeen probably originated in the libraries of two Buddhist monasteries near Tun-huang. They comprise not only copies of well-known Buddhist texts like the *Lotus* and *Diamond* sūtras, but also thousands of prayers made by the donors who commissioned the copying of scriptures; lists of the holdings of monastery libraries; population registers from local temples; otherwise unknown texts, in a variety of languages, dealing with philosophical matters; funerary banners, hanging silk paintings, and painted paper scrolls depicting nearly the entire pantheon of medieval Chinese Buddhism; sermons and scriptures from the early stages of what later became the Ch'an (Zen) school; membership lists, newsletters, and club rules for small groups of Buddhist lay people; liturgies for confession, memorial rites, and the transfer of merit; and a large number of Chinese indigenous scriptures (so-called apocrypha), that is, texts written anonymously in China to answer specifically Chinese concerns, but which attempted to mimic the style and substance of scriptures translated from Indic originals into Chinese.

Some years after traveling to India, my itinerary trimmed to major Sinological libraries closer to home (Vermont, Southern California, New Jersey), I began to explore the significance of the Tun-huang finds for the study of Chinese Buddhism. Aware that grant agencies were conscious of productivity, I settled on what I thought would be a fascinating but easily managed topic, the study of a tenth-century apocryphal text describing purgatory and of its immediate historical context. The text, *The Scripture on the Ten Kings,* survived in over thirty manuscript copies from Tun-huang, most of which were accessible on microfilm; it had been the subject of good secondary studies by Japanese scholars in the 1940s and 1950s; and it was a logical successor to some of my earlier work, which examined the interaction between Chinese religion and Buddhism in the mythology and rituals of a slightly earlier period. The *Ten Kings* sūtra was the first surviving exposition of a multifaceted system that came to dominate Chinese culture after the medieval period in which it was born; more than just a theory about the afterlife, it resembled a complex *habitus* involving ritual, the practice of morality, concepts of personhood, the social hierarchy, and the institution of bureaucracy. As my research progressed, I realized that a simplistic presentation of text and context did justice neither to the evidence nor to the need to think through the texts and come to grips with the religious life of which they were merely one small part. I therefore began to shift the way I conceived of the project, trying to take seriously both the idea of purgatory as a vision of a necessary but terrifying passage to the next life and the practices—the prayers, funerals, memorial observances, telling of stories, sermons, songs, dreams, and picture-shows—by which the idea was created and sustained. Consequently, much of this book is filled with what come close to being ethnographic details about medieval religion. I have placed special emphasis on the particulars of Buddhist piety, because outside of the Tun-huang materials they are usually either unavailable or derided. As scholars of European history have taught us, one way to advance the study of medieval society is to focus on, rather than to presume or to summarize, everyday religious life. The first two parts of this book are not intended to be a

derivative study of the background to a more fundamental text; by placing a consideration of ritual (Part One) and textual practice (Part Two)
before the annotated translation in Part Three, I hope to invert the
usual priority of *textus receptus* over everything else.

The approaches I have cobbled together are the ones I have found
most helpful in trying to understand what some of my students like to
call "real Buddhism." I have drawn on a variety of fields, in some of
which I am a rank beginner, as the evidence allows: philology and linguistic analysis, the history of Buddhism and Chinese religions, the
social history of medieval China and the local history of Tun-huang, the
technology of writing and book-production, and art history. The most
daunting and at the same time the most rewarding foray I have had to
make is into the field of Tun-huang studies. From the time of their "discovery" in 1907 well into the 1970s, the Tun-huang manuscripts and
artistic materials had been the subject of study by a few dozen Chinese,
Japanese, and European scholars. Microfilms of many of the original
manuscripts could be consulted at a few institutions each in North
America, Western Europe, the Soviet Union, China, and Japan; facsimile reproductions were beginning to appear; and once the academic
codes for designating the manuscripts had been broken, one could reasonably expect to finish reading the secondary scholarship on any particular topic within about one undisturbed year. With the calming of the
chaos wrought by the Cultural Revolution in the People's Republic of
China in the late 1970s and early 1980s, the entire field entered a
renaissance, ushered largely by Chinese scholars. From all corners of
China they brought as-yet-unknown manuscripts out of storage, publishing descriptions of the "newly discovered" materials and initiating
their dissemination to the world through photographic editions. And
they brought together scholars of the highest caliber from a variety of
traditional disciplines to cooperate in reassessing our knowledge of the
Chinese past. Their efforts have been echoed and redoubled by well-
funded research teams in Japan and France, and by individual scholars
working in Japan, Europe, and the United States. If this book has any
value to the international academic community, I hope that it is to demonstrate what the recently reborn field of Tun-huang studies can contribute to our understanding of a small but significant slice of Chinese
Buddhism.

A word should also be said about what this book does not attempt to
do. With some exceptions the evidence gathered here comes from
China between the years 650 and 1000; Part Two in particular looks
almost exclusively at Northwest China in the tenth century. To expand
that framework would have meant writing a different kind of book. A
competent overview in English of Chinese, Buddhist, and Chinese Buddhist concepts of the afterlife remains to be written. In articles published

elsewhere I have begun to move in that direction, but it is hard to imagine improving upon Paul Mus's inspired study of Buddhist concepts, especially in South and Southeast Asia (*La lumière sur les six voies*, published in 1939) or Sawada Mizuho's learned, captivating account of Chinese and Japanese beliefs (*Jigoku hen*, published in 1964). In both history and anthropology in the past twenty years death has, it seems, come back to life. Work by such authors as Phillipe Ariès, Maurice Bloch, and Jacques Le Goff exercises a deservedly strong influence on the study of *homo mortus*. Nevertheless, aside from occasional theoretical elaborations—which some readers may already consider excessive—the comparative implications of the Chinese Buddhist notion of purgatory lie outside the scope of this study. Parallels to conceptions of purgatory in late antiquity, Islam, medieval Europe, and other cultures are enticing and deserve to be treated at greater length elsewhere.

Despite its limitations, this book could not have been written without the kind assistance of a number of individuals and institutions, to whom I would like to express my heartfelt gratitude. My research on this project culminated in a week in 1992 spent at the Tun-huang Research Academy (Tun-huang yen-chiu-yüan), a ten-minute walk south in the desert from the Mo-kao caves near Tun-huang. The Director of the Institute, Tuan Wen-chieh, arranged for me to see otherwise inaccessible caves, to examine manuscripts, and to meet with two research fellows working in related areas. Shih P'ing-t'ing shared with me her unpublished work on tenth-century Tun-huang, and she and Li Cheng-yü personally unrolled two scrolls for us to read together. Yu Jen-te, Director of Display and Preservation at the Tientsin Art Museum (T'ien-chin-shih i-shu po-wu-kuan), allowed me to examine a long text from Tun-huang. Along with my host, Li Shih-yü, we spent a memorable afternoon in Tientsin. I also spent two weeks in Peking studying Tun-huang documents at the National Library of China (Pei-ching t'u-shu-kuan), thanks to the Director of Rare Books, Fang Kuang-ch'ang. His staff was extremely helpful in locating materials, and the Deputy Director of the library, T'ang Shao-ming, provided hospitality. The general host for my stay in China was Wang Pang-wei, Associate Professor in the Department of Foreign Languages at Peking University (Pei-ching ta-hsüeh), who brought new meaning to the concept of graciousness. He amassed the sheaf of official letters required to conduct academic business in China, and together with Feng Tan he put together ideal lodgings and the tastiest Szechwanese meal available in Peking. Pai Hua-wen, Professor Emeritus at Peking University, served as my unofficial host, offering encouragement and letters at every turn.

Monique Cohen, Chief Curator of the Division of Oriental Manuscripts at the Bibliothèque nationale, generously opened the Pelliot collection of manuscripts for study when I visited Paris in 1990. At the

Musée Guimet Jacques Giès, Curator of Chinese Painting, guided me
through the Pelliot collection of art. Michel Soymié, Director of the
Équipe de Dunhuang, sponsored jointly by the Centre Nationale de la
Recherche Scientifique and the École Pratique des Hautes Études,
welcomed me warmly to the meetings of the group. Kristofer Schipper,
among other posts the Director of the Institut des Hautes Études Chinoises, shared Taoist liturgical texts from his own collection and made
my time in Paris, both inside and outside the library of the Institut, go
happily. Franciscus Verellen, now a member of the École Française
d'Extrême-Orient, hosted me and helped to negotiate the many do-
mains of French Sinology.

In 1990 I also visited London. Elizabeth McKillop, Curator of the
Chinese Collection at the British Library, showed me numerous manuscripts and educated me about the history of the Stein collection. At the
British Museum Anne Farrer, Assistant Keeper of Oriental Art, helped
me view some of the Stein paintings. Roderick Whitfield, Director of
the Sir Percival David Foundation of Chinese Art, took time out from a
busy schedule to share his knowledge of medieval art. My time in England went smoothly, thanks to the help and advice of Timothy Barrett,
Head of the Department of History at the School of Oriental and African Studies of the University of London.

Colleagues and friends have helped immeasurably in my efforts to
transform research into writing. Jan Nattier signed up for the project at
an early stage, guiding me through scholarship on Central Asia and,
with the help of Kahar Barat, translating Uighur texts. Several scholars
shared their unpublished research and encouraged me through many
stages of writing: Jean-Pierre Drège, Bernard Faure, Lothar Ledderose, Victor H. Mair, Michel Strickmann, and Chün-fang Yü. Many
people responded helpfully and critically to material presented in lectures at various institutions, including University of California at Los
Angeles, Harvard University, University of Illinois at Champaign-
Urbana, University of Michigan, National Central Library (Taipei),
Peking University, University of Pennsylvania, Princeton University,
and University of Southern California. Others offered suggestions on
earlier drafts or assisted in producing the book: Stanley Abe, John Blazejewski, Alan Cole, Edward L. Davis, Jean DeBernardi, Glen Dud-
bridge, Patricia B. Ebrey, Wen Fong, John G. Gager, Robert M.
Gimello, Howard L. Goodman, Peter N. Gregory, Helen Hardacre,
Robert Hymes, Matthew Kapstein, Terry Kleeman, Li-ying Kuo, William R. LaFleur, Miriam Levering, Fu-shih Lin, Yang Lu, Jennifer
Noering McIntire, John R. McRae, Frederick W. Mote, Susan Na-
quin, Ch'iang Ning, Anita O'Brien, Charles D. Orzech, Daniel L.
Overmyer, Robert Sharf, Jacqueline I. Stone, Jeffrey Stout, Kyoko
Tokuno, Timothy Y. H. Tsu, and Stanley Weinstein. The staff of Gest

Oriental Library has been extremely helpful in locating various materials; I am especially indebted to Antony Marr, Martin Heijdra, and Soowon Kim.

I am fortunate to have been given the time and space needed to complete this project on purgatory, which corresponds more or less, fortuitously or not, to my term as an assistant professor. Between 1987 and 1992 I submitted twelve separate grant applications, not an unusually high number for humanities scholars. Organizations that have provided leave time, travel funds, or research materials include the D. T. Suzuki Preceptorship at Princeton University, the Translations program and the Travel to Collections program of the National Endowment for the Humanities, and the University Committee on Research in the Humanities and Social Sciences at Princeton University.

My family has been an unending source of pleasure and has endured the uncertainties of writing far more gracefully than have I. Virginia W. Jackson has been an inspiration. She insisted that I think reflectively about what I was writing about, especially when I was most prone to hide under technicalia. Her raised eyebrow has done away with many infelicities in my prose, and her patience and forbearance in her own work and in our life together made this project possible in the first place. Our two children, each born during years when I was on research leave, helped me in more ways than I can tell.

As I was just beginning to define this project, mutual friends put me in touch with Anna K. Seidel, formerly of the Kyoto section of the École Française d'Extrême-Orient. Although the major part of her work was devoted to early Taoism, Anna probably had a better scholarly understanding of the Chinese Buddhist concept of purgatory than anyone else in the world. She wrote only a few, very short articles on the topic, but what she did not publish she shared, out of reflex, with anyone who asked. Anna taught as a Visiting Professor at the University of California at Santa Barbara for several months in 1987 and 1988 when I was living in Los Angeles, which allowed me to experience first-hand the compassion and intellectual charm for which she was famous. This world suffered a great loss when she passed away in San Francisco in September 1991, and it is to her memory that the merits of this book are dedicated.

Abbreviations and Conventions

AM	*Asia Major*
BEFEO	*Bulletin de l'École Française d'Extrême-Orient*
BN, *Catalogue*	Bibliothèque nationale, Département des Manuscrits, *Catalogue des manuscrits chinois de Touen-houang (Fonds Pelliot chinois)*
BSOAS	*Bulletin of the School of Oriental and African Studies*
Cft (L) or (ND)	"Ch'ien-fo-tung," numbered paintings and objects from Tun-huang, (L) held in British Museum, London; (ND) held in National Museum of India, New Delhi
Chang, *Ta-tz'u-tien*	Chang Ch'i-yün, *Chung-wen ta-tz'u-tien*
DBZ	*Dainihon bukkyō zensho*
Demiéville, *Hōbōgirin*	Paul Demiéville et al., eds., *Hōbōgirin: dictionnaire encyclopédique du bouddhisme d'après les sources chinoises et japonaises*
Dhk	Numbered manuscripts from Tun-huang in Dun'-khuanskogo Fonda held in Instituta Narodov Azii, St. Petersburg
EO	"Extrême-Orient," numbered paintings held in Musée Guimet (formerly in Louvre), Paris
Giles, *Catalogue*	Lionel Giles, *Descriptive Catalogue of the Chinese Manuscripts from Tunhuang in the British Museum*
HJAS	*Harvard Journal of Asiatic Studies*
Huang, *Pao-tsang*	Huang Yung-wu, *Tun-huang pao-tsang*
IBK	*Indogaku bukkyōgaku kenkyū*

Ikeda, *Shikigo*	Ikeda On, *Chūgoku kodai shahon shikigo shūroku*
JA	*Journal Asiatique*
Komazawa, *Daijiten*	Komazawa daigaku zengaku daijiten hensanjo, *Zengaku daijiten*
Lamotte, *Traité*	Étienne Lamotte, *Le traité de la grand vertu de sagesse de Nāgārjuna*
Mair, "Inventory"	Victor H. Mair, "Lay Students and the Making of Written Vernacular Narrative: An Inventory of Tun-huang Manuscripts"
Men'shikov, *Opisanie*	Lev N. Men'shikov et al., *Opisanie Kitaiskikh Rukopisei*
MG	Numbered paintings and objects held in Musée Guimet, Paris
MIK	Numbered items held in Museum für Indische Kunst, Berlin
Mochizuki, *Daijiten*	Mochizuki Shinkō, *Bukkyō daijiten*
Morohashi, *Jiten*	Morohashi Tetsuji, *Dai kanwa jiten*
Nakamura, *Daijiten*	Nakamura Hajime, *Bukkyō go daijiten*
Ono, *Daijiten*	Ono Gemmyō, *Bussho kaisetsu daijiten*
P	Numbered manuscripts from Tun-huang in Fonds Pelliot chinois held in Bibliothèque nationale, Paris
P tib.	Numbered manuscripts from Tun-huang in Fonds Pelliot tibétain held in Bibliothèque nationale, Paris
Pelliot/Lu, "Shu-mu"	Paul Pelliot, "Pa-li t'u-shu-kuan tun-huang hsieh-pen shu-mu," trans. Lu Hsiang
Pk and Pk *hsin*	Numbered manuscripts from Tun-huang held in National Library, Peking
S	Numbered manuscripts from Tun-huang in Stein collection held in British Library, London
Sakai, "Jūō shinkō"	Sakai Tadao, "Jūō shinkō ni kan suru shomondai oyobi *Enraō juki kyō*"
San	Numbers assigned to "miscellaneous" manuscripts from Tun-huang in Wang, *So-yin*
Sch	Numbering system for works in *Tao-tsang* in Kristofer Schipper, *Concordance du Tao-tsang*

T	*Taishō shinshū daizōkyō,* ed. Takakusu Junjirō, Watanabe Kaigyoku
TB, *Mokuroku*	Tōyō bunko tonkō bunken kenkyū iinkai, ed., *Seiiki shutsudo kanbun bunken bunrui mokuroku,* 4 vols.
TG	*Tōhō gakuhō* (Kyoto)
Th Institute	Numbered manuscripts from Tun-huang held in Tun-huang yen-chiu-yüan, Tun-huang, Mo-kao-k'u
Th Museum	Numbered manuscripts from Tun-huang held in Tun-huang-hsien po-wu-kuan, Tun-huang
Th Cave	Numbers assigned to Tun-huang caves by Tun-huang yen-chiu-yüan
Tokushi, "Kōzō"	Tokushi Yūshō, "*Jūō shōshichi kyō* sanzuken no kōzō"
Tp	Numbered manuscripts from Tun-huang held in Kuo-li chung-yang t'u-shu-kuan, Taipei
TP	*T'oung Pao*
TT	*(Cheng-t'ung) Tao-tsang*
Tts	Numbered manuscripts from Tun-huang held in T'ien-chin-shih i-shu po-wu-kuan, Tientsin
Tu, *Chiao-lu yen-chiu*	Tu Tou-ch'eng, *Tun-huang pen fo-shuo shih-wang ching chiao-lu yen-chiu*
V-N, *Bannières*	Nicole Vandier-Nicolas, *Bannières et peintures de Touen-houang conservés au Musée Guimet*
Waley, *Catalogue*	Arthur Waley, *A Catalogue of Paintings Recovered from Tun-huang by Sir Aurel Stein*
Wang, *So-yin*	Wang Chung-min, *Tun-huang i-shu tsung-mu so-yin*
Whitfield, *Art*	Roderick Whitfield, *The Art of Central Asia: The Stein Collection in the British Museum*
WW	*Wen-wu*
Z	*Dainihon zokuzōkyō*
repr.	reprint/reprinted in
reprod.	reproduced photographically in
trans.	translated by/in
transcr.	transcribed in/by/as

In translating from the Chinese I have tried to be as lexically precise as possible, while still trying to maintain an ear for both Chinese and English usage. Chinese words are transliterated in the Wade-Giles system, modified slightly by eliding superfluous diacritical marks (e.g., *she* instead of *shê*). Modern Mandarin, of course, differs considerably from the phonology of ancient Chinese, but reproducing the medieval pronunciations of all Chinese words would have been overly cumbersome. Where it is essential I rely on Karlgren, *Grammata Serica Recensa.* Variants in medieval manuscripts are often quite considerable. In general I try to make sense of unusual readings, and then offer emendations based on attested variants.

Chinese Buddhist vocabulary presents its own set of problems. When foreign (Sanskrit) words appear in the original Chinese, I render the word in Sanskrit, thus approximating in English the same mixture of native and foreign words as that in the original. In annotations I offer Sanskrit equivalents for some of the more important technical terms, but they are not intended to be philologically exhaustive, only to serve as a reference point for further research in Indic and Central Asian languages. All translations are my own unless otherwise noted.

One major departure from modern American academic style is the placement of note numbers within the text. Note numbers precede, rather than follow, extracts so that the reader is presented first with all information concerning the primary source and any secondary studies and then with notes addressing the interpretation and translation of specific words within the quote.

In discussing manuscripts, I try to use the designations currently in use in the various Tun-huang collections. My references are to the recto side unless verso (abbreviated as v) is explicitly noted. I refer to the unique manuscript (e.g., Pk *hsin* 836) rather than to the name of the text (e.g., *Ni-ts'e chan*) whenever details about textual variants, paleography, codicology, or dating are important. The bibliography contains a separate listing of manuscripts from Tun-huang. In notes I try to provide just one published source—either the clearest or the most readily accessible—in which to find the manuscript, either transcribed in print or reproduced photographically. (It is hoped that over the next fifteen years high-quality facsimile reproduction of most of the Tun-huang manuscripts will render most of those references obsolete.)

References to works bound in a traditional Chinese format include *chüan* number, page number, and side (e.g., 9.4v–10r, indicating *chüan* 9, pages 4 verso to 10 recto). When a traditional book is reproduced photographically in a work with modern pagination, modern pagination is added in parentheses. References to multivolume works in modern format include volume, page, and column (e.g., 2:703b, indicating volume 2, page 703, column b).

Dates are given in their Chinese order first (reign-name and year, sexagenary cycle/month/day, e.g., Ch'ang-hsing 5, *chia-wu*/VI/15) and then in their Western form (e.g., 29 July 934). In matters of chronology I rely on Tung, *Chung-kuo nien-li tsung-p'u,* and Hiraoka, *Tōdai no koyomi.* In translating office titles I generally follow Hucker, *A Dictionary of Official Titles in Imperial China,* for government positions, and Weinstein, *Buddhism under the T'ang,* for offices in the Buddhist order.

1. Introduction

The Idea of Purgatory

Humble and obscure in origin, aggressively diverse in its sources, *The Scripture on the Ten Kings* is one of the most obvious signals of the birth of a new concept of the afterlife in medieval Chinese Buddhism. That vision of the hereafter and its social realization are sufficiently analogous to the medieval European situation to merit the label of "purgatory," which may be defined as the period between death and the next life during which the spirit of the deceased suffers retribution for past deeds and enjoys the comfort of living family members. *The Scripture on the Ten Kings* was probably written in China in the ninth century, based on notions that crystallized sometime in the seventh. However, the historical significance of the idea of purgatory is not limited to medieval China. The fruit of a collaboration between Indic and Chinese civilizations, it in turn gave rise to new ideas and practices in Korea and Japan. Furthermore, for anyone who has watched a popular Chinese drama, read a morality book, looked at temple decorations, seen the burning of spirit-money, or attended a funeral service, purgatory remains a defining feature of modern Chinese culture. In contrast to the allegedly this-worldly humanism and meritocracy thought to define Neo-Confucianism, purgatory represents, literally, the dark side of Chinese civilization.

In theory purgatory is easily delimited in both time and space. It lasts from the moment of death until the spirit of the deceased is reborn in another bodily form, usually in the third year after death. Just as important as the beginning and ending points are the gradations marking the passage of time. During the first forty-nine days after death the dead person passes a critical juncture every seven days. The timing of the "seven seven" rites derives from Buddhism; in Tibet the same stretch is described in the *Bardo Thödol* (popularly known in the West as *The Tibetan Book of the Dead*). In the Chinese case the journey of the spirit is viewed less in psychological terms and more as a bureaucratic experience. On every seventh day the deceased, pictured as a prisoner, must undergo a trial administered by a judge. After the court clerks and jailers assemble the requisite paperwork and the mourning family dispatches acceptable gifts, the magistrate issues a judgment and sends the inmate to the next court. To the first seven nodes are added three more, based not on Indian but on Chinese custom. They occur on the one hundredth day, during the first month after the first full year, and during the third year after death. The location of purgatory is slightly more vague than its duration. There is no doubt that it is situated low in the

1

scheme of things: one of the terms most commonly used to refer to purgatory is "underground prisons" *(ti-yü)*, which, however, also designates the realm of hell to which one can be assigned after the last trial. In addition to its subterranean quality, purgatory is marked by a unique topography, including the River Nai (or "River of No Recourse," Naiho), which all shades must cross soon after death, and a large wheel of fortune from which they are projected into their next life. The space of purgatory also has an existential impact beyond its objective delineation. Magistrates always appear fully and formally dressed, positioned behind an elevated bench. Their prisoners are clad only in undergarments, shackled at the neck, hands, or ankles, and usually assume a cringing posture beneath guards and officials.

The ten judges of the underworld, each in charge of one court, constitute yet another way of defining the quality of life after death. *The Scripture on the Ten Kings* is the earliest surviving text that mentions all of them by name (see appendix 1). While some of their titles are tantamount to personal names (e.g., Ch'in Kuang wang, literally "King Kuang of Ch'in"), for the most part their names designate positions or office-titles rather than individuals. Their titles explain their function in the life of the dead. Some have geographical significance: Ch'u-chiang wang (King of the First River) is stationed at the River Nai. Some titles have a clearly necrological significance, like the name Pien-ch'eng wang (King of Transformations), which invokes the idea of change. Other titles appear to describe the actual duties of the post, but with a philosophical twist: Wu-kuan wang (King of the Five Offices), for instance, sounds reasonably bureaucratic, but also plays on Indian and Chinese understandings of the five senses.

The dual provenance of the ten kings is one of the clearest indications that the idea of purgatory is a Sino-Indian synthesis. The fifth and seventh kings provide the clearest examples. The Chinese name for the fifth king is Yen-lo wang (King Yama rāja), a soteriologically effective but philologically flawed rendering of the Sanskrit term, "Yama rāja." Yama rāja ruled the land of the dead in the pre-Buddhist mythology of India. Yama in Indian texts is usually understood as a personal name, although its meaning of "twin" (related to Avestan: Yima and Yimeh, and Latin: Gemini) is not without significance, since in fact the brother-sister pair of Yama and Yamī were believed to rule separate jails, segregated by sex, in the Vedic afterlife. The sound, but not the sense, of "Yama" is properly transliterated into Chinese as "Yen-mo." The second component of the term is "rāja," which means "king" (cf. Proto-Indo-European: *reg-, and Latin: rex) and is usually transliterated as "lo-she." "Yen-lo" in Chinese is an abbreviation of the full transliteration "Yen-mo lo-she." The last component of the Chinese word is *wang,* which is taken at face value as "king." From a philological perspective the Chinese usage is akin to saying in English "King Oed Rex," which abbreviates and redundantly translates and transliterates the original "Oedipus Rex." Thus, the Chinese rendering of Yama rāja attempts, albeit imperfectly, to preserve the foreignness, and hence the power, of the god by using a foreign sound, but it also invests him with an air of local authority by adopting the Chinese word for "king."

In contrast to Yama, the seventh king, the King of Mount T'ai (T'ai-shan wang), exercises overwhelmingly autochthonous power. Well before Buddhism came to China, Mount T'ai (in modern Shantung) was regarded as the abode of the dead. The shades who lived underneath the mountain were governed by the district official, the Magistrate of Mount T'ai (T'ai-shan fu-chün). To the extent that the ten kings can be said to have "conquered" China, they did so not by exterminating traditional Chinese practice, but by granting titles to and making new laws for some of the local governors. Whatever their origin and in whichever language their names were known, they were all accorded the rank of king *(wang)*. By the time that the ten kings ruled, that title (which, after the Han dynasty, brought emolument, land, and privilege, but no direct political authority) was sufficiently anachronistic to carry weight. Furthermore, the law that they administered was not bifurcated into Indian versus Chinese codes. It was more like the Dharma, which, to use a Buddhist metaphor, has a "single flavor."

It is worth considering in more detail just how the motivating ideals of two civilizations were merged into one system. Special care must be taken, I think, to avoid stereotyping what was in fact a complex and ever-changing process. It would be misleading to posit any single, enduring difference between the cultures we now dub "Indian" and "Chinese." The Indian concept of the afterlife is typified by the word *saṃsāra,* a nearly eternal round of birth and death driven by the effects of people's deeds. The Chinese philosophy of death is associated with the two pillars of Chinese social organization, the kinship system and the imperial bureaucracy: the former requires that the dead be venerated, the latter that they be registered and kept in line. It is undoubtedly valid, for purely analytical purposes, to consider the system of the ten kings as a synthesis of these two monolithic conceptualizations. Medieval translators, modern nationalisms, and even a few modern scholars find such ethnic imagining an extremely convenient tool for a wide range of implementations. But the reification involved is hopelessly wooden as soon as we confront history. The two cultures never lived up to their ideal types, and the clash between them was rarely so neat. Over the centuries China has produced many images of foreigners, but with notable exceptions there was little first-hand travel to India—and those who did make the trip did not experience a culture neatly and completely prefabricated.

If we are to take seriously the fact that culture is, and was, made, then we must attend, if the evidence allows, to the process by which the idea of purgatory was constructed. Indian concepts (much less *the* Indian concept) of the afterlife were never presented as *faits accomplis* to a Chinese audience. They were mediated by the hazards of translation, by their own profusion, and by the need to conform to the demands of a heterogeneous audience. What I will attempt to provide in the next three paragraphs, then, are idealized snapshots of the Chinese understanding of the afterlife at three points. The first is the conception of the afterlife prior to the influx of Buddhism. The second is the early medieval view, in which Indic notions as translated into Chinese were dominant. The third comes several hundred years later, when the idea of purgatory had taken hold.

In the early years of the Western Han dynasty, before the growth of Buddhism or the development of organized Taoism, Chinese belief maintained a relatively fluid boundary between this life and the next. Human existence was viewed as a temporary conglomeration of the two dominant forces in the universe, *yin*[b] and *yang*. Instead of being an uneasy union of material body and ethereal soul, the person was a harmonious blending of darker, heavier aspects (*yin*[b]) with lighter ones (*yang*). With the arrival of death, a person did not separate into two theologically opposed entities. Rather, the lighter parts of the person tended upward, and the heavier elements moved downward. Han dynasty sources describe the elaborate funerals, lavish tomb furnishings, and complicated sacrifices held at the graves of the aristocracy. A passion for immortality is also evident in this period, ranging from the prolongation of life on earth to the search for an unending existence in Heaven, various western paradises, or islands in the East. Another important feature of the otherworld was that it was, before any discernible influence from Buddhism or Taoism, organized along bureaucratic lines. Officers administered the empire of the dead, keeping records on every human being and taking charge of the spirit after death.

For the next several hundred years, up to roughly the seventh century, the most widespread conception of the afterlife in Chinese Buddhism was based on the circular hierarchy presented in Chinese translations of Buddhist *sūtras* (scriptures claiming to have been spoken by the historical Buddha). Ranging from the earliest collections of small discourses to Mahāyāna philosophy and nonsectarian morality tracts, such books propounded the view that this life is merely one short segment of a potentially unlimited circle, and that after death, some significant portion of the person will be reborn in a new life. That which underlies the process is not a unique or eternal soul, but rather the actions (Skt.: *karma*, Ch.: *yeh*) performed when in an unenlightened state. Until they are cleansed of all volition, actions in fact give rise to a transitory but unfortunately sensitive self that experiences all of the pain and discomfort attending reincarnation. Built into the system of rebirth is a scale of value: actions defined as good result in higher rebirth, actions defined as evil result in a lower one. The quality of the next life is determined by the moral balance of one's past life. The range of possible rebirths is conceptualized as a hierarchy of six levels or paths. Those who are fortunate are reborn in one of the three higher paths as a god, a titanlike being, or a human being. The lower three are animal, hungry ghost, and hell. Those reborn higher in the scheme enjoy only a temporary rest from suffering; gods live long and pleasant lives, but when they die they are invariably demoted. The attention of many Chinese Buddhists in the early medieval period was focused on the lower three paths, particularly that of hell (Skt.: *naraka*, Ch.: *ti-yü*). In most analyses, hell is located underground and consists of eight distinct levels; the lowest is Avīci (Ch.: *o-pi* or *wu-chien*), which literally means "without interval," so named because the pause between rounds of torture allowed in the seven other hells is not practiced there.

Sometime during the medieval period, probably by the time the ten kings are first mentioned in surviving sources in the seventh century, the Chinese Buddhist understanding of the afterlife changed. The earlier conception of time provided the framework for the new one. Within the nearly endless cycle of rebirths, special anxiety attached to the period surrounding death. Dying a good death meant preparing for purgatory. For some this meant taking last-minute refuge in the Three Jewels and facing the direction one hoped to go, while for others it meant leaving behind the appropriate relics or poems. In many ways the time of purgatory was not objectively deducible from the instant of death. Rather, the time between death and rebirth was dependent on the memory and diligence of living family members, who, according to most available evidence, usually had trouble mustering the resources to mark every sacrifice demanded by *The Scripture on the Ten Kings*. The wheel of the six paths continued to supply the basic understanding of where the dead might soon be found, but (to extend the Buddhist analogy) attention shifted from the spokes of the wheel to the spaces in between. Purgatory was that uncertain interstice where the spirit of the deceased awaited assignment to a new spoke. The motivating ethic of the system remained a karmic one, but rather than being understood in terms of the individual, *karma* was imagined under bureaucratic form. *Karma* was none other than the law administered by the ten kings and their staff. Rebirth was not a fact of nature; it was achieved only after submitting to a lengthy process of judgment overseen by powerful officials. Those ten judges may well represent the most unprecedented innovation in the conception of the afterlife in Chinese Buddhism, although it must be remembered that the Buddhist cosmology was already sufficiently elastic to include Buddhas, Bodhisattvas, gods, humans, demons, animals, ghosts, and hell-dwellers.

The idea of purgatory in Chinese Buddhism was made complete by a figure virtually required by the addition of the ten kings to the pantheon, the Bodhisattva known in China as Ti-tsang (Skt.: Kṣitigarbha, literally "Earth Matrix"). Buddhas and Bodhisattvas have always held an ambiguous position in Mahāyāna Buddhism: on technical grounds Buddhas have fully transcended the realm of suffering, and Bodhisattvas could have gone beyond but decided to remain behind to assist beings in need. Yet precisely how Buddhas and Bodhisattvas made themselves available to the unenlightened, and in what respect they differed from mere gods, were questions that remained, especially in practice, unanswered. Ti-tsang was the Bodhisattva who specialized in helping the dead to evade the reach of the ten kings. Ti-tsang was known in other Buddhist settings (in Indian and Central Asia as Kṣitigarbha, in Tibet as Sa'i snying-po), but usually as an undistinguished member of various groups of Bodhisattvas. It was in medieval China that his powers to deliver sinners from punishment were first celebrated on a broad scale. In early medieval times Ti-tsang's role was greatest near the fringes of orthodox Buddhist thought, occupying a prominent position in mass movements like the Teaching of the Three Stages (san-chieh chiao), in the monthly observances of lay Buddhists, and in Chinese Buddhist divination techniques. His appearance in the system of the ten kings is roughly contemporaneous with the apocryphal manufacture of a biography befitting a savior. *The Scripture on the Past Vows of Ti-tsang Bodhisattva* explains that, many lifetimes ago, Ti-tsang promised to deliver all sentient beings from suffering, especially those trapped in the lower regions of rebirth. Although he is mentioned only once in *The Scripture on the Ten Kings,* his picture appears prominently and repeatedly in the illustrations to the sūtra. As an advocate for inmates he simultaneously stands outside the courts of the ten kings and enters frequently into the gloomiest of chambers to dispense comfort and win acquittal for his clients. If the ten kings represent the rigidity of a familiar system of law, Ti-tsang's appearance justifies an equally realistic hope for vindication and release.

The Practices of Purgatory

It remains to consider the practices of everyday life through which the idea of purgatory emerged and was constantly remade. Since most of those practices make some allusion to the story contained in *The Scripture on the Ten Kings,* it is helpful to introduce the text in greater detail. The scripture opens with a surprising claim by the historical Buddha. Śākyamuni announces that the very same figure most widely feared for his consistency in dispensing punishment in the dark world, King Yama, will in a future lifetime become a fully enlightened one, a Buddha named P'u-hsien (Skt.: Samantabhadra). To his astonished audience Śākyamuni explains how someone like King Yama could compensate for his unsavory deeds sufficiently to achieve Buddhahood. All officers now stationed in the dark paths are in fact, says Śākyamuni, serving a higher purpose. In the past they either desired to bring as much help as possible to sinners located below ground or were forced to commit minor acts of evil—now requited by being assigned a post in purgatory—in the pursuit of a higher good. In either case, underneath their stern appearance and despite their complicity in torture, Yama and his associates are revealed to be agents of compassion. The story grounds the authority of the ten kings in the most hallowed virtues of Mahāyāna Buddhism, and the group vows in front of Śākyamuni to be lenient in their treatment of sinners. At the same time the text reinforces the less compassionate side of the regime by reviewing the titles of the ten kings and the tribulations endured by prisoners in each of their courts. The second plot line of the scripture, advanced more through pictures than words, is about the journey of the spirit through purgatory, beginning with the first court seven days after death and ending three years later in rebirth. The subtext here is largely pragmatic. The speaker (usually Śākyamuni) threatens the audience with the likelihood of punishment, but also holds open the prospect of escape. In lawyerly language he describes how written accounts of each suspect's previous actions accompany the deceased through each organ of the government. Release can be obtained if the grieving family sends offerings to each of the ten kings at the appropriate time. Such practices are not accepted on faith: Yama promises the Buddha that he will verify their observance by dispatching a messenger to each mourning household. Even more beneficial is the practice of sending offerings to the ten kings on one's own behalf while still alive.

The formal title of the sūtra draws attention to the story of King Yama and the importance of making offerings. Some copies are entitled *Fo-shuo yen-lo wang shou-chi ssu-chung yü-hsiu sheng-ch'i wang-sheng ching-t'u ching* (The Scripture Spoken by the Buddha to the Four Orders on the Prophecy Given to King Yama Concerning the Sevens of Life to Be Cultivated in Preparation for Rebirth in the Pure Land). The name of the text was often shortened to *Yen-lo wang shou-chi ching* (The Scripture on the Prophecy Given to King Yama), or, in the three-character usage I will adopt throughout this book, *Shih-wang ching* (The Scripture on the Ten Kings).

Up until now I have assumed that the plot of *The Scripture on the Ten Kings* defines a unique and unchanging text, but that pretense obscures the fact that roughly the same plot was transmitted in a multiplicity of

forms. Three distinct recensions of the text survive among the Tun-
huang manuscripts; here I will refer to them as the long, medium, and
short recensions. The long recension, translated and annotated in Part
Three, constitutes a program for a wide range of performance styles,
some distinctly unliterary. The components of the text include:

1. Color illustrations, beginning with a frontispiece of Śākyamuni
   flanked by the ten kings and numerous assistants
2. An announcement that the scripture is about to be intoned, and
   directions to chant the name of O-mi-t'o (Amitābha) Buddha
3. The name and residence of the author
4. The formal title
5. Thirty-four hymns (tsan, cf. Skt.: stotra), consisting of four rhym-
   ing lines of seven characters, which were sung aloud
6. The narrative, which begins in the style of Buddhist sūtras ("Thus
   have I heard. Once, when the Buddha resided at . . . .") and is
   written in relatively straightforward Classical Chinese prose
7. Short, unrhymed ch'ieh-t'o, modeled on the Sanskritic gāthā, usually consisting of quatrains with five characters per line, which
   were chanted
8. An abbreviated title at the end.

The short recension contains only titles, narrative, and chants; it lacks
illustrations, hymns, and prefatory prayers. The middle recension contains most of the same elements as the short one, except its narrative is
slightly longer.

The Scripture on the Ten Kings is more than a written artifact. The long
recension involves singing, rhythmic chanting, and worshiping, presumably conducted in unison; the viewing of pictures; as well as the elements more dependent on knowledge of literary Chinese like title,
author, and narrative. The short and middle recensions involve chanting and reading. In later chapters, rather than isolating an original text
kept pure from misunderstanding, poor translation, and mere practice,
I shall attempt to demonstrate that there was a fluid relationship
between the narrative and the prayers, hymns, chants, and pictures.

The scripture names its own author. He was a monk named Tsang-
ch'uan who, the scripture says, lived at Ta-sheng-tz'u ssu in Ch'eng-tu.
Some evidence suggests that he wrote not the narrative portions of the
sūtra, but rather its hymns. In any case neither the standard nor the
marginal sources for Chinese Buddhism have anything more to say
about Tsang-ch'uan. The date for the composition of the scripture is
likewise shrouded in mystery. The earliest surviving manuscript of *The
Scripture on the Ten Kings* that can be dated conclusively was copied in the
year 908. It was presumably copied from a master version kept at one of
the eighteen temples in the garrison town of Tun-huang in Sha-chou

(near the modern town of Tun-huang in modern Kansu), but where *that* text came from we do not know.

To ascertain the date of an unusual text, scholars of Chinese Buddhism usually turn to the dozens of catalogues of the Buddhist canon written during the medieval and modern periods. Here too we meet with silence, but that silence may be instructive. Catalogues of Buddhist scriptures were not mere listings of library holdings. Compiled by the highest-ranking members of the Buddhist clergy, often at the urging of the emperor, they were prescriptions for what was accepted as part of the Dharma as it was understood in China and what was barred from contaminating it. *The Scripture on the Ten Kings* had probably not yet been written in the year 720, when the monk Chih-sheng (fl. 669–740) defined what would become the core of all later canons in his *K'ai-yüan shih-chiao lu* (Catalogue of Items of the Buddhist Teaching Compiled during the K'ai-yüan Era). Chih-sheng makes a point of discussing *other* texts, barred from the canon, that focus on the dark regions, but does not mention *The Scripture on the Ten Kings*. It is likely, then, that the text was put together sometime between 720 and 908. Although the sūtra was copied by hand from at least the tenth century and printed by woodblock by 1469 at the latest, it was not allowed into a Buddhist canon until 1912, by which time the canon was more of a scholarly than a religious institution.

Copied by hand in Buddhist monasteries, yet never accorded canonicity—such is the status of many texts situated in the nexus between Buddhism as an organized tradition and the longstanding religious practices of China. The distance between *The Scripture on the Ten Kings* and canonical scriptures is clear: it makes only a weak claim to have been transmitted from India, which no one appears to have taken very seriously anyway. It is populated by several figures with unambiguously Chinese origins, not only kings like the King of Mount T'ai, but also such lower-level functionaries as the Officer of Life Spans and the Officer of Records (Ssu-ming and Ssu-lu). And it is overwhelmingly concerned with the fate of the ancestors, the mainstay of Chinese religion. Yet scriptoria in Tun-huang had a strong interest in copying out the text, and some members of the Saṃgha encouraged its propagation.

In organizing a small-scale business in which lay people could pay to have *The Scripture on the Ten Kings* copied, thereby sending spiritual benefit to donors and their ancestors and bringing material gain to the Saṃgha, monks stood on firm textual ground. Like other Mahāyāna sūtras, the ten kings scripture emphasizes repeatedly the boons that accrue to those who commission the copying of the text or the carving of related images. Not only is the content of the scripture related to its form, but the diversity of styles in which the text was reproduced casts further light on how purgatory came to life. Some copies were produced as scrolls, some as bound booklets. The scrolls come in two formats. One includes illustrations and reproduces the long recension (which includes hymns). It was best adapted for use in a communal setting where a priest could show the pictures to a mourning family who joined in the singing of hymns. The other type of scroll is slightly smaller and lacks pictures and hymns (i.e., it contains the short recension). It was probably used most frequently at services where chanting by monks, rather than psalmody and pictures, was paramount. Likewise for most of the sūtras bound as booklets, the pages of which could be easily turned while chanting. One booklet, however, is different. It contains everything in the long recension except the pictures, and it is a miniature, small enough to fit into a pocket. It may have been used as a talisman to ward off the ten kings or as a private study-guide.

What could be called the textual practice of *The Scripture on the Ten Kings* includes one more dimension: the conditions under which the scripture was commissioned. Luckily colophons supply interesting answers to the questions of who paid for copying the text and why. *The Scripture on the Ten Kings* was copied for the same range of motivations as were other Buddhist texts: to cure sickness, to amass a stock of merit for oneself, to contribute to the welfare of others, or to practice selflessness. A copy of the scripture donated in the year 958 was made under less common circumstances. It was the fifth sūtra in a series of ten (only half of which were canonical) to be copied in perfect conformity to the teachings of the text itself. On each of the ten feast days after the passing of his wife, a local official in Tun-huang named Chai Feng-ta (fl. 902–966) had one scripture made. Chai's copy of *The Scripture on the Ten Kings* is a particularly telling reminder that in medieval times the making of a book was itself a religious service, and that the conditions of textual production are extremely important to our understanding of religious life.

The practices of purgatory were sometimes unrelated to *The Scripture on the Ten Kings*. Many of the ten kings, for instance, appear individually as part of the multimedia medieval performance involving song, pictures, and verbal recitation known as "transformations" *(pien)*. The most vivid reminder that the premodern experience of the afterlife was not bound to a text is artistic—the numerous paintings of Ti-tsang Bodhisattva surrounded by the ten kings that survive from tenth-century Tun-huang. The way in which Ti-tsang dominates the ten kings in these paintings suggests that they served as icons in worship services dedicated to Ti-tsang. Esoteric liturgies focusing on Ti-tsang do survive from the period, but ones accessible to the uninitiated do not. From other ritual programs, however, it can be extrapolated that the worship of Ti-tsang involved bowing, chanting, the saying or singing of prayers, and the offering of incense, flowers, and cash. Purgatory must have also figured prominently in another activity central to the propagation of

Chinese Buddhism, preaching. Such moralizing took place across a broad spectrum, ranging from homey lectures given in the spoken language to tracts analyzing examples of retribution written in Classical Chinese. Finally, it must be recognized that the practices of purgatory were not merely motivated by the fear of punishment in the next life. Rather, rituals addressed to the ten kings were an integral part of the Buddhist path, the following of a set of precepts based on noninjury and compassion.

The History of Purgatory

The growth of purgatory has significant implications for our understanding of the history of Chinese Buddhism, considered both as a particular instantiation of a pan-Asian tradition and more narrowly as a particular stage in the development of Chinese religion. Attributing significance to any local form of Buddhism depends, of course, on one's point of reference. We must be particularly cautious, I think, to avoid using "original Buddhism" as a standard of measurement. Most of the details of the Buddhist tradition during the time of the founder are simply inaccessible to critical historians, an admission made even more humbling by the inability of contemporary scholars to agree on which century the historical Buddha lived in. Furthermore, whichever sources one depends on to imagine an earliest Buddhism, the picture that emerges is one of a tradition that was, in its doctrine, practice, and institutions, always fluid—or, to use the grammar of Mādhyamika, never not indeterminate.

The Chinese variation on the standard Buddhist cosmology can be profitably contrasted with a few examples from other Asian cultures. Virtually all traditional Buddhist cultures inherited from Indian sources a complex and already aggregated picture of the world. In general terms, that chart included three levels. At the bottom were the six paths of rebirth, constituting the realm of desire (Skt.: *kāmadhātu*). The second realm included heavenly beings and states of meditation subject to the effects of action, constituting the realm of form *(rupadhātu)*. The third and highest realm, postulated to account for progressively rarefied states of meditative absorption, was the realm of no-form *(arupadhātu)*. Most Buddhisms paid lip service to the opinion that ultimate salvation was not to be found in any of these realms, but diverged in focusing attention on different parts of the map. Some representations (seen now, for instance, in many Tibetan monasteries) follow the directions given in early sources for painting a wheel of life *(bhāvacakra)* in the halls of temples. In the central circle are the three poisons (desire, hatred, and delusion) represented by a chicken, a snake, and a pig. They are surrounded by a six-segment circle of the six paths of rebirth, surrounded in turn by a circle marking the twelve links in the chain of causation, all of which is grasped, in mouth, hands, and feet, by the demon Māra. This interpretation of Buddhist cosmology can be said to supply a philosophical analysis of why sentient beings remain trapped in the cycle of rebirth in the six paths, of how the illusory and painful world ruled by Māra is maintained by the first of the twelve causes of suffering, ignorance. In contrast to the wheel of life, traditions of meditation involving visualization of celestial Buddhas in their Buddha-lands aspired to realms not contained in the earlier cosmography. In these techniques of visualization, after proper cleansing and devotion the practitioner proceeded systematically to create an eidetic image of each detail of an other realm. The realms included those of the Buddhas of the ten directions, Amitābha's Land of Bliss in the West, and the Tuṣita Heaven, where Maitreya currently resides. The focus of the Chinese notion of purgatory, on the other hand, was on the space between one rebirth and the next, the transition of which required help from the living.

The Chinese Buddhist theory of purgatory constitutes an important chapter in the history of what could be called Buddhist "theology." "Pantheism" is somewhat of a misnomer in the Buddhist case: true, because a variety of gods are thought to be as "real" as human beings are; yet beside the point, because unlike Buddhas and Bodhisattvas, who have achieved some form of enlightenment, gods suffer from ignorance. Gods are unwillingly subject to reincarnation and suffering and hence have only a minor role to play in liberating other sentient beings from the cycle. Within these general parameters, however, a variety of elaborations was possible, especially in the styles by which indigenous gods were linked to Buddhism. The method utilized in the Tantric traditions was to multiply, often by doubling, the number of spiritual beings in the cosmos. Wrathful gods were balanced by compassionate ones, personifications of expediency by personifications of wisdom, and so on. In some instances the Tantric system was organized in psychological terms by a useful dualism, according to which local gods were associated with chthonic values while Buddhist figures were viewed as pure. Another method, found throughout the Buddhist world, was to adopt local gods as guardians for Buddhist temples. The process can be seen in the traditional placement of fierce warrior gods at the entrance to temples dedicated to Buddhas or Bodhisattvas (perhaps akin to the life-size photograph of His Holiness the Dalai Lama and Richard Gere protecting the entryway to the Asian Art Museum of San Francisco for its 1991 exhibition of Tibetan art). In Japan the question of who was guarding whom was debated openly from medieval times to the early modern period. Sometimes *kami* were viewed as the temporary manifestations of ontologically more significant Buddhas and Bodhisattvas, sometimes vice-versa. Chinese Buddhism used a slightly different strategy. The system of the ten kings dealt with the issue by assigning posts to local and foreign figures in a single administration, the members of which all swear fealty to Buddhist ideals. For other deities, the belief in reincarnation was adapted to the style of traditional Chinese hagiography, resulting in stories of how Kuan-yin Bodhisattva manifested himself in female form as Miao-shan, whose local cult was active in western China from at least the twelfth century, or of how a Korean prince famous for his magical powers at Chiu-hua shan (in modern Szechwan) was really Ti-tsang Bodhisattva.

The Chinese Buddhist understanding of purgatory should also be a part of an unfortunately neglected side of Buddhist studies, the investigation of beliefs and practices distributed widely across a given culture. Purgatory was an ingredient in the more universal form of Buddhist-influenced culture which, in medieval and early modern China at least, was shared by most social classes (whether ranked by economic, social, or educational status) and most regions, regardless of explicit religious affiliation. To this basic and most widespread form of Buddhism, distinctions between Buddhist schools or lineages were largely irrelevant. Rebirth in the Pure Land of Amitābha Buddha is important as a general religious goal in *The Scripture on the Ten Kings,* and his name is chanted at the opening of the text, but he plays no significant role, intermediate or ultimate, in the passage through the ten courts described therein. Similarly, the text contains several symbols drawn from the Hua-yen school, but the ten kings are not mentioned in the biographies of any of the T'ang-dynasty Hua-yen masters. In Japan, where sectarianism became a reality in the late medieval period, the ten kings were included in the mortuary practice of every sect except the True Pure Land School *(jōdo shinshū),* which denied in principle that the dead could receive any benefit from the living. The significance of purgatory will be better understood when scholarship takes more seriously the common forms of Buddhism—funerary observances and cosmology, morality and everyday ritual—throughout the cultures of Asia.

The cosmology of the ten kings was by no means the only view of the afterlife in medieval Chinese Buddhism. Pure Land–style rituals were available to many people already in the Six Dynasties period. In those rites, chanting the name of Amitābha Buddha would cause Amitābha or one of his attendants to descend to the bedside of the person near death and to transport him or her directly to the Pure Land. Such practices may have competed, in theory or in fact, with rites addressed to the ten kings. There appears to be a conflict between the symbolism of the bureaucratic passage characterizing purgatorial rites and that of final deliverance to an unstained realm typical of Pure Land forms, but only further research into the world of death in Chinese Buddhism can clarify the potential oppositions. Still other metaphors appear to dominate the funeral rituals for Ch'an abbots described in some of the Sung dynasty monastic regulations. In that literature, abbots are portrayed as patriarchs, and their disciples are enjoined to carry out practices similar to those that younger male members of the kinship group were required to perform for their ancestors. The apparent discrepancies between these different forms of Chinese Buddhist mortuary ritual are not easy to dismiss.

The historical significance of the idea of purgatory is not limited to medieval China. Looking further ahead in time, I would argue that purgatory constitutes an important component of the culture of early modern China. Born on the borders of the Buddhist church, it continued to dominate most forms of Chinese religion well after Buddhism lost the institutional strength attributed to it during the T'ang dynasty. To cast the issue in terms of the "decline" of Buddhism is to miss the point. In its medieval forms, the Buddhist ideas and practices evident in the system of the ten kings were already heavily—and, I believe, not inconsistently—Confucianized. Similarly, the presence of Buddhist symbols in modern times in obviously non-Buddhist contexts like funeral dramas or literati-sponsored morality books needs to be understood as something more than just a "survival" of elements long since fossilized. This study of purgatory thus forms one volume in a series that might be called, to paraphrase Joseph Levenson, "Buddhist China and Its Confucian Fate."

Purgatory helps to illuminate two particular facets of Chinese religion, the placing of the dead and the bureaucratization of the other world. Some of the earliest written documents for Chinese history already exhibit a consistent flexibility in imagining the dead. Once they have died, people are found in or near their graves, visiting ancestral halls and family banquets, and lodged in specific sites like Hao-li or the Yellow Springs (Huang-ch'üan). Accompanying these *topoi* was a philosophy of personhood which, as noted above, viewed human life as a temporary embodiment of a multiplicity of forces, some *yin*[b] and some *yang*. Although the coming of Buddhism did require the reworking of some aspects of Chinese cosmology, both indigenous Chinese and imported Buddhist conceptions viewed selfhood as a fluid process. Neither tradition possessed a creator god or an eschatology that would make a unique and eternal soul the precondition for salvation. Hence purgatory emerged after Buddhism arrived in China not through a battle over souls, but rather through a process of supplementation. To an originally fluid and multilocal vision of the afterlife, Buddhism added one more option: that the person could be reborn in another bodily form.

In much the same way, Buddhist notions of karma refined and completed a system of judgment after death that had been in place for centuries. Archaeological discoveries made nearly every year cause us to place at an earlier point in time the date for the existence of a hierarchy of bureaucrats ruling the afterlife. Han dynasty sources—and now, apparently, pre-Han documents accompanying the dead—make it clear that although the living were sad to see their loved ones pass away, they also feared that the dead might return to haunt them. Hence they petitioned the authorities in the other world to insure that their ancestors were kept in their proper place. The pre-Buddhist regime enforced the law through surveillance by an unseen host of agents. Some resided in the body, others looked over each person's shoulders during life; they all reported to their superiors after death. The addition of karma heightened both the logic and the terror of the underworld government. It made it more rational since the magistrates administered an explicit, universal, and immutable law. And it made it even more terrifying, since the darkness and unpleasant crowding after death were now inflated by Buddhist inspiration into specific, grisly tortures. Buddhism provided a new means for expressing the ambiguous sentiments, long a part of Chinese family religion, of fear of the dead and respect for the ancestors. Purgatory thus represents the last stage in the imposition of a bureaucratic metaphor on the experience of death.[1]

1. Writing in 1931, Arthur Waley justified the five pages that he devoted to the subject of "The World of the Dead" by claiming that *The Scripture on the Ten Kings* "represents so strange a fusion of ideas as to merit a longer treatment" (Waley, *Catalogue*, p. xxvi). In the past sixty years several scholars have followed Waley's lead in treating *The Scripture on the Ten Kings* and pursuing Tun-huang studies in general. This book builds on their research, a brief introduction to which is in order. The most important studies of *The Scripture on the Ten Kings* are: Hsiao, *Tun-huang su-wen-hsüeh lun-ts'ung*, pp. 175–292; Izumi, "*Jūō kyō* no kenkyū"; Mochizuki, *Daijiten*, pp. 2216a–18a; Ogawa, "*Enraō juki kyō*"; Sakai, "Jūō shinkō"; Sawada, *Jigoku hen*, pp. 23–30; Tokushi, "Kōzō"; Tsukamoto, "Inro bosatsu shinkō ni tsuite," pp. 168–79; and Tu, *Chiao-lu yen-chiu*. The implications of the finds at Tun-huang for the study of Chinese Buddhism have been addressed in a number of works, including: Kao, *Tun-huang min-su-hsüeh*; Makita, *Gikyō kenkyū*; Makita and Fukui, *Tonkō to chūgoku bukkyō*; Overmyer, "Buddhism in the Trenches"; Shinohara and Tanaka, *Tonkō butten to zen*; and Strickmann, "India in the Chinese Looking-Glass." The study of the movable evidence as well as the wall paintings in the caves near Tun-huang now constitutes a field in its own right; for a sampling, see: *Cahiers d'Extrême-Asie*, no. 3 (1987), *Numéro spécial: Études de Dunhuang*; Fujieda, "The Tun-huang Manuscripts: A General Description"; Soymié, ed., *Contributions aux études de Touen-houang*, vol. 3; Tun-huang wen-wu yen-chiu-so, *Tun-huang mo-kao-k'u*, 5 vols.; and recent issues of the three journals in the field: *Tun-huang yen-chiu*, *Tun-huang-hsüeh*, and *Tun-huang-hsüeh chi-k'an*.

PART ONE

Traces of the Ten Kings

IN EXPLORING the background of a religious text historians are often tempted to focus exclusively on scripture and doctrine. That temptation is all the more compelling because for premodern times the lack of appropriate sources prevents us from understanding the dynamics of social life and the complexity of social action. *The Scripture on the Ten Kings,* however, takes us directly to the realm of practice. Not only are the surviving copies of the sūtra padded with ritual formulae, but the message of the text itself is overwhelmingly consequential: the Buddha proclaims that the sufferings of the spirit after death can be obviated only by worshipping the ten kings.

Part One of this study attempts to document the worship of the ten kings by examining their manifestations in medieval culture outside of the major scripture advocating their cause. It asks how was knowledge of the ten kings transmitted; in which practices were they invoked; and in what media did they appear. How widespread was belief in the ten kings; in what areas of China and in which groups of society was it found? How did belief in the ten kings gain legitimacy; since they were never mentioned as a group in the traditional Buddhist canon, what stories were told to support their authenticity?

Although it is tempting to organize this part by time from beginning to end, the chance survival of evidence means that any simplistic chronology would tell us mostly about the limitations of our sources. Instead, I have chosen to adopt a thematic presentation emphasizing the importance of memorial rites and religious art in Chinese culture.

The usual sources for medieval religion are notoriously silent about how beliefs were put into practice by the vast majority of people who could neither read nor write. Answers can be found, though, by looking outside the offically sanctioned repositories of Chinese Buddhist doctrine. Texts from the Buddhist and Taoist canons provide some help, but the most important information about memorial services is contained in indigenous Chinese Buddhist scriptures. These so-called apocrypha, some of which were later made canonical, were written in Chinese to answer Chinese concerns, but they maintain some of the linguistic conventions and philosophical presuppositions of Indian Buddhist texts. Another important source is the genre of apologetic literature known imprecisely as the Chinese Buddhist miracle tale. Written in literary Chinese but often preserving traces of oral transmission, some of these legends offer details on the unseen powers of Buddhist images. Others demonstrate that the reign of the ten kings was so effective that people saw them in their dreams and suffered their judgment after death. Artistic sources constitute another fund of information about the ten kings. Although some evidence is available in medieval writings about artists and their work, the ten kings survive most vividly in materials unearthed at Tun-huang, paintings on silk and scriptural illustrations. Such pictures are an important reminder that the ten kings cannot be understood by looking solely at the words of scripture.

2. Memorial Rites

EVERY FOREIGN CREED seeking followers in China had to adjust itself to the most visible and enduring form of Chinese religion, the sacred ties between past and present generations of the kinship group. The responsibilities of junior members of the family toward their seniors began during life and continued, intensified, after the elders passed away. One particularly influential formulation of the ideal of "filial devotion" (hsiao) is attributed to Confucius. Elaborating on his definition of filial devotion as "not being disobedient," Confucius said:[1]

> When parents are alive, serve them according to ritual [li^a]. When
> they die, bury them according to ritual and sacrifice to them
> according to ritual.

Nearly 1,500 years later many families sacrificed to their ancestors according to a code of ritual unknown to Confucius, by sending offerings to the ten kings.

This section assembles evidence for the evolution of memorial rites addressed to the ten kings through the tenth century and investigates

---

1. *Analects* 2:5, in *Lun-yü cheng-i,* annot. Liu Pao-nan (1791–1855), p. 25; largely following Legge, trans., *Confucian Analects,* p. 11.

the reasoning behind the practice. One consistent historiographical problem is terminological: different writers use the same term to refer to a variety of rituals. Philology does not suffice to unlock such puzzles. I have used source criticism and a consideration of context whenever possible, but in some cases my interpretation remains admittedly hypothetical.[2]

References to ten memorial rituals in *The Scripture on the Ten Kings* are purely normative; they do not document the circumstances in which the services were performed. One of the earliest descriptions of the practice is only slightly less tangential. That piece of evidence is contained in *Wang Fan-chih shih-chi* (Collected Poems of Brahmācārin Wang), an anonymous collection of didactic, semivernacular verse that Demiéville dates approximately to the middle of the eighth century. One poem portrays "the feast of one hundred days" *(pai-jih chai)*, eighth in the series of ten, as the limit of collective memory—and respect—for the deceased. The poem warns that after the completion of the eighth feast, family members will move on from mourning to other concerns. The poem states:[3]

> After celebrating the feast of one hundred days
> Your wife[4] will forget you;
> Your money and goods will be used by others
> As if it had always been thus.

Formal prayers addressed to the ten kings are offered in a composition by the poet and statesman Ssu-k'ung T'u (837–908), whose last years coincided with the end of T'ang dynastic rule. Ssu-k'ung's family was from the area of present-day Shansi, and he held a variety of posts in the central government, including Palace Censor, Recorder in the Court of Imperial Entertainments, Vice Director of the Ministry of

2. The term "ten feasts" *(shih-chai)* is a good example of the problem of labeling practice. The term can refer to the ten services performed as a memorial to an ancestor or to preparatory services undertaken on one's own behalf. The latter services, in turn, could be dedicated to the standard set of ten kings, to an exclusively Buddhist set of ten deities, or to Taoist gods. References to the first seven feasts *(ch'i-ch'i chai)* are quite common before the T'ang dynasty, but there is usually no way of knowing whether three more services were added for a total of ten.

3. *Wang Fan-chih shih-chi*, in Demiéville, *L'oeuvre de Wang le zélateur*, 7J; and Hsiang, *Wang Fan-chih shih chiao-chu*, p. 45. I follow Demiéville (pp. 7–16) in dating the text to ca. 750; for other opinions, see Chang, *Wang Fan-chih shih chiao-chi*, pp. 333–62; Chu, *Wang Fan-chih shih yen-chiu*, pp. 43–110; Hsiang, *Wang Fan-chih shih chiao-chu*, preface, pp. 1–42; Iriya, "Ō Bonji ni tsuite"; and idem, "Ō Bonji shishū kō."

4. *Hun-chia* (which Demiéville, p. 55, and Hsiang, p. 48, n. 8, interpret as "the whole family") was a T'ang colloquialism for "wife"; see Wang et al., *Kuo-yü tz'u-tien (Gwoyeu Tsyrdean)*, p. 1716a.

Rites, and Drafter in the Secretariat.[5] Ssu-k'ung entitled one of his essays "Shih-hui chai wen" (A Prose Composition on the Feasts of the Ten Assemblies). Although it is undated and its context unknown, some usages in the piece suggest that the "feasts" mentioned in the title were memorial rituals addressed to the ten kings. Ssu-k'ung refers several times to the salvation of the deceased and raises the theme of prosperity for the family and the community. He begins:[6]

> Distress takes ten thousand different forms, but spiritual kindness brings universal deliverance in the mysterious darkness. The ten assemblies are carried out separately, but the paths of the kings all consist of impartiality.

Ssu-k'ung also invokes the ten kings and their underlings to discharge their duties with compassion. He writes:

> I humbly pray that the various kings together with the true officers of the five paths and the six ministries serve forever as honored spirits, bringing benefit to [those in] the good paths and causing [those in] the mysterious darkness to look upward.

Evidence for the practice of posthumous rituals involving the ten kings is far more compelling in ninth- and tenth-century Tun-huang. The best-documented case is the full complement of ten feasts sponsored in 958–960 by a local offical named Chai Feng-ta (fl. 902–966) to benefit his deceased wife. For each feast Chai commissioned the copying of one Buddhist scripture, followed by a formal note of the circumstances and a prayer for the woman's salvation (see chapter 9).

We have knowledge of memorial services for several other Tun-huang residents (or former residents) thanks to the survival of written requests for monks to attend the rites (see appendix 2). These invitations generally follow a standard form: the grieving family, headed by the father or eldest son, usually a low- or middle-ranking local official, invites a handful of monks, each named, to come to the house for the

---

5. For early biographies of Ssu-k'ung T'u, see *Chiu t'ang shu*, Liu Hsü (887–946), pp. 5082–85; and *Hsin t'ang shu*, Ou-yang Hsiu (1007–1072), pp. 5573–74. The *Hsin t'ang shu* (p. 1608) attributes one work to him, *I-ming chi*, in thirty *chüan*. Some of his surviving poems are collected in *Ch'üan t'ang shih,* ed. P'eng Ting-ch'iu (1645–1719), pp. 7243–89, 10,000–02, and 10,069–70. His prose works are contained in *(Ch'in-ting) Ch'üan t'ang wen,* ed. Tung Kao (1740–1818), chs. 807–10 (pp. 10,693–747). The *Chiu t'ang shu* (p. 5082) states that he was from Lin-huai (modern Chekiang), but I follow the *Hsin t'ang shu* (p. 5573), which traces his family's origins to Yü-hsiang (modern Shansi). For a study of his poetry and poetics, see Wang, *Ssu-k'ung T'u hsin-lun.*

6. "Shih-hui chai wen," in *(Ch'in-ting) Ch'üan t'ang wen,* 808.3v (p. 10,708b), 808.4r (p. 10,708c), respectively.

"posthumous remembrance" *(chui-nien)* of the deceased to be held on a specific date. Most of the invitations are signed and dated, ranging from 887 to 993. Most are written on the back sides of older texts or on small scraps of paper.

While these examples do not provide a complete picture, they do justify some generalizations about the incidence of memorial rites dedicated to the ten kings. By the ninth century such rituals were held according to the schedule promulgated in *The Scripture on the Ten Kings.* The families of lay people apparently took responsibility for organizing the services; we do not know who organized monks' services, since contemporaneous evidence is lacking. The feasts of remembrance were an important occasion for monks and families to cooperate in fulfilling their mutual duties. Some families invited monks to their homes to perform services, presumably consisting of preaching and chanting, in which the Samgha's privileged spiritual position brought aid to the deceased. In return lay people made donations to the Order. Other families took advantage not of the verbal arts but of the training in literacy some monks claimed; they commissioned copies of sacred texts and dedicated the merit to their ancestors on each of the ten feasts.

The inspiration for holding ten memorial services is partly (one is tempted to say seven-tenths) Buddhist in origin. Even before the development of Mahāyāna schools, several sects of Indian Buddhism (the Sarvāstivādin, later Mahīśāsaka, Vātsīputrīya, Sammatīya, and Pūrvaśaila) propounded the idea of an "intermediate existence" (Skt.: *antarābhava,* Ch.: *chung-yu*), a period beginning at death and lasting until one is reborn in another form. The argument was founded on the principle of karma, the doctrine that every act has a result, which provided a grounding for Buddhist morality. Applied to the problem of the afterlife, belief in karma implied that there could be no gap of chance separating the moment of death from the moment of rebirth; these two forms of life had to be connected by an intermediate stage.[7] Scholastic Buddhist sources portray the anxieties that beings suffer in the intermediate state. Possessing only a frail body, constantly in search of nourishment, and beset by unknown shapes, sounds, and smells, such beings struggle for rebirth in a more settled form. The opportunity to exit the liminal stage occurs only once every seven days. When the seventh day comes, the karmic circumstances must be just right—for example, the person's prospective parents happen to be having intercourse at the right juncture—for the person to be implanted in its new mother's

---

7. See *O-p'i-ta-mo ta p'i-p'o-sha lun (Mahāvibhāṣā),* Hsüan-tsang (602–664), *T* no. 1545, 27:356c–58a; and Bareau, *Les sectes bouddhiques du Petit Véhicule,* p. 283.

womb. If the seven-day rhythm is not fortuitous, then the being has to pass another period of seven days, repeated up to seven times for a total of forty-nine days, before achieving rebirth.[8]

Chinese Buddhism offered a variety of rituals to resolve the uncertainties of the forty-nine days. One mid-fifth-century source provided a technique for guiding the deceased directly from the intermediate state to the lands of bliss located in the ten directions. *Sui-yüan wang-sheng shih-fang ching-t'u ching* (The Scripture on Rebirth in Accordance with One's Vows in the Pure Lands of the Ten Directions), which constituted chapter 11 of the *Kuan-ting ching* (The Consecration Scripture), states:[9]

> In the intermediate darkness [*chung-yin*] the body of the person whose lifespan has ended is like a small child. Because sins and blessings have not yet been decided, you should cultivate blessings on its behalf. You should pray that the spirit of the deceased be born in the unlimited *kṣetra*-lands[10] of the ten directions. When it inherits this merit it will definitely be reborn.

The sponsorship of seven memorial rituals held every seven days began well before the development of the ten kings and their corresponding ten rituals, and it continued, undiluted, long after belief in the ten kings had become popular. One of the earliest injunctions to perform the ritual occurs in the *Fan-wang ching* (Scripture on Brahmā's Net), a Chinese composition based loosely on Indian materials that dates from the middle of the fifth century. The thirty-ninth precept of that text instructs monks to chant scriptures for lay and religious alike during the seven weekly feasts. It states:[11]

> On behalf of all sentient beings, Bodhisattvas must also preach the scriptures [*sūtras*] and regulations [*vinaya*] of the Greater Vehicle. If someone is sick, if the country is in danger, if there is rebellion, or if it is the day on which parents, siblings, monks, or *ācāryas* pass into extinction, or the third seventh day, the fourth or fifth seventh day, up to the seventh seventh day, Bodhisattvas must also preach the scriptures and regulations of the Greater Vehicle.

8. See, for example, *O-p'i-ta-mo chü-she lun (Abhidharmakośaśāstra)*, Vasubandhu, trans. Hsüan-tsang, *T* no. 1558, 29:46a–47a; and *Yü-ch'ieh-shih ti lun (Yogacārabhūmiśāstra)*, Hsüan-tsang, *T* no. 1579, 30:282a–b.

9. *Kuan-ting ching*, Hui-chien (fl. 457), *T* no. 1331, 21:529c. On the dating, content, and context of the work, see Strickmann, "*The Consecration Sūtra: A Buddhist Book of Spells.*"

10. "*Kṣetra*-land" reproduces the redundancy of the original, *sha-t'u*.

11. *Fan-wang ching*, attrib. Kumārajīva (350–409), but probably written ca. 431–481, *T* no. 1484, 24:1008b; see also de Groot, *Le code du Mahāyāna en Chine*, p. 72; and Ishida, *Bommō kyō*, pp. 229–33. Chapters 11 and 12 of the *Kuan-ting ching* repeatedly mention seven weekly memorial feasts and are dominated by septenary symbolism; see *Kuan-ting ching*, *T* 21:528c–32b, 532b–36b.

Beginning in the sixth century, memorial services timed to coincide with the forty-nine days of intermediate existence are recorded for several individuals who have biographies in the standard histories.[12] Evidence scattered in medieval collections of miracle tales shows that seven-seven services often became the occasion for the confirmation of prophecies and the manifestation of other auspicious signs.[13] Memorial rituals appear in the writings of T'ang Confucian figures as examples of extravagance in ritual. In his "Ch'ü fo-chai lun" (Essay on Abolishing Buddhist Feasts), Li Ao (772–841) refers disapprovingly to a work on mourning ritual by a roughly contemporaneous figure named Yang Ch'ui. Yang describes the practice: "For feasts of the seven weeks, on each feast day one sends clothing to the deceased at Buddhist temples in order to extend posthumous fortune."[14] Taken as a whole, these citations show that the holding of seven weekly feasts was continuous from the fifth century onward, but given the lack of background information, they do not justify any significant conclusions about the geographical spread or the appeal to different social classes of this Buddhist practice.

The inspiration for the last three of the ten memorial services derived from indigenous Chinese ritual practice, a fact that Buddhist clerics were proud to announce. Writing in the thirteenth century, the historian Chih-p'an (fl. 1258–1269) found copious precedents in Buddhist sources for the first seven rites. For the last three, however, he turned to the words of Confucius as an authority. He writes:[15]

12. The most complete citations of material from the standard histories are contained in *Heng-yen*, Ch'ien Ta-hsin (1728–1804), p. 94; and *Heng-yen kuang-cheng*, Ch'en Chan (1753–1817), p. 74. For modern surveys, see de Groot, *Le code du Mahāyāna en Chine*, pp. 146–47; and Kao, "Lun tun-huang min-chien ch'i-ch'i chai sang-su," pp. 106–8. Seven-seven rituals are recorded for Hu Kuo-chen, Prince Cho of Nan-yang, Wang Yüan-ch'i, and Meng Luan in the *Pei shih*, by Li Yen-shou (fl. 629); for Ho Shih-k'ai in the *Pei-ch'i shu* by Li Te-lin (530–590) and Li Pai-yao (565–648); and for Yao Ch'ung in the *Chiu t'ang shu*, by Liu Hsün (887–946).

13. See, for example, the account of services for the monk Hui-yüan (d. 455), in *Ming-hsiang chi*, Wang Yüan (fl. 424–479), cited in *Fa-yüan chu-lin*, Tao-shih (d. 683), *T* no. 2122, 53:1003c–04a; also collected in Lu, *Ku hsiao-shuo kou-ch'en*, pp. 442–43; and the memorial services for Lady Hsiao (d. 665), wife of Ts'ui I-ch'i, in *Fa-yüan chu-lin*, *T* 53:911a–12a.

14. Li Ao, "Ch'ü fo-chai lun," in *(Ch'in-ting) Ch'üan t'ang wen*, 636.11r (p. 8158a). Yang Ch'ui was the grandfather of Yang Tung-ch'ien (fl. 907–923); see *Shih-kuo ch'un-ch'iu*, Wu Jen-ch'en (1628?–1689?), p. 888; and *Hsin t'ang shu*, p. 2363.

15. Translation from *Fo-tsu t'ung-chi*, Chih-p'an (fl. 1258–1269), *T* no. 2035, 49:320c; cf. Ch'en, *Buddhism in China*, p. 54. Chih-p'an was not the first Buddhist to note the Confucian basis of the last three rites. The same point had been made in *Shih-men cheng-t'ung*, Tsung-chien (fl. 1237), *Z*, 2b, 3:404vb. Four hundred years before Chih-p'an, apologists had affirmed that the institution of

Confucius said, "It is not till a child is three years old that it is allowed to emerge from the arms of its parents."[16] That is why children must reciprocate with the three-year mourning. Buddhist scriptures say that it is only after the seven-seven days following death that one is allowed to emerge from the paths of intermediate darkness. That is why one carries out the method of the feasts of seven. As for our contemporaries who perform Buddhist services on the one-hundredth day after death, the *hsiao-hsiang,* and the *ta-hsiang,* although they follow the institutions of mourning of the Confucian pattern, they are still able to cultivate the blessings of strict Buddhist practices.

Chih-p'an was probably not historically accurate in tracing all three of the memorial services back to Confucius (551–479 BCE), but his general point still holds. Since the Latter Han dynasty (25–220) the three commemorations were all identified with state-sponsored ritual. The rite held one hundred days after death can be traced to imperial pronouncements by Emperor Ming (r. 57–75).[17] The observances called *hsiao-hsiang* (lesser auspiciousness) and *ta-hsiang* (greater auspiciousness) are stipulated in the *I-li* (Rites and Ceremonials), a Han dynasty compilation of materials originating in the fourth or third century BCE.[18] The ceremony of *hsiao-hsiang* was usually held in the thirteenth month after death, thus marking the elapse of one year. Medieval commentators disagree over the precise timing of the *ta-hsiang;* some suggest the twenty-fifth month after death, some the twenty-seventh. In any event the last memorial feast was held in the third year after the passing of the deceased.

Although *The Scripture on the Ten Kings* avoids using the Confucian names for the rites, the Confucian scheduling of the last three is unmistakable: services are to be held on the one hundredth day after death, during the first year after death, and during the third year after death. Other sources written under the aegis of Buddhism, including invitations to monks to perform the services, mix freely the Buddhist designations for the first seven feasts with the Confucian names for the last three feasts.

The time for performing rituals addressed to the ten kings was not

---

a three-year mourning period applied to Buddhists as well as to Confucians; see *Pei-shan lu,* Shen-ch'ing (d. ca. 806–820), *T* no. 2113, 52:608c–9b.

16. The full passage is contained in *Analects,* 17:19, in *Lun-yü cheng-i,* pp. 380–83; and Legge, trans., *Confucian Analects,* pp. 190–92.

17. For Han dynasty references, see *Ch'ün-shu i-pien,* Wan Ssu-t'ung (1638–1702), 4.16r–v; and Kao, "Lun tun-huang min-chien ch'i-ch'i chai sang-su," pp. 107–8.

18. On the *hsiao-hsiang* and *ta-hsiang* services, see *I-li cheng-i,* annot. Cheng Hsüan (127–200), ch. 33 (*ts'e* 14, pp. 60–62).

limited to the period after death. While their results were never considered negligible, in terms of efficacy the seven weekly feasts ranked rather low on the scale of posthumous benefit. Even before belief in the ten kings developed in China, the Buddhist tradition engineered a set of premortem services, the merit from which could be held in reserve until after one's death. As Ti-tsang explains in *The Scripture on the Original Vows of Ti-tsang Bodhisattva,* ritual acts carry the greatest weight if performed by the person while still alive. Second in effectiveness is the period of forty-nine days after death. Ti-tsang states:[19]

> In the future or the present, if on the day they approach the end of their lifespan sentient beings manage to hear the name of a Buddha, Bodhisattva, or Pratyekabuddha, then regardless of whether they have sinned or not, they will all attain liberation. If there is a man or woman who during life did not cultivate good causes or who committed many sins, and if after his or her lifespan has ended, descendants engage in creating good fortune, no matter how much or how little, then of all the religious services, out of seven parts the deceased will receive only one. Six parts of the merit will profit the living.

Rituals performed for the deceased were deemed salutary because of the general assumption that the actions of the kin group always had an effect—before, during, and after death—on the condition of the deceased. According to the Buddha's formulation in *The Scripture on Rebirth in Accordance With One's Vows in the Pure Lands of the Ten Directions,* good acts by others not only can free the deceased from the torments of the liminal state, but can assure the attainment of extinction. The Buddha states:[20]

> Whether one's lifespan has not yet ended or whether it has already passed or even on the day it ends, parents, relatives, associates, and friends can, on behalf of the one whose lifespan has ended, cultivate various acts of blessing. They should fast and observe the precepts with a single mind, wash and purify the body, and put on fresh, clean clothes. With one mind they should reverence the Buddhas of the Ten Directions. They should also offer flowers and incense to the various Buddhas. If they do, then the deceased will achieve deliverance from the troubles of suffering, be raised up to heaven, and attain the way of *nirvāṇa.*

19. *Ti-tsang p'u-sa pen-yüan ching,* attrib. Śikṣānanda (652–710), but probably written ca. 936–943, *T* no. 412, 13:784b; cf. Bhikṣu Heng-ching et al., trans., *Sūtra of the Past Vows of Earth Store Bodhisattva,* p. 172. For other references to posthumous offerings returning only one-seventh of the principal, see *Kuan-ting ching, T* 21:530a, 531b; and *Yü-lan-p'en ching shu,* Tsung-mi (780–841), *T* no. 1792, 39:509a–b.
20. *Kuan-ting ching, T* 21:531b.

Although in the eyes of Chinese Buddhists the memorial rituals performed while the deceased traversed the intermediate state did not produce as much merit as premortem acts, nevertheless the general principles on which the rituals were based were never subject to doubt. No one questioned the belief in an afterlife: after death the deceased lives in a liminal stage lasting forty-nine days, possessing a body that is not fully human. The stay in purgatory ends in accordance with the dead person's own karma and the solicitude of the family in sponsoring mortuary rituals. In concept and in performance, death was not a single event but a series of processes. Mortuary rituals occupied a continuum; the deceased took part in them while still alive, and the family of the deceased continued them after death, making merit every seven days.

In light of the continuities between Buddhism and Taoism in the medieval period, especially in the areas where those two religions intersected with ancestral religion, it is not surprising to find that the Taoist church placed premortem and postmortem services on a similar footing. A mid-sixth-century text entitled *T'ai-shang tung-hsüan ling-pao yeh-pao yin-yüan ching* (The Scripture on Karmic Retribution and Causes and Conditions of the Most High Numinous Jewel that Penetrates Mystery) describes the Taoist underpinnings at some length. In that book T'ai-shang tao-chün (Most High Lord of the Way) explains how gods oversee all aspects of life and death. Human beings are born into this world in accordance with their past karma. Each person is endowed with multiple deities residing in different parts of the body. Those internal guests together with ranks of gods in the external world cooperate in recording each act that an individual performs, keeping tally on a balance-sheet that determines the date and hour of death. The balance of good and evil is affected not only by one's deeds but also by acts of offering; sacrifices to the gods both before and after death are beneficial. T'ai-shang tao-chün states:[21]

> Thus at death, during the first seven, the second seven, up to the seventh seven and the one hundredth day, relatives of the deceased should hold services of deliverance so that the deceased will be reborn in a good place and be able to experience happiness. Making this merit is most essential.

The bureaucratic structure of the otherworld, the correlation of gods in the cosmos with gods inside the body, and the quantification of morality all ensured that offerings to the gods could be sent either before or after death.

---

21. *T'ai-shang tung-hsüan ling-pao yeh-pao yin-yüan ching,* Sch no. 336, *TT* 174–75, 8.6v. Soymié ("Les dix jours de jeûne du taoïsme," p. 6) dates the text to the mid-sixth century. A later text mentions the full complement of ten posthumous rites, "from the first of the sevens to the three auspiciousnesses"; see *T'ai-shang tz'u-pei tao-ch'ang hsiao-tsai chiu-yu ch'an,* ed. Li Han-kuang (d. 769), Sch no. 543, *TT* 297–99, 10.7v.

The sixth- and seventh-century Taoist sources mention only the schedule of ten memorial rites, not the deities to whom they are addressed. By the twelfth century the Taoist church had produced its own brigade—actually several brigades—of deities by explicit analogy to the ten kings. The most complicated version of that Taoist administration is described in a liturgy entitled *The Ceremonial for Deliverance of the Ten Kings of the Dark Prefects (Ti-fu shih-wang pa-tu i)*, probably dating from the twelfth century. The text assumes a basic understanding of the ten kings of purgatory and builds a distinctively Taoist set of gods on that basis. Each court is described in detail. At the first court the text states:[22]

> We burn incense and make offerings at the first court of the dark prefects, the True Lord of Great Plainness and Mysterious Breadth [T'ai-su miao-kuang chen-chün], whom people in our time call the Great King Kuang of Ch'in [Ch'in Kuang ta-wang]. In his underground prisons there are long snakes breathing flames and metal dogs puffing smoke. During the first seven the deceased arrives at this court. The Original Celestial Venerable [Yüan-shih t'ien-tsun] takes pity and brings deliverance to deceased souls, releasing them from the dark paths. Then he sings a hymn.

The first hymn praises one of his assistants, the Celestial Venerable Jade Jewel, Augustly Exalted (Yü-pao huang-shang t'ien-tsun), and is followed by a second hymn praising another assistant, the Celestial Venerable Who Saves from Darkness and Plucks Out Sinners (Chiu-yu pa-tsui t'ien-tsun), on whom sinners can also call for help. Both the phrasing and the structure of the system are worth examining further. The text presupposes that its audience is already familiar with the "standard" set of deities described in *The Scripture on the Ten Kings;* it explicitly links each of the major Taoist gods to the standard ones with the locution "whom people in our time call" *(shih-jen so-wei)* or, in other courts, "whom the current generation calls" *(hsien-shih yüeh)*. This wording suggests that at some point in the late medieval period, Taoist practitioners took cognizance of the widespread appeal of offerings to the ten kings of purgatory and attempted to popularize their own list of ten gods as an alternative. The Taoist gods are organized by rank. Each court is under the charge of a Chen-chün (True Lord), who is assisted by two T'ien-tsun (Celestial Venerables) (see appendix 3). In this Taoist cosmos—staffed by members of the Taoist bureaucracy, but

22. *Ti-fu shih-wang pa-tu i,* Sch no. 215, *TT* 84, p. 4r; the whole system is described pp. 4r–11v. The text is undated, but because its deities are similar to those in ch. 172 of *Ling-pao ling-chiao chi-tu chin-shu,* Lin Wei-fu (1239–1303), Sch no. 466, *TT* 208–63, 172.6v–12r, Yoshioka assigns it to the twelfth century; see Yoshioka, "Chūgoku minkan no jigoku jūō shinkō ni tsuite," pp. 262–63.

modeled at significant points on the generic ten kings of purgatory—
offerings before and after death have the same effect.[23]

Returning to the manifestations of this idea in Buddhist-influenced
ritual, one finds that preparatory rituals in *The Scripture on Rebirth in
Accordance With One's Vows in the Pure Lands of the Ten Directions* are called
"preparatory cultivation" *(ni-hsiu)* for the forty-nine days between
death and rebirth. *The Scripture on the Ten Kings* uses the same terminology *(ni-hsiu* and its variant, *yü-hsiu)* in reference to premortem feasts for
the ten kings. *The Scripture on the Ten Kings* does not rule out deathbed
services, but it recommends semimonthly services, held on the fifteenth
and the thirtieth of each month, as the best way to prepare for one's
demise. Although they are not "memorials" in the modern sense of
keeping alive the remembrance of the deceased, these anticipatory rituals are linked philosophically to the ideas motivating the rituals held
after death.[24] It makes a difference whether services are held before or
after death, but the differences are not absolute. In Chinese Buddhism
death reduces the rate of return on one's ritual "investment" from full
benefits to only one-seventh of the offering. It also shifts responsibility
for performing the rites from the prospective decedent to the bereft
descendants. But the logic of the services remains the same: the act of
making offerings has a positive result that can be reserved for the enjoy-
ment of the departed after death. The ritual preparation for one's own
demise and the formalized wailing by one's descendants accomplish an
identical end, as a piece in *The Collected Poems of Brahmācārin Wang* makes
clear:[25]

> All the members of my family having died out,
> When I die no loved ones will offer lamentations.
> So I'll quickly sell off my belongings
> To sponsor a feast of preparatory cultivation.

23. Premortem and postmortem services are mentioned together in two
related texts: *Ling-pao ling-chiao chi-tu chin-shu,* ch. 172; and *Yüan-shih t'ien-tsun
shuo feng-tu mieh-tsui ching,* Sch no. 73, *TT* 32, pp. 1v–2r. Yoshioka ("Chūgoku
minkan no jigoku jūō shinkō ni tsuite," pp. 262–63) dates the latter text to the
twelfth or thirteenth century.
24. From a philosophical perspective both premortem and postmortem practices involve mindfulness, keeping death in mind. Comparative philology offers
interesting connections: Proto-Indo-European: **(s)mer,* "to remember," "to be
concerned"; **mi-moro,* "mindful"; Skt.: $\sqrt{smr}$, "to remember," "to recollect,"
in the *Ṛg Veda* meaning "to remember or think of with sorrow or regret"; usually rendered in Chinese as *nien,* "thought," "mindfulness," "remembrance";
Latin: *memor,* "mindful"; *memoria,* "memory"; Old English: *murnan,* "to
mourn"; see Pokorny, *Indogermanisches etymologisches Wörterbuch,* 1:969–70; and
Monier-Williams, *A Sanskrit-English Dictionary,* p. 1271c.
25. *Wang Fan-chih shih-chi,* in Demiéville, *L'oeuvre de Wang le zélateur,* 3A; and
Hsiang, *Wang Fan-chih shih chiao-chu,* p. 17.

3. Artistic Representations

THE PRODUCERS of books and the preachers responsible for educating lay people about the fate of the dead understood well that displaying pictures of bodies in pain tends to have a more significant impact than simply writing or talking about them. This section focuses on the two principal kinds of pictures of the ten kings in medieval China, illustrated scriptures and hanging silk paintings. Most of them are undated, but their execution can reasonably be assigned to the tenth century.

Five of the surviving copies of the long recension of *The Scripture on the Ten Kings* are illustrated (see appendix 4).[1] Another scroll contains illustrations to the sūtra but no text. It was probably intended to serve as the major prop in a sermon, since the placement of some of the pictures leaves no room for writing. Among the Tun-huang manuscripts there also survives a collection of notes written on the back of another text. The notes record ritual formulas, the words of *The Scripture on the Ten Kings,* and some details specifying the colors and identifying the figures in illustrations to the text. It is unclear whether they were written by an artist, a storyteller or preacher, or an observer.[2] Fragments of scrolls on the ten kings also come from the workshop of Uighur artists active in Qočo (Ch.: Kao-ch'ang). The text is in the Uighur language, and the illustrations betray a strong Central Asian influence.

The illustrated versions of *The Scripture on the Ten Kings* are produced in the format of the handscroll, that is, a long scroll typically placed on a

1. Studies of the iconography of the illustrated scripture include Gabain, "Kṣitigarbha-Kult in Zentralasien: Buchillustrationen aus den Turfan-Funden"; Ledderose, "The Ten Kings and the Bureaucracy of Hell"; Matsumoto, "Jizō jūō zu to inro bosatsu"; idem, *Tonkō ga no kenkyū,* 1:402–16; Tokushi, "Kōzō," pp. 274–87; Watanabe, "An Iconographic Study of 'Ten Kings' Paintings," pp. 17–29; and Whitfield, *Art,* 2:338–39.
2. The notes are part of P 3304v, reprod. Huang, *Pao-tsang,* 127:370a–72b, portion dealing with the ten kings on pp. 370a–b. Soymié ("Un recueil d'inscriptions sur peintures," pp. 170–79) maintains that they were written by an artist for reference in completing illustrations. Roderick Whitfield suggested to me in a private conversation (July 1990) that since artists sometimes used stencils but probably did not work from written notes, the manuscript might represent the hurried notes of a student or interested onlooker. I would also raise the possiblity that the manuscript is an artifact of a ritualized telling of the story, recorded either by an officiant or an observer. This would explain the inclusion of the words "Homage to Ti-tsang Bodhisattva" (*nan-wu* Ti-tsang p'u-sa) at the beginning, the use of storyteller's nomenclature (*shih,* "This is the time when . . . [Mu-lien converted the jailer and saved his mother]") to identify the last scene, and the hurried writing of the notes on the back side of an already used Taoist text.

31

table and viewed horizontally, one segment at a time. In height they range from 27.8 to 30 cm. Placed as scenes throughout the text, the pictures offer glimpses of the passage of the spirit through the underworld. They introduce the characters in the story, advance the narrative, and bring it to a close.

Most copies contain fourteen pictures. Each one is discussed at greater length in Part Three. Here I am interested in their artistic aspects. The first illustration (plates 1a, 1b) is a frontispiece, depicting the audience described at the beginning of the text. The second and third illustrations (plates 2, 3a, 3b) decorate the narrative, providing instructive details about what the minor figures, whom the scripture merely cites by name, actually look like.

The next ten illustrations (plates 4–13b), interspersed throughout the text, show the courts of the ten kings. These illustrations form the core of the narrative. By picturing the movement of the deceased through the tribunals underground, they repeat in a different medium the passage of the spirit described in prose and verse. Each scene is accompanied by a hymn *(tsan)* in four lines of seven syllables. As I will argue more fully in chapter 15, the connection between hymns and pictures is not accidental. Not only were *tsan* as "hymns" an important genre of liturgy in both Buddhism and Taoism, but *tsan* in the sense of "eulogy" had long functioned, before the entry of Buddhism into China, as the textual accompaniment to portraits. Pictures and hymns had a historically sanctioned linkage.

In other respects the pictures accompanying the text go beyond the words. Many of the scenes flesh out, in a sense, the grisly prospects only hinted at in the scripture. The sūtra promises that meritorious actions will bring release from suffering in the dark regions, while the illustrations make the contrast between good and evil deeds frighteningly real. In almost every scene there appear virtuous people, identifiable not only by the scrolls and statues that they have donated to the Saṃgha and now carry in their hands, but also by their lovely clothing, upright posture, and among women their hairpins and rouge. Sinners, however, are clad only in pants or undergarments, usually bound by fetters or manacles or wearing the cangue. The long handle protruding from some of the wooden collars provides jailers with an easy tool for managing prisoner flow, but when that is lacking guards use less subtle methods. The artist's rendering in plate 6b, for instance, shows a guard yanking on a sinner's hair to bend back his head to an unnatural degree, while two disquieted donors clutch nervously at their scrolls. Other scenes (plate 11b) depict the wounds sustained by inmates being beaten with sticks.[3]

3. See also the seventh court in S 3961, reprod. Whitfield, *Art,* 2: pl. 64. To my mind these depictions of punishment and the sinner nailed down to a table

Movement toward a fate measured by the gradations of karma is shown especially clearly in some of the illustrations of the second court, administered by the King of the First River. In the second week after death, the spirit must cross the River Nai. Plate 5a is one of the simplest representations of this scene. It shows eight figures attempting to cross the river. The two at the top are nearly drowning, the virtuous woman crosses effortlessly by a bridge, the next three wade through shallows, and the two at the bottom have already crossed. The story behind this depiction must have circulated widely in medieval China, but in written sources it survives only in a medieval Japanese text that builds upon *The Scripture on the Ten Kings*. The Japanese text refines the spiritual ranking by specifying that people can cross the river at three fords: at the shallows of a mountain stream, at a deep river, or by bridge. The Japanese text also makes sense of the imagery in other versions of this scene (plate 5b), in which sinners' clothes hang from a tree on the banks of the river. The tree is actually a scale, says the Japanese text, that measures the worth of people's past actions. The text also names two figures missing from the Chinese illustrations, Datsueba (Old Woman Who Pulls Off Clothing) and Den'eō (Old Man Who Hangs Up Clothing), whose jobs explain how the tree-scale comes to function.[4]

Other illustrations betray the recognition that the technique of heaping terror upon terror can, without subverting its own moralistic intent, give rise to entertainment or laughter. The court of King Yama, fifth in the sequence after death, was especially fertile for the medieval sense of humor. In King Yama's hall was located the karma mirror, a preternatural surface capable of reflecting a person's past life. The hymn describes how sinners are coaxed to consult the mirror:

> With their hair yanked and their heads pulled up to look into the
>   mirror of actions,
> They begin to know that affairs from previous lives are rendered
>   distinct and clear.

One depiction of this court (plate 8b) demonstrates how justice can be served even when the karma mirror, like the mind of the slow Zen stu-

---

in the final scene (plates 14a–c) are as graphic as the tenth-century scrolls get. In light of the descriptions of hell in earlier Chinese literature and the mutilations depicted unflinchingly in paintings and sculpture beginning in the twelfth and thirteenth centuries—to say nothing of medieval European, Islamic, and Japanese pictures of hell—the renderings in *The Scripture on the Ten Kings* are rather mild.

4. The explication of the scene is found in *Jizō bosatsu hosshin innen jūō kyō, Z,* 2b, 23:381va–b. On the old man and old woman in Japanese mythology, see Seidel, "Datsueba."

dent, has collected too much dust. In that scene three animals—a boar, a snake, and a rooster—march toward King Yama's bench carrying in their mouths and beak the plaints they have filed against the humans who treated them violently in a previous life.[5]

After the tenth court comes the final scene in *The Scripture on the Ten Kings*. It proposes a different attitude, perhaps a solution, to the ordeal of judgment just described. There, standing outside the city of hell to which some people are consigned for their next life, stands an embodiment of compassion. In some versions that figure is Ti-tsang Bodhisattva: in plate 14c he dispenses broth to a weary sinner. By releasing prisoners from their shackles, he provides a glimmer of hope to those contemplating a journey through the dark regions.

Given the gaps in our knowledge about medieval religious art, we can never arrive at a certain assessment of the influences on the illustrations to the ten kings text. Some of the sources, though, are clear. Some basic features of geography and cosmology were based on the understanding of the fate of the dead diffused throughout the Buddhist world.[6] Some of the conventions in the illustrations can be traced only as far as other medieval Chinese representations; some were purely formal, such as the word for "king" *(wang)* written on the cap of each king,[7] while other portrayals reflected life aboveground, like the sticks used for beating prisoners and the size of the cangues around their necks, both of which are specified in T'ang and Sung codes of penal law.[8] Some of the pictures contain more details or different stories altogether than those in the text of the scripture. And among the surviving scrolls there is considerable variation in the depiction of specific scenes.

The second major format for picturing the ten kings was the hanging scroll. Rather than unfolding a story about the ten kings, these vertical paintings portray the kings in positions subordinate to their major subject, the glory of Ti-tsang Bodhisattva. Thanks again to the arid climate of the Northwest and the expeditions of Stein and Pelliot, some one

5. The motif is repeated in paintings during the Southern Sung dynasty. See, for example, painting at Kōtōin, reprod. Suzuki, *Chūgoku kaiga sōgō zuroku*, JT 12-001, 7/11; painting at Jōdoji, reprod. ibid., JT 20-001, 5/10; painting at Eigenji, reprod. ibid., JT 108-001, 5/11; painting at Hōnenji, reprod. ibid., JT 62-001, 5/11; painting at Seiganji, reprod. ibid., JT 13-001, 7/11; painting in collection of Morimura Yoshiyuki, reprod. ibid., JP 9-001, 2/3; and a Muromachi painting at Hōfukuzenji, reprod. ibid., JT 68-001, 3/11. For nineteenth-century examples, see *Shih-tien yen-wang*, pls. 6, 39.

6. See, for example, Matsumoto, *Tonkō ga no kenkyū*, 1:412–16, who speculates about Central Asian influences.

7. Illustrations to P 4524, entitled *Hsiang-mo pien-wen*, depict King Prasenajit sitting on a platform with the graph for "king" written on his cap; reprod. Vandier-Nicolas, *Śāriputra et les six maîtres d'erreur*.

8. See Niida, "Tonkō hakken *jūō kyō* zuken ni mietaru keihō shiryō."

dozen paintings from the ninth and tenth centuries are now held in the major collections of Tun-huang artifacts. Like the illustrated scriptures, they vary considerably in both composition and style, meriting a fuller treatment elsewhere. My comments are intended only to raise a few questions about the portrayal of the ten kings. (For details on the surviving paintings, see appendix 5.)[9]

The paintings may be divided for analytical purposes into two groups according to the relative autonomy and distinctiveness of the ten kings. One kind of painting (fig. 1) places the ten kings indiscriminately at the base of Ti-tsang's throne. The ten kings are closest to the viewer, kneeling in two unordered clumps to the right and left. They are not identical, but the minute variations in costume and expression provide no clue as to which king is which. They do not rank highly enough to command individual assistants; the four clerks (two on each side), the Boys of Good and Evil (one at each side), and the monk Tao-ming (at right) are simply part of the crowd. Aside from depicting them in bureaucratic garb with the word "king" written on their caps, the painting tells us little about what role they might perform in their own right. Instead, the kings are subservient entirely to Ti-tsang. This representation of Ti-tsang matches the composition of paintings lacking the kings that portray Ti-tsang as master of the six paths of reincarnation.[10] He is shown in hooded form, carrying his standard attributes, with halos surrounding him and a simple canopy suspended overhead. At each side three of the paths of rebirth are shown: the halls of heaven, humans, and *asuras* at right, hungry ghosts, animals, and hells at left.

At the other extreme are paintings in which the special function of the

9. For studies of paintings from Tun-huang depicting Ti-tsang and the ten kings, see Kawahara, "Tonkō ga jizō zu shiryō"; Kwon, "Ten Kings of Hell"; Ledderose, "The Ten Kings and the Bureaucracy of Hell"; Matsumoto, "Hibō jizō bosatsu zō no bumpu"; idem, *Tonkō ga no kenkyū*, 1:368–401; Petrucci, "Essai sur les peintures bouddhiques de Touen-houang: les maṇḍalas," pp. 1422–23; V-N, *Bannières*, 14:235–57; Watanabe, "An Iconographic Study of 'Ten Kings' Paintings," pp. 7–16; and Whitfield, *Art,* 2:317–19. The literature on art featuring the ten kings made after the tenth century is quite large. For studies of Sung, Yüan, and Ming paintings, see Ledderose, "A King of Hell"; idem, "Kings of Hell"; Suzuki, *Mindai kaiga shi kenkyū: seppa*, pp. 105 ff.; Tanaka, "Riku Shinchū jūō zu"; and Watanabe, "Kanki aru sō gen butsuga." On Korean paintings of the ten kings, see Nakano, "Chōsen no jizō jūō zu ni tsuite"; and Pak, "The Cult of Kṣitigarbha." On Japanese paintings of the ten kings, see Kajitani, "Nihon ni okeru jūō zu no seiritsu to tenkai." On related Japanese paintings, see Peschard-Erlih, "Les mondes infernaux et les peintures des six voies dans le Japon bouddhique."

10. For paintings of Ti-tsang as master of the six paths without the ten kings, see, for example, Cft lvi.0017 (L), reprod. Whitfield, *Art,* 2: fig. 43; Cft lviii.003 (L), reprod. ibid., 2: pl. 22, figs. 25–27; and MG 17664, reprod. V-N, *Bannières,* 14: pl. 11; 15: pl. 113.

1. Hanging silk painting of Ti-tsang Bodhisattva, master of the six paths, with the ten kings. MG 17793. Musée Guimet. ©Réunion des Musées Nationaux.

ten kings, now shown as fully independent actors, assumes greater importance (see fig. 2). Ti-tsang is still the central icon, but each king now commands his own staff, usually consisting of two assistants. Each king is endowed spatially with his own court; he is seated on a chair behind a desk placed at an angle of three-quarters to the viewer, suggestive of the independent palaces of deities in *maṇḍala* paintings. At each desk the tools for inscribing judgment are displayed. The kings gain in authority by more thorough differentiation, King Yama shown at bottom left, the last king dressed as a general at top right. The kings' role is made even clearer by including at the bottom an actual scene of judgment: a sinner wearing a cangue stands in front of the mirror of karma.

Although Tun-huang paintings constitute our richest store of information about medieval representations of the ten kings, written sources prove that pictures of the ten kings were not limited to the Kansu corridor. In central China a man named Chang T'u (fl. 907–922) painted some of the first recorded examples of Ti-tsang and the ten kings.[11] Chang T'u painted many murals in the temples of his home town of Lo-yang. Some of the most famous were drawn at Kuang-ai ssu as part of a contest of skill. Traditional Chinese art criticism dwells on his unusual technique, apparently self-taught, of painting landscapes by "slinging ink" *(p'o-mo)* and notes his proficiency in portraying large figures. Over one hundred years after Chang T'u, the art historian Liu Tao-ch'un (fl. 1060) wrote down his response to one of Chang T'u's paintings of Ti-tsang and the ten kings. Liu does not mention that Chang T'u's portrayal of the ten kings inspired fear, but he does note that the painting as a whole conveyed compassion, a virtue that, given the subjects involved, could only be attributed to Ti-tsang. Liu writes:[12]

> Once at the home of Wu Tsung-yüan [otherwise unidentified] I contemplated a scroll that T'u had painted of the ten kings and Ti-tsang. It had many fine points, and it preserved the aspect of compassion. To this day it is still kept as a treasure. It can be ranked as a spiritual piece.

Another painter associated with the ten kings is Wang Ch'iao-shih (fl. 907–960). In the middle of the eleventh century Kuo Jo-hsü (fl. 1010–

11. The biographical sketch offered below follows *Wu-tai ming-hua pu-i*, Liu Tao-ch'un (fl. 1060), 2v–3v (p. 437a–b). A few further details are available in *T'u-hua chien-wen chih*, Kuo Jo-hsü (fl. 1010–1074), p. 25; Soper, trans., *Kuo Jo-Hsü's Experiences in Painting (T'u-Hua Chien-Wên Chih)*, pp. 32, 144–45, n. 332; *P'ei-wen-chai shu-hua p'u*, Sun Yüeh-pan (1639–1708) et al., 49.3v–4v (pp. 1042b–43c); and Chu and Li, *T'ang sung hua-chia jen-ming tz'u-tien*, pp. 246c–47c.

12. *Wu-tai ming-hua pu-i*, 3v (p. 437b).

2. Hanging silk painting of Ti-tsang Bodhisattva, master of the six paths, with the ten kings. Cft 0021 (L). ©British Museum.

1074) noted that a great number of Wang Ch'iao-shih's paintings of the ten kings had been preserved. He wrote:[13]

> Wang Ch'iao-shih was skilled at painting Buddhist and Taoist subjects and secular figures. He especially loved painting images of Ti-tsang Bodhisattva and the ten kings; in all there are over a hundred versions circulating in our time.

We do not know precisely where or when Wang lived, but some tangential evidence places a Taoist priest with a similar name at the court of Kao-tsu (r. 936–943).[14]

Images of the ten kings were not restricted to paper and silk. Archaeological and architectural studies currently underway will probably uncover further evidence of the artistic manifestations of the ten kings, but brief mention can be made here of stone statues and wall paintings executed in the early tenth century.[15] A modern epigraphical collection shows that a full set of statues of the ten kings was made at a temple in Anhwei in the year 903. It preserves an inscription accompanying the carving in stone of the *Diamond* sūtra commissioned by a layman named Li Tsung-ta on T'ien-fu 3/VII/25 (20 August 903) at Pao-lin ssu (later renamed Kuang-fu ssu) in Feng-t'ai hsien (modern Anhwei). The inscription also refers to four sets of statues and dedicates the merit from their carving to Li's family. The four sets are: "Images of Śākyamuni, one set [*i-p'u*]. The Western Pure Land, one set. The Merit of Layman Vimalakīrti, one set. Images of the ten kings, one set."[16] An inscription preserved in another collection notes simply that a man named Tu Liang and others commissioned images of the ten kings to be carved in a grotto in Tzu-chou (modern Szechwan) on Wu-ch'eng 3/XI/26 (30 December 910).[17]

13. *T'u-hua chien-wen chih*, p. 23; cf. Soper, trans., *Kuo Jo-Hsü's Experiences in Painting*, p. 29. I assign Wang the vague floruit of 907–960 because this source classifies him as a Five Dynasties painter.

14. Outside of *T'u-hua chien-wen chih*, the only possible—but still unlikely—reference to the painter comes in a note written by Wu Jen-ch'en (fl. 1669). He states that "Wang Ch'iao, a Taoist priest" (Wang Ch'iao, *tao-shih*) wrote a copy of the *Scripture on Salvation (Tu-jen ching)* during the reign of Kao-tsu (r. 936–943); see *Shih-kuo ch'un-ch'iu*, Wu Jen-ch'en, p. 676.

15. The most comprehensive study of artistic representations of the ten kings through the tenth century outside of Tun-huang is still Tsukamoto, "Inro bosatsu no kenkyū," pp. 172–75. Current research into sites in Szechwan promises to add to our knowledge; see Hu, "Lun ti-yü pien-hsiang t'u."

16. *Shan-yu shih-k'o ts'ung-pien*, Hu P'in-chih (fl. 1898), 9.44v. I emend the text, changing *t'u-wang hsiang* to *shih-wang hsiang*, following Tsukamoto, "Inro bosatsu no kenkyū," p. 172.

17. Inscription in *I-feng-t'ang chin-shih wen-tzu mu*, Miao Ch'üan-sun (1844–1919), 7.9r (p. 19,637a). Tu Liang may be the same person whose eulogy of

T'ang dynasty sources state that scenes of hell were painted frequently on the walls of Buddhist temples, but give no indication what these "transformation tableaux of the underground prisons" *(ti-yü pien-hsiang)* actually looked like.[18] Perhaps the earliest mention of a wall painting depicting the ten kings is contained in a text that was carved in stone on T'ien-yu 4/V/14 (27 June 907) in a temple named Shen-fu-shan ssu (at Fang-shan in modern Shansi). The text, "Shen-fu-shan ssu ling-chi chi" (A Record of the Numinous Traces at Shen-fu-shan ssu), written by a certain Wang Chü-jen and inscribed by a man named Wang Ch'ung-yü, narrates the vissicitudes of the temple complex. It concentrates on the miracles associated with one of the temple's most famous residents, the Hua-yen philosopher Li T'ung-hsüan (646–740). It describes the destruction of buildings and images during the Hui-ch'ang era (841–846) and mentions the subsequent rebuilding of the temple. Its survey of notable images that existed in 907 includes a mural of the ten kings and Ti-tsang.[19] Since most of the buildings at the temple were destroyed during the Hui-ch'ang suppression, I would hypothesize that the mural of the ten kings was painted sometime between 846 and 907.

The grottoes at Mo-kao-k'u near Tun-huang were also decorated with paintings of the ten kings. Those wall paintings were made during the tenth, eleventh, and twelfth centuries. Some portray only the ten kings, and others join the ten kings with Ti-tsang Bodhisattva or pictures of transmigration in the six paths.[20]

The evidence surveyed above demonstrates that the ten kings appeared in a broad range of art forms in the ninth and tenth centuries. Artists added them to some copies of *The Scripture on the Ten Kings,* dispensed with the text and painted the same images on handscrolls used in storytelling, placed them as minor attendants or as judges in their own right in silk paintings of Ti-tsang, carved their forms into statues, and painted scenes of their courts on temple walls. Despite the variety of artistic and literary evidence, however, there are very few direct clues

---

T'ai-tsung (r. 626–649) is contained in *(Ch'in-ting) Ch'üan t'ang wen,* 860. 15v–16r (p. 11,372a–b).

18. See Mair, "Records of Transformation Tableaux *(Pien-hsiang)*"; and Teiser, " 'Having Once Died and Returned to Life': Representations of Hell in Medieval China."

19. Inscription in *Shan-yu shih-k'o ts'ung-pien,* 9.45r–48r; mention of ten kings and Ti-tsang, 9.47r; editor's (Hu's) note to the text, 9.48r–v.

20. According to Tun-huang wen-wu yen-chiu-so, ed., *Tun-huang mo-kao-k'u nei-jung tsung-lu,* the caves containing wall paintings of the ten kings and their dates of construction are Th Cave 6 (907–959), 176 (960–1035), 202 (960–1035), 314 (1036–1226), 375 (960–1035), 379 (907–959), 380 (960–1035), 384 (907–959), 390 (907–960), 392 (907–960), and 456 (960–1035).

about the context of these representations. Hence for some conclusions we must rely on what we know of other medieval renderings of the dark regions.

We know in the first place that pictures of hell proper—the set of underground prisons to which some sinners were sentenced after passing before the ten kings—were used in a variety of religious settings.[21] The same appears to be true of portrayals of the ten kings. The narrative scrolls were probably used for entertainment and education, although we cannot be certain of the background of the tellers—theatrical or priestly—or of the demography of their audience. The illustrated scriptures were linked to the memorial observances that families carried out for their dead. The paintings on silk undoubtedly helped to popularize devotion to Ti-tsang Bodhisattva and may have been used as devices in meditation, allowing monks to re-create and then eidetically destroy the world of birth and death. As life-size manifestations of the kings, statues were fit to receive offerings. And wall paintings probably served most of these functions, decorating the walls of Buddhist temples with soteriologically relevant, and amusing, paintings of other realms.

Some scholars have advanced hypotheses about changes in the iconography of the ten kings based on a comparison of the tenth-century specimens with Sung, Yüan, and Japanese paintings. The most convincing analysis is that of Lothar Ledderose, who proposes "a typological sequence which is meant to suggest the general line of iconographic development as well." He argues that earlier pictures make no significant distinctions between the ten kings, while the later ones grant them greater autonomy, portraying them with separate desks, their own attendants, and, in the illustrated scripture and in thirteenth-century samples, their own scenes of judgment.[22] Although Ledderose's theory is a plausible explanation of changes in artistic composition, it is proba-

21. See, for example, Teiser, " 'Having Once Died and Returned to Life,' " esp. pp. 459–63; and Jera-Bezard and Maillard, "Le rôle des bannières et des peintures mobiles dans les rituels du bouddhisme d'Asie centrale." For an earlier period, see Hou, "Recherches sur la peinture du portrait en Chine."

22. See Ledderose, "The Ten Kings and the Bureaucracy of Hell"; quotation from p. 11. Whitfield draws explicitly on Ledderose's typology in arranging the relevant entries in Whitfield, Art, 2: passim. Watanabe also offers an insightful analysis of the iconography of the paintings of the ten kings; see Watanabe, "An Iconographic Study of 'Ten Kings' Paintings," pp. 7–35. At one point, however, she posits an invariant link between these iconic paintings (as opposed to illustrations to the scripture) and the short (unillustrated) recension of the ten kings text, and claims further that both were grounded exclusively in *postmortem* rituals. Part Two of this study offers several examples of the *premortem* commissioning of the short recension, while Jera-Bezard and Maillard ("Le rôle des bannières et des peintures mobiles") demonstrate that the composition of a painting alone is not a reliable index of its actual use.

bly unwise to posit an unchanging relationship between specific iconographic types, on the one hand, and distinct schools of thought, specific
rituals, or actual specimens, on the other. The move from logical priority to chronological development is undermined by the apparently random and still poorly understood process by which the Tun-huang paintings and illustrations managed to survive. Furthermore, very few
samples are dated, and the conservatism of Chinese art—in this case,
the anachronistic reproduction of earlier, logically simpler compositions
—is especially true of religious art produced by semiskilled artists for
audiences that were not part of a metropolitan elite.

For conclusions about composition and style, perhaps the best
method is simply to explain more fully, and more critically, the terms of
analysis I have already applied, namely, the distinction between narrative and iconic modes of representation. The former is exemplified in
illustrated scriptures, the latter in hanging silk paintings.[23] Seemingly
trite differences in the physical limitations of the two genres provide a
helpful starting point.

What I have called the "narrative" mode may be defined as a connected series of relatively small, simple scenes, which, because Chinese
handscrolls are usually not laid out entirely flat but are unrolled one
stretch at a time, must be viewed consecutively. The pictures are never
viewed all together; the story they tell unfolds one scene at a time. Most
episodes are dominated by an event or action. The narrative form is
suited ideally to depict movement; this particular narrative describes
the transit of the deceased from the moment of death to the instant of
rebirth. In general the organizing principle is the passage of time; in
these scrolls the law of cause-and-effect explains why sinners suffer in
each court. To borrow an analogy from Ch'an Buddhism extended frequently to the criticism of painting and poetry, the narrative mode could
be defined as "gradual" (chien[b]). If forced to specify the subject of these
illustrations, one would have to say that they are about the experience
of the spirit after death.

The "iconic" mode may be defined as a single, relatively large, complex scene organized hierarchically around a single focus. Usually suspended on a wall, such paintings are viewed in their entirety. They are
static and make no reference to time. Although no one would claim to
understand them fully at first sight, they are viewed "all at once" or in
"subitist" fashion (tun). Their logic is spatial, and they are composed
symmetrically. Like many maṇḍalas, the figures in these paintings are

23. I offer a definition of these two modes tailored to pictures of the ten kings,
but the distinction itself is not new. For other interpretations, see Mair's distinction between maṇḍala and pien-hsiang in Mair, "Records of Transformation
Tableaux," esp. pp. 3–4; and the distinction between "iconic" and "episodic"
in Wu, The Wu Liang Shrine, pp. 132–41.

ranked according to their distance from the center. The major deity is enthroned in the central circle. In this book I have placed these paintings under the rubric of the ten kings, but there can be no doubt that their primary subject is Ti-tsang. His power and compassion dominate the ten kings, their assistants, and other members of the bureaucracy. In fact in one exceptional painting the kings appear not as severe bureaucrats but as devoted worshippers of Ti-tsang. I have seen only a poor reproduction of the painting (now kept in New Delhi), but the rough description published in 1921 conveys a good idea of its iconic nature:[24]

> [The kings, here called "judges"] sit with hands in adoration behind their benches, on which are brazen altar vessels instead of scrolls. . . .
>
>   . . . function of judges lost sight of even in original tracing, where brazen vessels transform their benches into altars; they themselves, devoid of their rolls of office, have adopted pose of subsidiary adoring Bodhisattvas in Paradise pictures.

Although the distinction between narrative and iconic modes of representation may help to clarify the analysis of different renderings of the ten kings, we must also remember that the distinction is modern and arbitrary, and at times impedes an understanding of medieval culture. Some pictures contain a mixture of the two styles. At the very beginning of the illustrated scripture—the definitive form of narrative illustration —the frontispiece (plate 1a) portrays Śākyamuni as a central icon and the ten kings and other attendants as subsidiary figures arrayed around him. Conversely, some of the Ti-tsang *maṇḍalas* include details that effectively draw the viewer's attention away from the center. At the bottom of one painting (fig. 2) a sinner in King Yama's court is shown standing in front of a mirror, his cruelty toward animals reflected there as proof of past misdeeds. The scene is still tied spatially to the dominating figure of Ti-tsang, but it also becomes an episode linked chronologically to the passage of the spirit through the prisons of purgatory. It hints at Yama's cruelty and retribution rather than the compassion and forgiveness associated with Ti-tsang.

Folktales recorded by the monk Ch'ang-chin (fl. 989) present a more sophisticated analysis of the relationship between narrative and iconic modes in the portrayal of the ten kings. Entitled *Ti-tsang p'u-sa hsiang ling-yen chi* (A Record of the Numinous Verifications of Images of Ti-tsang Bodhisattva), the book consists of thirty-two tales, culled from an

24. The painting is Cft 00355 (ND), reprod. Matsumoto, *Tonkō ga no kenkyū*, 2: pl. 111a. The description is contained in Stein, *Serindia*, p. 991. Stein credits Miss F. M. G. Lorimer, who in 1914 organized a temporary exhibition of artifacts from the second expedition at the British Museum, with writing most of the descriptions in this section of *Serindia;* ibid., 1:xiv.

original corpus of approximately one hundred, about the miraculous events caused by paintings, murals, and statues of Ti-tsang. The twenty-ninth story concerns a *maṇḍala*-like painting of Ti-tsang and the ten kings like those discussed above. Because of its importance I translate the story in its entirety below.[25]

> Śramaṇa Chih-yu was from western India. He came [to China] during the T'ien-fu[b] era [936–943] and lived at Ch'ing-t'ai ssu.
>
> Among the images and scriptures he brought with him were a transforming image of Ti-tsang Bodhisattva and a *Scripture on the Merit of [Ti-tsang's] Original Vows* bound in Brāhma-style boards. The special marks of the Image were that in the central circle the Image of the Bodhisattva was drawn wearing a cap and carrying a jewel and metal staff.[26] To the sides were images of the ten kings, five on each side. The five on the left were: one, King Kuang of Ch'in. . . . [The ten kings are listed in their usual order.] Each of them was accompanied by the Officer of Life-span and the Officer of Emoluments, magistrates,[27] and various administrators.
>
> Chih-yu explained their origins. He said, "Formerly in western India there lived a Bodhisattva who was compassionate and brought salvation to the world. He took a great vow to paint an Image of Ti-tsang in order to bring salvation to sentient beings suffering in the three paths. He went to the city of the ten kings and declared, 'I have vowed to bring salvation to the sufferings of the three paths. I seek your help in bringing benefit to those who suffer.' The ten

25. *Ti-tsang p'u-sa hsiang ling-yen chi,* Ch'ang-chin (fl. 989), *Z*, 2b, 22:184rb–vb; cf. abridged trans. in Mochizuki, *Daijiten,* pp. 2216c–17a. Aside from the preface and postface to the work, the only mention of the author I have found places him at the imperially sanctioned translation bureau (*i-ching yüan*) in K'ai-feng (modern Honan) in the year 982, serving as a secretarial and literary assistant to the translator T'ien-hsi-tsai (d. 1000); see *Fo-tsu t'ung-chi,* Chih-p'an (fl. 1258–1269), *T* no. 2035, 49:398a. With one exception, events cited in the text date from 665 (second tale) to 980 (twenty-sixth tale). The exception is the thirtieth tale, dated 1163–1164, which is probably the interpolation of a later editor. According to Ono (*Daijiten,* 4:275a), the *Z* edition of the work is based on a manuscript held in the library of Kyoto University; see also Manabe, *Jizō bosatsu no kenkyū,* pp. 157–59.

26. The term *pao-hsi* could mean "jewelled staff," but given the standard iconography of the hooded Ti-tsang in the tenth century, I interpret the term as two separate words. The first refers to the wish-fulfilling gem (*ju-i pao-chu,* Skt.: *cintā-maṇi*), the second to the monk's staff with tin rings (*hsi-chang,* Skt.: *khakkara*) carried by Ti-tsang; see Mochizuki, *Daijiten,* pp. 4132c–33c, 2152c–53c, respectively.

27. The text reads simply *fu-chün* (magistrates), and I do not emend it, but most similar lists refer here to T'ai-shan fu-chün (the Magistrate of Mount T'ai).

kings assented respectfully by bringing their palms together. They lined up in order to the left and the right and told the Image [of Ti-tsang], 'All sentient beings belong to the Great Sage. If you should wish to transform them, then we will serve as companions to help in the process of sagely transformation.' At that time the Image gave a subtle smile [and said], 'Excellent! The sinful acts of sentient beings will soon be lessened.' Then it emitted a beam of light that illuminated the suffering vessels in the three paths. All of the sufferings of the sentient beings who received illumination were relieved."

[Chih-yu continued,] "Such is the great profit that was bestowed when the Indian[28] Bodhisattva entered the *samādhi* of bringing benefit to sentient beings and prayed to the ten kings. That Bodhisattva himself made into a picture the forms that he had seen and added the ten kings and the others to the original Image. This [painting that I have brought from the West] is the numinous Image."

[The author, Ch'ang-chin, adds,] Originally this happened in the western regions. [Traveling to China] he was very careful with them and preserved two images.

[Chih-yu continued,] "While crossing the desert I encountered a seductive demon. Beseeching the Bodhisattva [Ti-tsang] through invocation,[29] I was able to hold up my metal staff and, maintaining my tranquility,[30] apprehend her."

[Chih-yu continued,] "Another time when a great rainstorm came at night, we lost our light and didn't know East from West. Vicious beasts howled and there was pandemonium among people and horses. Then the Image emitted a ray that made things as bright as morning; the vicious beasts calmed down and our way was clear."

[Chih-yu continued,] "Another time there was a great river one-half *li* wide. The water was so rough we couldn't tell how deep it was. It was so easy to drown in it that even leaves which we placed on the surface wouldn't float—imagine what would have happened to a boat! We invoked the transforming Image and all of a sudden saw a *śramaṇa* and two boys riding in a boat. One boy held up a banner, the other one

---

28. I emend *tz'u chi tu p'u-sa . . . yeh* to *tz'u yin-tu p'u-sa . . . yeh*. In addition to the orthographic similarity, the word *yin-tu* is abbreviated to *yin^d*, not *tu*, and in this construction the particle *chi* would be redundant.

29. "Beseeching through invocation" renders *ch'i-nien*. The text gives no clue as to whether the invocation was purely mental or included chanting as well. The same ambiguity marks the phrase below, "invoking the transforming Image" *(nien pien-hsiang)*.

30. I am uncertain of my translation of *ning-shang* as "maintaining my tran-quility."

rowed the boat, and the *śramaṇa* carried Brāhma-style boards. They ferried us across. When we reached the eastern shore we took our leave and departed. At that time the *śramaṇa* set down the Brāhma-style boards."

[The author, Ch'ang-chin, concludes,] The powers of this transforming Image to do away with obstacles are truly inconceivable. In this land both religious and lay made tracings of it, but still everyone felt differently and quarreled over the style. Two years later no one knew where Chih-yu or his Image was. Everyone suspected that they returned to India. Perhaps [Chih]-yu was a transformational incarnation of Ti-tsang!

Before addressing the "inner" stories here—the meditative encounter between the Indian Bodhisattva and the ten kings and Ti-tsang, and the events Chih-yu witnessed on his journey—it is helpful to examine how the author, Ch'ang-chin, has framed the account.[31] Ch'ang-chin begins by identifying the owner of the image and describing its special characteristics. He then relates the explanation of the icon's origins offered by the owner, perhaps as mediated through written or oral folklore. Resuming the role of narrator, he closes by noting the impact of the image upon pious Chinese people and by extolling the miraculous nature of the image and its owner. It is clear from Ch'ang-chin's crafting of the piece that not only were paintings of the ten kings with Ti-tsang in vogue during the tenth century, but their iconography was hotly contested. The major part of the account (Chih-yu's testimony) is no doubt supposed to put an end to the "quarrels over style" *(ching-mo)* by Ch'ang-chin's contemporaries. It is more difficult to assess whether Ch'ang-chin's presentation of Chih-yu's story was in its own time very convincing. The temple named Ch'ing-t'ai ssu where Chih-yu settled was probably in Chekiang, but we have no other information about his residence there.[32] Several usages in the account suggest that the original story circulated in a milieu somewhat removed from that of the usual literati miracle tale. Ch'ang-chin states unequivocally that the original story was spoken, not written. The monk who told it is supposed to be Indian, yet Ch'ang-chin provides only his Chinese name. Aside from the monk's eventual cenobitical home on Chinese soil, no place names are listed for his itinerary. Similarly, the particular format of the scripture delivered by the *śramaṇa* borne in a boat inspires little confidence in

31. I here follow the distinction between "inner" and "outer" stories advanced in Dudbridge, "Yü-ch'ih Chiung at An-yang," p. 43.
32. Ch'ing-t'ai ssu in Tung-yang chün (modern Chekiang) was the first monastic residence of the T'ien-t'ai monk Hsüan-lang (673–754); see *Hung-tsan fa-hua chuan*, Hui-hsiang (fl. 667), *T* no. 2067, 51:48a; and *Sung kao-seng chuan*, Tsan-ning (919–1001), *T* no. 2061, 50:875b–76a.

its Indic origins. In the inner story itself, Chih-yu claims merely that the mysterious monk carried "Brāhma-style boards" *(fan-chia);* the text is named only in Ch'ang-chin's introduction. Thus, the tenth-century physical description of the manuscript is congruent with the opinion of modern scholarship about the authenticity of the sūtra: it was a late Chinese creation placed consciously in Indian packaging.[33]

The stories related by Chih-yu explain the origins of two objects, image and text. In fact the story of the painting's creation is told at third hand: Ch'ang-chin records the story that Chih-yu told about the experiences of an anonymous Indian Bodhisattva. As part of his formal assumption of the Bodhisattva path, the unnamed Indian vows to paint pictures of Ti-tsang. For help with the picture he travels to what we can assume was Ti-tsang's field of activity, "the city of the ten kings" *(shih-wang ch'eng).* In responding to the aspiring Bodhisattva's request, the ten kings position themselves in the pattern that he would later reproduce in painting. Chih-yu attempts to guarantee the accuracy of the depiction by attaching an authoritative-sounding name to the meditative state in which the Bodhisattva traveled to the underworld.

Through unspecified means the image passes to its second owner, Chih-yu, and saves him from danger several times. In the last episode Chih-yu's devotion to the image is rewarded by a ferry-mounted monk, who leaves him an Indian scripture after carrying him across a river.

Ch'ang-chin's story offers a sophisticated and critical perspective on the categories of "iconic" and "narrative" we have used thus far in analyzing artistic representations of the ten kings. It suggests that icon and text were constantly interacting, and that we can make sense of one mode only in terms of the other. At the beginning of the story, within the time frame of the legend itself, the picture precedes the text: first the anonymous Bodhisattva paints a picture of his experiences, then Chih-yu's invocations of the painting call forth the bestowal of a text. Yet the collector of the legend subverts the priority of the icon; Ch'ang-chin's handling of the legend suggests an additional point about the relation between icon and narrative. Ch'ang-chin's account shows that what we have considered the quintessentially iconic representation of the ten

33. In medieval Chinese usage *fan-chia* connoted Indian-style binding, in which the leaves of a tree (or, as in the case of many Tun-huang exempla, paper cut in the shape of palm leaves) were pierced once or twice in the center, tied together with string, and protected on top and bottom with boards; see Mochizuki, *Daijiten,* pp. 4180c–81b. The text Ch'ang-chin refers to as [*Ti-tsang*] *pen-yüan kung-te ching* is almost certainly *Ti-tsang p'u-sa pen-yüan ching,* T no. 412. Modern scholarship proposes that it was composed in the ninth or early tenth century. It is not listed in catalogues compiled in 730 or 800, it is not cited in extant T'ang dynasty sources, and it is not mentioned by Japanese pilgrims to T'ang China. Ch'ang-chin's account of Chih-yu's journey contains the earliest known reference to the work; see Mochizuki, *Daijiten,* pp. 3602c–3c.

kings derives from a series of incidents, that the authenticity of the image is explained best by telling a story. Like the illustrated versions of *The Scripture on the Ten Kings*, it accepts the validity of a *maṇḍala*-like picture, but makes sense of that arrangement by placing it as one scene within an ongoing narrative.

4. Other Manifestations

MEMORIAL RITES and paintings were probably the most frequent contexts in which the ten kings appeared in medieval times, but the rulers of the underworld were by no means limited to those two media. Within China their presence can be detected in essays, encyclopedias, dreams, sermons, and Buddhist and Taoist liturgies for related monthly services. Outside of China they appeared in Uighur texts and in Japanese scriptures and hymns. This section assembles such fragmentary, often less-than-certain evidence to speculate on the distribution of the ten kings across space and time and their manifestations in a number of religious settings.

The earliest reference to the ten kings is preserved in a work that catalogues Buddhist books and provides brief biographies of their authors, compiled by the highly placed cleric Tao-hsüan (596–667) in the year 664. Tao-hsüan records the names of two treatises written by a monk named Fa-yün, who was active in Ch'ang-an in the middle of the seventh century. Tao-hsüan writes:[1]

> *An Essay Assessing the Three Teachings,* one work in three scrolls.
> *An Essay on the True Karma of the Ten Kings,* one work in ten scrolls.
> These two essays in thirteen scrolls were written by Śākya Fa-yün, a *śramaṇa* of Hsi-ming ssu in the capital. Yün was originally from Chiang [modern Shansi]. When young he roamed the mysterious shop [of meditative practice?] and stayed in the room of concentration. He arrived promptly at clever insights, so that even though he was not well acquainted with scriptural writings, [he had only] to pass them before his eyes and know mysteriously their basic meaning. Whenever he saw people consulting rulers with base currents, false discussions, or the Three Teachings leveled into one school, thus muddying the way of government in the common fashions of the time, he would carefully sort out the names and principles and thoroughly investigate the

---

1. *Ta-t'ang nei-tien lu,* Tao-hsüan, *T* no. 2149, 55:282a.

mysterious [Taoism] and the *ju* [Confucianism]. In writing these two essays he opened the way for enlightening the base.

Tao-hsüan's biography of Fa-yün is not long, but it does draw a rough sketch of Fa-yün's background and writings. Tao-hsüan probably knew Fa-yün personally, which adds further value to his testimony.[2] Fa-yün's book-learning appears to have been founded primarily on his meditative experience. His métier, according to Tao-hsüan, was neither translating Sanskrit texts nor writing commentaries, but rather explaining Buddhism to people in a written language they could understand. He took aim at what he regarded as "base" *(su)* and "false" *(hsieh[b])* attempts at syncretism. His work was probably directed toward an audience more interested in practical effects than in doxological subtleties. Fa-yün's *Essay on the True Karma of the Ten Kings* was still in existence in the eleventh century, but was not preserved after that.[3] Judging from its title, it was written in the style of a prose essay, and it explained the operations of karmic retribution, perhaps devoting one chapter each to the evil actions punished in the ten courts of purgatory. The written sources and the liturgical background to Fa-yün's treatise are unknown, but Tao-hsüan's account suggests that it was an apologia dealing with rebirth and the principles of morality.

After this early reference the historical record becomes much fuller in demonstrating the place of the ten kings in memorial rites, art, and scripture. Those manifestations are discussed elsewhere in this study; here my concern is with more fragmentary evidence. The ten kings appear next in a more refined literary work, a tenth-century encyclopedia designed as a Buddhist version of the lists of flowery vocabulary available to men of letters. Entitled *Shih-shih liu-t'ieh* (Buddhist Items under Six Headings), the work was put together by the monk I-ch'u (fl. 945–976).[4] I-ch'u's secular surname was P'ei, and his family was from Honan. He became a novice at age seven and took full precepts at

2. A conservative floruit for Fa-yün would be 658–664. Hsi-ming ssu was completed in 658. Tao-hsüan was abbot *(shang-tso)* there until his death in 667. Furthermore, both Tao-hsüan (in this work) and his contemporary, Tao-shih (d. 683) (in *Fa-yüan chu-lin, T* no. 2122, 53:1023b), who also resided at Hsi-ming ssu in mid-century, situate Fa-yün's writings just before those of Tao-hsüan.

3. It is cited in the bibliographical treatise in *Hsin t'ang shu,* Ou-yang Hsiu (1007–1072), p. 1526.

4. *Shih-shih liu-t'ieh,* I-ch'u, in Makita, *Giso rokujō.* The brief biography offered here is based on the prefaces and postface to *Shih-shih liu-t'ieh* in Makita's edition (a Japanese printed edition preserved at Tōfukuji, based on a Chinese edition of 1103); *Sung kao-seng chuan,* Tsan-ning (919–1001), *T* no. 2061, 50:751b–c; *Ts'e-fu yüan-kuei,* Wang Ch'in-jo (962–1025), 52.17r–v (p. 584a); *Fo-tsu t'ung-chi, T* 49:392b; and Makita, "Giso rokujō ni tsuite," in Makita, *Giso rokujō,* pp. 1–5.

twenty-one. He specialized in the study of Abhidharma works and in his mature years lived at K'ai-yüan ssu in Ch'i-chou (modern Shan-tung). In the preface to *Buddhist Items under Six Headings,* I-ch'u expresses the hope that it will help correct mistakes in the use of Buddhist expressions. He claims to have read through the Buddhist canon three times, compiling the book between the years 945 and 954. The title alludes to the phrase book edited one hundred years before by Pai Chü-i (772–846), *Pai-shih liu-t'ieh shih-lei chi* (Mr. Pai's Collection of Classified Items under Six Headings). The Buddhist encyclopedia was submitted to the throne, and Emperor Shih-tsung (r. 954–959) thought so highly of the work that he had it sent to the Bureau of Historiography for printing.

Because Chinese encyclopedias typically comprise citations of pre-existing works and involve little or no writing by the author, clues to the individuality of an encyclopedia can be found only in the logic of arrangement and the nature of the sources. I-ch'u's discussion of the ten kings comes at an interesting location. He does not refer to the ten kings in his subsection entitled "The Underground Prisons" *(ti-yü).*[5] That subsection describes the traditional, pan-Buddhist system of eight major hells that make up the lowest of the six paths of rebirth. The sources for the citations in that part are primarily canonical works translated from Indian languages. The ten kings, on the other hand, appear in a later subsection, entitled "Yama Rāja" (Yen-lo), which is the first subsection in the section entitled "Ghosts and Spirits of the Mysterious Darkness" *(yu-ming kuei-shen).*[6] Some of the sources in that part are canonical, others are not. Under the phrase "The Prophecy Given to Yama Rāja" (Yen-lo *shou-chi*), I-ch'u paraphrases several sentences from the long recension of *The Scripture on the Ten Kings,* detailing the Buddha's prediction of Yama's Buddhahood, his explanation of Yama's past life, and his description of Yama's current position. I-ch'u's citation of the scripture suggests that by the middle of the tenth century in eastern China, *The Scripture on the Ten Kings* was recognized as a noncanonical and indispensable source on King Yama.

Unlike the conscious attempts to popularize and explain belief in the ten courts of purgatory discussed thus far, the next snippet on the ten kings derives from folklore about the dreams of no less a Confucian than Ou-yang Hsiu (1007–1072). The historian Chih-p'an (fl. 1258–1269) appends a report of Ou-yang Hsiu's dream experience to a notice on his death. Chih-p'an notes carefully that his source is the "Account of Conduct" *(hsing-chuang)* drawn up by Wu Ch'ung (1031–1080), the

5. *Shih-shih liu-t'ieh,* 4.17r–20v (pp. 71a–72b).
6. *Shih-shih liu-t'ieh,* 16.30r–v (p. 362b).

father of Ou-yang's oldest son's wife, who heard the original tale from one of Ou-yang's grandsons. Chih-p'an writes:[7]

> When Yung-shu [Ou-yang's courtesy name] was first called to government service, he suffered from many illnesses. Once he dreamt that he went to a place where he saw ten people wearing the imperial cap [*mien*] and seated in rows. One of them said, "You served in the government—how could you come to this?"
>
> Yung-shu asked, "Aren't you gentlemen what the Buddhists call 'the ten kings of the dark offices' [*ming-fu shih-wang*]?"
>
> The king said, "Yes."
>
> "Then I would like to ask," [Yung-shu continued,] "when people in our world feed monks and commission scriptures, does any profit result?"
>
> [The king] replied, "How could there be no profit?"
>
> When [Yung-shu] awoke his sickness was cured. From then on he knew better about respecting the Buddha.

Although Wu Ch'ung's original biography, probably written for inclusion in ancestral ceremonies, does not survive, Chih-p'an's scrupulousness in citing his source and, in turn, its source indicates that not long after Ou-yang Hsiu's death, his experiences with the ten kings were discussed widely. In his waking hours Ou-yang may well have tried to furnish Confucian alternatives to Buddhist rituals, but folklore suggests that the ten kings still exercised a hold upon him when darkness fell.[8]

By the twelfth century the ten kings were an easily recognized metaphor for pain and evanescence in sermons on the Pure Land. They are mentioned in a short essay on the impermanence of life written by the layman Wang Jih-hsiu (d. 1173).[9] Wang lived most of his life in Anhwei and wrote books on such topics as the *Book of Changes* and the *Spring and*

---

7. *Fo-tsu t'ung-chi*, *T* 49:414b; cf. Mochizuki, *Daijiten*, p. 2217a.

8. Ou-yang's daytime attitude is nicely expressed in his "Pen-lun" (Essay on Fundamentals): "The cult of Buddhism has plagued China for over a thousand years. . . . It is clear then that Buddhism took advantage of this time of decay and neglect to come and plague us. This was how the illness was first contracted. And if we will but remedy this decay, revive what has fallen into disuse, and restore once again to the land kingly rule in its brilliance and rites and righteousness in their fullness, then although Buddhism continues to exist, it will have no hold upon our people"; trans. de Bary, *Sources of Chinese Tradition*, 1:387. On Ou-yang's attitudes toward Buddhism, see Liu, *Ou-yang Hsiu*, pp. 155–72. On general trends in the Neo-Confucian opposition to Buddhist mortuary practice, see Ebrey, *Confucianism and Family Rituals in Imperial China*, pp. 68–101; and idem, "Cremation in Sung China."

9. For Wang's biography, see the prefaces to *Lung-she tseng-kuang ching-t'u wen*, Wang Jih-hsiu, *T* no. 1970; *Le-pang wen-lei*, Tsung-hsiao (d. 1214), *T* no. 1969a, 47:196b–97a; *Fo-tsu t'ung-chi*, *T* 47:284a–b; and *Sung yüan hsüeh-an pu-i*, Huang Tsung-hsi (1610–1695) et al., 4.123r.

Autumn Annals. He collected many of his essays on Buddhist topics in a work called *Lung-she tseng-kuang ching-t'u wen* (Revised and Expanded Pieces on the Pure Land from Lung-she). Wang raises the specter of the ten kings midway through one of the essays. He places the ten kings, in keeping with their purgatorial function, between the ills of this lifetime and the sufferings of the next. In this life, Wang explains, even those who achieve longevity are subject to pain: their bodies are a home to parasites, and their health is always uncertain. Whether death comes early or late, all people must pass before the ten kings. Wang describes the experience:[10]

> On the road ahead you see no light, and looking around you are entirely without companions. When you reach the shore of the River Nai you see them, all in desperate pain. Everyone going through the portal at the Ghost Gate trembles with fear. In the world above only seven days have passed, but in the dark regions you are forced to have an audience with the ten kings. The officers of the bureau who hold the case books lack all human feeling, and the prison guards who carry pitchforks never smile.

Wang next explains what happens after passing through the ten courts: good people are reborn in heaven or as humans, while those with any trace of evil are reborn in the hells. He describes life in hell in generic terms, mentioning the various forms of torture (boiling inmates, forcing them to drink molten iron, making them climb trees sprouting knives) and the cruelest form of justice, the cool wind of karma, which refreshes prisoners just enough to let them experience the next round of punishment. Wang's interest is ultimately didactic; once one realizes that bodily existence is the root of suffering, he says, then the practices of lay Buddhism offer a means of salvation. As he puts it, "If you can't study the Way or practice meditation, then be diligent in upholding the feasts and invoking the Buddha, giving up evil and returning to the good . . . ."[11] In this context, passing through the ten courts underground is not the worst horror of life and death. Instead, the ten kings are considered to be just one part of the process of *saṃsāra,* all of which is tinged with pain. The courts are accepted as points of transit between present and future suffering, escape from which can only be secured by the practice of simple Buddhist morality.

A moral order similar to that administered by the ten kings was the basis for regular observances in the medieval lay organizations of both Buddhism and Taoism. What makes those practices worth mentioning in this study of the ten kings is that they too involved deities organized

10. *Lung-she tseng-kuang ching-t'u wen,* *T* 47:286c.
11. Ibid., *T* 47:287a.

in brigades of ten. In a Buddhist context the rituals, which consist of holding special feasts, repeating the precepts, and making offerings, are called "the ten feasts [or fasts]" *(shih-chai)*, while Taoist sources refer to similar practices as "the ten feasts" *(shih-chai)* or "the ten feasts of uprightness" *(shih-chih-chai)*.

Evidence for this kind of Buddhist and Taoist lay religion is fragmentary, difficult to date, and still imperfectly understood. One may, however, accept the conclusions of Michel Soymié, who judges that the basic idea of holding ten feasts per month grew out of the Buddhist practice of *uposadha*, which originally designated the recitation of monastic regulations and confession of faults by members of the Samgha twice each month. That custom gave rise to a practice, verified in fifth-century Chinese apocrypha, of holding six feasts per month.[12] According to one such text, the four kings of heaven, under the authority of the god Indra, oversee the inspection of people's good and evil deeds six times every month. The scripture states:[13]

On the eighth day of every month, [the four kings of heaven] dispatch messengers to inspect the empire. They investigate emperors and kings, ministers and common people, dragons and ghosts, and insects that crawl, fly, squirm, and wiggle as to whether their thoughts, words, and actions are good or evil. On the fourteenth day they dispatch princes. On the fifteenth day the four kings of heaven themselves descend. On the twenty-third day the messengers descend again. On the twenty-ninth day the princes descend again. On the thirtieth day the four kings descend again. On days when the four kings descend, all of the gods among the sun and the moon, the five planets, and the twenty-eight constellations descend together.

The move from six feasts per month to ten was made for the first time, according to surviving evidence, in Taoist circles in the sixth century. A number of Taoist texts set forth a monthly schedule for lay feasts, detailing the day of the month, the direction responsible for each feast, the chief god dispatched, his assistants, and the nature of deeds under investigation (see appendix 6).[14] Many of the gods are stellar dei-

12. See Soymié, "Les dix jours de jeûne du taoïsme"; idem, "Les dix jours de jeûne de Kṣitigarbha"; and Yoshioka, "Chūgoku minkan no jigoku shinkō ni tsuite," pp. 254–68.
13. *Ssu-t'ien-wang ching*, Chih-yen (fl. 394–427), Pao-yün (376–449), *T* no. 590, 15:118b; following Soymié, "Les dix jours de jeûne du taoïsme," pp. 9–10.
14. For representative texts, see *Yüan-shih wu-lao ch'ih-shu yü-p'ien chen-wen t'ien-shu ching*, Sch no. 22, *TT* 26, 3.1r–8r; cited with minor variations in *Wu-shang pi-yao* (ca. 574), Sch no. 1138, *TT* 768–79, 9.4v–10r; *T'ai-shang tung-hsüan ling-pao yeh-pao yin-yüan ching* (ca. mid-sixth century), Sch no. 336, *TT*

ties: T'ai-i is 42 or 184 Draconis, Pei-tou is Ursa Major, and Pei-ch'en means "Northern Asterism," the group around the North Star.

The ten lay feasts sponsored by the Buddhist church appear somewhat later in the historical record, beginning in the tenth century. They are held on the same days of the month as are the Taoist ones and rely on the dispatch of deities and their functionaries to inspect behavior on earth. Some of the gods are unmistakably Buddhist, and there are no connections to stars or directions (see appendix 7). Many of the texts specify that if the feast is performed correctly, then after death one's sins will be wiped away for a specific number of *kalpas* and one will avoid suffering in a specific hell. One schedule begins:[15]

> On the first day of the month the Boys [of Good and Evil] descend. If one invokes Ting-kuang ju-lai [Dīpaṃkara Tathāgata] Buddha and upholds the feast,[16] then one's sins will be wiped away for forty *kalpas* and one will not fall into the underground prison of knives and swords.
>
> On the eighth day of the month the Princes descend. If one invokes Yao-shih liu-li kuang [Bhaiṣajyaguru vaiḍūryaprabha] Buddha and upholds the feast, then one's sins will be wiped away for thirty *kalpas* and one will not fall into the underground prison with powdery grass.[17]

The system of ten monthly feasts in lay Buddhism provides an interesting contrast to that of the ten kings. Like the ten kings, the monthly pantheon combines bureaucrats with Buddhist deities in a web of cosmic surveillance. But the theology of the ten feast days is dualistic. On one side stand ten bureaucrats, some of them associated with Buddhism to be sure (e.g., King Yama, Śakra), but each discharging the duties of his office and holding a rank, either civil or military, in the bureaucratic empire that intruded into all spheres of Chinese life and death. On the other side float ten deities of distinctly Indian provenance, all of whom retain their Sanskritic identification as "Buddha" *(fo)* or "Bodhisattva" *(p'u-sa)*.

The monthly feasts in Buddhist and Taoist lay life make no reference to the ten kings of purgatory as a group (although the Buddhist set over-

---

174–75, 4.10r–v; and *Tung-hsüan ling-pao liu-chai shih-chih sheng-chi ching*, Sch no. 1200, *TT* 875, 1v–r; cited in *Chai-chieh lu* (ca. late seventh century), Sch no. 464, *TT* 207, pp. 2v–3r.

15. *Ta-sheng ssu-chai jih*, S 2567, transcr. *T* no. 2849, 85:1299c.

16. Here and in the next paragraph I emend *ch'u-chai ch'u-tsui* (wipe away the feast and one's sins will be wiped away) to *ch'ih-chai ch'u-tsui* (uphold the feast and one's sins will be wiped away), following the locution in similar texts like *Ti-tsang p'u-sa shih-chai jih*, S 2568, transcr. *T* no. 2850, 85:1300a.

17. I render *fen-ts'ao* as "powdery grass" (see Morohashi, *Jiten*, no. 26872.28), but it could also mean grass that slices its victims into powder.

laps with the fifth and seventh kings), nor are they connected overtly with mortuary ritual. Nevertheless, like some of the premortem memorial rites discussed in chapter 2, they are based on many of the same principles as the offerings to the ten kings. The feasts combine elementary rules of morality with the making of offerings, and their primary effect is to improve one's condition after death. They depend upon a view of the cosmos as a bureaucracy, with higher-level deities sending down their assistants to inspect deeds and to forward reports on what they have observed.

The traditional conceit that places China in the middle of the world is aptly reflected in the diffusion of the ten kings westward and eastward. German expeditions to Central Asia in the first decade of the twentieth century unearthed literary and pictorial references to the ten kings dating from the eleventh century or later. The expeditions, led by Alfred Grünwedel and Albert von Le Coq, concentrated on the modern district of T'u-lu-fan (Turkish: Turfan), formerly Kao-ch'ang (Turkish: Qočo), located in what is now called the Xinjiang Uighur Autonomous Region, known to earlier European explorers as Chinese Turkestan.[18] The Uighur people migrated there from their homeland in Mongolia in 840, following their defeat by the Kirghiz. The new Uighur state, based in the oasis town of Qočo on the edge of the Tarim Basin, became a thriving crossroads in East-West trade between 850 and 1250. Buddhism, Manichaeism, and Nestorian Christianity all flourished there, as did a pageant of cultural groups. Ethnically and linguistically the Uighurs were Turks. They spoke a kind of Old Turkish that was recorded most often in a form of the Sogdian alphabet that had been developed in Central Asia prior to the arrival of the Uighurs. The majority of Uighur texts surviving from Qočo (now housed in several German collections and elsewhere), including those referring to the ten kings, are written in this form. For philologists and Buddhologists they constitute an especially vexing corpus: Uighur is basically a Turkic language in the Altaic family, it preserves vocabulary from Indo-European languages (Prakrit, Sanksrit, Sogdian, Tokharian A, Tokharian B) and Chinese, and it is written in a Sogdian script, which in turn derives from the writing system of Aramaic, a Semitic language.

For the purposes of this study the most important body of Central

18. I must here acknowledge the gracious assistance provided by Jan Nattier, who translated Uighur texts and led me through the web of linguistic and historical problems involved in studying Central Asia. Good introductions to the medieval Uighur empire in Chinese Turkestan include von Gabain, *Das Leben im uigurischen Königreich von Qočo (850–1250)*; Hamilton, *Les Ouïghours à l'époque des Cinq Dynasties d'après les documents chinois*; and Moriyasu, "Uiguru to tonkō." Von Gabain's work on the Uighur language also provides a helpful starting point: see von Gabain, *Alttürkische Grammatik*; and idem, "Das Alttürkische."

Asian evidence consists of thirty-five manuscript fragments, comprising at least two separate copies, of a Uighur version of an illustrated book about the ten kings (see appendix 8).[19] Judging from both pictures and words, the Uighur text presents a rough translation not of the entire *Scripture on the Ten Kings,* but only of the hymns accompanying the illustrations. The selective translation into Uighur of only those parts that were rhymed poetry in Chinese is particularly interesting. Although the evidence is piecemeal, the pieces that do survive raise the possibility that the Uighur translators and artists based their work either on a Chinese original that contained only hymns and pictures, or on the aboriginal practice of memorializing the dead.[20] Seven of the Uighur fragments can with some assurance be declared to be translations of the Chinese *Scripture on the Ten Kings.* Sometimes the match is iconographic, or the Uighur is a straightforward translation of the sense of the Chinese. In other cases, phenomena specific to the rituals addressed to the ten kings appear in the Uighur: the days or years in which sacrifices are performed, the trident held by the guards of hell, and so forth. In at least one other case the Uighur text transliterates the Chinese name of one of the ten kings. I would conclude, then, that the Uighur fragments of *The Scripture on the Ten Kings* were translated from the Chinese, probably between the years 1050 and 1250.[21]

Although the Chinese influence is dominant in these Central Asian traces, it is by no means complete. We know from other literary sources that Indian Buddhist notions of transmigration were translated into Uighur, sometimes via texts written in Tocharian.[22] Uighur social conventions also played a role, as seen in the short veil, a prerogative of the Uighur aristocracy, that some of the kings wear in the illustrations to the

19. For a superb study (plus photographic reproductions) of the Uighur fragments, see von Gabain, "Kṣitigarbha-Kult in Zentralasien, Buchillustrationen aus den Turfan-Funden"; cf. shorter treatments in idem, "The Purgatory of the Buddhist Uighurs"; and idem, *Das Leben im uighurischen Königreich,* pp. 193–96. Ten fragments of the Chinese version of the long recension of the scripture, including illustrations, were also found at Qočo; see appendix 10.

20. Note that the Chinese "original," if there truly was one such text, might in fact be preserved in ten Chinese fragments discovered at Qočo, which contain only hymns and pictures. Hymns and prayers form a large portion of the Buddhist literature in Uighur based on Chinese models: see von Gabain, "Die Alttürkische Literatur," esp. pp. 221–30.

21. For details on the match between the Uighur fragments and the Chinese original, see appendix 8. The dating of the translation of the Chinese *Scripture on the Ten Kings* into Uighur is based on von Gabain's dating of the surviving fragments to "approximately the eleventh to the thirteenth century" ("The Purgatory of the Buddhist Uighurs," p. 25).

22. Bang, Rachmati, "Uigurische Bruchstücke über verschiedene Höllen aus der Berliner Turfansammlung."

Uighur ten kings text.[23] Other manuscript fragments written in Uighur draw on the same system as that of *The Scripture on the Ten Kings*, but betray Iranian influences. They prescribe the same series of feasts for the deceased as those in the Chinese text and refer to King Yama (Uighur: Ärklig Qan), but place the proceedings under the aegis of the constellation Pleiades (Skt.: Kṛttikā; Uighur: Ülkär).[24]

The eastward and southward transmission of the ten kings through rituals, art, and literature is a fascinating and complex topic deserving treatment in its own right. The bulk of the evidence survives from Japan, on which I will focus.

The names of the ten kings and the process of judging the dead were part of Sino-Japanese commerce during the medieval period. The first contact of underworld cultures that can be dated with certainty is described by the Japanese pilgrim-monk Jōjin (1011–1081), who traveled in China between 1072 and 1081. Jōjin reports that in the year 1072 in Chekiang he saw a text entitled *Ti-tsang shih-wang ching* (Ja.: *Jizō jūō kyō* [or *gyō*]; The Scripture on Ti-tsang and the Ten Kings) as well as statues of the ten kings arrayed around one of Ti-tsang.[25] Unfortunately Jōjin offers no details about the contents of the scripture or the nature of the icons, although the text may well be related to the Ti-tsang scripture to be discussed below. We do know that within two hundred years of Jōjin's journey, at least one copy of the Chinese version of the *Scripture on the Ten Kings* had been taken to Japan, because a thirteenth-century

23. Von Gabain ("Kṣitigarbha-Kult in Zentralasien," p. 55) offers this interpretation of the costume of the king in one of the fragments, MIK 3:6327; reprod. ibid., fig. 57.

24. Von Gabain includes a discussion, transcription, and translation of these fragments in "Kṣitigarbha-Kult in Zentralasien," p. 65. The Sanskrit-Uighur correspondences for Yama and Pleiades are from Bazin, "Über die Sternkunde in alttürkischer Zeit"; and idem, "Les noms turcs et mongols de la constellation des Pléiades"; cf. Clauson, "Early Turkish Astronomical Terms." Von Gabain also discerns Iranian influence in the appearance of Ursa Major (Uighur: Yetikän, literally "seven lords") atop the hat of one of the ten kings in the Uighur fragments (MIK 3:6670; reprod. von Gabain, "Kṣitigarbha-Kult in Zentralasien," fig. 81); discussed ibid., p. 64; and idem, "The Purgatory of the Buddhist Uighurs," pp. 32–33; cf. Clauson, "Early Turkish Astronomical Terms." The possible Iranian influence must also be weighed against the association made in Chinese lore between Yama-as-Emperor and Ursa Major. In many of the pictures of King Yama in *The Scripture on the Ten Kings,* for instance, his imperial hat *(mien)* has Ursa Major on top; see chapter 16 and plate 8a, below. For a discussion of Taoist influences on Buddhist materials dealing with the stars, see Franke, "The Taoist Elements in the Buddhist *Great Bear Sūtra (Pei-tou ching).*"

25. *San tendai godaisan ki,* Jōjin, in *DBZ,* 72:232c, 252c; cf. von Verschuer, "Le voyage de Jōjin au mont Tiantai," p. 10, n. 21.

source cites the title and quotes verbatim from the narrative.[26] Pictures
of the ten kings became a trading commodity not long after that. Several sets of hanging paintings of Ti-tsang and the ten kings made in the
workshops of Ningpo (in modern Chekiang) in the late twelfth and early
thirteenth centuries are preserved in Japan.[27] They were brought there,
no doubt, by devoted Japanese tourists.

The paradigm of unilinear diffusion on which I have relied thus far is
less helpful in understanding the development of rituals addressed to
the ten kings in their Japanese context. Foreign inspirations were soon
fashioned into rites and symbols that satisfied local tastes. Such a fusion
of influences is clear in the richest literary source on the ten kings in
medieval Japan, entitled *Bussetsu jizō bosatsu hosshin innen jūō kyō* (also
pronounced *gyō*) (The Scripture Spoken by the Buddha on the Causes of
Bodhisattva Jizō [Ti-tsang] Giving Rise to the Thought of Enlightenment and the Ten Kings). Modeled in part on the Chinese *Scripture on the
Ten Kings,* the text was probably put together by anonymous Japanese
authors sometime between 1000 and 1300.[28] To distinguish it from the
Chinese text, I will follow scholarly usage in referring to it as *The Scripture on Jizō and the Ten Kings (Jizō jūō kyō).*

The Scripture on Jizō and the Ten Kings outlines the journey of the spirit
through the ten courts of purgatory. Like the Chinese *Scripture on the Ten
Kings,* it defines a schedule of seven seven-day periods plus the one hundredth day, one year, and three year observances. The geographical
tour is more dominant in the Japanese scripture than in the Chinese
one. In addition to reproducing the hymns of the Chinese text for each

26. *Hōji san shiki,* Ryōchū (1199–1287), in *Jōdōshū zensho,* p. 15a (4:47a).
27. See the studies cited in chapter 3 by Kajitani, Ledderose, Peschard-
Erlih, Suzuki, Tanaka, and Watanabe.
28. The text is available in *Z,* 2b, 23, based on Japanese printed editions of
1594 and 1688. Important studies and translations include Ishida, trans., *"Bussetsu jizō bosatsu hosshin innen jūō kyō,"* pp. 183–277, 337–41; Izumi, *"Jūō kyō no
kenkyū";* Ono, *Daijiten,* 4:273b–74a; idem, *Bukkyō no bijutsu to rekishi,* pp. 646–
51; Pelliot, review of Waley, *A Catalogue of Paintings Recovered from Tun-huang by
Sir Aurel Stein,* pp. 384–90; Soymié, "Les dix jours de jeûne de Kṣitigarbha,"
pp. 155–56; idem, "Notes d'iconographie chinoise: les acolytes de Ti-tsang,"
part 1, p. 48, n. 3, and p. 51; Yabuki, trans., *"Bussetsu jizō bosatsu hosshin innen
jūō kyō";* and Waley, *Catalogue,* p. xxvii. The text is attributed to Tsang-ch'uan,
the putative author of *The Scripture on the Ten Kings.* The colophon to the text is
dated T'ien-sheng 10, which must be 1023. A different version of the colophon
is recorded in *Jizō jūō kyō senchū,* Zenshin (d.u.), cited in Izumi, *"Jūō kyō no
kenkyū,"* pp. 312–13. Neither the attribution to Tsang-ch'uan nor the veracity
of the colophon can be trusted. I discuss below the reasons for regarding the text
as a Japanese creation put together partly on the basis of Chinese materials
between 1000 and 1300. The earliest dated quotation from the text as we know
it is in *Jōdo kenmon shū,* Zonkaku (1290–1373), in *Shinshū zensho,* 48:340a–47b,
but the text must have circulated widely before that.

court, the Japanese text several times adds the locution, "Next I will preach about the court of . . . ." The Japanese scripture expands upon the sufferings of the deceased at the hands of the underground bureaucracy. It devotes special attention to the fifth court, that of King Yama. The fifth court is the focus of *The Scripture on Jizō and the Ten Kings* not because of its chief administrator, but because Yama's offices are where the deceased can glimpse the Bodhisattva Jizō (Ch.: Ti-tsang). Here the book describes the rewards for those reborn in Jizō's Pure Land, lists the vows to relieve people's suffering that Jizō took in a previous lifetime, and explains how Jizō will manifest himself in six different bodily forms to those in need. Thus, where the Chinese text grapples with the problem of King Yama, the Japanese apocryphon is concerned with the prospects for salvation offered by Jizō.

In language and literary form *The Scripture on Jizō and the Ten Kings* shows that Chinese components were revised for a Japanese-speaking audience. The narrative portions are written in classical Chinese prose *(kanbun),* and the seven-syllable hymns (Ch.: *tsan;* Ja.: *san*) describing the ten courts in the Chinese *Scripture on the Ten Kings* are repeated verbatim. At three of the ten courts, however, *The Scripture on Jizō and the Ten Kings* appends a second hymn to the Chinese one. All three follow the style of Japanese Buddhist hymns *(wasan).* The Japanese text adds considerably to the story told in the Chinese text, most notably by giving the dead a voice. At the seventh court, for instance, *The Scripture on Jizō and the Ten Kings* notes:[29]

> The deceased are forced into suffering. Grieving over their problems, they chant:

> > We wait for seven-times-seven days,
> > Without food or drink, forced into the cold,
> > For our sons and daughters to use our belongings
> > To do some good, soon to support us.

> > Barred from entering prison on their relatives' behalf,
> > Our sons stay home, probably relieved.
> > What fears have we of suffering Yama's prison?
> > Already the fires in our heads are no metaphor.

As a literary piece, the one extant version of *The Scripture on Jizō and the Ten Kings* appears unpolished: it contains different numbers of hymns at the different courts, and its prose portions are very long at the beginning and middle but quite short elsewhere. This asymmetry perhaps reflects an early stage in the transmission of the text or indicates that this version grew out of an oral tradition.

29. *Jizō jūō kyō, Z* 2b, 23:384rb; cf. Ishida, trans., *"Bussetsu jizō bosatsu hosshin innen jūō kyō,"* pp. 262–64.

In terms of content *The Scripture on Jizō and the Ten Kings* attempts a fascinating synthesis of Chinese and Japanese materials. Whoever put the text together—in a process that may have spanned several centuries and included Chinese and Japanese versions now lost—had a very thorough grounding in Chinese concepts of the afterlife. The scripture represents the first time in East Asian history that the theory of three *hun*-spirits and seven *p'o*-spirits (Ch.: *san-hun ch'i-p'o;* Ja.: *sankon shichihaku*) was linked explicitly to the ten courts of the underworld. It is also the first surviving text to join the ten feast days of Chinese lay practice and their ten Buddhas and Bodhisattvas (discussed above) to the ten kings of purgatory. At the fifth court in *The Scripture on Jizō and the Ten Kings,* King Yama himself promulgates the monthly calendar for observing the feasts and bestows a *dhāraṇī* that will assure long life and a good rebirth. The Japanese text also draws on the apocryphal Chinese version of Ti-tsang's career as a Bodhisattva to explain the vows he took in the past to bring salvation to all sentient beings.[30]

As a convincing Japanese Buddhist creation, *The Scripture on Jizō and the Ten Kings* weaves into the text several features of the underworld unique to medieval Japan. Most striking from a historical point of view is the pairing of the ten kings with the first ten Buddhist deities that would eventually emerge as the standard list of thirteen Buddhist gods invoked in a schedule of thirteen memorial services. The thirteen figures were one of the later developments in the form of Japanese theologizing generally called *shinbutsu shūgō* (unification of [Shinto] gods and Buddhas) and more specifically *honji suijaku* (original ground and subsequent manifestation).[31] Although the strategies for matching indigenous and foreign gods saw many changes between the Heian and Meiji periods, by the twelfth century the Buddhist figures were usually regarded as the "original ground," the Shinto deities as their later traces. It is probably in that context—the attempt to provide a Buddhist rationale for symbols and rituals of mixed pedigree—that we should place the appearance of the ten Buddhist figures in *The Scripture on Jizō and the Ten Kings.* The text cites the name of the corresponding Buddhist deity in smaller, commentarial-style writing, directly after each court. In later centuries three more Buddhas and Bodhi-

30. The discussion of Jizō's past life can be found in *Jizō jūō kyō, Z* 2b, 23:383rb–va. The original story is contained in *Ti-tsang p'u-sa pen-yüan ching,* attrib. Śikṣānanda (652–710), *T* no. 412, 13:780b–81c.

31. The literature on the matching of Buddhist to indigenous deities is voluminous. Helpful overviews include Murayama, *Honji suijaku;* idem, *Shinbutsu shūgō shichō;* Matsunaga, *The Buddhist Philosophy of Assimilation;* and Sakurai, *Shinbutsu kōshō shi kenkyū.* A fascinating angle on the whole phenomenon is now available in English in Grapard, *The Protocol of the Gods.*

sattvas were appended to the list, adding *yahrzeit* observances at the tenth, thirteenth, and thirty-third years (see appendix 9). As proof that the text was put together in Japan, scholars also point to the use of vernacular Japanese words to describe various features of the underworld (e.g., "Yomi no kuni" for Yama's city) and to details of the subterranean administration that do not appear in Chinese accounts.[32]

A cursory sampling of the better-known figures of Kamakura Buddhism shows that by the end of the period, the ten kings played a role in the mortuary rituals of many Japanese Buddhist movements.[33] The third patriarch of the Pure Land School *(jōdo shū)*, Ryōchū (1199–1287), explains a line in a prayer attributed to the Chinese master Shan-tao (d. 662) by citing from the Chinese *Scripture on the Ten Kings*.[34] Ryōchū's choice of sources indicates that in Japanese Pure Land circles, *The Scripture on the Ten Kings* was considered a sufficiently authentic Chinese scripture to serve as an explanation for a hymn that in fact predates the scripture. The ten kings also form the topic of a short piece attributed to Nichiren (1222–1282).[35] The text discusses most of the landmarks of purgatory mentioned in *The Scripture on Jizō and the Ten Kings*. Whoever wrote the text was well versed in the doctrinal controversies of the day. The author quotes extensively from earlier Buddhist literature, refers often to positions of the Shingon sect and the True Pure Land school *(jōdo shinshū)*, and touches on the topic of the end of the Dharma *(mappō)*. In discussing the *honji suijaku* correspondences mentioned in *The Scripture on Jizō and the Ten Kings*, the author emphasizes that the Buddhist figures serve to ground the entire system of retribution in the Buddhist virtue of compassion. In the more radical criticism of self-assertion propounded by the True Pure Land School, the act of making offerings to the ten kings, either on behalf of oneself or for one's ancestors, was considered counter-productive. Thus Zonkaku (1290–1373) describes the underworld at length and mentions some of the rituals

32. See Izumi, "*Jūō kyō* no kenkyu," pp. 306–18; and Seidel, "Datsueba," respectively.

33. The role of the ten kings in the "funerary Buddhism" of medieval Japan is an important and complex topic. For fuller treatments, see Bodiford, *Sōtō Zen in Medieval Japan;* Fujii, *Jōdo shū;* Goodwin, "Shooing the Dead to Paradise"; Matsuura, *Zenke no sōhō to tsuizen kuyō no kenkyū;* Tanaka, *Bukkyō minzoku to sosen saishi;* and idem, *Sosen saishi no kenkyū*.

34. Shan-tao refers to King Yama and lesser functionaries in *Chuan-ching hsing-tao yüan wang-sheng ching-t'u fa-shih tsan*, Shan-tao, T no. 1979, 47:428b. Ryōchū's explanation can be found in *Hōji san shiki*, p. 15a (4:47a).

35. The piece, of which only the first of two chapters survives, is *Jūō sandan shō,·* Nichiren, in *Shinshū shiryō shūsei*, 5:241–52. See also Nakamura, "Nichiren shōnin no *jūō sandan shō* o yomite."

addressed to the ten kings in his day, but his whole account is intended to demonstrate the perils of merit-making and the need for faith (*shinjin*).[36]

This Sinocentric survey of materials ranging from Central Eurasia to Japan is far from complete, nor is it intended to do justice to the complexity of religious life in any of those locales. Similiarly, the Chinese evidence considered throughout this study demonstrates how much would be lost in treating belief in the ten kings as a phenomenon that could be traced unambiguously thorough the filiation of a single text. Nevertheless, some trends in the diffusion of the ten kings can be identified. The languages for discussing the bureaucrats of purgatory were as different as Uighur and Japanese, and their rule was explained in a variety of literary forms. The paraphernalia of the subterrestrial regions often mirrored the changing landscape above ground, and tortures varied from place to place. The ten kings were matched to different sets of Buddhas, Bodhisattvas, True Lords, and Celestial Venerables, and were placed under the jurisdiction of powerful local gods. Along with these divergences, however, there was consistency in the bureaucratic structure of judgment after death and in the faithful transmission of the names of the ten kings. And the preservation of hymns to the ten kings in both medieval Central Asia and medieval Japan suggests that the diffusion of belief was achieved largely through liturgical continuity.

36. See *Jōdo kenmon shū,* Zonkaku, 48:34a–47b, esp. 345b–47a.

5. Origin Legends

THE ISSUE OF authenticity was never far from the minds of Chinese Buddhist apologists. However "sinicized" their religion might have become, even after the T'ang dynasty they traced its beginnings to Śākyamuni Buddha and enunciated its teachings in a form of Chinese still tinged with Sanskrit. But authenticity had two sides. Looking westward, Buddhists in China were compelled to demonstrate a living connection to India. Looking to the east, they had to explicate that foreign grounding in a style that was unquestionably Chinese. Hence, the ambiguous status of Buddhism in China produced a wealth of origin legends, which may be defined as narratives that explain the existence of ideas, books, or practices by linking them to events, usually of an extraordinary nature, that occurred in the lives of important persons in the significant past.[1]

The demand for legitimation was especially pressing in cases like that of *The Scripture on the Ten Kings,* in which practices were suspected of being untraditional and scriptures were deemed noncanonical. That is perhaps why the first attempt at a rationale for the ten kings is contained in the text itself. *The Scripture on the Ten Kings* addresses the issue in several places. Śākyamuni provides an explanation of the underground bureaucracy in general: the officers of purgatory, he says, are not mindless functionaries but Bodhisattvas exercising compassion toward the group of sentient beings currently moving through the intermediate state. Lest there be any doubt, later in the scripture the Buddha commissions all members of the bureaucracy to honor the sacrifices sent to their halls, saying, "The Law is broad and forgiving. I allow you to be lenient with the compassionate and filial sons and daughters of all sinners." To this the chief administrator, King Yama, replies that his officers will vow to carry out the Buddha's directive. Thus *The Scripture on the Ten Kings* founds the system of ten memorial rituals on the authority of the historical Buddha, who explains its logic and guarantees its efficacy by directing each king to take a formal pledge of responsibility.

The origin story internal to *The Scripture on the Ten Kings* was not, however, fully convincing; the text also required validation of its authorship and assurance of its historicity from outside sources. In the several hundred years after the ten kings first appeared in China, three legends about their origins gained widespread acceptance. This section examines the formation of those legends and reflects briefly on their significance.

One of the first systematic attempts to explain the beginnings of *The Scripture on the Ten Kings* is found in *Shih-men cheng-t'ung* (roughly, The Correct Lineage of the Buddhists), completed in 1237 by the śramaṇa Tsung-chien.[2] Tsung-chien lived in Liang-chu (modern Chekiang). As

---

1. Most of the origin legends combine characteristics of what Thompson distinguishes as *"Sage"* ("local tradition" or "local legend") and "explanatory tale"; see Thompson, *The Folktale,* pp. 8–9.

2. It is important to note that *Shih-men cheng-t'ung* contains much older material. Tsung-chien did not begin writing from scratch. He started with a work already entitled *Shih-men cheng-t'ung* by Wu K'o-chi (1142–1214) and added more material; see *Shih-men cheng-t'ung,* Tsung-chien (fl. 1237), *Z,* 2b, 3:446vb–47ra; and *Fo-tsu t'ung-chi,* Chih-p'an (fl. 1258–1269), *T* no. 2035, 49:132a–b. On Tsung-chien and his works, see Tsung-chien's preface in *Shih-men cheng-t'ung, Z,* 2b, 3:357ra; *Fo-tsu t'ung-chi, T* 49:132a–b; Mochizuki, *Daijiten,* pp. 2159b–60a; Ogawa, "Shūkan *shakumon shōtō* no seiritsu"; Ono, *Daijiten,* 5:33d–34c; Schmidt-Glintzer, *Die Identität der buddhistischen Schulen und die Kompilation buddhistischer Universalgeschichten in China,* pp. 96–108; and Ts'ao, "Lun *Shih-men cheng-t'ung* tui chi-chuan t'i-ts'ai te yün-yung."

a historian he consciously assumed what had become a rather sectarian outlook in the T'ien-t'ai Buddhism of his day, partially in response to what he perceived to be the misrepresentations of the Ch'an school. Nevertheless he remained ecumenical at least in terms of coverage, taking care to include biographies of figures associated with the schools of *ching-t'u, ch'an, fa-hsiang* (Yogācāra), *lü* (Vinaya), and *mi* (Tantra). Like other Buddhist histories written during the Sung, *Shih-men cheng-t'ung* is very much a work of traditional Chinese historiography: its first chapters are labeled "basic annals" *(pen-chi)*, and its later sections include genealogies *(shih-chia)*, treatises *(chu-chih)*, biographies *(lieh-chuan)*, and sources *(tsai-chi)*.[3] Tsung-chien places the article on the ten kings in a chapter entitled "Benefitting Life" *(li-sheng)*, which discusses releasing live animals, donating food to wandering ghosts, prayers for the spirits of water and land, the ten kings, and donating goods (including paper money) to spirits. Tsung-chien cites two sources on King Yama, reviews the legends on the origins of the ten kings, and then offers his own assessment. He writes:[4]

> Then there are the "ten kings." In *The Scripture on [the Points of] Mind-fulness of the True Law* there is only [one king], King Yama Rā[ja].[5] His name is translated as "the Twin Kings" [Shuang-wang] because the brother is in charge of the men's prison and the sister is in charge of the women's prison.[6]
>
> According to *The Record of Retribution from the Dark World*, it is said,[7] "The Emperor of Heaven exercises universal authority over the six paths; these are called 'Heaven's Sections.' [The jurisdiction of] King

3. On Sung Buddhist historiography, see Dalia, "The Political 'Career' of the Buddhist Historian Tsan-ning"; Franke, "Some Aspects of Chinese Private Historiography in the Thirteenth and Fourteenth Centuries"; Jan, "Buddhist Historiography in Sung China"; idem, *A Chronicle of Buddhism in China*, pp. 1–10; Makita, "Sannei to sono jidai"; idem, "Sōdai ni okeru bukkyō shigaku no hatten"; Ogawa, "Myōshinji shunkōen shozō sō hongaku *rekidai hennen shakushi tsugan*"; idem, "Shūkan *shakumon shōtō* no seiritsu"; Schmidt-Glintzer, *Die Identität der Buddhistischer Schulen*, passim; Takao, *Sōdai bukkyō shi no kenkyū*, pp. 139–48; and Ts'ao, "Lun *fo-tsu t'ung-chi* tui chi-chuan t'i-ts'ai te yün-yung," pp. 121–80.

4. The entire section is in *Shih-men cheng-t'ung*, Z, 2b, 3:400ra–402ra. Translation from ibid., Z, 2b, 3:401va–b; cf. the translation in Mochizuki, *Daijiten*, p. 2216b. This account was the model for Tsan-ning's brief treatment of the same topic; see *Fo-tsu t'ung-chi*, T 49:322a–b.

5. The text is *Cheng-fa nien[-ch'u] ching*, Gautama Prajñāruci (fl. 538–543), T no. 721. It refers to King Yama dozens of times, usually under the name of Yen-mo-lo (Yama Rā[ja]) or Yen-lo wang (King Yama Rāja); see *Taishō shinshū daizōkyō sakuin*, 9:33b, c.

6. For this etymology of "Yama," see chapter 16.

7. In this paragraph Tsung-chien paraphrases *Ming-pao chi*, T'ang Lin (fl. 600–659), T no. 2082, 51:793b. Cf. the partial translation in Teiser, *The Ghost Festival in Medieval China*, p. 188.

Yama Rāja is called 'Earth's Prefectures,' just like the Son of Heaven among humans. The Magistrate of Mount T'ai is like the Director of the Department of State Affairs. The Great Spirits, Recorders in the Five Paths[8] are like the Ministers of the Six Ministries. The other offices in the path of ghosts are like those in prefectures, districts, and so on."

Aside from this there are the names of the ten courts, which are divided into various offices. The T'ang monk Tao-ming, having entered the dark regions, explained them fully one by one. Based on this he standardized their names and made sense of retribution and response. In the beginning the world was not confused [about their names], but later, as the systems of government offices of succeeding generations differed, [their names] underwent changes in accord with the time.

Then there is *The Scripture on the Ten Kings*. It was composed by [*chuan*[b]] *śramana* Tsang-ch'uan of Ta-sheng-tz'u ssu in Ch'eng-tu Prefecture. In addition the preface to *A Ceremonial for [the Feast of] Water and Land* states, "Illustrations of their form [began] with Old Kuo, the immortal [Kuo-lao, hsien-jen]. (I.e., during the T'ang dynasty Chang Kuo-lao drew the pictures.) The teaching began with the monk Taoming."

Although the names of the ten kings are found in the dark regions, nevertheless there is not a word about them in the Library Hall.[9] I have investigated the causes of this and come up with a rough explanation. In order to display the power of the Twin Kings, their administration was divided into ten courts by the forcible addition of extra names. [In our day] some people revere the method of posthumously bestowing luck on the dead. Others convene assemblies for preparatory cultivation before their demise.

8. Lu wu-tao ta-shen is a problematic term. The editors of *Shih-men cheng-t'ung* (Z, 2b, 3:401va), Mochizuki (*Daijiten*, p. 2216b), and Oda ("Godō daishin kō," p. 25) punctuate the sentence differently than I, making "lu" the last character in the previous sentence. But this leaves "Shang-shu ling-lu," which is even more problematic. Ling-lu was used as an official title, but not until the Sung dynasty, when it referred generically to highly ranking officials in the local administration, a category that would not be associated with the Department of State Affairs (Shang-shu). By contrast, Shang-shu ling (Director of the Department of State Affairs) was a standard term for over a thousand years; see Hucker, *A Dictionary of Official Titles in Imperial China*, nos. 3764, 5049, respectively. I follow the editors of the Taishō edition of *Ming-pao chi* in reading it as Lu wu-tao ta-shen; T 51:793b. T'ang Lin or his redactors probably confused two standard terms, Ssu-ming ssu-lu (Officer of Life Spans and Officer of Records) and Wu-tao ta-shen (Great Spirit of the Five Paths).

9. "Library Hall" translates *tsang-tien*, literally "hall of the storehouse." The term is a synonym for *ching-tsang*, "storehouse of scriptures"; see Komazawa, *Daijiten*, pp. 225d–26a; and Mochizuki, *Daijiten*, pp. 597c–99a.

Rather than referring specifically to the ten kings, Tsung-chien's first two citations concern the underground bureaucracy in general. Simply in terms of length the first source, *Cheng-fa nien-ch'u ching* (The Scripture on the Points of Mindfulness of the True Law), was the most comprehensive canonical statement on the underworld written in Chinese. It was a natural first reference for matters relating to the underworld. Tsung-chien puts the second quotation to a rather different use. It is part of a speech given by an officer in the dark world named Ch'eng Ching, who explains the workings of the bureaucracy of the subterranean prisons to a recent arrival named Mu Jen-ch'ien. The extract outlines the general principles of the system by analogy to the government on earth headed by the emperor.

Tsung-chien broaches the topic of the ten kings proper in turning to the near-death experiences of the T'ang monk named Tao-ming, the protagonist of the first major origin legend to be considered here. Medieval Chinese folklore contains not one but a variety of traditions about monks named Tao-ming. Eventually one of those Tao-mings was associated with the Bodhisattva Ti-tsang in a story entitled "Huan-hun chi" (Record of a Returned Soul). Once that legend was established, Tao-ming was in turn claimed by historians like Tsung-chien and the author of *The Ceremonial for the Assembly of Water and Land* to be responsible for propagating pictures and texts dealing with the ten kings. In some materials he was even portrayed as a minor saint capable of bringing comfort to spirits of the dead.[10]

Surviving sources contain the biographies of over a dozen Buddhist monks with the name "Tao-ming."[11] Such an abundance is hardly surprising, given the significance and simplicity of his name, which might be translated literally as "Illumination of the Path" or "Knowledge of the Way." Three of these early Tao-mings are especially noteworthy for our purposes.

The first is described in a collection of miracle tales illustrating the efficacy of faith in the *Lotus* sūtra compiled in the late seventh century.[12]

10. I follow Matsumoto in giving an evolutionary cast to the history of Tao-ming's legend, but it should be noted that most of the materials are undated; see Matsumoto, *Tonkō ga no kenkyū,* 1:368–40. Arthur Waley was one of the first scholars to emphasize the earlier figures named Tao-ming; see Waley, *Catalogue,* pp. xxx–xxxii. Other studies of Tao-ming include Matsumoto, "Hibō jizō bosatsu zō no bunpu," pp. 141–69; idem, "Jizō jūō zu to inro bosatsu," pp. 265–70; Sakai, "Jūō shinkō," pp. 43–45; Sawada, *Jigoku hen,* pp. 29, 119–20; Soymié, "Jizō no shishi ni tsuite"; Teiser, "Dreamer, Painter, and Guide: Tao-ming's Career in Hell"; idem, " 'Having Once Died and Returned to Life,' " pp. 447–50; and Tokushi, "Kōzō," p. 272.
    11. See *Taishō shinshū daizōkyō sakuin,* 28:90a, b, and 29:190a.
    12. *Fa-hua chuan-chi,* Seng-hsiang (a.k.a. Hui-hsiang, fl. 667), *T* no. 2068, 51:82c–83a. The story is also contained in *Shih-men tzu-ching lu,* Huai-hsin (fl. 843), *T* no. 2083, 51:819b–c.

It relates that a monk named Hsüan-hsü is forced to spend the night at an unfamiliar temple inhabited by surreal monks undergoing torture. While there, Hsüan-hsü meets his deceased friend, Tao-ming. Tao-ming asks Hsüan-hsü to make good on a loan of firewood that Tao-ming neglected to repay before he died. The living monk complies, returning one hundred bundles of kindling to the temple supply and commissioning a copy of the *Lotus* sūtra. Later Tao-ming reports to Hsüan-hsü in a dream that the repayment has caused him to be released from suffering and to be reborn in the Pure Land. The form of the story is that of a Chinese Buddhist miracle tale, wherein the fate of the dead is improved by devotion to sacred scriptures. It does, though, set an important precedent, in that a monk named Tao-ming appears in a tale in which a monk wanders from his own temple into hell and has first-hand experiences with residents of the dark regions.

A second early monk named Tao-ming had connections with the cult of Ti-tsang. This *śramaṇa* was from Shih-chi ssu and served as one of seven monks who "verified the meaning" *(cheng-i)* in helping Hsüan-tsang (602–664) translate a Ti-tsang scripture late in the year 650 in Ch'ang-an.[13]

The third early figure was associated not with Buddhism but with the religion of light in China, Manichaeism. The famous Manichaean hymn scroll, probably dating from the eighth century, was translated by a person who identifies himself as Tao-ming. In discussing the infernal regions, related Manichaen texts mention not only Ti-tsang but also the "Impartial King" (P'ing-teng wang), the eighth of the ten kings, and "the great kings of the ten heavens" (shih-t'ien ta-wang).[14] Some scholars have explored possible connections between the ten kings and deities in the Manichaean pantheon, but the diverging soteriologies of *The Scripture on the Ten Kings* and of Manichaeism make a Manichaean inspiration unlikely.

Whatever the status of these early figures, the attention of medieval China was captured by the Tao-ming who first appears in a brief story entitled "The Record of a Returned Soul."[15] It describes how in the

13. See *Ta-sheng ta-chi ti-tsang shih-lun ching,* Hsüan-tsang (602–664), *T* no. 411, 13:728a.

14. For the translator's name, see *Mo-ni-chiao hsia-pu tsan, T* no. 2140, 54:1279c. For references to Ti-tsang and Shih-t'ien ta-wang, see *Po-ssu-chiao tsan ching, T* no. 2141b, 54:1282c. On the relations between Manichaeism and Buddhism, see Bryder, *The Chinese Transformation of Manichaeism,* pp. 102–3; and Sakai, "Jūō shinkō," pp. 621–24.

15. "Huan-hun chi" (The Record of a Returned Soul) is S 3092, reprod. Huang, *Pao-tsang,* 25:667b–68a. The manuscript is not dated; Matsumoto (*Tonkō ga no kenkyū,* 1:378) places it in the tenth century. I offer a paraphrase of the story here because I have translated it elsewhere; see Teiser, "Dreamer, Painter, and Guide," pp. 13–19; and idem, " 'Having Once Died and Returned to Life,' " pp. 448–49, 464; unfortunately neither of these makes ref-

year 778 a monk from K'ai-yüan ssu named Tao-ming was arrested in broad daylight by two messengers who escorted him to the dark offices for a meeting with King Yama. After a brief interrogation, King Yama declared that Tao-ming from K'ai-yüan ssu was a victim of mistaken identity. The person who should have been arrested had the same name as Tao-ming, but hailed from a different temple, Lung-hsing ssu. Having noted the error in his files, King Yama released Tao-ming to return to the path of the living.

Before Tao-ming reaches the human world, however, he encounters an imposing figure. Tao-ming confesses that he does not recognize the mysterious person and is shocked to learn he is Ti-tsang Bodhisattva. Tao-ming explains that Ti-tsang looks nothing like his pictures in the world above and recounts exactly how the Bodhisattva is portrayed in paintings and statues. Ti-tsang then instructs Tao-ming to return home and dedicate himself to correcting the mistaken impression that people have formed. He makes sure that Tao-ming notes clearly his dress and proportions and that he commits to memory a *mantra* that people can invoke to ask him for help. After a few more exchanges explaining the identity of a lion accompanying Ti-tsang, the story ends with Tao-ming carrying out Ti-tsang's instructions: "Tao-ming left and in the space of an instant was back in the temple of his old home, breathing once again. There he set to work mixing his paints, making portraits of Ti-tsang's correct countenance that he passed down to the world."

"The Record of a Returned Soul" draws strongly on the genre of tours of the other world in Chinese folklore. It includes such stock devices as a descent to hell; a comical, nearly tragic mix-up of names in the registers of King Yama; frequent references to the inevitability of karmic retribution and the need to maintain the precepts; and a resuscitation of the main character, who resumes life with a new mission. Aside from these traits, the story seems especially concerned with the issue of iconographic authenticity. Tao-ming's experiences in hell justify a new artistic style. The deity himself commands Tao-ming to propagate the cult through proper visual and auditory means.

Up to this point (probably sometime during the ninth century) Tao-ming was associated solely with the popularization of pictures of Ti-tsang Bodhisattva. From there it was but a short step to claim Tao-ming as the source of paintings and texts of the ten kings, since he already served that purpose for representations of Ti-tsang. In a variety of tenth-century art the legitimacy of the ten kings was grounded in the famous after-death experiences of a Buddhist monk. In some paintings

---

erence to the complete transcription and translation into Japanese by Soymié, "Jizō no shishi ni tsuite," pp. 48–51.

(fig. 2) the claim is not yet explicit, since the composition is dominated by Ti-tsang, not the ten kings. Some frontispieces to *The Scripture on the Ten Kings* (plate 1a) dispense with Ti-tsang, allowing the relationship between Tao-ming and the ten kings to emerge as a subject in its own right.[16] Although Tao-ming is still a comparatively minor figure, he serves as an emblem not for Ti-tsang but for the ten kings. Here the originator of the story is painted into the text itself. This is the tradition to which Tsung-chien refers.

Other sources contain another version of the legend of Tao-ming, in which Tao-ming himself is a savior capable of rescuing sentient beings from the torments of purgatory. The first indication of Tao-ming's soteriological vocation occurs in the last scene illustrating some versions of *The Scripture on the Ten Kings,* in which a monk helps people escape from hell. In some versions (plate 14c) the monk is clearly Ti-tsang Bodhisattva, while in others (plate 14a) there can be no doubt that he is Tao-ming. Tao-ming's role as helpful guardian in purgatory is made even clearer in later years, when one finds his name written with homophonous characters, Tao-ming[b], literally "Guide to the Dark Regions." It is in this guise that he is portrayed in a twelfth-century collection in which a functionary of hell explains to a recent arrival, "Here is the monk Tao-ming[b]. This monk guides the *hun* and *p'o* of all ordinary people."[17] Having first met Ti-tsang on his own return from death, Tao-ming became a figure capable of dispensing aid to others journeying to their next life.

The second major figure cited in Tsung-chien's account had his name, but not his picture, inscribed in *The Scripture on the Ten Kings.* In all of the surviving long recensions of the scripture (containing hymns), but in none of the other recensions, the name of Tsang-ch'uan is written after the opening invocation, just before or after the formal title of the text: "Recorded by [*shu*[b]] *śramaṇa* Tsang-ch'uan of Ta-sheng-tz'u ssu in Ch'eng-tu Prefecture."[18] Another tenth-century manuscript from Tun-huang contains on its verso a series of writing exercises, one of which adds the information that "the hymns were recorded by" *(tsan-shu)* Tsang-ch'uan.[19] Whether Tsang-ch'uan wrote the words of the

16. Tao-ming appears in eleven of the thirteen paintings of Ti-tsang surrounded by the ten kings listed in appendix 4. Tao-ming, the lion, and Ti-tsang also appear as inferior figures in the donor panel of a painting of Thousand-Armed Kuan-yin, MG 17659, reprod. V–N, *Bannières,* 15: pls. 103, 103 *bis.* Tao-ming and the lion accompany the ten kings in three of the frontispiece illustrations to *The Scripture on the Ten Kings* listed in appendix 4.

17. *I-chien chih,* Hung Mai (1123–1202), *i chih,* ch. 4 (p. 213).

18. *Shu* here could mean "written," "recorded," or "edited." It is no accident that Buddhist usage is not very rigorous in relation to authorship; see Demiéville et al., *Répertoire du canon bouddhique sino-japonais,* p. 11.

19. P 2249v, reprod. Huang, *Pao-tsang,* 118:62b. *Tsan-shu* could also mean "set to hymns and recorded by."

scripture or was the originator of the hymns added to a preexisting text is unclear. What is certain is that Tsang-ch'uan's name was associated with *The Scripture on the Ten Kings* early in the tenth century.[20]

The only other clue to Tsang-ch'uan's identity is his reputed residence at Ta-sheng-tz'u ssu in Ch'eng-tu (in modern Szechwan). The origins of Ta-sheng-tz'u ssu are connected with Emperor Hsüan-tsung's (r. 712–756) residence in Ch'eng-tu during 756 and 757 (from Chih-te 1/VII until Chih-te 2/X).[21] None of the available evidence about the history of the temple mentions the name of Tsang-ch'uan, but one anecdote does indicate that pictures of hell already adorned its walls when the T'ang court again sought refuge there over one hundred years later. At some earlier time (probably 825–827) the Szechwanese painter Tso Ch'üan (fl. 825–860) had painted a transformation tableau of the underground prisons *(ti-yü pien-hsiang)* on the lower part of To-pao pagoda (To-pao t'a) of Ta-sheng-tz'u ssu. It was still in existence when Chu Ch'ien (fl. 873–881), a painter attached to Hsi-tsung's (r. 873–888) court, accompanied the imperial retinue to Ch'eng-tu in 881. One source reports that Chu Ch'ien hoped to paint a mural of hell scenes when he arrived there, but was disappointed to find that Tso Ch'üan had already painted one.[22] Our sources do not refer to the content of the

20. The style of the hymns is discussed in chapter 15. Many modern scholars accept Tsang-ch'uan as the author of *The Scripture on the Ten Kings;* see, for example, Hsiao, *Tun-huang su-wen-hsüeh lun-ts'ung,* pp. 178–79; Ogawa, *"Enraō juki kyō,"* p. 642; and Tsukamoto, "Inro bosatsu shinkō ni tsuite," pp. 170–71.

21. See *Fo-tsu t'ung-chi, T* 49:376a; the same facts are repeated in abridged form in ibid., 49:464a. *T'ang hui-yao,* Wang P'u (922–982), p. 853, notes the founding of two other temples in Ch'eng-tu (Sheng-shou ssu and Nan-p'ing ssu) in the year 807, but says nothing about Ta-sheng-tz'u ssu. The designation *ta* (literally "Great" or "Imperial") covered a wide range of official temples during the T'ang; see Forte, "Daiji (Chine)." The name of the temple might be connected to one of the honorific names (Ta-sheng, literally "Great Sage") given to Hsüan-tsung. According to *Tzu-chih t'ung-chien,* Ssu-ma Kuang (1019–1086), p. 7049, the title Kuang-t'ien wen-wu ta-sheng hsiao-kan huang-ti was bestowed upon the retired emperor in Chih-te 2/XII/[21], *chia-tzu* (3 Feb. 758). The entry in Tz'u-i, *Fo-kuang ta-tz'u-tien,* p. 5586a–b repeats the account in *Fo-tsu t'ung-chi,* but adds that the temple was destroyed by fire in 1435 and rebuilt ca. 1644–1661, when it was renamed Sheng-tz'u ssu. A Ming gazetteer locates the temple, then named T'ai-tz'u ssu, inside the east gate of the city and says that the name plaque written by Hsüan-tsung was still in existence; see *(Hsin-hsiu) Ch'eng-tu fu chih,* Feng Jen (Ming), Chang Shih-yung (Ming), 3.41v.

22. On Tso Ch'üan's painting of hell at Ta-sheng-tz'u ssu, see *I-chou ming-hua lu,* Huang Hsiu-fu (fl. 1006), p. 8. On Chu Ch'ien's disappointment at finding such a mural already painted, see ibid., p. 25. For further biographical information on these two painters, see *T'u-hua chien-wen chih,* pp. 17, 18, respectively; and Soper, *Kuo Jo-hsü's Experiences in Painting (T'u-hua chien-wên chih),* pp. 23, 24, respectively. The two imperial sojourns in Ch'eng-tu had important implications for artistic styles in later years and were largely responsible for the

painting, so we do not know if it contained the ten kings. They do, however, establish that during the middle and late T'ang Ta-sheng-tz'u ssu in Ch'eng-tu was credited with being a home to painters as well as hymnodists of the underworld.

The lack of much hard data about Tsang-ch'uan does not justify a very strong argument against accepting him as an author, since very few figures residing outside of the capitals or standing low in the Saṃgha hierarchy found a place in the surviving historical record. Furthermore, the grounds usually adduced for suspecting a late, spurious attribution of authorship are in this case lacking. In many examples of anonymous authorship, later sources assign the text to a famous figure from an earlier period. But our figure was hardly famous. Tsang-ch'uan's consistent obscurity makes it quite possible that sometime between 756 and the early tenth century, a person by that name composed the hymns or the text of *The Scripture on the Ten Kings*.

There is no independent evidence verifying Tsung-chien's account of the third major figure, Chang Kuo (fl. 690–756), but a brief discussion of legends about Chang Kuo casts some light on the mythology of the ten kings. In medieval times Chang Kuo was probably the most famous of the three legendary originators, yet judging from surviving sources he had the most tenuous connection to the ten kings. His contacts with the T'ang court were sufficiently well documented to earn him separate entries in the two standard histories of the T'ang dynasty. In addition he appears frequently in medieval miracle tales, Taoist hagiography, and Buddhist histories. The differences between these accounts are quite large, but on the whole there is no evidence of a consistent pattern in the evolution of his legend. Some of his greatest feats, for instance, were performed in the presence of Emperor Hsüan-tsung and thus made their way into the early biography contained in the *Old T'ang History*. In the biographical sketch that follows I offer a core narrative based on the more conservative sources and then add a few relevant details drawn from the slightly more credulous ones.[23]

---

flourishing state of Buddhist temples there. Wai-kam Ho ("Aspects of Chinese Painting from 1100 to 1350," p. xxxi) notes that Ta-sheng-tz'u ssu "was known nationwide as a great center of Buddhist art and Buddhist propagation."

23. The legend of Chang Kuo is a complex topic that goes beyond the confines of this study. One could begin, for instance, by reconstructing the pericopes contained in the books on which our existing sources draw, including *Hsüan-kuai lu*, Niu Seng-ju (779–848); *Hsüan-shih chih*, Chang Tu (fl. 847–859); *Kao-tao chuan* (?); and *Ming-huang tsa-lu*, Cheng Ch'u-hui (T'ang). The "core" biography below is based on *Chiu t'ang shu*, pp. 5106–07; *Hsien-yüan pien-chu*, Wang Sung-nien (fl. tenth century), Sch no. 596, *TT* 329–30, 3.23r–v; and *Hsin t'ang shu*, pp. 5810–11. Later sources following this form of the legend include: *T'an-chin wen-chi*, Ch'i-sung (1007–1072), *T* no. 2115, 52:676a; *Fo-tsu*

By all accounts Chang Kuo was popularly thought to be already a few hundred years old during the time of Empress Wu (r. 690–705). He lived at Chung-t'iao shan (modern Shansi) and traveled often between there and the region of Chin (modern Hopei). When Empress Wu called him to court he feigned death to avoid sullying himself with affairs of state. In the year 733 he repeated the action, this time ceasing to breathe in the presence of the imperial envoy. Only after Emperor Hsüan-tsung sent another highly ranking official bearing a personal letter did Chang consent to go to the capital. In Ch'ang-an he was lodged at the Academy of Scholarly Worthies (Chi-hsien yüan) and allowed to enter the palace in a sedan chair. He met many times with the emperor, sometimes in such esoteric circumstances that no one else knew the substance of their conversations. Hsüan-tsung tried unsuccessfully to forge an alliance between Chang and the Yü-chen Princess, a younger devotee of Taoism. Chang received many honors: he was acknowledged as "Hsi-huang shang-jen" (Supreme Man of the Time of Emperor Fu-hsi), bestowed the title "T'ung-hsüan hsien-sheng" (Teacher Who Penetrates Mystery), and granted the rank of Grand Master of Imperial Entertainments with Silver Seal and Blue Ribbon. The emperor built a temple for him when Chang returned to a hermitage at Heng-shan (modern Hopei), where he died and was liberated from the corpse in the early years of the T'ien-pao era (742–756). Chang Kuo wrote a variety of books, some of which still survive.[24]

---

t'ung-chi, T 49:377b, 459c; *Shih-shih chi-ku lüeh,* Chüeh-an (fl. 1266–1355), *T* no. 2037, 49:826c; and *Fo-tsu li-tai t'ung-tsai,* Nien-ch'ang (d. 1341), *T* no. 2036, 49:593b. The details I add later are based on *Hsü-hsien chuan,* Shen Fen (late T'ang), Sch no. 295, *TT* 138, 2.4v–6r; and *T'ai-p'ing kuang-chi,* Li Fang (fl. 978), pp. 192–94, 199–200. These in turn form the basis for later biographies in *Yün-chi ch'i-ch'ien,* Chang Chün-fang (fl. 1008–1029), Sch no. 1032, *TT* 677–702, 15.1v, 64.12r–v, 64.15r–v, 113b.21r–22v; *San-tung ch'ün-hsien lu,* Ch'en Pao-kuang (Sung), Sch no. 1248, *TT* 992–95, 7.12r–v, 10.3v, 15.5v–6r; *Hsüan-p'in lu,* Chang T'ien-yü (fl. 1335), Sch no. 781, *TT* 558–59, 5.3r; *Li-shih chen-hsien t'i-tao t'ung-chien,* Chao Tao-i (Yüan), Sch no. 296, *TT* vols. 139–48, 37.4r–7r; and *Sou-shen chi,* Chang Kuo-hsiang (Ming), Sch no. 1476, *TT* 1105–06, 2.22v. Chang Kuo is discussed briefly in Sakai, "Jūō shinkō," pp. 646–48; and even more briefly in Tokushi, "Kōzō," p. 279; and Ogawa, *"Enraō juki kyō,"* p. 232.

24. Three complete, book-length works by Chang survive. They are: 1. *Huang-ti yin-fu ching chu,* Sch no. 112, *TT* 55; also contained in *Yün-chi ch'i-ch'ien,* 15.1r–11r; attested in *Chiu t'ang shu,* p. 5106; 2. *T'ai-shang chiu-yao hsin-yin miao-ching,* Sch no. 225, *TT* 112; preface also contained in *Ch'üan t'ang wen,* 923.2v (p. 12,133b); and 3. *Yü-tung ta-shen tan-sha chen-yao ching,* Sch no. 896, *TT* 587; attested in *Hsin t'ang shu,* p. 1521. A poem also survives: "T'i teng chen-tung," in *Ch'üan t'ang shih,* p. 9718; as does a preface to a nonextant work, "Tao-t'i lun hsü," in *Ch'üan t'ang wen,* 923.1r–2r (p. 12,133a–b). *Hsin t'ang shu* (p. 1521a) attributes three additional works to him: *Ch'i-chüeh, Shen-hsien t'i-tao ling-yao ching,* and *Wang-hsiang ch'eng-ming t'u.*

The more circumspect sources also agree on the nature of Chang's skills and on several of his more notorious performances. Chang owed his longevity to his proficiency at embryonic respiration *(t'ai-hsi)*. He could go for several days without eating, and when he did eat he consumed only a small amount of wine and pills of gold. After Chang arrived in the capital, Hsüan-tsung enlisted his two best diviners to gain further knowledge of Chang's background, but both were unsuccessful: the horoscopist could not determine Chang's age, and Chang made himself invisible to the clairvoyant. Later Hsüan-tsung arranged a more convivial ordeal. The emperor had heard that only true holy men could consume celery juice without injury. He waited until mid-winter and then invited Chang to a banquet of celery juice. After drinking a few goblets, the guest remarked with some understatement "This is not fine wine" and promptly fell asleep. When he awoke he asked for a mirror, in which he could see that his teeth had burned to a crisp. He knocked out the charred roots, put them in his pocket, and then from a vial he happened to have brought along applied medicine to his gums. Before the banquet ended he sprouted fresh, white teeth.

Other sources embellish the biography of Chang with further exploits. One story bears a resemblance to the banquet adventure recounted just above. It describes a drinking contest, also arranged under Hsüan-tsung's auspices, between Chang and a teenage disciple. When the emperor forces Chang to drink well beyond a mortal capacity, his hat falls off, lands upright on the floor, and turns into a wine cup, positioned perfectly to catch a fountain of wine spouting from the top of his head. Another story claims that Chang travels several hundred *li* per day on a white donkey that he folds up and stores in his pocket like a piece of paper, using water to reconstitute it. Another tale describes how Hsüan-tsung humbles himself to Chang in order to bring back to life a less skilled disciple stricken dead when he revealed Chang's true identity. And other sources tell of Chang's encounter with an even older sage named Wang Chang.

Confirmation of the persistence of the tale of Chang Kuo over the centuries comes from an unlikely—and hence relatively trustworthy—quarter, Buddhist historiography. The earliest mention of Chang Kuo places him over one hundred years before the reign of Empress Wu. An early biography of the T'ien-t'ai monk Chih-i (538–597) states that in the year 578 a Taoist immortal named Chang Kuo prophesied the imminent death of Chih-i's older brother, Ch'en Chen (d. 593). When he heard of the prediction, Chih-i held a repentance service for his brother, which put off his death for another fifteen years. A later Buddhist source states explicitly that the Chang Kuo active during the reigns of Empress Wu and Emperor Hsüan-tsung was the same person who made the prediction in 578.[25] Thus, even Buddhist historians, who for apologetic reasons could have easily disputed not just the sagacity but also the longevity of Chang Kuo, refrained from doing so.[26]

For our purposes what is most remarkable about the legends surveyed above is that none of them links Chang Kuo to the ten kings. That association is made, according to Tsung-chien's account, in a work entitled *Shui-lu [chai] i-wen* (A Ceremonial for the [Feast of] Water and Land). Unfortunately the liturgy itself does not survive, but we do know that it was written by a man named Yang O between 1068 and 1077 and that some fifty years later it was used widely in Szechwan.[27] The tradition that Chang Kuo was the first to paint illustrations of the ten kings was local to Szechwan in the eleventh and twelfth centuries. Compared to those of Tao-ming and Tsang-ch'uan, the legend of Chang Kuo was probably established earliest and disseminated most widely. But until the eleventh century Chang was famous primarily for his old age, not for creating *The Scripture on the Ten Kings* or its pictures.

Tsung-chien concludes his discussion with yet another explanation of the genesis of the ten kings. Having apparently found all of the legends unsatisfactory, Tsung-chien falls back upon a partly etymological, partly theological rationale. Since Yama's name literally means "twin," he reasons, the ten kings must be the product of multiplying the twins by five. To this he appends a brief note describing the world outside the Library Hall, where beliefs about the ten kings were put into practice. His contemporaries performed both premortem and postmortem rituals. Thus, in Tsung-chien's time, although doubts about the authorship of *The Scripture on the Ten Kings* may have remained unresolved, and new explanations were still offered in origin legends, none of these pangs of illegitimacy stopped people from sending offerings to the ten kings.

What kind of conclusions can be drawn from this study of origin legends? From a purely chronological point of view, one finds the repeti-

25. The original reference is in *Sui t'ien-t'ai chih-che ta-shih pieh-chuan,* Kuanting (561–632), *T* no. 2050, 50:197c. The later source is *Fo-tsu t'ung-chi, T* 49: 353a, 377b.

26. Chang Kuo's relationship to organized Buddhism may not have been entirely adversarial. A tenth-century source notes that the Buddhist monk Chen-chün[b] (847–924) was a descendant of Chang Kuo; see *Sung kao-seng chuan,* Tsan-ning (919–1001), *T* no. 2050, 50:810a.

27. A work completed in 1204, *Shih-shih t'ung-lan* (Tsung-hsiao [1151–1214]), contains three selections from works by Yang O: 1. *Shui-lu ta-chai ling-chi chi,* dated 1071 (*Z,* 2a, 6:220va–21rb); 2. *Shui-lu i* (*Z,* 2a, 6:223rb–25va); and 3. "Shui-lu chai i-wen hou-hsü" (*Z,* 2a, 6:225va–b). *Shih-men cheng-t'ung,* completed in 1237, states (*Z,* 2b, 3:401va): "During the Hsi-ning era [1068–1077], Yang O of Tung-ch'uan [modern Szechwan] wrote the first *Old Rules* and composed *A Ceremonial* in three scrolls. Most recently they are circulating in Shu [i.e., Szechwan]."

tion of a pattern found frequently in the history of religions. The earliest putative author (Chang Kuo) appears latest, and with the greatest wealth of documentation, albeit irrelevant, in the historical record. Conversely, concerning the latest alleged author (probably Tsang-ch'uan), sources are both sparse and late, but by empirical standards most believable.

Some answers can also be offered to the question of what counted for Chinese Buddhists as an adequate and appealing explanation of origins. What is most interesting, perhaps, are the tropes missing from Tsung-chien's account. He does not allude to the antiquity of the system, evidenced by Śākyamuni commissioning the officers of the ten courts to exercise compassion. He makes no attempt to reinforce the credibility of the scripture by attributing its translation from an Indic language to any early, famous figure. Nor does he try to justify the undoubtedly tardy appearance of the text by revealing the special circumstances of its preaching. Instead, Tsung-chien appeals, in the case of Tao-ming, to the verisimilitude of near-death experience. Like the story of the bestowal of paintings on Chih-yu (translated in chapter 3), Tao-ming's recall from death was a reasonable explanation of the genesis of pictures of Ti-tsang and the ten kings. Tao-ming's adventure fit the pattern of other dream reports and tales of resuscitation; his personal audience with Ti-tsang Bodhisattva may have made his story even more convincing than most. Tsung-chien does perpetuate a legend about the authorship of *The Scripture on the Ten Kings,* but he makes no claims connecting the text to India. The small bit of specific information Tsung-chien offers about the "author" Tsang-ch'uan may have caused his readers to appreciate his concern for detail, but offers little basis for either belief or skepticism. Not so with the immortal Chang Kuo. Although no earlier tradition connected him with the ten kings, Chang Kuo was well established in popular mythology. What the modern historian would evaluate as his distance from *The Scripture on the Ten Kings* did not matter. If his skill in transformation was convincing to more than one Chinese emperor, then most people would have had little reason to doubt his knowledge of the fate awaiting them after death.

6. The Making of the Ten Kings

ALTHOUGH A BUDDHIST scripture is the major topic of this study, we must take seriously the fact that religious life in medieval societies did not revolve around books. The written record is indeed the major source of the historian's knowledge of the past, but that limitation should not delude us into thinking that texts were the primary vehicles of knowledge for most people in medieval China. Other options—stating the theoretical issue as the need to balance text and context, or merely lamenting the disdainful silence of literate elites toward the practices of the majority—still perpetuate a bibliocentric bias. As the evidence assembled above has shown, the afterlife was described not just in religious texts but in paintings, murals, statues, prayers, dedications, essays, folktales, and invitations to funerals. In a culture where only a few could engage in reading or studying, religious life was defined rather by mourning and remembering, worshiping, meditating, commissioning copies, listening to stories, or watching pictures.

If traces of the ten kings are to be found primarily outside of sūtras, how then can we analyze the transmission of religious culture in medieval China? It is convenient to begin by summarizing the cultural practices in which the ten kings appeared. The concept of "praxis" is not uncomplicated, but it does avoid positing an unhelpful dichotomy between the written and the oral. That disjunction too often depends upon the assumption that the "elite" used writing to express complicated ideas, while the "folk" told stories related to their unsophisticated practice. The discussion of memorial rites has shown that ritual performances involved both literary and verbal components, and the survey of artistic representations has demonstrated just how much of medieval culture is ignored by focusing merely on the written and the oral. Without implying the universal applicability of the following categories, I would propose four kinds of practice in which the ten kings figured prominently and four corresponding genres or media through which knowledge of the ten kings was disseminated.

Given the severity of their rule, it is not surprising to find the ten kings mentioned most often, perhaps, in prayer—prayer both as the act of making reverent petition to a deity and as the petition itself. As I discuss more fully in Part Three, the "hymns" *(tsan)* in the long recension of *The Scripture on the Ten Kings* were a subgenre of medieval religious song. They were sung by a group without musical accompaniment at a wide range of services, including memorial rituals. At the other extreme is Ssu-k'ung T'u's prayer, which was written in a polished form of the literary language and was probably never read aloud in a public setting.

Somewhere between these two examples are the dedications to individual copies of *The Scripture on the Ten Kings* discussed in detail in Part Two. These prayers are formulaic: the vows and unique circumstances of the commissioners are recorded in a limited range of forms. The original wishes were expressed orally and then recast in liturgical language.

The second practice was the worship or reverencing of images. Offering flowers, incense, or simply devotion to icons had always been central to Chinese Buddhism, which was since the Han dynasty known as "the religion of images" *(hsiang-chiao)*. Paintings of the ten kings usually adopted what I have called an "iconic" style, with Ti-tsang, the most important deity, enthroned in the center, and the ten kings seated in subservient but still dignified fashion at his sides. Such representations used the principle of hierarchy and other rules of artistic grammar common to Chinese Buddhist *maṇḍalas*. The worship of images was dependent not only on icons but on stories attesting to the sanctity of icons. The tales about Chih-yu and Tao-ming examined above attempted to justify a specific style of representing Ti-tsang and to encourage cultic activities devoted both to him and, it may be assumed, to the ten kings. Both were written in classical prose but show signs of oral derivation. Both were originally tied to specific locales and later achieved wide circulation.

The ten kings figure prominently in a third important activity, the telling of stories in which narrative, in both scriptural and pictorial formats, was the primary genre. *The Scripture on the Ten Kings* was the paradigmatic literary prototype. Written in the Chinese of Buddhist sūtras, this text addressed several topics. It offered a rationale for the power of Yama and the other kings, it told a story about the processing of the spirit after death, and it insisted upon a regimen of Buddhist rites. When the narrative took artistic form, the plot was less cluttered, dealing exclusively with the judgment of the dead and the rewards to be gained by sending offerings on their behalf. Several formats can be distinguished within pictorial narratives: illustrations added to a scripture, a scroll containing scenes but not words, and wall paintings. Unlike other media for propagating belief in the ten kings, narrative illustrations did not require (nor did they exclude) any knowledge of the written language either on the part of performers and explainers or of viewers.

When the narrative was lost, the telling of stories turned easily into a fourth form of cultural practice, moralizing. Although the surviving evidence is limited, preaching was probably carried out in a variety of settings: exegetical lectures to organized lay groups, sermons about karmic retribution delivered in homes and temples, as well as strictly literary forms. Attested examples of this genre include Brāhmacārin Wang's poetry and treatises like Fa-yün's essay on karmic retribution. The former was written in a mixture of the literary and vernacular languages. The latter, which does not survive, was probably written in simple literary Chinese. Both undoubtedly made frequent use of clichés and had a distinctly didactic tone.

Another important issue in the history of the ten kings is that of distribution: among which groups and in what areas were the ten kings popular? The issue cannot be confined merely to texts, their authors, and their audiences. Rather, the question is best formulated by asking who engaged in the forms of practice outlined above, who produced the literary or artistic tools and provided the services essential to the act, and who was capable of understanding the language in which the practice was carried out?

The practice of making prayers for the welfare of one's ancestors was in theory open to everyone, because the ten kings required only timely offerings, not unchanging allegiance, and the Buddhist church placed no sectarian limitations on worshipers once they finished praying. Finding incontrovertible proof for this hypothesis is, as one would expect, not possible. The strongest evidence for medieval offerings to the ten kings is contained in the invitations to memorial services sent by low-level officials to monks of several Tun-huang monasteries. There is no doubt that the Buddhist church charged families for the hymns that monks sang, a fact that would in itself suggest that only those families with resources to spare could afford to seek help from the ten kings. In the case of medieval ritual, however, poverty gave rise to the sharing of resources: families banded together in mutual-aid "societies" *(she)* organized expressly for the purpose of defraying the cost of funerals. Although it is possible that such organizations allowed people of little means to sponsor memorial services, the surviving documents do not explicitly mention the ten kings, thus leaving the issue unsettled. Individuals with sufficient resources registered their prayers in a slightly different fashion. As will be discussed in Part Two, they paid to have *The Scripture on the Ten Kings* copied, dedicating the merit in a formal prayer to members of their family (usually deceased) or to themselves (soon to die). In both cases the actual inscribing of prayers, as well as the copying of the scripture, was carried out by monks who had been taught to read and write in temple schools.

It is more difficult to establish the profile of the group that engaged in worshiping images of the ten kings. Although most icons were paid for by private individuals—the merit usually dedicated to a deceased family member—paintings and statues of Ti-tsang and the ten kings were usually housed in Buddhist temples. There they were revered by monks and by a range of lay people about whom surviving sources are silent.

Like prayer, the stories associated with the ten kings were in principle open to all. The recital of the tale contained in the scripture was probably limited to memorial rites. The narrative of the picture-scroll (of which only one example survives), however, may well have been used outside of liturgical settings. Matsumoto even argues that because this particular scroll was designed to include only pictures, not text, preachers or storytellers were able to reach an audience that included a significant number of the uneducated.[1]

Because it strived to instill a consciously Buddhist scheme of ethics in a seemingly unsympathetic congregation, the practice of moralizing may have been less widespread than the other three. Fa-yün's treatise was probably available only to literati, and although Wang Fan-chih scattered vernacular expressions throughout his poems, as far as we know they were still confined to the written medium.

The geographical distribution of the ten kings in medieval China is easier to chart than their diffusion among different social groups, but the resulting map may not be very meaningful. We can begin by putting to rest the claim that the ten kings were limited to or originated in the border area of Tun-huang. Judging only from unambiguous evidence interpreted conservatively, in the ninth and tenth centuries traces of the ten kings could be found across most of northwestern, northern, central, and eastern China. Rituals, texts, and paintings are attested in the modern area of Kansu; prayers and paintings in Shansi; a text in Shantung; statues in Szechwan; paintings in Honan; statues in Anhwei; and paintings in Chekiang. The only place they were not found was the south (corresponding to the economic macroregions of the Southeast Coast, Lingnan, and the Southwest), but that apparent gap may only be due to the chance survival of manuscript and archeological evidence from the northwest deserts and to the northern bias of so many of the T'ang and Five Dynasties historical sources. The authorship and proximate origins of some of the Tun-huang copies of *The Scripture on the Ten Kings* have been traced to Szechwan, but there may well have been other recensions with different geographical filiations circulating in other parts of the empire. At any rate the distribution of manifestations of the ten kings across so much of China within the span of one hundred years, together with the gaps in our knowledge, make it unwise to posit a precise roadway of diffusion.

The chronological parameters are rather clear, but again, in light of the contingent preservation of artifacts and the radically incomplete coverage of written sources, they may not mean much. The existence of the ten kings may with reasonable certainty be dated as early as 658–664, the floruit of Fa-yün, the author of *An Essay on the True Karma of the Ten Kings*. The next significant event in the time line of the ten kings is a reference in *The Collected Poems of Brāhmacārin Wang,* dated roughly to the

1. Matsumoto, *Tonkō ga no kenkyū,* 1:403.

middle of the eighth century, to a set of ten memorial rituals. After that
the evidence is thicker: invitations to monks to attend memorial rites
survive from the year 887, wall paintings of the ten kings are datable to
846–907, paintings on silk are attested around the year 900, and statues
were carved in 903. The first dated copy of *The Scripture on the Ten Kings*
was produced in 908. For both artistic and scriptural representations it
is clear that the specimens we know of were copies of earlier versions,
but it is unknown how far back the original images and texts can be
traced. It is of interest to note that, judging from the surviving evidence, the writing down of *The Scripture on the Ten Kings* falls latest in
time. History preserves notice first of moralizing about karma, next of
practicing memorial rituals, next of drawing images, and last of putting
the story of the ten kings into the written form of scripture.

One issue remains: how do we explain the success of the ten kings?
That is, given that they were worshiped across the breadth of late medieval China, by what devices did they assume and maintain power?

Perhaps the clearest guarantee of authority in medieval Chinese Buddhism was to be deemed canonical. Canonical status was an assurance
not only of textual authenticity—that a scripture transmitted accurately
the words of the Buddha, or that a treatise propounded an interpretation acceptable to the highest echelons of the Buddhist church—but also
of physical survival. Noncanonical Buddhist texts from the medieval
period do survive, but in very small proportion to their historic numbers. By contrast, texts placed in the Buddhist canon were copied regu-
larly with high levels of funding and were disseminated widely.

Although the Buddhist canon was both a religious and political institution, it would be a mistake to treat it as a single entity. In fact it was
not a collection, but rather a series of attempts to define a collection of
books. Before the Sung dynasty there were scores of such attempts,
some official, some unofficial, to designate an authoritative corpus.[2]
What is important for our purposes is that *The Scripture on the Ten Kings*
was not included in any of them.

The issue of canonicity merits further consideration because it helps
to show why this particular mode of legitimacy was denied to texts like
The Scripture on the Ten Kings. Chinese Buddhist canons were defined in
works called "catalogues" *(mu-lu)* by a process of exclusion: after discussing all works he has known or seen and providing information
about the books' contents and authorship, the writer of the catalogue
draws up a listing of works deemed "canonical" *(ju-tsang)* and works

2. The best study of the Chinese Buddhist catalogue as a standard of
canonicity is Tokuno, "The Evaluation of Indigenous Scriptures in Chinese
Buddhist Bibliographical Catalogues." See also Buswell, "Introduction: Prolegomenon to the Study of Buddhist Apocryphal Scriptures"; Hayashiya, *Kyōroku
kenkyū,* vol. 1; Yabuki, *Meisha yoin kaisetsu,* part 2, pp. 156–319; and Yao, *Chung-
kuo mu-lu-hsüeh shih,* pp. 229–300.

deemed "suspect" *(i-huo)* or "spurious" *(wei)*. Unfortunately *The Scripture on the Ten Kings* is never cited by name—even to be declared spurious—in any surviving catalogue, but some catalogues do refer to texts that are similar to the *Ten Kings* sūtra.

The scripture that may have come the closest of all medieval Chinese texts to *The Scripture on the Ten Kings* does not survive, but its existence is noted in the first official catalogue compiled for the Sui dynasty.[3] Its title, *Yen-lo wang tung t'ai-shan ching* (Scripture on King Yama Rāja and Mount T'ai in the East), names two of the figures who would later be ranked among the ten kings. Although the compilers of the catalogue remain silent about what troubles them about this particular text, relegating it simply to the category of "spurious and fallacious" *(wei-wang)*, they do explain their aversion to the category as a whole. Such scriptures, they state:[4]

> bear the mark of perverting truth. Some interpolate the golden words [of the Buddha] at the beginning and include songs and prophecies [*yao-ch'an*] at the end. Some first discuss secular techniques [*shih-shu*], but later rely upon phrases from the Buddhist Law. Some draw upon the concepts of *yin*[b] and *yang* or good and bad luck. Others explain the world of spirits and ghosts or calamities and blessings. All such scriptures are clearly spurious and fallacious. They should, then, be kept from the public and be exterminated in order to rescue the world from trouble.

If *The Scripture on King Yama Rāja and Mount T'ai in the East* bore further similarities, beyond its cast of officials, to *The Scripture on the Ten Kings*— a proposition that can only be indulged as a thought experiment—then one could deduce several grounds for its exclusion from the canon: it mimics the form of a sūtra but appends unacceptable verse forms; it is modeled on the popular practice of making offerings for the departed; it depends upon indigenous cosmological beliefs involving *yin*[b] and *yang* about what happens after death; and it is concerned primarily with the fate of the ancestors, who, it is hoped, will be placated by blessings rather than returning to haunt their families.

Other texts dealing with the underworld and probably resembling *The Scripture on the Ten Kings* were consistently excluded from later canons.[5] Descriptions of purgatory appear to have excited the strongest

3. The title is first noted in Chinese sources in *Chung-ching mu-lu* (594), Fa-ching (d.u.) et al., *T* no. 2146, 55:138c.

4. Translation from *Chung-ching mu-lu* (594), *T* 55:139a; slightly modified from Tokuno's translation of the nearly identical passage at *T* 55:127c; see Tokuno, "The Evaluation of Indigenous Scriptures," p. 41.

5. One example is *Yen-lo wang shuo mien ti-yü ching* (The Scripture Spoken by King Yama Rāja on Escaping the Underground Prisons), which is noted and declared spurious for the first time in the catalogue of Empress Wu's Chou

official denial from Chih-sheng (fl. 669–740), who molded the canon compiled during the K'ai-yüan era (713–741). The texts and their reasons for exclusion are especially worth examining because of the pivotal role Chih-sheng's catalogue played in the history of Chinese Buddhism. Defined by Chih-sheng's work, the K'ai-yüan canon not only served as the norm for later Buddhist canons in the age of the manuscript, but became the unquestioned basis for all xylographic printings, official and private, of the Chinese Buddhist canon.

Traditional historiography often describes Chih-sheng as a critical, nearly modern judge of literary and doctrinal authority.[6] He also had strong opinions about texts dealing with the hell regions. *Ti-yü ching* (The Scripture on the Underground Prisons), for instance, had up until his time been admitted into the canon under the rubrics of "anonymous authorship" *(shih-i)* and "abridged edition" *(ch'ao-ching)*.[7] Chih-sheng placed it in the category of "spurious and fallacious, bringing disorder to the truth" *(wei-wang luan-chen)*.[8]

We are fortunate in being able to glimpse Chih-sheng's justification for excluding a text on hell about which we know comparatively much. Portions of the book, entitled *Ching-tu san-mei ching* (The Scripture on the Samādhi of [Bodhisattva] Ching-tu), were cited in medieval anthologies, and fragments have been preserved among manuscripts in Japan and Tun-huang.[9] The sūtra can be linked to *The Scripture on the Ten Kings* not so much because of its overt message, which encourages Buddhist lay people to follow a schedule of six days of feasting per month and to practice a set of ethical rules stated partly in Buddhist, partly in Confucian terms, but rather due to the sanctions it invokes if such practices are contravened. If the precepts are not observed, warns the Buddha, then after death the morally lax will be remanded to a set of thirty

---

dynasty; *Ta-chou k'an-ting chung-ching mu-lu* (695), Ming-ch'üan (d.u.) et al., *T* no. 2153, 55:474a.

6. Demiéville, ("Les sources chinoises," p. 460), for example, advises students of Buddhism about Chih-sheng, "To him one can turn with confidence for any quick reference." For a good corrective to this view of Chih-sheng, see Forte, "The Relativity of the Concept of Orthodoxy in Chinese Buddhism."

7. The *Ti-yü ching* in one scroll is listed as an anonymous work in *Ch'u santsang chi chi*, Seng-yu (445–518), *T* no. 2145, 55:27c; *Ta-t'ang nei-tien lu*, Taohsüan (596–667), *T* no. 2149, 55:225c; and *Ta-chou k'an-ting chung-ching mu-lu*, *T* 55:440c. It is listed as an abridged work in *Chung-ching mu-lu* (594), *T* 55:137b; and *Chung-ching mu-lu* (602), *T* 55:170a.

8. *K'ai-yüan shih-chiao lu*, Chih-sheng (fl. 669–740), *T* no. 2154, 55:673a.

9. The most complete study of the text, including transcriptions of some of the manuscript versions, is Makita, *Gikyō kenkyū*, pp. 247–71; an earlier version of part of this study was translated by Antonino Forte as "The *Ching-tu san-mei ching* and the Tun-huang Manuscripts." See also Sunayama, "Don'yō to *jōdo sanmai kyō*"; and Teiser, *The Ghost Festival in Medieval China*, p. 180.

administrators who amount to an earlier and parallel formulation of the
system of the ten kings. Yama is not among the thirty. Instead he is the
emperor ("Son of Heaven," T'ien-tzu) over all those who superintend
the prisons. Beneath him stand the eight great kings *(pa ta-wang),* and
under them serve the thirty kings. The thirty kings are all portrayed as
bureaucrats, and their names are not personal names but for the most
part describe their function. (This too is a precedent for some of the
names of the ten kings.) Although *The Scripture on the Samādhi of Bodhi-*
sattva Ching-tu was accepted as part of earlier Buddhist canons, Chih-
sheng withdrew it from the canon.[10] Chih-sheng knew of at least four
different versions of the text. After studying one in detail, he wrote:[11]

> I have examined closely the words of the text. It is crude and shallow,
> and its principles are confounded. It is all about human contrivances
> and could hardly be a classic of the Sage. Therefore I have listed it in
> the record of doubtful texts rather than giving it a respectable position
> among the true scriptures.

Texts like *The Scripture on the Ten Kings* were banned from the official
repository of Buddhist teachings, but there were other mechanisms
available in medieval China for gaining legitimacy. One such mecha-
nism, controlled from the top by the Saṃgha but subject to considerable
local and unofficial influence, was the practice of lay Buddhism. Lay
Buddhism was located socially midway between monks, who left their
families to devote themselves full-time to the religious life, and common
people, who hired Buddhist specialists when they could afford them and
visited temples when they could not afford not to. Lay Buddhists were
householders who undertook an explicit, but not necessarily exclusive,
commitment to follow identifiably Buddhist practice. As a general rule,
lay Buddhist religion was organized by middle-level monks at individual temples and was modulated by the monthly calendar of feast-days.
As discussed above (chapter 4), this is the Buddhist institution in which
one sees, if not the ten kings themselves, at least their shadows. I noted
the attempt to combine a decile of compassionate figures with ten members of a bureaucracy, the avoidance of tortures after death, and in some
cases an overlap between the functionaries of the ten feast days and the
ten kings. While it would not be accurate to cite this form of lay practice

10. Chih-sheng places a three-scroll version by Hsiao Tzu-liang (fl. 490) in
the category of "doubtful" *(i-huo)* and an abridged version in one scroll in the
category of "spurious and fallacious, bringing disorder to the true" *(wei-wang*
luan-chen); see *K'ai-yüan shih-chiao lu, T* 55:671c, 680a, respectively.

11. Translation from *K'ai-yüan shih-chiao lu, T* 55:632b. Cf. the garbled transcription of this passage in Makita, *Gikyō kenkyū,* p. 248; and the garbled
English translation of that transcription in Makita, "The *Ching-tu san-mei*
ching," p. 353.

as an example of direct institutional support for worship of the ten kings, it is clear that the two practices shared some of the same principles and were located in overlapping social milieux. Proponents of the system of lay feast days may also have attempted to preempt the less legitimate, but more widespread custom of memorial offerings, thus lending an ambiguous air of authority to the ten kings. Given the gaps in our knowledge, however, the borrowing could just as well have run in the other direction, with proponents of the ten kings trying to gain respectability by crafting their practice after the examples provided by lay Buddhism and lay Taoism.

Given the exclusion of the ten kings from the canon and from organized lay practice, origin legends may have been the most influential means of legitimation. As far as I have been able to discover, the only hard claim for the Indic origins of *The Scripture on the Ten Kings* is made in the text itself, which as a sūtra begins with the formula, "Thus have I heard. Once, when the Buddha . . . ." Another story, told by Chih-yu and collected by Ch'ang-chin, adduces the meditative experience of an unnamed Indian bodhisattva as the source for paintings of Ti-tsang and the ten kings. All other attempts to justify belief in the ten kings and to encourage their worship look not to India or the Western regions but to China. No one, it seems, took seriously the Indian pedigree that *The Scripture on the Ten Kings* claimed for itself. Instead, apologists sought to persuade people of the validity of the ten kings by grounding them in Chinese experience. Some traditions provided the ten kings with a mantle of authenticity by connecting them to famous wonder-workers. Chang Kuo used Taoist techniques to achieve immortality and charm emperors, while Tao-ming was a Buddhist monk who died and returned to life; both were effective guarantors of the ten kings. Perhaps most convincing of all, however, was the story of the monk Tsang-ch'uan, whose skill was neither wisdom, nor meditation, nor saintly powers, but the singing of hymns.

PART TWO

Production of the Scripture

LIKE MOST SŪTRAS of Mahāyāna Buddhism, *The Scripture on the Ten Kings* insists upon its own reproduction. More than once the text promises that, regardless of one's station in life or degree of commitment to the Buddhist path, one can gain incalculable benefit simply by paying a scribe to make a copy of *The Scripture on the Ten Kings*. Śākyamuni himself encourages his followers to disseminate the book:

> a person can during life commission this scripture or the various images of the Honored Ones, and it will be noted in the dark registry. On the day one arrives, King Yama will be delighted and will decide to release the person to be reborn in a rich and noble household, avoiding [punishment for] his crimes and errors.

Even more than the living, the dead depend upon the propagation of the text to escape the torments marking their path to the next life. As they stand before the ninth king one year after death, the *Ten Kings* sūtra states:

> At one year they pass here, turning about in suffering and grief,
> Depending on whatever merit their sons and daughters have
>   cultivated.
> The wheel of rebirth in the six paths is revolving, still not
>   settled;
> Commission a scripture or commission an image, and they will
>   emerge from mistaken crossings.

Although the scripture intimates that the living and the dead virtually require the duplication of the text for their salvation, it leaves entirely open the question of how that task is to be fulfilled. It is silent about writing materials, formats for binding, copyists, assignment of benefits, or how the resulting book is to be used.

Part Two of this study attempts to demonstrate that the scripture's promises were not ignored in medieval China. It documents the variety of people and the diversity of motives involved in copying the text. It raises the questions: Who copied the scripture, and how? Who commissioned it, and why? In what settings was the text used? Who owned copies of *The Scripture on the Ten Kings,* and where did they store them?

Answers to those questions are not generally found in the Buddhist canon or in studies of Buddhist doctrine. In a tradition like Chinese Buddhism, which required that the words of the Buddha be passed down without change or interruption, most details of textual practice were relegated, quite literally, to the margins of the text. Fortunately a large number of Tun-huang manuscripts preserve precisely the kind of endnotes needed to answer these questions. Almost one-half of the surviving copies of *The Scripture on the Ten Kings* contain dedications that may be compared systematically to the colophons of other medieval manuscripts. In addition to colophons, the details of book composition and sources on the history of Tun-huang will be used to examine the conditions for the production of the text. In a number of cases this codicological approach allows us to date precisely several copies of the scripture that have so far eluded scholarly grasp. I devote special attention to the prayers appended as dedications to many copies of *The Scripture on the Ten Kings.* Those prayers are extremely important for our knowledge of medieval religion, yet they have not, I believe, been taken seriously enough either as literary genre or as religious act. Some of them provide the most detailed knowledge we have about how the doctrines of the text were put into practice. They are an invaluable form of commentary on how the scripture was understood.

7. Scrolls

THE SCRIPTURE ON THE TEN KINGS specifies no particular format for the reproduction of the scripture, so it is perhaps fitting that the surviving samples of the text are constructed in the two most common styles of book manufacture in the Chinese world of the tenth century. Over two-thirds of the specimens are scrolls, some of which contain illustrations. The others are bound booklets of varying sizes, discussed in the next section. (For an overview of the physical characteristics of the manuscripts, see appendix 10.)

In the history of Chinese bookmaking the "scroll" (*chüan-tzu* or *chüan-chou*) developed as an imitation of the method used for storing an earlier

form of the book.[1] Until the third or fourth century Chinese books had
been written on wooden and bamboo strips, which were then stitched
together with leather or cloth and rolled up. These early "scrolls"—
rolls of wooden strips—gave way to scrolls made of paper and silk for a
variety of reasons. The technology for making paper was perfected and
diffused throughout China in the first few centuries of the common era.
Paper was a less respected material for books than was silk, but it was
cheaper and easier to make. Scrolls made out of a long continuous strip
of paper, made by gluing together individual sheets, were also much
more convenient to manipulate than bundles of wooden strips. When a
chain of wooden strips broke, the text became jumbled and portions frequently disappeared. When a paper scroll deteriorated, it often lost only
its cover or its last few, most tightly curled, lines. When holes appeared
they did not necessarily threaten the integrity of the whole book and
could be repaired with relative ease. At any rate, by about the year 300
an increasing number of books in China were constructed of paper
wound in scrolls, and by the year 500 that format was used widely in
Central Asia.

The physical characteristics of the surviving nonillustrated scrolls of
The Scripture on the Ten Kings may be summarized as follows. Sheets of
paper were cut to a fairly uniform size. Sheets for canonical Buddhist
and Taoist works averaged 25.9 cm in height by 46.2 cm in length.
Paper for most of the scrolls of *The Scripture on the Ten Kings* is near this
average, but other noncanonical and private writings varied considerably from this standard.[2] Scribes set to work on individual sheets of
paper. They laid out top and bottom margins and inserted ruling,
sometimes with a pencil, before beginning to write. In most cases there

---

1. This section and the next draw on an earlier essay, Teiser, "Hymns for the
Dead in the Age of the Manuscript." The literature on the Chinese scroll is
voluminous. For an important overview of the physical characteristics of Tun-
huang scrolls and a methodology for dating them, see Drège, "Papiers de
Dunhuang"; idem, "Notes codicologiques sur les manuscrits de Dunhuang et
de Turfan"; and idem, "Étude formelle des manuscrits de Dunhuang conservés à Taipei." Other important studies of the Chinese scroll include idem,
"Le livre manuscrit et les débuts de la xylographie"; Fujieda, *Moji no bunka shi;*
idem, "Tonkō shutsudo no chōan kyūtei shakyō"; Ma, "Chung-kuo shu-chi
chih-tu pien-ch'ien chih yen-chiu"; and Mote and Chu, *Calligraphy and the East
Asian Book.* On the composition and manufacture of paper, see P'an, *Chung-kuo
tsao-chih chi-shu shih-kao,* pp. 66–107, 171–78; idem, "Tun-huang shih-shih
hsieh-ching chih te yen-chiu" *WW* 1966, no. 3 (no. 185) (March 1966): 39–47;
Harders-Steinhaüser, "Mikroskopische Untersuchung einiger früher, ostasiatischer Tun-huang-Papier"; and Clapperton, *Paper: An Historical Account of Its
Making by Hand from the Earliest Times Down to the Present Day,* pp. 1–26, esp. pp.
22–26.
2. Drège, "Papiers de Dunhuang," esp. pp. 339–57, offers the most complete and up-to-date analysis of dated samples.

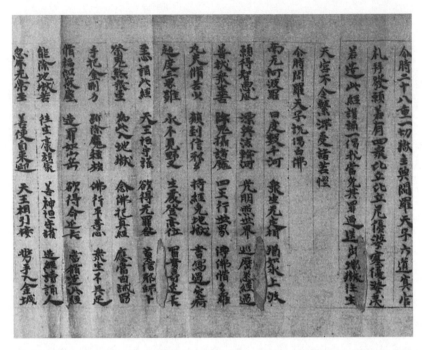

3. Short recension of *The Scripture on the Ten Kings* in scroll format. This portion includes prose narrative and five-syllable chants. S 3147. ©British Library.

were seventeen characters per vertical line and twenty-five lines per sheet, but here too there was variation. The layout also varied in the spacing of five-syllable chants on the page (see fig. 3).[3] The scroll was put together after the text was copied. Individual sheets were glued together to form one continuous strip of paper. Sometimes a roller made of wood was fastened to the end (the inside edge) of the manuscript. Reinforcement was also added to the beginning (the leading, outside edge) of the scroll. Usually an extra length of paper or cloth was glued on; when the scroll was wound up, this cover, on which the title was usually written, provided extra protection. Once the writing of the text and construction of the physical scroll were completed, only one step remained. The final margin of the scripture was inscribed with a dedi-

3. S 2489, reprod. Huang, *Pao-tsang,* 20:175a–76b, with eighteen characters per line, contains three verses per line, but Pk 8045, reprod. Huang, *Pao-tsang,* 109:430b–31b, also with eighteen characters per line, contains four verses per line. It is unknown whether these variations in composition are due to differences between the original recensions used as a standard in each of the scriptoria, the preferences of individual scribes, or inattention or random factors.

cation, noting the persons or beings whom the commissioner wished to receive the benefits of the act of copying.[4]

Like the imperial central library ("Department of the Palace Library," Pi-shu-sheng), each scriptorium in Tun-huang must have possessed an archival recension of the text on which all of its copies were based. Great care was taken to eliminate errors in the copying of texts. Judging from other texts produced at Tun-huang and from over two score surviving scriptures made in Ch'ang-an, we know that techniques to insure accuracy included the counting of characters, repeated proof-reading by up to three people, revising of mistakes by as many as six copyeditors, and certifying of the finished product by the supervisors of the copying office.[5] Almost all scrolls of *The Scripture on the Ten Kings* contain evidence of corrections: characters are written over, reverse marks are placed in the margins, patches with the correct characters are glued on top of mistakes, incorrect characters are blotted out and corrections placed alongside, and where the paper is decayed the text has been patched and rewritten.

Despite the wealth of physical details, much remains unknown. Not one copyist recorded his name in a colophon to *The Scripture on the Ten Kings*. We do not know in which temples the text was copied, nor do we know the precise institutional arrangement of Tun-huang scriptoria. We can only estimate how long it took a scribe to copy the text, and we have no direct evidence about how the scroll was wrapped up or where it was shelved in monastery libraries.[6]

4. Judging from the handwriting—never a certain guide—dedications were not written by the same person who copied the text.

5. For comprehensive studies of the manufacture and storage of texts in medieval Buddhist libraries, see Drège, "Les bibliothèques en Chine au temps des manuscrits (jusqu'au Xe siècle)," pp. 261–364; and Fang, *Fo-chiao ta-tsang-ching shih*, esp. pp. 274–355. Drège makes the intriguing suggestion (pp. 312–13) that each monastic library may have been divided into an upper and lower collection, the former for archiving the official canon, the latter—in which *The Scripture on the Ten Kings* may have been kept—for shelving copies of texts that saw frequent use. For details on the best-documented example of the copying of texts in medieval China, the reproduction of the *Lotus* and *Diamond* sūtras in Ch'ang-an between 671 and 677, see Fujieda, "Tonkō shutsudo no chōan kyū-tei shakyō," esp. pp. 655–59. For the Japanese system based on this model, see Ishida, *Shakyō yori mitaru nara chō bukkyō no kenkyū*.

6. Based on Fujieda's estimate that it took one scribe two full days to copy a scroll of average length, it probably took a scribe one to two working days to copy out the relatively short text of the short recension of *The Scripture on the Ten Kings*; see Fujieda, "Tonkō shutsudo no chōan kyūtei shakyō," pp. 661–65. Wrappers *(chih[b])* made of silk, paper, and other materials were used to enclose bundles of scrolls, usually numbering ten. For studies and photographs of wrappers uncovered at Tun-huang, see Riboud and Vial, *Tissus de Touen-houang*

The primary deployment of *The Scripture on the Ten Kings* bound as a scroll without illustrations must also remain a matter of speculation. The act of commissioning the copying of the text or collecting it was itself a ritual, often quite involved and lasting over several years. But that phase of the production of texts (discussed at length below) rarely influenced the disposition of the text itself. Although some copies of the scripture were probably housed at least briefly in the private library of a family in tenth-century Tun-huang named Chang,[7] most copies were undoubtedly kept in Buddhist temples, where they served a variety of purposes. Sometimes they were unrolled for study, recitation, and memorization, while other times they may have been used in a more crowded setting as the basis for a sermon or for chanting by monks.

All of the scrolls without illustrations reproduce the short or middle recensions of *The Scripture on the Ten Kings*.[8] By contrast, all copies of *The Scripture on the Ten Kings* produced as scrolls that do contain illustrations present the long recension of the text. In terms of their physical characteristics the illustrated scrolls differ only slightly from those without illustrations. They are slightly larger and contain more characters per line, which provides the extra space needed for a consistent laying out of the sections of poetry.[9]

The inclusion of illustrations means that in addition to paper makers,

---

conservés au Musée Guimet et à la Bibliothèque nationale, pls. 1, 2, 3, 4, 39, 43, 44, 45, 94, 95, 99, and 100; and Whitfield, *Art,* 3: pls. 6, 7, and 29–2. For an important article collating the call numbers on the wrappers of Tun-huang manuscripts with T'ang dynasty sūtra catalogues, see Fang, "Han-wen ta-tsang-ching chih-hao t'an-yüan." The only surviving external reference to the location of copies of *The Scripture on the Ten Kings* is contained in an inventory of books collected from private donors and deposited in the library of San-chieh ssu in Tun-huang in 934 by the monk Tao-chen; see below, chapter 13. Other lists of books survive from Tun-huang, but to my knowledge none mentions *The Scripture on the Ten Kings*. Some are formal listings of titles loaned by one monastery to another for copying; some are official records of deficiencies in particular libraries; some are simply titles jotted down on scraps of paper. For overviews see Okabe, "Tonkō zōkyō mokuroku"; Kyōdo, "A Study of the Buddhist Manuscripts of Dunhuang"; and Fang, "Tu tun-huang fo-tien ching-lu cha-chi."

7. The manuscripts are S 3147 and Pk 6375, discussed in chapter 13.

8. The short and middle recensions contain the story of King Yama told in prose, the instructions to cultivate sacrifices to the ten kings, and several segments of five-syllable *gāthās* suitable for chanting, but no mention of an author, no ritual invocations at beginning or end, and no hymns—all elements of the long recension.

9. A good example is P 2003, reprod. Huang, *Pao-tsang,* 112:24b–34b. Its sheets average 29.5 by 50 cm. There are nineteen to twenty-one characters per line. Hymns containing four verses of seven syllables are arranged neatly with two verses in a line. The chants, consisting of eight verses of five syllables, are laid out four verses per line.

copyists, and binders, these scrolls passed through the hands of artists as well. The historical record is even blanker concerning Tun-huang artists than for local scribes, so all of our knowledge is deduced from the scrolls themselves. The process for producing scrolls with illustrations was very similar to that for making nonillustrated manuscripts described above. It appears that illustrators set to work, sketching outlines in ink and then brushing in colors, before sending the scrolls to copyists. In several examples scenes were drawn so close together that the text had to be squeezed in clumsily or superimposed upon the picture.[10]

10. The third illustration to P 2870 is too close to the fourth, as a result of which part of the text was written (and later corrected with a patch) on top of the foot of the attendant leading the black messenger's horse; reprod. Huang, *Pao-tsang*, 124:588b.

8. Booklets

THE OTHER MAJOR format for medieval copies of *The Scripture on the Ten Kings* substitutes the convenience and speed of flipping the pages of a folio for the pleasure of unwinding a long scroll. First appearing in China during the T'ang dynasty, this style of book binding, known under a variety of names (*ts'e^b-tzu* or *ts'e-tzu^b*, "booklet," *ts'e-yeh*, "album of individual leaves"), soon became the dominant shape for written texts.[1]

When it was time to search for a hazily remembered passage or to join in the recitation of chants, the earlier form of the scroll was much more cumbersome to manipulate than was the booklet. Booklets were also easier to store and to transport than were scrolls. The paper sheets from which booklets were constructed were generally smaller in size than the sheets joined to make scrolls. That smaller size was heavily favored by a development that would have tremendous implications for

1. Recent discoveries of physical remains have prompted a reinterpretation of the terms used by Sung dynasty authors to describe styles of binding and a reassessment of the place of the booklet and related forms in the history of Chinese book production. The most helpful overviews are Drège, "Les cahiers des manuscrits de Touen-houang"; and idem, "Les accordéons de Dunhuang." Other important studies include Ch'ang, "T'ang-tai t'u-shu hsing-chih te yen-pien"; Fujieda, "Sutain tonkō shūshū e'iri *kannon gyō* sasshi"; idem, *Moji no bunka shi*, pp. 188–92; Li, "Ku-shu hsüan-feng-chuang k'ao-pien"; and Ma, "Chung-kuo shu-chi chih-tu pien-ch'ien chih yen-chiu."

the transmission of knowledge in East Asia (and later throughout the world), printing with wooden blocks. The topic of the printing of books on the ten kings is fascinating, but goes well beyond the confines of this study.[2] The fact remains that all Tun-huang copies of *The Scripture on the Ten Kings* manufactured as booklets were written by hand, not printed.

In addition to indigenous trends, foreign influences played an undeniable role in the popularization of the booklet. Indian customs provided two models for gathering individual leaves into a stack. In one particular technique that appears in some Chinese texts from Tun-huang, scribes wrote in long columns upon paper cut into long, rectangular strips, a shape imitating the leaves of the palm tree. The strips were placed atop one another, numbered, and either left unbound or secured loosely with one or two strings running through holes punched in the middle of the page. The other technique, seen in Chinese manuscripts from Tun-huang as well as in printings of the Buddhist canon beginning in the twelfth century, was to fold a long strip of paper in alternate directions in the form of an accordion *(ching-che-chuang).*[3] Whatever its origins, the binding of individual leaves into the form of a notebook is represented in approximately four hundred specimens of a variety of texts from Tun-huang. The earliest is dated 899, the latest 982.

Three specific forms of booklets of *The Scripture on the Ten Kings* are discussed below; all of them bear a resemblance to the codex of late antiquity in the West.[4] Several features are common to all three morphologies. As stock, the sheets of paper used to make them measured thirty by forty-five centimeters. The raw material was usually cut three times, and the resulting leaf was folded in half to form a page measuring fifteen by eleven centimeters. The dimensions are close to those of the *Cliffs Notes* series seen frequently on American college campuses. One method for binding the leaves did not involve the use of string:

2. One of the earliest surviving xylographic editions of *The Scripture on the Ten Kings,* presumably bound as a booklet, is a Korean edition of 1469; transcr. Z, 2b, 23:4. The editors identify it simply as "a Korean printed edition"; ibid., p. 385ra. Its colophon is dated Ch'eng-hua 5/V (1469); ibid., p. 387rb.

3. On the binding of books as accordions and related styles, see Drège, "Les accordéons"; and Li, "Ku-shu hsüan-feng-chuang k'ao-pien." The Buddhist canon was first bound in the format of an accordion with the private edition produced at Tung-ch'an ssu in Fu-chou in two stretches of work between 1080 and 1103 and between 1112 and 1176; see Fang, "Sung-tai fo-chiao tui chung-kuo yin-shua chi tsao-chih chih kung-hsien," p. 447; Ono, *Bukkyō kyōten sōron,* pp. 781–808; and Ts'ai, *Erh-shih-wu-chung tsang-ching mu-lu tui-chao k'ao-shih,* pp. 469–70.

4. See the definition of "codex" offered in Roberts and Skeat, *The Birth of the Codex,* p. 1: "a collection of sheets of any material, folded double and fastened together at the back or spine, usually protected by covers."

glue was applied along the edge of one fold, another folded leaf was placed on top, glue was applied to the new fold, and so on until the requisite number of pages was bound. In the other method for binding, several sheets together were folded in half to form a signature, and several signatures were stitched together to form a booklet. The leaves bound by both methods could then be protected by paper jackets glued around the spine. The texts were inscribed using a wooden pen, which was the most common writing implement in Tun-huang for over 250 years. In the arid northwest the use of brushes to write characters depended upon regular contact with bamboo-producing regions in central and southern China, which was ended by the Tibetan takeover of the Tun-huang area in 748. At first scribes used the wooden pen to copy texts in the Tibetan language. Then copyists improvised the use of a wooden stylus to imitate the form of Chinese characters achieved by using a brush. After the government of Tun-huang was reclaimed by local Chinese families, continuing economic isolation from the rest of the Middle Kingdom meant that pens were used even more frequently. Fujieda estimates that 60 to 70 percent of all surviving Tunhuang manuscripts were written with a pen.[5] In time the pen was even adapted by Chinese artists to make paintings, banners, and ink sketches.

In the most common form of *The Scripture on the Ten Kings* bound as a booklet, the manuscript is bound together leaf-by-leaf (see fig. 4). Although the pages are relatively small, thus restricting the amount of text a scribe can write on each readable page (with the book opened flat, presenting the verso of one page and the recto of the next page), scribes exercised considerable latitude in laying out the text. In most copies, for instance, they managed to squeeze the entire section of recited *gāthās* onto one surface, thus saving the reader from having to turn the page mid-chant. All of these booklets present the short recension of *The Scripture on the Ten Kings*.

Most of the booklets bound in this fashion contain not one text, but two. Before *The Scripture on the Ten Kings* comes one of the most influential statements of Mahāyāna philosophy, the *Diamond* sūtra—but not just a random copy of the *Diamond* sūtra. Recent studies by Hirai Yūkei and others have demonstrated a nearly bewildering variation in the presentation of the *Diamond* exempla from Tun-huang. By documenting the different versions and the considerable differences in prefatory material and back matter, they have proven that outside of Ch'ang-an the *Diamond* sūtra was not a single, standard text.[6] The form in which

5. Fujieda, *Moji no bunka shi,* p. 198; and idem, "Sutain tonkō shūshū e'iri kannon gyō sasshi," p. 6.

6. For a superb study of the different forms in which the *Diamond* sūtra circulated, see Hirai, *"Kongō hannya kyō";* and Makita, "Kan'yaku butten denshōjō

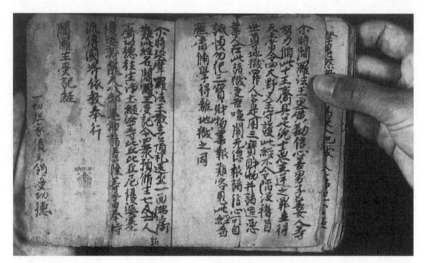

4. Short recension of *The Scripture on the Ten Kings* in format of large booklet. This portion includes narrative, concluding title, and colophon. S 5450. ©British Library.

the *Diamond* sūtra is presented in the booklets containing the *Ten Kings* text is probably not an accident; codicological and textual details about the *Diamond* sūtra offer important clues about the production of *The Scripture on the Ten Kings*.

The *Diamond* sūtra was written earlier and copied more frequently than most other Prajñāpāramitā literature—despite the fact that it never once uses the word "emptiness" (*k'ung*, Skt.: *śūnyatā*)—so one would naturally expect textual variation to accompany proliferation. In monastic folklore the text was associated with the enlightenment experience of the allegedly illiterate Ch'an master Hui-neng (638–713), and medieval collections of miracle tales tout the supernatural abilities of the text.[7] The Sanskrit versions of *Vajracheddikā prajñāpāramitā* (The Perfection of Wisdom that Cuts like a Thunderbolt [or Diamond]) were translated numerous times into Tibetan, Khotanese, and Chinese, and versions also survive in Sogdian, Mongolian, and Manchu. Of the six

---

no ichimondai." There are excellent studies on the textual and philosophical aspects of the *Diamond;* see, for example, Conze, *Vajracchedikā prajñāpāramitā;* and Kajiyoshi, *Kongō hannya kyō.*

7. On the place of the *Diamond* sūtra in Chinese Buddhism, see Hirai, *"Kongō hannya kyō";* idem, "Tonkō bunsho ni okeru *kongō kyō* sho"; Kamata, *Chūgoku bukkyō shi,* pp. 220–22; O, *"Kongō hannya kyō shū genki* kenkyū"; and Soymié, "Notes d'iconographie bouddhique: des Vidyārāja et Vajradhara de Touen-houang."

surviving Chinese translations completed between 402 and 703, how-ever, the *Diamond* texts that are bound together with *The Scripture on the Ten Kings* reproduce only the translation by Kumārajīva (350–409).[8] All of those that survive intact contain a sixty-character section the authen-ticity of which has been disputed in Buddhological circles since medie-val times.[9] Although other handwritten copies of Kumārajīva's transla-tion are divided into both twelve and thirty-two sections, these copies present only the text in thirty-two divisions. They all claim descent from one specific recension, referred to at the end of the scripture as "the true printed copy of the Kuo family of Hsi-ch'uan." And they all close with a series of three *dhāraṇī*, which find no parallel in the Sanskrit version.

Why do these details matter? Hirai singles out the factor that, more than all the others, helps to explain the binding together of this version of the *Diamond* sūtra with *The Scripture on the Ten Kings*. He sketches the following scenario for the transmission of the *Diamond* sūtra:[10]

> The Sanskrit original, at least as far as surviving manuscripts from India are concerned, does not have the style of the Chinese text of the scripture, in which such elements as the scene illustrating the preach-ing of the Law, the *dhāraṇī*, and the names of the eight Vajras occur before and after the main text of the scripture. Of course the text in this form does not exist in the Taishō canon, nor does it appear in very many Tun-huang manuscripts. Thus, in the process of the circulation of the scripture, this particular guise was added for purposes of recita-tion (or copying), and the format of this popular edition took shape.

If Hirai is correct, then we have a link of primary importance between two texts that otherwise, in terms of content, share very little. The *dhāraṇī* associated with the *Diamond* were not mere embellishment, added as an afterthought to the main body of the text. They were an essential part of a religious service in which scriptures achieved their effect by being recited aloud by a group. Dividing the text into many short sections—precisely the choice taken in producing the *Diamond*

8. The modern edition is *Chin-kang po-jo po-lo-mi ching,* Kumārajīva (350–409), *T* no. 235.

9. The intact copies containing the interpolation are S 5450 and S 5544. The interpolation was probably contained in the printed version of the *Diamond* from Szechwan on which these copies were based. Following Sung Buddhist historio-graphy, Makita suggests that these lines, popularly called "*gāthās* from the dark offices" *(ming-ssu chi),* may have been dropped inadvertently from the earliest copies of Kumārajīva's translation and were reinserted beginning in the T'ang dynasty; see Makita, "Kan'yaku butten denshōjō no ichimondai," p. 128, n. 10.

10. Hirai, *"Kongō hannya kyō,"* p. 24.

copies bound together with the *Ten Kings*—also made the text liturgi-
cally convenient.

Two more textual details about the *Diamond* sūtra must be mentioned. Even in the realm of practice, the connection between these two
texts was not universal, a fact attested by the existence of manuscript
booklets containing the *Diamond* sūtra alone or the *Diamond* sūtra
together with other texts of Chinese Buddhism. The same recension of
the text—Kumārajīva's translation divided into thirty-two sections,
based on a printed master edition from Szechwan—is found by itself in
a number of bookets; the dated ones range from 905 to 943. The same
recension is also found in booklets containing between two and six texts,
one of which is dated 969.[11] These variations render the joint replication
of the *Diamond* and the *Ten Kings* in one book (in five surviving samples)
all the more significant. The survival of these booklets in the caves of
Tun-huang makes it extremely unlikely that the two sūtras were associated merely by scribal caprice. It is much more likely that a scriptorium in a Buddhist temple bound them together repeatedly, and in an
easily chanted format, because monks used the two texts frequently in a
program of religious services.

The other detail about binding implies that some Tun-huang copies
of *The Scripture on the Ten Kings* may be traced to Szechwan, one of the
cradles of the woodblock printing industry. Only three of the five surviving copies of the text bound together with the *Diamond* scripture are
intact enough to contain the ending of the *Diamond* text, but all those
that do include a note on filiation, placed after the *Diamond* sūtra and
before the *dhāraṇī*, stating that the text is based on "a true printed copy
of the Kuo family of Hsi-ch'uan" (Hsi-ch'uan Kuo-*chia chen yin-pen*).[12]
The same copyright occurs in other Tun-huang copies of the *Diamond*
sūtra, some bound singly in booklets, others produced as scrolls. They
range in date between 908 and 943.[13] The printed edition belonging
originally to the Kuo family, then, must have been revered so highly in
at least one Tun-huang scriptorium that it served as the master version

11. Copies of this recension of the *Diamond* sūtra bound individually as a
booklet include S 5444 (dated 905), S 5451 (906), S 5534 (905), S 5669 (906), S
5965 (906), P 2876 (906), P 3398-1 (same manuscript also designated P 3493)
(943), Pk 8909 (907), and Th Museum 53 (906). Copies of this recension of the
Diamond sūtra bound together with other texts include S 5450, S 5544 (911?),
S 5585, S 5646 (969), P 5580 (probably), and *san* 262.
    12. They are S 5450, S 5544 (dated 911?), and *san* 262.
    13. Other copies of the *Diamond* sūtra with the notation "based on the true
printed copy of the Kuo family in Hsi-ch'uan" bound as a booklet include
S 5444 (dated 905), S 5451 (906), S 5534 (905), S 5669 (906), S 5965 (906),
P 2876 (906), P 3398-1 (same manuscript also designated P 3493) (943), and
Pk 8909 (907). *Diamonds* with the same notation bound as scrolls include
S 6276 (926?) and P 2094 (908).

for the production of many copies.[14] Did the text bound together frequently with the Kuo family *Diamond*, that is, the short recension of *The Scripture on the Ten Kings*, share the same filiation? Without other evidence the question cannot be answered, but the correlation would reinforce—on evidence slightly less flimsy—the tradition reported in Part One of this book that traces the origins of the long recension to a Buddhist monk active in Szechwan.

Only one copy survives of *The Scripture on the Ten Kings* bound in the second style of booklet. That is a volume consisting of stitched signatures, eight leaves folded in half (making sixteen pages, with writing on recto and verso sides) per signature. Compared to the glued booklets, the pages of the stitched booklet are smaller, containing fewer characters per line and fewer lines per page. Its composition makes it slightly easier to read than the glued booklets.

The stitched booklet contains a total of ten texts. They deal with specific deities (Kuan-yin Bodhisattva, Ti-tsang Bodhisattva, the goddess Mārīci), seek the prolongation of life and the avoidance of sickness, and offer *dhāraṇī* for the pacification of enemies. The last text is the *Heart* sūtra. The booklet lacks a dedicatory colophon but ends with a notation of the date in the sexagenary cycle, "the twentieth day of the twelfth month of the *keng-ch'en* year" (31 January 921?).

The use of this stitched booklet must remain purely conjectural. Other manuscripts bound as booklets that contain three or more Buddhist sūtras do exhibit some consistency: they are predominantly *dhāraṇī* collections and texts on specific Bodhisattvas.[15] Do the design and customary content of these booklets suggest that they were intended to be temple copies, used by monks performing a priestly function in a wide range of practical services?

Questions also remain about the third form of *Ten Kings* booklet, a

14. I have not been able to find any other information concerning the Kuo family of Hsi-ch'uan. Hsi-ch'uan was the name used in T'ang times for part of Wei-chou in western Szechwan; see *Chiu t'ang-shu*, Liu Hsü (887–946), p. 1690; and *T'ai-p'ing huan-yü chi*, Yüeh Shih (930–1007), 78.7v–8r (1:601b–c). These are not the only Tun-huang texts that can be traced to Hsi-ch'uan. P 2292 was apparently copied in Hsi-ch'uan in 947; reprod. Huang, *Pao-tsang*, 118:554a–62b, colophon on p. 562a. For others, see Mair, *T'ang Transformation Texts*, p. 180, n. 33. Hsi-ch'uan was an important center for printing as early as the middle of the ninth century. In his catalogue of books brought home to Japan, the monk Shūei (fl. 809–884), who traveled in China between 862 and 866, records two works printed in Hsi-ch'uan, one the *T'ang-yün* in five chapters, the other the *Yü-p'ien* in thirty chapters; see *Shin shosha shōrai hōmontō mokuroku*, Shūei (fl. 809–884), *T* no. 2174, 55:1111b; and Hsiang, "T'ang-tai k'an-shu k'ao," pp. 124, 126–27, 132.

15. Booklets containing three texts include S 5646 (dated 969), P 3136, and Cft xxii.0026. Five texts: S 5458, and Th Museum 77. Six texts: S 5581 and P 3915. Seven texts: P 3920. Ten texts: S 5531 (921?) and P 3916.

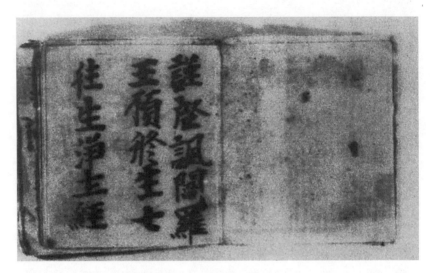

5. Short recension of *The Scripture on the Ten Kings* in format of tiny booklet. Closed, cover page. P 3761. Photograph courtesy of Bibliothèque nationale, Paris. Actual size.

single specimen that is probably the most fetching textual representation of the sufferings endured in the netherworld. The booklet measures 5.3 by 4.9 centimeters, a size that may be translated for the modern reader's benefit as the dimensions of a pack of Lucky Strikes (see fig. 5). The booklet is bound in the same fashion as the first type discussed above, with each leaf glued to the next along its fold, but here the copyist has chosen to write on only one side of the page. Unlike all the other booklets, this one contains the long recension of *The Scripture on the Ten Kings*. Despite great constraints on layout, the copyist varied the size of characters and the length of lines, in order, apparently, to keep the book handy—even when that required him to squeeze in characters inconsistently at the bottom of the page (see fig. 6).

Other manuscripts of this size—easily transported? hidden in a sleeve? used surreptitiously? studied in private?—do survive among Tun-huang collections.[16] In terms of content they betray concerns similar to those of *The Scripture on the Ten Kings:* identifying and invoking the aid of benevolent deities, averting misfortune, and offering prayers.

16. Other tiny manuscripts include S 5924, an accordion-style booklet, 6 × 5 cm; P 3759, a bound booklet containing two texts, 5.1 × 4.7 cm; P 3760, an accordion-style booklet containing three texts; and Cft 00213, a bound booklet, 6.4 × 6.5 cm.

6. Short recension of *The. Scripture on the Ten Kings* in format of tiny booklet. Open to page showing end of narrative and layout of seven-syllable hymns. P 3761. Photograph courtesy of Bibliothèque nationale, Paris. Actual size.

This copy of *The Scripture on the Ten Kings* might be seen as performing the same personal, perhaps talismanic, functions as do other tiny texts.[17] Yet it is not likely that *The Scripture on the Ten Kings,* especially in its long recension, was ever reserved for strictly personal use. The tiny booklet reproduces faithfully the invocation of Amitābha Buddha, part of a communal ceremony, that opens the long recension. It does not contain paintings, but it does record the hymns, presumably sung during services, accompanying each of the pictures in the illustrated scrolls. Given the cost of producing and the difficulty in acquiring illustrated scrolls of *The Scripture on the Ten Kings,* coupled with the shadowy, compelling demand for large-scale memorial services with all the trappings, a booklet this size would serve as a perfect study guide for an officiating priest.

17. For a tiny manuscript booklet of the gospel of St. John of similar dimensions (7.1 × 5.1 cm.) that was probably worn as a talisman, see Bischoff, "Kreuz und Buch im Frühmittelalter und in den ersten Jahrhunderten der spanischen Reconquista," p. 288.

9. Chai Feng-ta, in Memory of His Wife

A HANDWRITTEN COPY of *The Scripture on the Ten Kings* "rediscovered" only recently in the collection of the Tientsin Municipal Art Museum helps to clarify the social background and religious significance of the production of the *Ten Kings* sūtra. Unlike other medieval examples of the reproduction of scriptures for the spiritual benefit of the commissioner, this unique copy of *The Scripture on the Ten Kings* proves that the copying of the sūtra was performed in strict accordance with its message. The Tientsin manuscript was once the first of a set of three scrolls containing ten separate texts. The second scroll is now housed in the National Library of China in Peking, and the third scroll was taken by Pelliot to Paris.[1] The three scrolls were produced by an unidentified scribe in the Tun-huang region beginning in the year 958 to the order of a local official named Chai Feng-ta (fl. 902–966). Chai commissioned the copying of ten scriptures in memory of his deceased wife, née Ma. After each text Chai had prayers written, which I translate in full below.

The first scroll in the series consists of four scriptures, each followed by a colophon. The first colophon states:

> On the night of the first day of the third month of the fifth year of the Hsien-te era, designated *wu-wu* in the sequence of years [23 March 958], the body of our mother,[2] the lady Mrs. Ma, passed away. On the

1. Several scholars quickly realized that the Tientsin manuscript provided the missing link in the series; see Shih, "I-chien wan-cheng te she-hui feng-su shih tzu-liao"; and Kao, "Lun tun-huang min-chien ch'i-ch'i chai sang-su," esp. pp. 111–16. The Tientsin manuscript is Tts 175; colophon transcr. Liu and Li, "T'ien-chin-shih i-shu po-wu-kuan ts'ang tun-huang i-shu mu-lu." The second scroll is Pk 4544, reprod. Huang, *Pao-tsang*, 109:435b–38a. The third scroll is P 2055, reprod. Huang, *Pao-tsang*, 113:278a–88a. One of the most encouraging signs of the renaissance of Tun-huang studies in the People's Republic of China in the 1980s was the bringing to light of several thousand manuscripts that had been hidden—some truly forgotten, some intentionally consigned to dark, safe corners—since the early years of the twentieth century. A good idea of the significance of the newly publicized manuscripts can be gained from Drège, "À propos de quelques collections 'nouvelles' de manuscrits de Dunhuang."

2. "Our mother" translates *chia-mu*, which means literally "the mother of our family." Scholarship is divided over whether the woman was Chai's wife or his mother. Given the lack of references to the woman outside of this manuscript, the issue is impossible to settle definitively, but most evidence suggests that it was his wife. Fujieda interprets the word as "the elder woman of the house"; see Fujieda, "Tonkō rekijutsu fu," p. 437. In the colophon to the tenth

seventh day [29 March 958] we hold the feast of the opening seven. The Acting Vice Director of the Ministry of Public Works in the Department of State Affairs, Chai Feng-ta, in remembrance reverently copied *The Scripture on Impermanence* on one scroll and reverently painted one picture of the Thus Come Buddha Pao-chi. For every week until the third full year, on each feast one scroll of scripture will be copied as a posthumous blessing. We pray that Mother's shadow be entrusted[3] and her spirit roam to be reborn in a fine place, and that she not fall into the calamities of the three paths.[4] Offered fully and forever.

The second colophon states:

On the fourteenth day [5 April 958] for the feast of the second seven we make an offering for posthumous blessing. We pray that her spirit be born in the Pure Land and that she not fall into the difficulties of the three paths. May Mrs. Ma receive the field of blessings.[5]

---

text Chai refers to her as "my deceased wife" *(wang-kuo ch'i)*, a term that would not be applied to one's mother. The evidence from Chai's biography, presented below, also makes it extremely unlikely that the woman could have been his mother. Born in 883, Chai was seventy-five years old when the woman died. The author of the entry on P 2055 in BN, *Catalogue,* disagrees, translating *ch'i*^{c} as "his mother." Kao seems to treat the deceased as Chai's mother, arguing that he referred to her as both "mother" and "wife" in order to glorify her fulfillment of both social ideals; Kao, "Lun tun-huang min-chien ch'i-ch'i chai sang-su," p. 113. Shih also believes that the deceased was Chai's mother, citing as evidence the use of three colloquial terms for "mother" in the colophons to the ten texts *(a-p'o, a-niang,* and *a-niang*^{b}). Given the context, however, there is no problem in construing all three terms as references to the eldest woman of the family, i.e., "the old lady" or "our mother." Below I translate *a-p'o* as "lady" and both *a-niang* and *a-niang*^{b} as "Mother." For further references, see *Shuo-wen chieh-tzu,* 10:226b; and Mair, "Oral and Written Aspects of Chinese Sutra Lectures *(Chiang-ching-wen),* " p. 327, n. 86.

3. "Shadow be entrusted" translates *t'o-ying,* which is similar to traditional terms describing the way a bird "entrusts its body to the sun" *(t'o-t'i t'ai-yang)* and the way a human being "dispatches his spirit to the spirits and immortals" *(t'o-ling shen-hsien);* see *P'ei-wen yün-fu,* pp. 1746c–47a, 1235c.

4. "The three paths" *(san-t'u)* are the lower three paths of rebirth: animals, hungry ghosts, and hell beings.

5. "Field of blessings" translates *fu-t'ien* (Skt.: *puṇyakṣetra*), often rendered into English as "field of merit." In my translation I prefer to differentiate between two terms that overlap in meaning, *kung-te,* which I translate as "merit," and *fu*^{c}, which I translate as "blessings." The whole concept is based on an agricultural metaphor. The lay person is like a farmer, his or her act is like a seed, the Order or immediate recipient of the offering is like the field in which a seed is planted, the resulting merit is like the crop, and the deceased is like the person who benefits from or harvests the crop. The general idea was susceptible to a wide range of interpretations throughout the Buddhist world; see, for example, Collins, *Selfless Persons,* pp. 218–24; Filliozat, "Sur le domaine sémantique du *puṇya*"; and Tokiwa, *Shina bukkyō no kenkyū,* 2:471–98.

The third colophon states:

> On the twenty-first [12 April 958] is the feast of the third seven, held in order to provide posthumous blessings for our mother, Mrs. Ma. May every bit of the merit from copying this scripture be received as a field of blessings. Offered fully and forever.

The fourth colophon states:

> The twenty-eighth day [19 April 958] is the feast of the fourth seven. We pray that our mother, Mrs. Ma, see every bit of the blessings made for her, that the calamities and obstructions she faces be wiped away, and that she receive the field of merit. Offered with a single mind.

The second scroll in the series consists of three more scriptures, each followed by a colophon. The fifth colophon states:

> The fifth day of the fourth month [26 April 958] is the feast of the fifth seven. This scripture is copied as posthumous blessing for Mother, Mrs. Ma. May Yama rāja,[6] Son of Heaven, serve to authenticate[7] that she receives the merit of the scripture and is born in a happy place.

The sixth colophon states:

> The twelfth day of the fourth month [3 May 958] is the feast of the sixth seven. This scripture is copied for posthumous blessing. May Mrs. Ma receive every bit of the merit from copying this scripture. We pray that she be born in a good place.

6. The current state of this scroll, Pk 4544, makes it impossible to read the first colophon in its entirety. For all of the first text and most of the second text (numbers five and six in the complete set), the manuscript is a series of jagged strips held together in just a few places. I am able to make out the fifth colophon up to the word "Yama rāja" (Yen-lo), and after that I rely upon the transcription of the colophon published by Hsü Kuo-lin in 1937, presumably when the manuscript was not so badly deteriorated; see Hsü, *Tun-huang shih-shih hsieh-ching t'i-chi*, p. 11r. Hsü's transcription, however, has several readings that are questionable on philological grounds and by comparison with other colophons. I have emended his transcription in one place. Here Hsü reads "Yen-lo *chih tzu*" (Yama rāja's son), which makes no sense because to my knowledge Yama's son is nowhere mentioned in popular Chinese scriptures or in other colophons. *Chih tzu*, however, is an easy misreading of T'ien-tzu (Son of Heaven), the epithet given to King Yama throughout Chinese sources. Hence I emend Hsü's reading of *chih tzu* to T'ien-tzu. The remaining two colophons on this manuscript (sixth and seventh) are legible.

7. *Cheng-ming*, which I translate as "to authenticate [our act of offering]," also occurs in the tenth colophon in its variant form, *cheng-ming*[b]. The term is used frequently in Buddhist literature when gods "witness" an oath or a vow or when authorities "certify" a disciple's achievement; see Nakamura, *Daijiten*, p. 738a.

The seventh colophon states:

> The nineteenth of the fourth month [10 May 958] is the concluding
> feast of seven. This scripture is copied on one scroll as posthumous
> blessing for Mrs. Ma. May she be born in a fine place, encounter good
> people, and always meet with kindness and goodness.[8] Offered for per-
> petual circulation by her family.

The third scroll in the series consists of three scriptures, each followed
by a colophon. The eighth colophon states:

> The eleventh day of the sixth month [1 July 958] is the feast held one
> hundred days after death. This scripture was copied on one scroll as a
> posthumous blessing on behalf of our deceased mother, Mrs. Ma. We
> pray that her spirit may roam in the Pure Land and never fall into the
> three paths.

The ninth colophon states:

> On behalf of our deceased mother this scripture was copied on one
> scroll as a posthumous blessing one full year after her death. We pray
> that her shadow be entrusted to a fine place and that she not fall into
> the calamities of the three paths.[9] [For] the Buddha's disciple, Mrs.
> Ma. Offered with a single mind.

The tenth colophon states:

> The disciple, Gentleman for Court Discussion, Acting Vice Director
> of the Ministry of Public Works in the Department of State Affairs,
> Chai Feng-ta, in order to gain posthumous blessings for his deceased
> wife, Mrs. Ma, copied one scroll of scriptures on each feast. The titles
> are listed as follows:
>   On the feast of the first seven *The Scripture on*
>   *Impermanence* was copied on one scroll.
>   On the feast of the second seven *The Scripture on Kuan-yin*
>   *and the Moon on Water* was copied on one scroll.
>   On the feast of the third seven *The Scripture on Chants for*
>   *Demons* was copied on one scroll.
>   On the feast of the fourth seven *The Scripture on the*
>   *Questions Asked by a God* was copied on one scroll.

8. The original manuscript reads *shan-ho* with the word *hui*[b] (reverse) written
in the margin. Accordingly I read the term as *ho-shan* (kindness and goodness),
which is attested as early as the Han dynasty; see Morohashi, *Jiten,* no.
3490.256.
9. For "the calamities of the lower three paths of rebirth" the original text
reads *san-t'u chih tsai*[b] *tsai*[c]. The scribe must have written *tsai*[b] (an exclamatory
particle) incorrectly, realized the mistake, and corrected it with the correct
homophone *tsai*[c], but then forgot to blot out the original mistake.

On the feast of the fifth seven *The Scripture on Yama Rāja*
was copied on one scroll.
On the feast of the sixth seven *The Scripture on Protecting
All Children* was copied on one scroll.
On the seventh feast[10] *The Scripture on the Heart of
Prajñāpāramitā* was copied on one scroll.
On the feast held one hundred days after death *The Scripture
on Yü-lan Bowls* was copied on one scroll.
On the feast held one year after death *The Scripture on the
Buddha's Mother* was copied on one scroll.
On the feast held three years after death *The Scripture on
Good and Evil Causes and Results* was copied on one
scroll.

The merit from copying the scriptures itemized above is dedicated
as a posthumous blessing to the departed, Mrs. Ma. We respectfully
invite dragons, gods, and the eight classes of beings;[11] Kuan-shih-yin
Bodhisattva, Ti-tsang Bodhisattva; the four great kings of heaven,[12]
and the Eight Chin-kang[13] to authenticate it. May she receive every
bit of the field of blessings, be reborn in a happy place, and encounter
good people. Offered with a single mind.

Before considering the content of the ten scriptures copied on these
three scrolls, it is important to note the scheduling of the whole production. The prayers record the day on which Chai's wife died as well as
the dates on which the first eight scriptures were copied for her benefit.
The timing is precise. Each scripture was dedicated at exactly the
moment when Mrs. Ma passed before one of the ten kings.

10. "On the seventh feast" renders *ti-ch'i chai*. Here the scribe breaks the
symmetry used to describe the six previous feasts, "On the feast of the nth
seven" *(ti-mou-ch'i chai)*.
11. "Dragons, gods, and the eight classes of beings" *(lung-t'ien pa-pu)* occur
frequently as members of the celestial audience for the Buddha's sermons and
as protectors of the Buddhist Law. Some scholars suggest emending the reading
of this term to *lung-wang pa-pu* (the eight dragon kings); see de Jong, review of
Giles, *Descriptive Catalogue of the Chinese Manuscripts from Tunhuang in the British
Museum*, p. 229. The original reading occurs in a variety of colophons, so I prefer not to emend it. Since dragons and gods are two of the eight classes of
beings, the phrase should be understood as "dragons, gods, and [other members of] the eight classes of beings." See below, chapter 17, note 10.
12. The "four great kings of heaven" *(ssu-ta t'ien-wang)* are usually identified
as Dhṛtarāṣṭra in the East, Virūḍhaka in the South, Virūpākṣa in the West, and
Vaiśravaṇa in the North. See chapter 17, note 14.
13. The eight Chin-kang (Skt.: Vajra) are probably protective deities drawn
from the classes of Ming-wang (Skt.: Vidyārāja) and Chih-chin-kang shen
(Skt.: Vajrapāṇi). Their names and pictures occur frequently in medieval copies of the *Diamond* sūtra. For a detailed study, see Soymié, "Notes d'iconographie bouddhique: des Vidyārāja et Vajradhara de Touen-houang."

From physical characteristics[14] I would hypothesize that the scriptures themselves were copied in batches. The first seven texts (on two scrolls) were probably written in one set, and the prayers were added one-by-one on each of the first seven memorial feasts. Sometime during the forty-nine days a label was made for the first scroll, noting a title and the purpose of copying.

Chai's choice of scriptures reveals much about memorial services and the reproduction of *The Scripture on the Ten Kings*. The first text he had copied was the *Wu-ch'ang ching* (Scripture on Impermanence; Skt.: *Anityatāsūtra*), which frequently played a role in the death rituals offered by the Buddhist order in China. The text of the scripture is quite short. It contains a simple sermon of Śākyamuni Buddha, narrated in both prose and verse, concerning the three facts of old age, sickness, and death. This presentation of the painful side of existence is sandwiched between brief poems, suitable for chanting, that describe the workings of karmic retribution and the rewards of following Buddhist morality. The existence of a scripture by this name is first noted in a catalogue compiled in the year 664, but the widespread popularity of the text probably dates from retranslations issued in 701 and 721.[15]

The full significance of the scripture is not apparent in the text itself.

14. According to Fujieda, the texts and dedications on the last of the three scrolls (P 2055) were written not with a brush but with a wooden pen; see Fujieda, "Tonkō rekijutsu fu," p. 438. Judging from the handwriting, the texts of the scriptures on this scroll were probably written by one copyist. The dedications following the texts, however, appear to be written in a single hand different from the hand that copied the texts themselves. On the outside cover of the first scroll (Tts 175) appears the title of the first text together with a notation: "*The Scripture Spoken by the Buddha on Impermanence* and others in seven chapters. Intended as posthumous blessing for our deceased mother. One chapter for each feast."

15. Fa-chü (fl. 290–306) is credited with translating the *Wu-ch'ang ching* in *Ta-t'ang nei-tien lu* (664), Tao-hsüan (596–667), *T* no. 2149, 55:238a. Fa-li (fl. 290–306) is named as cotranslator in *Ta-chou k'an-ting chung-ching mu-lu* (695), Ming-ch'üan (fl. 695) et al., *T* no. 2153, 55:426b. Their translation does not survive. I-ching (635–713) completed another translation in the year 701; Ratnacinta (Pao-ssu-wei) completed one in 721; see *Chen-yüan hsin-ting shih-chiao mu-lu* (800), Yüan-chao (fl. 778), *T* no. 2157, 55:868b; and *K'ai-yüan shih-chiao lu*, Chih-sheng (fl. 669–740), *T* no. 2154, 55:567c. I-ching's translation (available as *T* no. 801) is the only one that survives; it appears to have been very popular in Tun-huang. Among some forty-five copies from Tun-huang, one scroll (S 2926, reprod. Huang, *Pao-tsang,* 24:485a–91a) bears the date of Yen-ho 1/VI/20 (28 July 712) (date of copying of text on verso), and one copy (S 5447, reprod. Huang, *Pao-tsang,* 42:600a–3a) is in the form of a booklet bound together with the *Heart* sūtra. For lectures and commentaries, see P 2305 verso, transcr. Wang, *Tun-huang pien-wen chi,* pp. 656–71, which records a lecture in mixed poetic form and a more scholarly commentary entitled *Wu-ch'ang ching shu,* the latter written by Cheng-yen.

Appended to *The Scripture on Impermanence* in many of its early editions is a memorandum, nearly as long as the text itself, providing detailed instructions to monks on conducting death-bed rituals. The memorandum is not included in the copy of *The Scripture on the Ten Kings* that Chai commissioned for his wife, but it has been dated to the second half of the tenth century.[16] Entitled "Lin-chung fang-chüeh" (Last Rites for Approaching the End), the piece covers rites administered to both lay people and monks. It instructs the officiating monks to set up an altar in the sick person's room, to hang up a painting of a deity, and to make offerings of flowers and incense. Then the head priest is told to preach to the dying person. After asking her in precisely which Buddha-land she wishes to be reborn, he should describe to her the delights that await her there and lead her in chanting the name of that Buddha. He should perform the most rudimentary practices of lay Buddhism: he should administer the Three Refuges, lead her through a simple repentance ritual, and confer upon her the Bodhisattva Precepts. As the preacher turns the sick one (or directs her attention) to each of the ten directions, he should describe how the Buddhas and Bodhisattvas in each direction will welcome her spirit after death. The "Last Rites" discuss the distribution of the person's property after she has stopped breathing and the placement of the body in the coffin. Finally, all of the monks in attendance are instructed to chant *The Scripture on Impermanence*. Thus, according to the "Last Rites," the deceased receives the benefits of having *The Scripture on Impermanence* chanted only after she has taken the formal vows of the lay person, performed repentance, meditated upon the Law, visualized Buddhas and Bodhisattvas, and achieved some form of enlightenment.[17]

Although the surviving manuscript commissioned by Chai does not describe the actual last rites administered to his wife, nevertheless the employment of *The Scripture on Impermanence* in late medieval times suggests strongly that the words of this particular text were chanted for Mrs. Ma in her final moments. Its premortem use would also make it a logical choice for the lead scripture to be copied in a series of memorial offerings.

16. For the dating of the text, see Terasaki, "Konponsetsu issaiubu ni tsuite no ichi kōsatsu," p. 567.

17. "Lin-chung fang-chüeh" occurs in *Wu-ch'ang ching* (701), I-ching (635–713), *T* no. 801, 17:746b–47a. Most of the manuscript copies of the *Wu-ch'ang ching* found at Tun-huang do not contain "Lin-chung fang-chüeh," but the editors of the Taishō edition state that two of the Sung dynasty printed editions and Yüan and Ming dynasty printed versions all contained it; see *T* 17:746, n. 11. For studies, see Matsuura, *Zenke no sōhō to tsuizen kuyō no kenkyū*, pp. 10–13; Satō, "Chūgoku bukkyō ni okeru rinjū ni matsumeru gyōgi"; and Terasaki, "Konponsetsu issaiubu ni tsuite no ichi kōsatsu."

Chai's dedication notes that for the first memorial service, in addition to having *The Scripture on Impermanence* copied, he commissioned the painting of a Buddha named Pao-chi (Jeweled Coiffure).[18] This figure was known in two principal guises in medieval China. As one of the Buddhas of the past, his life follows many of the conventions of Buddhist hagiography. Miraculous signs accompanied his birth, chief among them the sudden appearance of jewels in his hair. Like the historical Buddha, Śākyamuni, the young boy was a prince, and court diviners declared that when he grew up he would become either a powerful monarch or a great holy man. The boy chose the latter course and carried out a long and successful ministry. He issued two important prophecies. He predicted that in a future lifetime his current sister would become a Buddha named Śākyamuni, and that one of his monastic disciples would become a Buddha named Dīpaṃkara (Ch.: Ting-kuang fo).[19] In his second guise the Thus Come One Pao-chi played a role in Tantric rituals that had been introduced in the Chinese capital cities in the eighth century.[20]

18. Pao-chi is sometimes given as Pao-kuang, Pao-tsang, or Chieh. Sanskrit reconstructions include Ratnaśikhin, Ratnacūḍaḥ, Ratnaketuḥ, and Maṇicūḍaḥ. See Akanuma, *Indo bukkyō koyū meishi jiten*, p. 543b; Hirakawa, *Abidatsuma kusharon sakuin*, 2:432a; Mochizuki, *Daijiten*, p. 3419a; and Ogiwara, *Bon kan taiyaku bukkyō jiten*, nos. 23.13, 65.24, and 168.22.

19. The story of Pao-chi's former life is contained in numerous sources from the third, fourth, and fifth centuries. See *Liu-tu chi ching*, K'ang Seng-hui (d. 280), *T* no. 152, 3:14c–15a; *Tseng-i a-han ching (Ekottarāgama)*, Gautama Saṃghadeva (fl. 383–398), *T* no. 125, 2:757a–58c; and *Hsien-yü ching*, Huichüeh (fl. 445), *T* no. 202, 4:371b–c.

20. In some rituals Pao-chi is listed as one among many deities who should be invoked before chanting *dhāraṇī;* see *Pu-k'ung hsüan-so shen-pien chen-yen ching*, Bodhiruci (fl. 693–727), *T* no. 1092, 20:229a. Some sources explain that Pao-chi was able to become a Buddha because of his mastery of Tantric techniques; see *Wu fo-ting san-mei t'o-lo-ni ching*, Bodhiruci, *T* no. 952, 19:281b; and *I-tzu chi-t'e fo-ting ching*, Amoghavajra (705–774), *T* no. 953, 19:289c. Pao-chi was also well known as a Bodhisattva, not a Buddha, to whom Śākyamuni explained the practices of the Bodhisattva; see the early text attributed to Dharmarakṣa (fl. 265–313) called *Pao-chi p'u-sa hui*, contained in *Ta pao-chi ching (Mahāratnakūṭa)*, Bodhiruci, *T* no. 310, 11:657a–72c. For a similar text and a related commentary, see *Ta-fang-teng ta-chi ching*, Seng-chia (fl. 586–594), *T* no. 397, 13:173b–84a; and *Pao-chi ching ssu-fa Yu-p'o-t'i-she*, attributed to Vasubandhu, trans. Vimokṣaprajñārṣi (fl. 516–541), *T* no. 1526, respectively. One final possibility—which must, I think, be ruled out—is that Chai Feng-ta knew of the Buddha Pao-chi because of the activities of the monk T'ien-hsi-tsai (Devaśanti? later named Fa-hsien, d. 1000), who is credited with translating a *dhāraṇī* named after Pao-chi, contained in *Hsiao-ch'u i-ch'ieh tsai-chang pao-chi t'o-lo-ni ching*, *T* no. 1400. The connection is tantalizing because of the fact that T'ien-hsi-tsai, a native of Magadha, passed through Tun-huang and was detained by the local ruler on his way to the Sung capital of K'ai-feng, where he arrived in 980. See *Sung hui-yao chi-kao*, Hsü Sung (1781–1848), 8:7877d–78a. It is highly

None of the surviving sources describing the Buddha Pao-chi's past life or his role in esoteric ceremonies draws any clear connections to the afterlife, but here again the "Last Rites" appended to the text of *The Scripture on Impermanence* might explain how such a picture was used. Pao-chi might well have been the deity portrayed in the picture that, as noted above, was supposed to be suspended in front of the dying woman. Such scrolls were intended not only to edify but also to enlighten the viewer before she passed on. The "Last Rites" describe the process:[21]

> Hang a colored image on the altar. Have the sick person connect her thoughts one to the other, observe the deity's attributes and good marks,[22] and distinguish them clearly. This will cause her to produce the thought of *bodhi.*[23]

For the second feast of remembrance Chai commissioned *The Scripture on Kuan-yin Bodhisattva and the Light of the Moon Shining on Water.* This manifestation of the Bodhisattva Kuan-yin is attested in artistic form as early as the eighth century.[24] The scripture, however, does not discuss this particular representation of Kuan-yin. Instead it contains a generic series of prayers that one may address to the Bodhisattva to help one follow the precepts, achieve enlightenment, assist people in need, achieve rebirth in the heavens, and escape from being born as a hungry ghost or being in hell.[25]

---

unlikely, however, that T'ien-hsi-tsai could have been detained in Tun-huang for over twenty years (between 958 when Chai's wife died and 980 when T'ien-hsi-tsai arrived in the capital). For details on T'ien-hsi-tsai's life, see Jan, "Buddhist Relations between India and Sung China," pp. 34–37.

21. *Wu-ch'ang ching, T* 17:746b.

22. "Attributes and good marks" translates *hsiang-hao* (Skt.: *lakṣaṇânuvyañjana),* a conjunction of two technical terms denoting the thirty-two attributes and the eighty good marks of a Buddha; see Nakamura, *Daijiten,* p. 866b.

23. On the "thought of *bodhi* [i.e., enlightenment]" *(p'u-t'i hsin;* Skt.: *bodhicitta),* see Nakamura, *Daijiten,* p. 1257a; and Komazawa, *Daijiten,* p. 1156a–b.

24. Chou Fang's (fl. 766–796) painting of Kuan-yin and the moon reflected in water is cited in *Li-tai ming-hua chi* (847), Chang Yen-yüan (fl. 847–874), p. 123. See also Wang, *Chou Fang,* esp. pp. 6–7. On medieval paintings of Kuan-yin, see Howard, "Tang and Song Images of Guanyin from Sichuan"; and Wang, "Tun-huang shui-yüeh kuan-yin hsiang." In iconographical compendia Kuan-yin and the Moon in Water is one of the thirty-three manifestations of Kuan-yin; see *Besson zakki,* Shinkaku (fl. 1117–1180), *T* no. 3007, 88:209c–14b, including pls. 86 and 87. For other representations of Kuan-yin in medieval China, see Satō, "Rikuchō jidai no kannon shinkō"; and Kobayashi, "Tōdai no daihi kannon narabi ni honchō ni okeru senju shinkō no kigen ni tsuite."

25. *Shui-yüeh-kuang kuan-yin p'u-sa ching,* Tts 175, is only seventeen lines long. It largely follows the text of two Tantric scriptures on Kuan-yin: *Ch'ien-shou*

On the third feast the *Chou-mei ching* (Scripture on Chants for Demons) was copied. This text, probably created in China sometime during the sixth century, first animates the world with malevolent forces and then offers a potent weapon to fight them. It describes how in a previous age an old fox populated the earth with demons and venomous insects *(mei-ku)*. Some demons infect people from the inside, crawling into their eyes, stomachs, and pores, while others take the form of horses, sheep, dogs, chickens, pigs, insane people, or amputated, chattering human heads. To aid the fearful in disarming these hordes, the Buddha teaches a chant to Ta-li (Skt.: Mahābala, or "Great Strength") Bodhisattva. The chant gains its effectiveness by calling the demons by their proper names. Particularly resistant demons receive harsher treatment. By calling upon those who know the chant—Buddhas, Bodhisattvas, the spirit-kings of the four directions, deities of the sun, moon, stars, and constellations—one can cause demons' heads to split into seven parts. Simply by reciting the scripture, people in distress not only gain relief from afflictions, but can achieve rebirth amid the pleasures of heaven as well.[26]

The *T'ien ch'ing-wen ching* (Scripture on the Questions Asked by a God) comes fourth in the series. It contains nine catechistic questions put to the historical Buddha by a visiting god and the Buddha's nine responses. It discusses basic Buddhist concepts concerning rebirth, morality, and the religious life. It was translated by Hsüan-tsang (602–664) and was the subject of several commentaries written during the T'ang dynasty.[27]

The next text was the *Yen-lo wang shou-chi ching* (Scripture on the Prophecy Received by King Yama Rāja), otherwise known as *The Scripture on the Ten Kings*. As other sections of this study make clear, its con-

---

ch'ien-yen kuan-shih-yin p'u-sa kuang-ta yüan-man wu-ai ta-pei-hsin t'o-lo-ni ching, Bhagavaddharma (fl. 650–660), *T* no. 1060, 20:106c–7a; and *Ch'ien-shou ch'ien-yen kuan-shih-yin p'u-sa ta-pei-hsin t'o-lo-ni,* Amoghavajra (705–774), *T* no. 1064, 20:115c. I am indebted to Chün-fang Yü, who helped in tracing sources.

26. The *Chou-mei ching* is not listed in *Ch'u san-tsang chi-chi,* Seng-yu (445–518), *T* no. 2145. It is first cited in *Chung-ching mu-lu,* Fa-ching (fl. 594), *T* no. 2147, 55:174b, where it is classed among the apocryphal scriptures, of which Fa-ching says, "Although their names appear to be correct, in content they are close to being human fabrications"; ibid., 55:172b. In addition to Tts 175, it survives in numerous Tun-huang manuscripts, two of which (S 418 and S 2517) have been printed as *T* no. 2882. For brief studies, see Ono, *Daijiten* 5:106a–b; and Yabuki, *Meisha yoin kaisetsu,* 2:201–2.

27. *T'ien ch'ing-wen ching* (*Devatāsūtra*), Hsüan-tsang (602–664), is represented in many Tun-huang manuscripts. It is printed as *T* no. 592. The commentary entitled *T'ien ch'ing-wen ching shu* survives in several Tun-huang manuscripts. For documentation on other commentaries, see the five listed in Ono, *Daijiten,* 8:108a.

tent was concerned with the passage of the spirit of the deceased through the courts of the ten kings. It occupies the fifth place in the sequence of the ten feasts and scriptures that Chai had copied for his wife because, as the scripture itself teaches, during the fifth week after death one passes through the court of King Yama.[28]

The *Hu chu-t'ung-tzu t'o-lo-ni ching* (Scripture on the *Dhāraṇī* for Protecting All Children) was copied for the next feast. This brief scripture, attributed to Bodhiruci (fl. 508–537), records the speech of a god from Brahmā's Heaven. The god names fifteen ghosts and spirits who specialize in threatening children. Some of them cause children to be frightened or to manifest a variety of disorders like involuntary twirling of the eyeballs, twitching of the shoulders, or refusal to nurse. Other demons prevent conception, bring about stillbirth, or put infants to death. The benevolent deity pronounces a short *dhāraṇī* that mothers can use to ward off attacks on the young.[29]

For the feast held forty-nine days after the death of his wife, Chai commissioned the copying of one of the most pithy Mahāyāna scriptures, the *Heart* sūtra. The text is entitled *Po-jo po-lo-mi-to hsin ching* (Scripture on the Heart of *Prajñāpāramitā*). The version presented here is that prepared by Hsüan-tsang. The *Heart* sūtra makes the problematic declaration "Form is emptiness; emptiness is form" and presents one of the most common *mantras* in the Buddhist tradition, *"gate gate pāragate pārasaṃgate bodhi svāhā."*[30]

The text copied one hundred days after death was the *Yü-lan-p'en ching* (Scripture on the Yü-lan Bowls), which was attributed to Dharmarakṣa (fl. 265–313) but was probably composed originally in Chinese sometime in the fourth or fifth century. The text served as the legitimating myth for one of the most widely celebrated Buddhist festivals in medieval China, the Ghost Festival. Known in its Buddhist guise as the "yü-lan bowl gathering" *(yü-lan-p'en hui),* it was celebrated in both temples and homes on the fifteenth day of the seventh lunar month. Like the offerings to the ten kings of purgatory, the Ghost Festival drew on Buddhist symbols and provided a Buddhist rationale for making offerings to ancestors. The scripture describes how a pious monk and devoted son named Mu-lien (Skt.: Maudgalyāyana) was unable to

28. *Yen-lo wang shou-chi ching* is Pk 4544.

29. *Hu chu-t'ung-tzu t'o-lo-ni ching,* Bodhiruci (fl. 508–537), *T* no. 1028A. In addition to Pk 4544 the text survives in numerous Tun-huang manuscripts. It is cited verbatim in *T'o-lo-ni tsa-chi ching,* Shih-hu (fl. 980–1017), *T* no. 999, 19:591a–92a.

30. *Po-jo po-lo-mi-to hsin ching,* Hsüan-tsang, is *T* no. 251. For a recent study of the text as it is reflected in Indian and Tibetan traditions, see Lopez, *The Heart Sūtra Explained.* For a study of the different versions of the Chinese text preserved in Tun-huang manuscripts, see Fukui, *"Hannya shin gyō."*

complete the sacrifices that his deceased mother needed in order to escape suffering in the underworld. In the story the historical Buddha assists his young disciple, Mu-lien, by establishing a model that even lay people could follow. He instructs them to make donations to the Buddhist Order each year on VII/15, precisely the time when monks are concluding their summer meditation retreat. Śākyamuni promises that the merit from this act will accrue directly to one's ancestors, who will enter heaven by being born miraculously in celestial flowers.[31]

The ninth scripture in the series was a noncanonical account of a reunion between Śākyamuni and his mother, Lady Māyā (Ch.: Mo-yeh). Its full title, *Ta-po-nieh-p'an mo-yeh fu-jen p'in ching* (The 'Lady Māyā' Chapter of *The Mahāparinirvāṇa Scripture*), claims it to be simply one portion of a longer canonical text, but in fact the surviving Chinese versions of the *Mahāparanirvāṇasūtra* contain no such chapter.[32] The manuscript attributes its translation to an otherwise unidentifiable monk named An of An-kuo ssu in the capital, but none of the catalogues of medieval Buddhist scriptures mentions the text.[33] At the end of the text the copyist gives its short title as the *Fo-mu ching* (Scripture on the Buddha's Mother).

The story presented in *The Scripture on the Buddha's Mother* differs from other legends concerning Lady Māyā known in medieval China.[34] It

---

31. *Yü-lan-p'en ching*, attrib. Dharmarakṣa (fl. 265–313), P 2055, reprod. Huang, *Pao-tsang* 113:278a–79a; very close to version printed as *T* no. 685. For a recent translation and a discussion of its authorship, see Teiser, *The Ghost Festival in Medieval China*, pp. 48–56. For an analysis of the festival in terms of mortuary ritual, see idem, "Ghosts and Ancestors in Medieval Chinese Religion." For a treatment of Tun-huang materials on the festival, see idem, *The Ghost Festival in Medieval China*, pp. 43–112; and Kanaoka, "Kuan-yü tun-huang pien-wen yü t'ang-tai fo-chiao i-shih chih kuan-hsi."

32. See *Fo po-ni-huan ching*, Po Fa-tsu (fl. 290–306), *T* no. 5; *Po-ni-huan ching*, anon. (ca. 317–420), *T* no. 6; *Ta-po-nieh-p'an ching*, Fa-hsien (fl. 399–416), *T* no. 7; *Ta-po-ni-huan ching*, Fa-hsien, *T* no. 376; *Ch'ang a-han ching (Dīrghāgama)*, Buddhayaśas (fl. 384–417), Chu Fo-nien (fl. 365), *T* no. 1, 1:11a–30b; *Ta-po-nieh-p'an ching*, Dharmakṣema (385–433), *T* no. 374; *Ta-po-nieh-p'an ching*, Hui Yen (363–443), Hsieh Ling-yün (385–433), *T* no. 375; and *Fo lin nieh-p'an chi fa-chu ching*, Hsüan-tsang, *T* no. 390.

33. Under entries for *Ta-po-nieh-p'an ching*, *Mo-yeh* and *Fo-mu ching* I have consulted the index to vol. 55 of *T*, *Taishō daizōkyō sakuin*, vol. 31: *Mokuroku bu;* and Tokiwa, *Gokan yori sōsei ni itaru yakkyō sōroku*.

34. Lady Māyā's ancestry and the events surrounding the birth of her son were widely disseminated in biographies of the Buddha. Those sources relate that after giving birth, Lady Māyā died and ascended to the Heaven of Thirty-three. They also narrate the story of how, before his own death, the Buddha ascended to the Heaven of Thirty-three to preach the Law to his mother; see, for example, *Chuan-chi pai-yüan ching (Avadānaśataka)*, Chih Ch'ien (fl. 220–252), *T* no. 200, 4:246c–47b; *Fo sheng tao-li-t'ien wei mu shuo-fa ching*, Dharmarakṣa (fl. 265–310), *T* no. 815; *Tao shen-tsu wu-chi pien-hua ching*, An Fa-ch'in (fl. 281–

begins just before the Buddha enters perfect extinction. He gathers together his disciples in order to pass on his teachings. To Ānanda he entrusts the *sūtras*, to Mahākāśyapā he entrusts the *vinaya*. Then he asks his disciple Upāli (Ch.: Yu-po-li) to inform his relatives of his impending death. That same night Lady Māyā, who predeceased her son and now dwells in the Heaven of Thirty-three, sees six inauspicious omens. When Upāli tells her of the Buddha's demise she is overcome with grief.

The Scripture on the Buddha's Mother next describes the scene in Kuśinagara where the funeral of the Buddha is already under way. Lady Māyā descends to the banks of the Ajitavati River and delivers a lament as the body of her son lies in a coffin. Upon hearing his mother's voice, the Buddha emerges from the sealed crypt and delivers a short sermon to her, touching on the theme of impermanence and noting that just as all sentient beings have a beginning and an ending, so too will mothers and sons eventually be separated. The Buddha's doubly posthumous lecture has an immediate effect upon Lady Māyā, who is freed from her female body and transformed into an *arhant* before ascending to heaven again.[35]

Aside from Chai Feng-ta's colophon, the historical record is silent about the use of *The Scripture on the Buddha's Mother* in religious practice. The content of the text, however, is too close to be mere chance: a deceased mother moves from her temporary resting place to permanent enlightenment after hearing a sermon of the Buddha. It is easy to imagine why Mrs. Ma's family would have chosen this sūtra for mimesis.

The last scripture that Chai had copied in memory of his wife was the *Shan-o yin-kuo ching* (Scripture on Good and Evil Causes and Results). The book was consistently excluded from the Chinese Buddhist canon, having first been defined as "spurious and absurd" in the year 695.[36]

---

306), *T* no. 816; *Tseng-i a-han ching (Ekottarāgama)*, Gautama Saṃghadeva (fl. 383–398), *T* no. 125, 2:703b–8c; *Tsa a-han ching (Saṃyuktāgama)*, Guṇabhadra (394–468), *T* no. 99, 2:134a–c; and *Mo-ho mo-yeh ching*, T'an-ching (fl. 479–502), *T* no. 383. Other texts relate the tale of the Buddha's aunt and foster mother, Mahāprajāpatī (Ch.: Ta-ai-tao), and how she passed away in the Buddha's presence because she could not bear to see her foster son die before she did; see, for example, *Ta-ai-tao po-ni-huan ching*, Po Fa-tsu, *T* no. 144; the chapter entitled "Ta-ai-tao po-nieh-p'an p'in" in *Tseng-i a-han ching (Ekottarāgama)*, *T* no. 125, 2:821b–23b; and *Fo-mu po-ni-huan ching*, Hui-chien (fl. 457), *T* no. 145.

35. This apocryphal scripture survives in many Tun-huang versions. My summary of the text is taken from the one commissioned by Chai Feng-ta, P 2055, reprod. Huang, *Pao-tsang*, 113:279a–81a. This version is lengthier and contains significantly different wording than other versions, e.g., S 2084, transcr. *T* no. 2919.

36. The catalogue of the Buddhist canon defined during the reign of Empress Wu calls the text "spurious and absurd" *(wei-miu);* see *Ta-chou k'an-ting chung-ching mu-lu*, Ming-ch'üan (fl. 695), *T* no. 2153, 55:474c.

Neither this copy nor other copies of the text found at Tun-huang contain any attribution of authorship. In the scripture Ānanda asks Śākyamuni why the good suffer and the evil prosper, and why some people live to an old age while others die young. The Buddha begins his response, a sermon on karmic retribution, with the words, "The different retribution received by those whom you ask about stems from the unequal ways in which people applied their minds in previous lives." In the first half of his lecture the Buddha dwells on the issue of theodicy. He explains that a person who has no teeth in this life probably loved to gnaw on skin and bones in a previous life, that a person born with sealed nostrils must have burned foul incense as an offering to Buddhas in the past, and that someone suffering from bad breath must have scolded people viciously in a past life. Similarly, the person who now enjoys great wealth must have been a selfless donor to the Buddhist Order in a past life. In the second half of the sermon Śākyamuni holds out great hope for the future. There are, says the Buddha, two kinds of mind or intent, good and evil. Evil intentions will result in rebirth in one of the woeful states as an animal, hungry ghost, or hell being. Even if an evil person is fortunate enough to be reborn as a human being, he or she will endure only a short life or will suffer from serious illness. The Buddha spells out in detail the various species of animals and the numerous levels of hell in which such people will be reborn. He also explains how the performance of good deeds can raise one's status in the scale of rebirth, leading to the pleasures of human existence or entry into one of the heavens.[37]

In both tone and content *The Scripture on Good and Evil Causes and Results* represents one of the oldest and most widespread forms of the sermon in the history of Buddhist thought. The punishment of evil and the reward of virtue were frequent topics of discussion throughout the Chinese Buddhist world.[38] What distingushes this scripture from others is its detailed listing, placed strategically at the end, of the various realms in which people are reborn in their next lives. In this connection it should be remembered that the merit gained from copying *The Scripture on Good and Evil Causes and Results* was dedicated to Chai's wife at precisely the time, three years after death, that she would be reentering

37. My summary is based on *Shan-o yin-kuo ching,* P 2055, reprod. Huang, *Pao-tsang,* 113:281a–87b. The translated passage is also found in a very similar version of the text, *T* no. 2881, 85:1380c. The *T* edition is based on two texts, a Tun-huang manuscript in the collection of Nakamura Fusetsu, and the printed edition in *Z,* 1, 1.

38. For recent studies on the topic of karmic retribution in Chinese Buddhism, see Jan, "The Chinese Understanding and Assimilation of Karma Doctrine"; Michihata, *Chūgoku bukkyō shisō shi no kenkyū,* pp. 189–224; and Yamazaki, *Zui tō bukkyō shi no kenkyū,* pp. 251–75.

the wheel of existence. While it insists on the ineluctability of karmic retribution, the sūtra concludes by favoring the prospect of a good rebirth.

Although I have written as if Chai personally chose each scripture for inclusion in the set, it is impossible to decide whether the selection of texts rested with Chai himself or a specific temple in Tun-huang, or whether it amounted to a standard decalogue used throughout China. Nevertheless, the ten scriptures that Chai had copied for his wife beginning in the year 958 enlarge our understanding of the ritualized reproduction of religious texts in medieval China.

The copying of these ten scriptures was neither a mechanical exercise divorced from religious practice nor a ritual deemed subsidiary to memorial services. Rather, the copying was itself the action specified in one of the ten, *The Scripture on the Ten Kings*. The texts were not ancillary to the ritual, they were its fulfillment; and the prayers inscribed at the end of each text constituted a kind of liturgy for the performance.

In the medieval world members of the gentry often donated money for the copying of religious texts, intending that the spiritual benefit from the act be dedicated to their deceased ancestors, and to this extent Chai's ten scriptures are not uncommon. But Chai's set of scrolls is one of the only surviving examples (the only one I know of) of a text produced as part of the memorial ceremonies addressed explicitly to the ten kings. As noted above, the dedications to the scriptures clearly specify the scheduling of the enterprise. In addition, at least three of the texts occupy a fixed position in the memorial sequence. In ministering to the dying, Buddhist priests often chanted *The Scripture on Impermanence* as part of the last rites, and it may well have supplied the last words that Chai's wife heard as her spirit left the realm of the living. *The Scripture on the Ten Kings* occupies the fifth place, in perfect synchronicity with the journey of Mrs. Ma's spirit, who was thought to suffer in King Yama's court during the fifth week after death. The tenth sūtra, dedicated just as she would be dispatched to a new incarnation, offers the hope that pious deeds will cause rebirth in a pleasant state of existence.

The ten scriptures dedicated to Chai's wife demonstrate a broad range of concerns, not limited to funerary and memorial functions, that was typical of medieval Chinese Buddhism. Although only half of them were deemed canonical in medieval times,[39] taken as a whole they represent a mainstream concern with impermanence, misfortune, and the practices required to achieve salvation.

39. Using Chih-sheng's catalogue as a yardstick of canonicity, only five were considered admitted to the canon: *Wu-ch'ang ching, T'ien ch'ing-wen ching, Hu chu-t'ung-tzu t'o-lo-ni ching, Po-jo po-lo-mi-to hsin ching,* and *Yü-lan-p'en ching;* see *K'ai-yüan shih-chiao lu* (730), Chih-sheng (fl. 669–740), *T* no. 2154, 55:718c, 718b, 711a, 701b, and 707b, respectively.

A discussion of the copying of texts and the contours of Chinese Bud-dhism cannot be isolated from the broader setting of medieval Chinese culture. Fortunately the name of Chai Feng-ta crops up in the titles and colophons of other Tun-huang manuscripts and cave inscriptions enough times to construct a reasonably complete biography. A proper study of his life and work goes beyond the scope of this book. The details I offer here are intended simply to develop further the social background of this particular set of scriptures and to throw more light on the significance of copying religious texts.[40]

Chai Feng-ta was no stranger to the world of the medieval scripto-rium. Chai was probably born in the year 883. At the age of twenty he was already proficient in the copying of texts and was attempting to write verse. In 902 he copied out a divination text and then recorded his own poems in the margins. Some of the allusions are especially impor-tant in demonstrating the level of literacy he had achieved and in sug-gesting the curriculum he may have followed. The first quatrain may be rendered roughly:[41]

> The great man is full of the three incipiencies,
> Unmatched the world over for his imposing manner and skill
>   in the humanities.
> The lad who studies not the reading of poetry and rhapsodies
> Resembles most the withered roots of flowering trees.

Chai's verse overflows with phrases taken from the standard "Confu-cian" or "secular" curriculum of T'ang dynasty schools. The "great man" *(ta-chang-fu)* is a paragon of unswerving righteousness discussed frequently in *Mencius*.[42] The Han dynasty collection of exempla of the

40. Studies touching on Chai Feng-ta, especially his calendrical works, include Chiang, "Tun-huang ching-chüan t'i-ming lu," p. 1069; Fujieda, "Tonkō rekijitsu fu," esp. pp. 434–39; Hsiang, "Chi tun-huang shih-shih ch'u chin t'ien-fu shih nien hsieh-pen *Shou Ch'ang hsien ti-ching*" (hereafter *"Shou Ch'ang hsien ti-ching"*); idem, "Hsi-cheng hsiao-chi"; Ogawa, "Tonkō butsuji no gakushirō," pp. 501–4; and Su, *Tun-huang-hsüeh kai-yao*, pp. 112–15. For a listing of works by Chai and a skeleton chronology of his government posts, see appendix 11.

41. Pk *hsin* 836, transcr. Hsiang, *"Shou Ch'ang hsien ti-ching,"* p. 439. On the recto is a text entitled *Ni-ts'e chan*. Its colophon identifies the date as 902 and the copyist as Chai Tsai-wen. In the margin is written "Tsai-wen's courtesy name is Feng-ta." Sometime after 902 Chai stopped using his given name and used only his courtesy name. Following this colophon on the recto are the poems, one of which is translated here, and the comment added later (translated below) on how ashamed he was of his early attempts at poetry. My attempt to translate Chai's verse pretends to be nothing other than bad poetry.

42. On the "great man" see, for example, *Mencius* 3B:2, in *Meng-tzu cheng-i*, annot. Chiao Hsün (1763–1820), pp. 244–47; and Legge, trans., *The Works of Mencius*, pp. 140–41.

Classic of Poetry defines the "three incipiencies" (or "three fonts," *san-tuan*) as the dangerous brush of the literatus, the sharp point of the swordsman, and the quick tongue of the logician.[43] The "humanities" (*liu-i*, literally "six arts"), comprising ritual, music, archery, charioteering, writing, and mathematics, were held up as the ideal curriculum for the cultivated man, even in the time of Confucius. "Imposing manner" (*t'ang-t'ang*) was a reduplicative term found in another basic text of Confucian education, the *Analects of Confucius*.[44]

It is clear, then, that as a young man Chai learned to read by copying texts and pursuing a course of study in the classics and some of the works of Confucianism. His tastes developed to the point that in his forties he could laugh at his own youthful verse. In a note following the poetry translated above, Chai would later record his embarrassment:[45]

> This was written in my youth, when I could hardly manage the road. Now it really makes me laugh how the young Ta moved his brush to write compositions. I was twenty years old when I wrote it. This year, seeing this poem by chance, I am simply mortified with shame.

The setting for such an education was the local, state-supported school. In a colophon to the text copied in 902 Chai refers to himself in polite terms as "a capable student in the prefectural school in the Tun-huang Commandery of Ho-hsi" (*Ho-hsi tun-huang chün chou-hsüeh shang-tsu tzu-ti*). In later years he would return to the local educational establishment as the head teacher-administrator, holding such titles as Erudite in the Prefectural School (Chou-hsüeh po-shih) in 945 and Acting Erudite of the Classics in Sha Prefecture (Hsing sha-chou ching-hsüeh po-shih) in 959.[46]

Modern scholarship has only recently begun to explore how important such local schools were in fostering both literacy and moral cultivation across a relatively broad range of social classes.[47] The details of Chai's life further reinforce one particular theory advanced in recent studies, namely, that there was considerable overlap between "secular" and "religious" training. In Chai's case it is clear that his early educa-

43. See *Han shih wai-chuan*, Han Ying (fl. second century B.C.), 7.5 (p. 59a).
44. See *Analects* 19:16, in *Lun-yü cheng-i*, annot. Liu Pao-nan (1791–1855), p. 406; and Legge, trans., *Confucian Analects*, p. 208.
45. The comment was probably written in T'ien-ch'eng 3 (928), along with the calendar for that year. Translation from Pk *hsin* 836, transcr. Hsiang, *"Shou Ch'ang hsien ti-ching,"* p. 439.
46. For documentation for all of Chai's official titles, see appendix 11. On education in Tun-huang, see Kao, "T'ang-tai tun-huang te chiao-yü"; and Li, "T'ang sung shih-tai te tun-huang hsüeh-hsiao."
47. See Kao, "T'ang-tai tun-huang te chiao-yü"; Mair, "Lay Students and the Making of Written Vernacular Narrative"; Ogawa, "Tonkō butsuji no gakushirō"; and Zürcher, "Buddhism and Education in T'ang Times."

tion in a Confucian curriculum was in no way inimical to his practice of Buddhism. As noted, late in his life Chai would rely heavily on Buddhist ideas and institutions in dealing with old age and death. Well before that, Chai took a strong interest in the *Diamond* sūtra. At the age of twenty-six he commissioned a copy of the *Diamond* sūtra, but he was not content to let the text stand by itself. He added to the scroll two works that would glorify and lend greater authority to the scripture. One appears to be his own composition, a collection of miracle tales demonstrating the rewards—often depicted as this-worldly benefits—of upholding, chanting, copying, or simply believing in the *Diamond* sūtra. He placed the text, entitled *Ch'ih-sung chin-kang ching ling-yen kung-te chi* (A Record of the Numinous Verifications and Merit to Be Gained from Upholding and Intoning *The Diamond Scripture*), at the very beginning of the scroll. Next on the scroll he copied a series of hymns. This text, entitled *K'ai-yüan huang-ti tsan chin-kang ching kung-te* (Hymns Extolling the Merits of *The Diamond Scripture* by the August Emperor K'ai-yüan), was ascribed to the T'ang emperor Hsüan-tsung (r. 712–756).[48] After that he wrote a list of deities, three *dhāraṇī*, and a dedication. The dedication offers a convenient picture of Chai's practice of Buddhism. He writes:[49]

> On the ninth day of the fourth month in the eighth year of the T'ien-fu era[50] of the T'ang, *wu-ch'en* in the sequence of years [11 May 908], the wearer of the common cloth Chai Feng-ta wrote *Hymns Extolling the Scripture* and *A Record of the Verifications and Merit to Be Gained*. He added to it and sent it into circulation. He hopes that ever after, for believers as well as departed and deceased spirits, including his current parents and people of the whole region, blessings will be the same as spring grasses, and sins be like autumn sprouts. It must certainly come about as everyone convenes a Buddhist service.

48. Some sources claim that Emperor Hsüan-tsung coauthored a commentary on the *Diamond* sūtra with the monk Tao-yin (d. 740) in 735, but neither the *Hymns* copied by Chai Feng-ta nor the surviving commentary by Tao-yin can be traced definitively to the emperor. Tao-yin's commentary is entitled *Yü-chu chin-kang po-jo po-lo-mi ching hsüan-yen*, P 2173, transcr. *T* no. 2733. On Hsüan-tsung's authorship, see *Chen-yüan hsin-ting shih-chiao mu-lu*, Yüan-chao (fl. 778), *T* no. 2157, 55:878c; *Sung kao-seng chuan*, Tsan-ning (919–1001), *T* no. 2061, 50:735a, 795b; *Ts'e-fu yüan-kuei*, Wang Ch'in-jo (962–1025), 51.19v–20r (p. 575a–b); and *Fo-tsu t'ung-chi*, Chih-p'an (fl. 1260), *T* no. 2035, 49:375a. For modern studies, see Ch'en, "Kuan-yü li t'ang hsüan-tsung yü 'chu' *chin-kang ching*"; and Weinstein, *Buddhism under the T'ang*, pp. 167–68, n. 18.
49. P 2094, reprod. Huang, *Pao-tsang*, 114:126b.
50. Properly speaking, the T'ien-fu era had only four years and was succeeded by the T'ien-yu era on the tenth day of the intercalary fourth month in 904; see Hiraoka, *Tōdai no koyomi*, p. 355. In Tun-huang the T'ien-fu reign period was used anachronistically as late as 910; see Dhk 295a.

In propagating miracle tales associated with the *Diamond* sūtra, Chai attempted to spread the Buddhist faith outside the ties of his own family. Although he makes no claim to reach the lower classes in particular, his dedication expresses the hope that other lay devotees and even his neighbors might reap the benefits of Buddhist piety.

Other important components of Chai's cultural background were his technical skills, which may have helped him in a number of government positions. We know, for instance, that in the year 945 Chai wrote a geographical survey of the area near Tun-huang.[51] Such work probably served him well in a government position he held fifteen years later, Acting Vice Director of the Ministry of Public Works in the Department of State Affairs (Chien-chiao shang-shu kung-pu yüan-wai-lang), in which capacity he would have been responsible for local construction projects, the upkeep of waterways and roads, and the standardization of weights and measures.

Chai's practical knowledge found its most enduring expression in the field of calendrical studies. Fully annotated calendars written by Chai for at least five different years survive among the Tun-huang manuscripts.[52] The creation of calendars like these was not a simple exercise in applying diachronic logic. In addition to calculating the length of the solar year, the placement of intercalary months, and the occurence of full moons and new moons, Chai drew upon a wide range of mantic knowledge. His calendar for the year Hsien-te 3 (956), for instance, notes the days when sacrifices to specific gods are appropriate, when the gods should be petitioned to send rain, and which days are lucky and unlucky for burial, cutting one's hair or nails, curing illness, taking medicine, cutting wood, repairing homes, planting seeds, and marrying. The passage of time is coordinated further with both the sexagenary cycle and the recurrence of the Five Phases *(wu-hsing)*. Reflecting over one hundred years of contact with Iranian-influenced Central Asian traders, Chai's calendar also includes a phonetic notation in red ink, placed every seven days, indicating the Sogdian word for "Sunday."[53] The last time Chai's name is mentioned in surviving sources is apparently the year 966, when he is mentioned in passing in some notes

51. The text, *san* 1700, is entitled *Shou Ch'ang hsien ti-ching*. It is described in Hsiang Ta, *"Shou Ch'ang hsien ti-ching"*; see also Fujieda, "Tonkō rekijitsu fu," p. 436; and Mori, "Shinshutsu tonkō sekishitsu isho toku ni *sushōken chikyō* ni tsuite."

52. The five calendars cover the years Chen-ming 10 (924), S 2404; T'ungkuang 4 (926), P 3247 and *san* 673; T'ien-ch'eng 3 (928), Pk *hsin* 836; Hsiente 3 (956), S 95; and Hsien-te 6 (959), P 2623. See appendix 11 for further details.

53. Chinese *mi* is an attempt to represent the Sogdian *mir*; see Uchida, *Koyomi to toki no jiten*, p. 273.

scribbled on the back side of a manuscript.[54] Chai's knowledge of calendrical arts did not vanish with his death. His style was carried on by a disciple named Chai Wen-chin, perhaps related to him, who wrote a calendar for T'ai-p'ing hsing-kuo 7 (982).[55]

I would conclude that Chai's motives for copying *The Scripture on the Ten Kings* and nine other texts had to do in the first place with an understanding of the afterlife in which the fate of the soul could be influenced by the pious actions of the living. The text as we have it is a product of Buddhist belief and a relic of Buddhist ritual. The details that can be pieced together from Tun-huang manuscripts suggest further that Chai's particular variety of Buddhism did not exist in isolation from the culture of medieval China. Confucianism, divination, the copying of a broad range of texts, secular education, technical skills, and lay Buddhism all played a demonstrable role in the life of Chai Feng-ta. Together these elements constitute the general cultural background against which the production of *The Scripture on the Ten Kings* must be understood.

54. See P 3197 verso, reprod. Huang, *Pao-tsang,* 126:559a. For the identification of Chai Feng-ta, see BN, *Catalogue.*
55. The calendar is S 1473, reprod. Huang, *Pao-tsang,* 11:143a–45a.

10. An Old Man of Eighty-five

NOT ALL DONORS followed the example of Chai Feng-ta in paying to have *The Scripture on the Ten Kings* copied for the benefit of the deceased. Many people dedicated the merit to themselves or to other living beings. In this method of preparatory cultivation (discussed in chapter 2), the difficult journey through the ten courts of purgatory could be shortened—or perhaps canceled altogether—if one had the text copied on one's own behalf while still alive. The motivation for such a deed only appears to lack altruism. In fact the practice could easily be justified in terms of Buddhist doxology, which had always placed an emphasis on the intentionality of actions. Offerings could be made and benefits could be assigned so long as they were undertaken in a selfless fashion. Enjoying the rewards oneself was also deemed more economical than transferring them to someone else; fewer parties to the transaction meant lower overhead, since the shadow of bribery was ever-present in the world underground.

One of the most philosophically interesting examples of copying *The*

Scripture on the Ten Kings for one's own benefit is the case of a gentleman who refers to himself simply as "an old man of eighty-five" *(pa-shih-wu lao-jen)*. In the years 908 and 909 he copied *The Scripture on the Ten Kings* at least three times. At the end of the first surviving scroll (now lost) he wrote a short dedication:[1]

> Written with his own hand[2] for transmission [by an old man][3] of eighty-five on the twenty-eighth day of the seventh month of the *wu-ch'en* year [27 August 908].

Three days later he copied the text again. He noted at the end:[4]

> Written with his own hand for transmission by an old man of eighty-five on the first day of the eighth month of the *wu-ch'en* year [30 August 908]. If I do not practice according to its teachings, may I be born in the underground prisons.

1. *San* 535, transcr. Wang, *So-yin, san* 535. I would hypothesize that the text is the short recension and is bound as a scroll, just like the next two the man commissioned. The manuscript once belonged to Li Sheng-to (1858–1935). Li was a high-ranking official in the Ministry of Education while the Chinese government was organizing the transfer of Tun-huang manuscripts from Kansu to Peking. According to Hsiang Ta, Li used his position to select some of the best ones for "his own pocket" *(ssu-nang);* Hsiang, appendix to Chang, *Mu-hsi-hsüan ts'ang-shu t'i-chi chi shu-lu,* p. 422. Li's grandfather and father were bibliophiles from whom he inherited a core of rare books. During the time he spent abroad he learned much from Japanese book collectors and began to secure his own rare editions. After 1911 he resided mostly in Tientsin, a good vantage point for acquiring rare books flooding the market. During the war with Japan he was rumored to have sent some of his holdings to Japan. He sold some of his books to the Harvard University Library, but gave most of them to Peking University. Many of the manuscripts alleged to have belonged to Li have been shown to be modern forgeries. Some of Li's manuscripts are held in the Kyoto National Museum, and some have appeared more recently in the Taipei and Peking collections. For further details on Li Sheng-to, see Li and Ch'en, *Chung-kuo ts'ang-shu-chia tz'u-tien,* pp. 300–1; Demiéville, "Récents travaux sur Touen-houang," pp. 90–92; Fujieda, "Tokka rishi hanshōkaku chinzō in ni tsuite"; and Chang, *Mu-hsi-hsüan ts'ang-shu t'i-chi chi shu-lu.*
2. Wang, *So-yin, san* 535, reads *san-hsieh liu-ch'uan* (written in three for transmission), but it is far more likely that the colophons to all three texts use the same phrase, *shou-hsieh liu-ch'uan* (written with his own hand for transmission), as attested unambiguously in the next scroll, Pk 1226. Wang's phrasing is also questionable because that meaning would be more fittingly conveyed by *san-hui* (three times) or by *san-chüan* (in three scrolls). On orthographic grounds *san* is easy to mistake for *shou.* Accordingly I emend the text to *shou-hsieh liu-ch'uan.*
3. "By an old man" *(lao-jen)* is my hypothetical reconstruction of a gap in the text, following the wording in the colophon to Pk 1226.
4. Pk 1226, reprod. Huang, *Pao-tsang,* 109:435a.

Just before the New Year celebration held four months later he made one last copy. The dedication states:[5]

> [Written with his own hand] for transmission [by an old man of][6] eighty-five on the fourteenth day of the twelfth month of the *wu-ch'en* year [8 January 909].

It is not known whether the man lived another sixteen days to celebrate his eighty-sixth year, since this is the last surviving manuscript in which such a name appears. It is clear, though, that he was especially interested in *The Scripture on the Ten Kings* very late in his life, taking care to write some of the copies himself. In the second dedication he contracted to put into practice what the scripture preaches. As an octogenarian who had read the text many times, he foresaw that breaking his promise would subject him to the tortures in the dark world described in the sūtra.

The hypothesis that *The Scripture on the Ten Kings* appealed especially to the elderly is given further weight by the existence of eight other manuscripts, none of them *The Scripture on the Ten Kings,* that the man copied in earlier years. Most of them contain definite dates: in addition to noting the year in the sexagenary system, seven of them record the reign-name and year in which they were copied. Like the three copies of

5. S 4530, reprod. Huang, *Pao-tsang,* 36:475b, transcr. Giles, *Catalogue,* no. 5457. When I consulted the original text in London in 1990 only seven of the characters in the colophon could be made out with any certainty: *shih-ssu jih pa-shih-wu . . . ch'uan* (. . . for transmission . . . eighty-five on the fourteenth day. . . .). Information supplied graciously by Elizabeth McKillop, Curator, Chinese and Korean Section, Oriental Collections, The British Library, allows us to reconstruct a rough history of the fate of the text in twentieth century. When Stein unearthed the text in 1906 it was already in poor condition: its beginning was missing, and it suffered from wear, many small rips and wrinkles, and some holes. Giles saw it in this condition and transcribed and translated the colophon (with one mistaken transcription of the Chinese, *mou-ch'en,* which should be *wu-ch'en*) in Giles, *Catalogue,* no. 5457. Sometime after Giles studied the text but before his catalogue was published—probably in the early 1930s—workmen in the British Library attempted to repair and conserve the text using the most up-to-date technology: they used an animal-base glue to affix it permanently to a stiff backing. In the process many of the small rips were exacerbated, and, especially in the area of the colophon, parts of the text were glued atop one another. Later scholars probably studied it in this condition; see Wang, *So-yin;* and Kanaoka, "Tonkōbon jigoku bunken kanki: awasete bakukōkutsu no seikaku o ronzu," p. 38, both of whose transcriptions differ from that of Giles. I follow Giles' transcription because he saw the text earliest, when it was in the best condition.

6. The original has a gap, which I reconstruct hypothetically as [*lao-jen shou-hsieh liu*]-*ch'uan,* following the wording in the colophon to the previous scroll, Pk 1226.

The Scripture on the Ten Kings, none of them contains a proper name. However, they may all be ascribed to the same man as our copyist with virtual certainty because of the recurring gerontonyms "old man" *(lao-jen)* or "old gentleman" *(lao-weng),* ages between eighty-two and eighty-five, and perfect matches of the sexagenary cycle (see appendix 12). All eight texts are copies of Kumārajīva's (350–409) translation of the *Diamond* sūtra, divided into thirty-two sections following a printed edition from Szechwan and bound as booklets (which is the same recension and format followed for copies of the *Diamond* sūtras bound together with the *Ten Kings* sūtra discussed in chapter 8). The old man copied three of them at the age of eighty-two, four when he was eighty-three, and one when he was eighty-four.

These eight copies of the *Diamond* sūtra show conclusively that the *wu-ch'en* year in which the three *Ten Kings* texts were copied was K'ai-p'ing 2 (908–909).

Taken as a whole, all eleven manuscripts allow us to gauge the relevance of the religious calendar to scripture-copying. The ten scrolls were copied on these days of the year: I/26, II/2, II/3, III/1, III/12, IV/5, IV/23, VII/28, VIII/1, XII/14, and XII/20.

In medieval times the scheduling of Chinese religious observances sometimes had a considerable effect upon when Buddhist texts were copied. Recent studies have demonstrated, for instance, a clear relation between the observance of feast-days *(chai-jih)* and the commissioning of texts.[7] Feast days were held according to at least three different schedules in medieval China. One schedule was derived from the Indian practice of *pu-sa* (Skt.: *upavasatha* or *upoṣadha,* Prakrit: *poṣadha*), the communal recitation of the *vinaya* by monks twice each month on the new and full moons. In China the *pu-sa* took numerous forms, the most frequent of which was the holding of religious services by lay and monk alike on six days of each month (days 8, 14, 15, 23, 29, and 30).[8] Another schedule prescribed ten feast days per month (on days 1, 8, 14, 15, 18, 23, 24, 28, 29, and 30) and found expression in both lay Buddhist circles and in lay Taoism.[9] A third schedule promised the remission of sins if Buddhas were worshipped on one different day in each of

7. See, for example, Magnin, "Pratique religieuse et manuscrits datés."

8. See, for example, *Feng-fa yao,* Hsi Ch'ao (336–377), in *Hung-ming chi,* Seng-yu (445–518), *T* no. 2102, 52:86b; trans. Zürcher, *The Buddhist Conquest of China,* pp. 164–65; and *Shih-sung lü (Sarvāstivādavinaya),* Puṇyatara (fl. 399–415) et al., *T* no. 1435, 23:158a–b. For brief surveys of other sources and schedules, see Mochizuki, *Daijiten,* pp. 4410a–11c; and Nakamura, *Daijiten,* p. 1175c–d.

9. See Soymié, "Les dix jours de jeûne de Kṣitigarbha"; and idem, "Les dix jours de jeûne du taoïsme." As discussed in Part One of this study, with their numerous sets of ten deities, both Buddhist and Taoist feast days preserve many echoes of the ten kings.

the twelve months.[10] What is interesting about the scheduling of the old
man's manuscripts is that there is no strong correlation with any of
these systems of feast-days. Only two of the manuscripts were copied on
the six feast-days, only four were copied on the ten feast-days, and not
one was copied on the twelve days of the year for the remission of sins.
We may hypothesize, then, that although he took a strong interest in
Buddhist thought and practice, he was probably not a regular member
of any lay Buddhist group. At any rate, the rhythms he followed in the
copying of scriptures were his own, as one might expect of a man of his
seniority.

The other religious calendar that could, in theory, have been relevant
to the copying of these ten texts was the cycle of seasonal observances.[11]
It seems, though, that only one of the ten manuscripts was copied on a
religious holiday, *The Scripture on the Ten Kings* copied on *wu-ch'en*/VIII/1
(30 August 908).[12] In the Tun-huang area the first day of the eighth
month was thought to be especially propitious for healing, and people
resorted to a wide range of therapies. One miscellany points to the benefits of bathing on that day:[13]

On the first day of the eighth month people often take water that flows
to the east and wash or bathe in it. It gets rid of internal filth [and saves

---

10. See Soymié, "Un calendrier de douze jours par an dans les manuscrits
de Touen-houang." Soymié's study includes seven Tun-huang manuscripts,
each with a different schedule.

11. Some festivals celebrated in Tun-huang were overtly Buddhist in nature:
Maitreya's birth on I/1, Kuan-yin's birth on II/19, and Śākyamuni's birth on
IV/8. Others, like the Ghost Festival on VII/15, had only a partial Buddhist
heritage, while others drew their inspiration entirely from indigenous mythology and non-Buddhist cults: the Lantern Festival on I/14–16, the parade of the
City God on X/1, and the dispatch of the Stove God on XII/23. Scholars have
only recently begun to read the Tun-huang manuscripts with an eye for seasonal religious observances, so firm conclusions are not yet possible; see Kao,
Tun-huang min-su-hsüeh, pp. 453–82, which emphasizes local and non-Han par-
ticularities; Lo, *Tun-huang pien-wen she-hui feng-su shih-wu k'ao;* and Magnin,
"Pratique religieuse et manuscrits datés."

12. It is possible that the manuscript of *The Scripture on the Ten Kings* that he
copied on VII/28 was related to the celebration of Ti-tsang's birthday or to the
closing of the gates of hell, but I have not been able to locate either of these
practices in medieval Tun-huang. The celebration of Ti-tsang's birthday on
VIII/30 is attested in Ming and Ch'ing dynasty sources in South China; see
Sawada, *Jigoku hen,* pp. 122–24. For a description of the closing of the gates of
hell late in the seventh month during the nineteenth century, see de Groot, *Les
fêtes annuellement célébrées à Émoui,* pp. 434–35. It should also be noted that two of
the manuscripts were copied near the middle and end of the twelfth month. It is
unclear whether their copying represented hopes for renewal near the advent of
the new year or whether their timing was random.

13. *Chu-tsa lüeh-te-yao ch'ao-tzu,* P 2661, reprod. Huang, *Pao-tsang,* 123:173b.

people from grief. The young will not][14] age, winter will not be cold, and summer will not be hot. It produces great results.

Another text describes the use of moxa:[15]

What is the first day of the eighth month? On this day people dot themselves with black, which is called "moxibustion" [*chih*]. It is used to treat the ten thousand illnesses. It is most excellent.

While it is clear that the day was a kind of religio-medical fair for curing, it is not known if the eighty-five-year-old engaged in hygienic bathing or the burning of moxa before he copied *The Scripture on the Ten Kings*.

Some of the prayers that the gentleman appended to his copies of the *Diamond* sūtra indicate that he enjoyed wrestling with the concepts of Mahāyāna Buddhist philosophy. His last thoughts might have been focused on avoiding hell, but just a few years earlier he was engaged in the practice of compassion and the understanding of emptiness.

The dedication to a copy of the *Diamond* sūtra made when he was eighty-three provides a good idea of the extraordinary lengths to which the man went in satisfying the standard Buddhist virtues. He writes:[16]

On the fifteenth day of the fourth month in the third year of T'ien-yu, *ping-yin* in the sequence of years [30 April 906], an old gentleman of eighty-three pricked himself to draw blood, which he mixed with ink. He wrote this scripture with his own hand for propagation to all of the believers in Sha Prefecture.[17] May the state and the land be still and peaceful; may the wheel of the Law turn forever. Should I die in writing it, I ask only that I quickly pass out of this world. I have no other prayers.

The man's hopes are not atypical of the dedications that lay believers appended to medieval scriptures. He wants to make the text more accessible to other lay believers and wishes for the prosperity of the secular and religious regimes.

The old man's particular method of copying the text was unusual, but not without precedent. The donation of one's own body for the

14. This portion, [*ling jen pu-huan, shao pu-*], appears as a hole in the reproduction in Huang, *Pao-tsang*, 123:173b. I follow the transcription in Kao, *Tunhuang min-su-hsüeh*, p. 468.

15. *Tsa-ch'ao*, S 5755, reprod. Huang, *Pao-tsang*, 44:433a.

16. P 2876, reprod. Huang, *Pao-tsang*, 124:622a.

17. The manuscript is unclear here. I read it as Sha-chou (Sha Prefecture), as do Pelliot/Lu, "Shu-mu"; and Ikeda, *Shikigo*, no. 2135. Others read it as Sha-t'u[b] ("land of Sha" or "land of sands"); see Ch'en, "Chung-shih tun-huang yü ch'eng-tu chih chien te chiao-t'ung lu-hsien: tun-huang-hsüeh san-ts'e chih i," p. 81; and Wang, *So-yin*.

reproduction of sacred texts was justified in a variety of canonical sources. Kumārajīva's compilation, *Ta chih-tu lun* (The Treatise on the Great Perfection of Wisdom), explains how a Bodhisattva employs the various parts of the body to fulfill the perfection of *ching-chin* (Skt.: *vīrya*, "energy," "vigor"). He writes, "If you truly love the Law, you should use your skin as paper, use your body and bones for the brush, and use your blood for copying."[18] The old man was not the only individual to follow the exhortation to loan one's blood for the copying of scriptures. A monk named Tseng-jen, whose legend was well known in the Tun-huang area, was reported to have sweetened enough ink with his blood over a fifty-nine-year lifetime to write a total of 283 scrolls.[19]

Vows that the man of eighty-something appended to another copy of the *Diamond* sūtra go beyond the sanguine expression of ardent Buddhist piety. His colophon to this manuscript, also copied in blood, states:[20]

On the third day of the second month in the third year of T'ien-yu, *ping-yin* in the sequence of years [28 February 906], an old man of eighty-three pricked the middle finger of his left hand. He drew blood to make the ink fragrant and wrote this *Dia[mond] Scripture*[21] for transmission to people of believing hearts. He is entirely without prayers. [Since] original nature is truly empty, there is no pleasure for which to pray.

This colophon is not as straightforward as it appears. Many dedications record the name of the commissioner, the date and circumstances of

18. *Ta chih-tu lun* (*Mahāprajñāpāramitāśāstra*), Kumārajīva, *T* no. 1509, 25:178c; see also Lamotte, *Traité*, p. 975. For other references to the practice, see *P'u-sa pen-hsing ching*, anon. (ca. 317–420), *T* no. 155, 3:119b; *Hsien-yü ching*, Hui-chüeh (fl. 445), *T* no. 202, 4:351b; *Fan-wang ching*, attrib. Kumārajīva but probably written ca. 431–481, *T* no. 1484, 24:1009a; Ishida, *Bommō kyō*, pp. 249–51; de Groot, *Le code du Mahāyāna en Chine*, pp. 79–80; and a collection of different pieces of poetry written during the Sung and Yüan dynasties on the occasion of copying scriptures with blood, contained in *Shinsen jōwa bunrui kokan sonshuku gejushū*, Gidō Shūshin (1325–1388), *DBZ* no. 819, 88:8b–10c.

19. The standard biography of Tseng-jen reports that his secular surname was Shih and that he flourished between 813 and 817. He painted pictures of Vairocana Buddha and was especially devoted to esoteric scriptures concerning Kuan-yin Bodhisattva; see *Sung kao-seng chuan*, Tsan-ning (919–1001), *T* no. 2061, 50:877a–b. Legends from Tun-huang concerning "Monk Shih" (Shih ho-shang) elaborated on the use of blood in copying texts; see, for example, *Ling-chou lung-hsing ssu pai-ts'ao-yüan shih ho-shang yin-yüan chi*, S 528, reprod. Huang, *Pao-tsang*, 4:301a–b; and the untitled text that begins "Ling-chou lung-hsing pai-ts'ao-yüan ho-shang su-hsing shih fa-hao tseng-jen . . . "; P 2680, reprod. Huang, *Pao-tsang*, 123:279a–80b.

20. S 5669, reprod. Huang, *Pao-tsang*, 44:300b.

21. The text reads *Chin ching*, an ellipsis for *Chin-kang ching*.

copying, and a brief series of prayers, usually composed of four-character phrases. This man follows the model in noting the time and circumstances of copying, but his capping phrases take an interesting twist. He ends by simply—and perhaps playfully—bringing the notion of emptiness to bear on the practice of making prayers (*yüan*ʿ, which can also be rendered as "vows"). The very act of praying for a stipulated end assumes the permanence of the one who prays and the reality of the result, be it the extinction of suffering or the arising of enlightenment. Instead, the eighty-three-year-old uses wording reminiscent of Prajñāpāramitā literature to throw the whole process of prayer into doubt.[22] If all constituents of existence are truly empty, he argues, then neither the person nor the pleasures such a person can experience possess significant reality. And if that is true, then seeking any result at all from the act of copying scriptures can only be foolish.

Despite the lack of further biographical data, colophons to eleven manuscripts suggest that one old man brought a variety of intentions and a nuanced understanding of Buddhism to the copying of *The Scripture on the Ten Kings*. As was perhaps typical for an educated Buddhist layman late in his life, he was moved by his infirmities and the terrors that awaited him after death. He practiced the ritualized shedding of blood to fulfill basic Buddhist devotion, yet he was also aware that the troubles occasioned by life and death could only be transcended through an understanding of emptiness.

22. The colophon reads "original nature is truly empty" (*pen-hsing shih k'ung*), a close reworking in four characters of a three-character phrase that occurs repeatedly in Prajñāpāramitā texts translated by Hsüan-tsang (602–664), "original nature is empty" (*pen-hsing k'ung*). See, for example, *Ta po-jo po-lo-mi-to ching (Mahāprajñāpāramitāsūtra)*, Hsüan-tsang, *T* no. 220, 5:13b. For other occurrences of the phrase, see *Taishō shinshū daizōkyō sakuin*, 3:326a.

11. Miao-fu, a Troubled Nun

THE SUFFERINGS that could be alleviated by the copying of religious texts were in no way limited to male lay believers. The sands of Tun-huang have preserved two copies of *The Scripture on the Ten Kings* that were originally commissioned in a batch of seven by a nun named Miao-fu. Their colophons are identical except for one word. They read:[1]

1. Pk 8045, reprod. Huang, *Pao-tsang*, 109:431b. The second colophon, noted in brackets, is S 2489, reprod. Huang, *Pao-tsang*, 20:176b. The texts

The disciple Miao-fu, a troubled nun[2] of An-kuo ssu, gave rise to the thought [of enlightenment][3] and reverently had this scripture written in seven separate scrolls. Offered with a single [the other colophon reads: full] mind.

Whether due to circumspection or simply to chance, Miao-fu or her scribe chose to leave the nature of her "troubles" *(huan)* entirely to the imagination of her unintended readers. The colophons do, however, note quite clearly that she commissioned seven copies as a single act of offering. A pattern of seven rituals is one of the strongest messages of *The Scripture on the Ten Kings*. This connection, together with the reference to her own difficulties rather than to the sufferings of a teacher or loved one, makes it most likely that she commissioned the scripture in preparation for her own demise.

Several other scraps of evidence allow us to conjecture that Miao-fu had these copies of *The Scripture on the Ten Kings* made sometime in the middle of the tenth century at the end of a life spent largely in the halls of the nunnery. Although the history of An-kuo ssu is known in outline from other sources, none of them places a nun named Miao-fu at An-kuo ssu.[4] The name of Miao-fu does crop up in two other Tun-huang

---

themselves reproduce the middle recension of the scripture. Unlike all other copies of *The Scripture on the Ten Kings* containing colophons, for each manuscript the handwriting of text and colophon appears to be the same. The page layout of the two specimens is slightly different, but information presented in the colophons and apparent similarities in handwriting suggest that they were produced by the same scriptorium. The manuscripts are undated.

2. "Troubled nun" translates *huan-ni*. Here I translate *huan* as "troubled" so that it can be used easily in noun form, "troubles," and because the nature of her troubles is unknown. The word could just as easily be rendered "ailments/ailing" (see Giles, *Catalogue,* no. 5454), "distress/distressed," "calamity/calamitous," or "grief/grieved."

3. I understand *fa-hsin* (gave rise to the thought) as short for *fa p'u-ti hsin* (gave rise to the thought of enlightenment, Skt.: *bodhi-cittôpādanata*); see chapter 9, n. 23.

4. The date of the temple's founding is unknown. Chiang (*Mo-kao-k'u nien-piao,* p. 649) suggests 847–960 for the temple's floruit. But the existence of the temple is probably noted earlier, in an informal tally of the local clerical population written about the year 800; see S 5676v, reprod. Huang, *Pao-tsang,* 44:323b; dated ca. 800 by Fujieda, "Tonkō no sōni seki," p. 314. The document gives a total of twenty-nine nuns for An-kuo ssu. Chikusa maintains that the temple was established sometime after 788; see Chikusa, "Tonkō no jiko ni tsuite," pp. 71–72, n. 6. The temple and the names of some of the nuns living there are recorded in four other documents between the years 865 and 938, but Miao-fu's name appears in none of them. They are: 1. Untitled register of nunneries, S 2669, reprod. Huang, *Pao-tsang,* 22:145b–49b; dated ca. 865 by Fujieda, "Tonkō no sōni seki," pp. 305–12; 2. Untitled register of monasteries and nunneries, S 2614v, reprod. Huang, *Pao-tsang,* 21:496b–505a; dated ca. 895 by Fujieda, "Tonkō no sōni seki," pp. 297–302; 3. Memorandum from

manuscripts, but these place her at Ling-hsiu ssu rather than An-kuo ssu. The first is a register of over 900 monks and nuns residing at thirteen temples in Tun-huang around the year 895.[5] Within each temple the names of monks and nuns are listed by rank. Of the thirteen temples, eight are monasteries, five are nunneries. The nunneries range in population from 49 to 189 nuns. A total of 142 nuns are registered at Ling-hsiu ssu: 99 are "*bhikṣuṇī* who have taken the great precepts" *(ta-chieh-ni);* 29 are "*śikṣamānā bhikṣuṇī*" *(shih-ch'a-ni);* 2 are "old *śrāmaṇerikā*" *(chiu sha-mi);* and 12 are "new *śrāmaṇerikā*" *(hsin sha-mi).* Miao-fu's name comes under the last category.

Assuming that the Miao-fu of An-kuo ssu was identical to the nun named Miao-fu at Ling-hsiu ssu, the classification of nuns in this registry provides a few helpful clues to Miao-fu's age. The system appears to be based on the division of the Buddhist sisterhood, well attested in a variety of Vinaya sources, into three levels.[6] The highest category was *bhikṣuṇī (pi-ch'iu-ni),* which corresponded to the highest level of monk, *bhikṣu (pi-ch'iu).* The minimum age requirement was twenty years. Ordination for women involved the acceptance of the full precepts, which traditionally numbered 500 but in practice ranged from 290 to

---

Hai-yen, Chief Controller of Monks, dated T'ien-ch'eng 3 (928), S 2575, reprod. Huang, *Pao-tsang,* 21:204b; 4. Untitled list of nuns, dated a *hsü*[d] year/ XI, P 3600, reprod. Huang, *Pao-tsang,* 129:236a–41; assigned to 926 or 938 by Fujieda, "Tonkō no sōni seki," pp. 303–4.

5. The registry is S 2614v, reprod. Huang, *Pao-tsang,* 21:496b–505a. The compiler writes that the number of nuns at Ling-hsiu ssu totals 143, but only 142 names are listed. Chiang (*Mo-kao-k'u nien-piao,* p. 658) estimates 713–975 as the period in which the temple flourished.

6. Details vary between different Vinaya sources. The account in this paragraph is based on *Ssu-fen lü (Dharmaguptavinaya),* Buddhayaśas (fl. 408–412) et al., *T* no. 1428, 22:922c–30c; and *T'an-wu-te lü-pu tsa chieh-mo,* K'ang Seng-k'ai (fl. 2522), *T* no. 1432, 22:1047c–50b. For a survey of other Vinaya sources, see Hirakawa, *Ritsuzō no kenkyū,* pp. 535–90. Most overviews of the ranks of ordination during the T'ang and Sung dynasties do not examine Vinaya sources or Tun-huang materials; see, for example, Ch'en, *Buddhism in China,* pp. 245–48; Huang, *Sung-tai fo-chiao she-hui ching-chi shih lun-chi,* pp. 357–78; and Michihata, *Tōdai bukkyō shi no kenkyū,* pp. 29–33. Most of these studies rightly emphasize the importance of the intermediary rank of "postulant" (*t'ung-hsing,* a contraction of *t'ung-tzu* [boys] and *hsing-che* [practicants]). Some, however, go too far in claiming that the stage of *śikṣamānā* did not exist in China; see ibid., p. 29. For studies that do attempt to integrate Tun-huang materials, Vinaya sources, and traditional historiography, see Tsuchihashi, "Chūgoku ni okeru konma no hensen"; idem, "Tonkō no ritsuzō"; idem, "Tonkō shutsudo ritten no tokushoku"; and Zürcher, "Buddhism and Education in T'ang Times," pp. 28–32. The close study of Tun-huang materials also provides new knowledge of ordination ranks in the Taoist church; see Schipper, "Taoist Ordination Ranks in the Tunhuang Manuscripts."

380 separate articles. By contrast, the number of precepts that full monks *(bhikṣu)* followed ranged from 215 to 263.[7] Like their male counterparts called *śrāmaṇera (sha-mi)*, women prepared for their full acceptance into the Buddhist Order by serving first as novices, called *śrāmaṇerikā (sha-mi ni* or *shih-lo-mo-na-li-chia)*. Most sources stipulated that women had to pass their twelfth year before entering the novitiate. To be ordained as a *śrāmaṇerikā*, women accepted ten precepts.[8] Between these two categories was inserted a third, called *śikṣamāṇā (shih-ch'a-mo-na)*. Women entered this rank at the age of eighteen and prepared for full ordination by following only the first six of the novice's ten precepts. This category finds no counterpart in the monkhood. Legend has it that the Buddha instituted this intermediary stage after a married woman left her family, very quickly took full ordination, and was then found out to be pregnant. To avoid future embarrassment to the Order, the Buddha decreed that the stage of *śikṣamāṇā* last for two years. An early eleventh-century Chinese account notes that these nuns-in-training let their hair grow long, waiting until their full ordination to be tonsured.[9] Since Miao-fu is classed among the "new *śrāmaṇerikā*," she was probably close to the minimum age of twelve when the register was compiled.

A second document corroborates the hypothesis that Miao-fu was close to the statutory age for ordination as a novice in 895. That document, dated Ch'ien-ning 2/III (895), is a memorandum addressed to an assistant aide in the prefectural office from a monk named Ch'ang-pi in the temple office of An-kuo ssu.[10] In the note Ch'ang-pi and other

7. Figures on the number of precepts are taken from Hirakawa, *Ritsuzō no kenkyū*, pp. 488–509.

8. According to one early source, the precepts are abstaining from 1. taking life, 2. stealing, 3. having sexual relations, 4. lying and slandering, 5. drinking alcoholic beverages, 6. using make-up or perfumes, 7. sleeping on a high, fancy bed, 8. listening to or participating in music or dance, 9. accumulating jewels, and 10. eating at the wrong times; see *Sha-mi-ni chieh ching*, anon. (ca. 25–220), *T* no. 1474, 24:937a–c. Enumerations of the "ten precepts" *(shih-chieh)* vary considerably; for brief surveys, see Mochizuki, *Daijiten*, pp. 2218c–21c; and Nakamura, *Daijiten*, p. 591c–d.

9. For discussions of the stage of *śikṣamāṇā*, see *Ssu-fen lü*, *T* 22:924a–c; *Ta chih-tu lun (Mahāprajñāpāramitāśāstra)*, Kumārajīva (350–409), *T* no. 1509, 25:161c; Lamotte, *Traité*, pp. 848–49; and Satō, *Ritsuzō*, pp. 354–55. The eleventh-century account is *Shih-shih yao-lan*, Tao-ch'eng (fl. 1019), *T* no. 2127, 54:262a.

10. The untitled memorandum is P 3167v, reprod. Huang, *Pao-tsang*, 126: 480a–b. The document begins "Ch'ang-pi and others in the temple office [*tao-ch'ang ssu*] at An-kuo ssu . . . ." Not having found any references to a specific governmental or monastic organ called *tao-ch'ang ssu*, I interpret it as a generic term. The document is addressed to the Chang-shih ssu-ma. Since a Chang-shih was in T'ang times an aide in a military commandery, I read the whole term as "Assistant Aide in the Governor General's Office." Cf. BN, *Catalogue*, which interprets it as two separate persons.

monks request the help of the local government in deciding the fate of some forty-one nuns, distributed among all five nunneries in Tun-huang, who present problems for the monastic officials. Miao-fu is the first of seven nuns listed under Ling-hsiu ssu: "[Ling-]hsiu [ssu]: The daughter of Li Nu-tzu, Miao-fu." Unfortunately the nuns' offenses are not specified individually, but Ch'ang-pi does provide a summary. At the end he writes:[11]

> Concerning the śrāmaṇerikā and those favored by the precepts[12] of the five nunneries listed above. Their parents all gave permission, and they were all happy to receive the precepts. However, some of them are too young. Some of them have not followed the teachings of the sage. Some of them have contravened secular statutes, and they must be controlled and disciplined.

In conclusion, it is a strong possibility that a young or underage Miao-fu sought ordination as a novice at Ling-hsiu ssu around the year 895, later moved to An-kuo ssu, and as an old woman there commissioned *The Scripture on the Ten Kings*.[13] If she was roughly ten years old in 895, she would have been born around 885, and between 930 and 960 she may have suffered from the unspecified ailments she hoped the copying of the text would relieve.

11. P 3167v, reprod. Huang, *Pao-tsang*, 126:480a–b.
12. "Favored by the precepts" renders *chieh-hui*. The wording is problematic. I follow Fujieda ("Tonkō no sōni seki," p. 321) in reading it as an informal term for those who have taken some precepts. It is possible that the term should be understood as *chieh-hui*ᵇ, "[those who] practice abstention and wisdom," perhaps shortened from *chieh-ting-hui*, "abstention, concentration, and wisdom"; see Chang, *Ta-tz'u-tien* 11816.22; and Komazawa, *Daijiten*, p. 140d.
13. The possibility should also be raised that the presumably elderly Miao-fu who commissioned seven copies of *The Scripture on the Ten Kings* and the novice—perhaps under the age of twelve—who presented problems for the authorities in 895 were not the same person. The first character of her name, which she would have taken when she entered the order, is quite common: in the register of nuns dating from ca. 895, ten other nuns at the same nunnery (Ling-hsiu ssu) have names that begin with "Miao-." When the full name is taken into consideration, however, each name is unique; S 2614v, reprod. Huang, *Pao-tsang*, 21: 496b–505a.

12. On Behalf of One Old Plowing Ox and Others

THE DEPTH OF historical detail offered above about rituals of production will be impossible to replicate in analyzing the seven remaining commissioner's colophons to *The Scripture on the Ten Kings*. Three of the seven record only the names of commissioners about whom nothing else is known, or they contain just a date.[1] The other four colophons consist of prayers that, given the lack of external evidence about their commissioners, can only be described as typical examples of Chinese Buddhist devotion. But, as I suggest below, their generic quality is not without interest.

The first colophon states:[2]

> Hsüeh Yen-ch'ang, the disciple of pure belief and wearer of the common cloth, gave rise to the thought of enlightenment and had this wondrous scripture written. Presented to make blessings for his kind departed father, so that he may not fall into the sufferings of the three paths. Secondly on behalf of his troubled mother, so that her sickness may quickly be cured. May the ghosts of his enemies receive the merit from writing the scripture, so that there be no [need for] further forgiveness. [May the benefits extend] to himself, so that he not be

1. The first manuscript is Pk *hsin* 1537, the colophon of which mentions the names Chai Ting-yu and Chang Yü-chien, to whom I have found no other references in Tun-huang materials. The second manuscript is Satō ms., reprod. Matsumoto, "Tonkōbon jūō kyō zuken zakkō," pls. 1–3. This scroll contains the long recension of *The Scripture on the Ten Kings* and includes pictures. Its colophon reads: "Copying and painting completed on the tenth day of the twelfth month of a *hsin-wei* year [2 Jan. 912? 30 Dec. 971?]. Written in his eighty-sixth year. Offered by the disciple Tung Wen-yüan." The manuscript includes an illustration of the commissioner, whose name I have not been able to find in other sources. The third manuscript is S 5531, reprod. Huang, *Pao-tsang*, 43:218b–50b. This short recension of *The Scripture on the Ten Kings* is the eighth text in a booklet containing ten scriptures. At the end of the last text is a colophon stating, "The twentieth day of the twelfth month of the *keng-ch'en* year [31 Jan. 921? 28 Jan. 981?]." I would guess that 921 is the most likely date, since most of the booklets containing three or more texts date from the first half of the tenth century; see the discussion of S 5531 and similarly bound booklets in chapter 8 above.

2. Nakamura ms. (*san* 799), colophon only transcr. Nakamura, *Uiki shutsudo bokuhō shohō genryū*, 3:19v; text only transcr. Tokushi, "Kōzō," pp. 259–67; and Sakai, "Jūō shinkō," pp. 631–38. Ellipses indicate holes in the original. The manuscript presents the short recension bound as a scroll. We know nothing about the other two scrolls mentioned in Hsüeh's dedication.

besieged by sickness, his years be lengthened, and his longevity increased. May this fortune be bestowed equally upon all people who read and intone this scripture in its three scrolls as well as upon all believers who transmit it. Offered fully and forever. Received and upheld on the two times with a believing heart . . . on the twenty-
. . . day of the twelfth month of the third year of Ch'ing-t'ai, a *ping-shen* year [937].[3]

Hsüeh, about whom nothing else is known, followed the primary model of Chinese religious practice since the Neolithic Age, that of making offerings to one's ancestors. His father's predicament is defined in Buddhist terms, and the specific measures Hsüeh took to rescue him involved paying for the copying of a Buddhist text. His prayer seeks benefits typical of Chinese religion: the healing of his mother, freedom from the visitations of ghosts, and long life for himself. The only exceptional concern is expressed at the end of the prayer, when he alludes to the practice, propounded in *The Scripture on the Ten Kings,* of making offerings—presumably to the ten kings—twice each month.

The healing of a mother's sickness is the focus of the second colophon, which is unsigned. The dedication reads:[4]

Presented so that the ailments of my kind mother may be speedily cured[5] and she escape from undergoing suffering in the underground prisons. First to make blessings for my living parents. Second so that I and my whole family, relatives of my own lineage and those of my wife's family,[6] and elders of families I do not even know, may not be

3. The twelfth month of Ch'ing-t'ai 3 (= T'ien-fu[b] 1) had only twenty-nine days. As noted below, the "two times" *(erh-shih)* of the month were typically the full moon (on the fourteenth or fifteenth of the month) and the new moon (on the twenty-ninth or thirtieth). If Hsüeh's practice indeed followed the precept, then this copy was probably executed on Ch'ing-t'ai 3/XII/29 (12 February 937).

4. Translation of colophon to S 6230, reprod. Huang, *Pao-tsang,* 45:144a; transcr. and trans. Giles, *Catalogue,* no. 5459. The manuscript presents the short recension bound as a scroll. This is the most corrupt colophon to the *Ten Kings* text. In at least two and probably four places it contains erroneous homophones. In addition, the gluing of the original manuscript to stiff backing in the binders' shop of the British Museum makes it difficult to read several characters.

5. The text reads *ch'üan-chieh,* "full sigh" or "complete crying out," which would make the sentence read, "Presented so that the ailments of my kind mother may quickly achieve full sigh . . . ." Such a meaning is possible only in the event that the son prayed for the mercifully quick and pleasant death of his parent. I follow Giles in emending it to *ch'üan-chieh[b],* "to be cured of sickness," the use of which is attested in a tenth-century work, *K'ai-yüan t'ien-pao i-shih,* Wang Jen-yü (880–956), cited in *P'ei-wen yün-fu,* p. 904c.

6. I follow Giles in emending *nei-wai ch'in-yin* to *nei-wai ch'in-yin[b].* I also follow Giles in understanding the meaning of the term. It could also be interpreted as

besieged by ailments but may forever be preserved in security and happiness. With the copying of this[7] scripture may the retribution for actions . . .[8] be escaped. Inscription of writing made on the sixth day of the sixth month in the fourth year of T'ung-kuang, a *ping-hsü* year [18 July 926].

As in many Chinese apotropaic rites, the benefits were not restricted simply to the sick person; the son registers the hope that good health will prevail beyond his extended family, among elders he does not know.

The third colophon presents an even clearer evocation of selflessness by assigning the merit gained from copying to the commissioner's foes. It comes at the end of a short recension of *The Scripture on the Ten Kings* bound as a booklet and preceded by the *Diamond* sūtra. The colophon to the text on the ten kings reads simply, "May all enemies and creditors receive the merit."[9] The wishes are amplified in the colophon to the preceding text of *The Diamond Scripture,* which states:[10]

On behalf of all enemies and creditors, for all those who have made the *saṃghârāma* impure, and so that all heavy sins may be wiped away.

The *"saṃghârāma" (ch'ieh-lan)* refers not to monks themselves but to the physical location—the grounds, comprising buildings, gardens, living quarters for slaves and attached households, and farmland—where members of the Order lived.[11] The commissioner (or the copyist, who may have inserted his own wishes or suggested stock phrases) was probably a monk or a nun, someone who would not only be likely to have commercial transactions and hence good cause to worry about creditors, but who would also be keenly interested in the purity of his or her habitat.

---

nei-ch'in and *wai-yin,* "relatives of my wife and those of marriage alliances"; see Morohashi, *Jiten,* no. 5750.22.

7. I follow Giles in emending *tz'u*[b] to *tz'u.*

8. As Giles suggests, *ti-yü* (in the underground prisons) is a likely phrase for the hole in the original.

9. S 5450, reprod. Huang, *Pao-tsang,* 42:622a; transcr. and trans. Giles, *Catalogue,* no. 1372 (2).

10. S 5450, reprod. Huang, *Pao-tsang,* 42:619b; transcr. and trans. Giles, *Catalogue,* no. 1372 (1). My translation differs from that of Giles; I understand the passage to be composed of three distinct vows, each preceded by a two-character term meaning "all" *(i-ch'ieh* or *so-yu).*

11. *Ch'ieh-lan* is an abbreviated form of *seng-ch'ieh-lan-mo* (Skt.: *saṃghârāma*), literally "garden for the Order." Tsan-ning explains what the term meant in the tenth century: *"Saṃghârāma* means the park for the Order. It refers to where members of the Order live"; *Ta-sung seng-shih lüeh,* Tsan-ning (919–1001), *T* no. 2126, 54:236c; see also *Fan-i ming-i chi,* Fa-yün (1088–1158), *T* no. 2131, 54:1167b.

Buddhist piety reaches one of its logical extremes in the fourth colophon. Like the third colophon, this dedication comes at the end of *The Scripture on the Ten Kings* written after *The Diamond Scripture* and bound in a booklet, and here too the dedications to the two texts are closely related. The dedication to the *Diamond* sūtra states:[12]

> Presented so that the spirit of an old plowing ox may be reborn in the Pure Land. When Maitreya descends to be born on earth, may we together hear the Sage's Law in the first assembly.

There was much disagreement in medieval clerical circles over the precise nature of Maitreya's heaven and whether or not it could be called by the same term used to refer to Amitābha's paradise in the West. The "Pure Land" *(ching-t'u)* mentioned here, however, appears to be the Tuṣita Heaven of Maitreya, the Buddha of the future. Although the particulars varied from one group to another, one standard theme of Maitreyan belief was that Maitreya would descend in the form of a Buddha to preach the Dharma. At that time inhabitants of Tuṣita Heaven and residents on earth will gather in a succession of audiences and, having heard his sermons, achieve enlightenment.[13]

The commissioner summarizes his vows in the colophon to the second text in the booklet, *The Scripture on the Ten Kings.* He writes:[14]

> Presented on behalf of one old plowing ox. The *Diamond* in one scroll and the *Prophecy* in one scroll were reverently written. I pray that this ox may personally receive the merit, be reborn in the Pure Land, and never again receive the body of an animal. May heaven's ministries and earth's prefects understand it clearly and handle it discreetly, so that there be no further enmity[15] or quarrel. The first month of a *hsin-wei* year.[16]

As in other colophons to *The Scripture on the Ten Kings,* the unspoken assumptions behind this prayer involve Buddhist cosmology. But in this dedication the principle of rebirth is put to use not on behalf of ancestors

12. S 5544, reprod. Huang, *Pao-tsang,* 43:361a; transcr. and trans. Giles, *Catalogue,* no. 1384 (1).

13. For an attempt to distinguish Tuṣita Heaven from Amitābha's Pure Land, see *Hsi-fang yao-chüeh shih-i t'ung-kuei,* K'uei-chi (632–682), *T* no. 1964. For modern studies on Maitreya, see Demiéville, "La Yogācārabhūmi de Saṅgharakṣa"; Hayami, *Miroku shinkō;* and Sponberg and Hardacre, *Maitreya, the Future Buddha.*

14. S 5544, reprod. Huang, *Pao-tsang,* 43:363b; transcr. and trans. Giles, *Catalogue,* no. 1384 (2).

15. I follow Giles in emending *ch'ou*[b] to *ch'ou*[c].

16. Possible dates are 791, 851, 911, and 971. The year 911 is the most likely because most other dated copies of the *Diamond* sūtra bound as booklets date from the first half of the tenth century; see chapter 8 for further details.

but for the benefit of a domestic animal. Compassion toward animals is simply one small and insufficiently studied example of the influence of Buddhism upon Chinese ethics. Better known—and, in terms of numbers, more effective—were efforts to "release life" *(fang-sheng)*, a practice in which animals otherwise consigned to the dinner table were purchased and then released in their natural habitats.[17] The anonymous commissioner of this booklet also performed rituals for the liberation of animals, praying that the beast alongside which he may have worked in the field would be released to a better life in the hereafter.

The colophons translated above have very few overt connections to the doctrines of *The Scripture on the Ten Kings*. Only one refers directly to practices mentioned in the text. The others express desires common to the copying of religious texts in medieval China. In the colophons to most medieval Buddhist texts—outside of the institutionalized copying of the Buddhist canon and the sponsorship of special projects by the state—commissioners pray for a better fate for their ancestors, seek peace among nations, or wish for their own longevity.[18]

The greatest value of the unexceptional dedications examined here is that they document a generic Chinese Buddhism in which cosmology and morality play a crucial, but rarely enunciated, role. They show how Buddhist ideas could be used to "relativize" every link in the chain of being. Given the postulate of multiple rebirths in a hierarchical but morally just system, it was impossible to confine the advantages of scripture-copying to just one person. Hence Buddhists—or perhaps just as often, common people who frequented Buddhist temples—dedicated the merit created by their donations not only to themselves but to ailing parents, renowned ancestors, parents of previous incarnations, the extended family, enemies, and unknown, unnamed sinners. Even ani-

17. A good survey of traditional sources is contained in *(Ch'in-ting) ku-chin t'u-shu chi-ch'eng*, "Po-wu hui-pien," "Shen-i tien," *chüan* 212, "Fang-sheng pu," 62:78a–87a. Modern studies include de Groot, "Miséricorde envers les animaux dans le bouddhisme chinois"; Michihata, *Chūgoku bukkyō shisō shi no kenkyū*, pp. 225–325; and the summary account in idem, *Chūgoku bukkyō to shakai fukushi jigyō*, pp. 225–35.

18. The prayers in medieval colophons are a significant literary genre in their own right and offer a relatively unfiltered glimpse of religious practice, yet they remain little studied. For basic accounts, see Kanda, "Chogen," pp. 1–7; Shiga, "Tonkō shakyō batsubun yori mita bukkyō shinkō"; and idem, "Kuyō no tame no tonkō shakyō." Other studies touching on the subject of dedications include Fujieda, "Tonkō shutsudo no chōan kyūtei shakyō"; Giles, "Dated Chinese Manuscripts in the Stein Collection," *passim;* idem, *Catalogue, passim;* Kanaoka, "Tonkō bunken ni mirareru shoshin shobasatsu shinkō no ichi yōsō"; Ikeda, *Shikigo*, pp. 9–13; de Jong, Review of Giles, *Descriptive Catalogue of the Chinese Manuscripts from Tun-huang in the British Museum;* Lin, *Tun-huang wen-shu-hsüeh*, pp. 271–353; and Mair, "Lay Students and the Making of Written Vernacular Narrative," *passim*.

mals could receive the benefits, since they too were related, not by blood or marriage, but by the ties of karma. If rebirth meant that all people were in principle part of the same line of descent, it also implied that other species deserved the same protection in the other world as did ancestors.

13. Received and Upheld by Bhikṣu Tao-chen

SOME COPIES OF *The Scripture on the Ten Kings* were ceremonially resurrected many years after they were first produced. Having been commissioned by a patron, copied by a scribe, chanted by monks, and consigned to the stacks of a library, some manuscripts then reentered the world of cause-and-effect. Owing to the scarcity of paper and, especially during the years of Tibetan rule, the interruption of trade with central China, damaged or unwanted texts in Tun-huang were often recycled. The sands of the Gobi preserve many examples of old scrolls and sheets, canonical and otherwise, that were filled with writing on their verso after the ink on their proper side had faded or been rubbed off. Two copies of *The Scripture on the Ten Kings* met a similar fate. If my guess is correct, these two copies were gathered from his own family's collection by a young monk of San-chieh ssu named Tao-chen (fl. 934–987), who patched their holes, corrected their mistakes, and then donated them to his monastery.

The scrolls themselves, one housed in the British Museum and one in the National Library in Peking, provide a starting point.[1] Each scroll contains only one text, the short recension of *The Scripture on the Ten Kings*. The two scrolls differ in layout and share very few textual variants, and the manuscript in Peking contains one entire paragraph lacking in the copy in London, all of which suggests that they were produced in two separate scriptoria or copied from different master texts. Whatever their origins, both texts appear to have been refurbished by the same pair of hands. At the beginning of each scroll has been pasted a piece of paper made of coarser—newer?—material that, when the scroll is rolled up, serves as a protective cover. The right side of each scroll is reinforced with a thin wooden splint to make the leading edge

1. The manuscripts are S 3147, reprod. Huang, *Pao-tsang,* 26:244a–46b; and Pk 6375, reprod. Huang, *Pao-tsang,* 109:422a–24a.

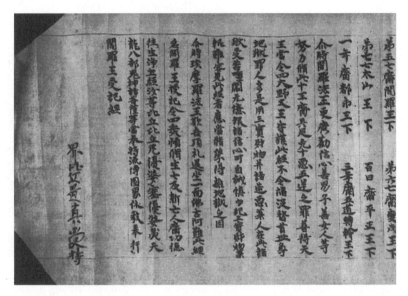

7. Short recension of *The Scripture on the Ten Kings* in scroll format. This portion shows end of narrative and colophon identifying Tao-chen. S 3147. ©British Library.

impervious to tearing. A string is anchored to the splint so that the scroll can be tied securely. To the trailing edge (i.e., the left side) of each scroll someone has affixed a small, rectangular paper tab, suitable for holding open the most curled part of the manuscript (see fig. 7). Both manuscripts show signs of repair. For large holes, a new strip of paper has been glued over the hole on the verso, and missing characters have been rewritten on the recto in a different hand than the original. At the end of each text is a brief colophon written in a hand different from that of the text itself. The colophon reads: "Received and upheld by the *bhikṣu* Tao-chen of [San-]chieh [ssu]."[2] Finally, the cover of each text contains the title, a number, and the name of the original owner. The Peking scroll reads: "*The Scripture Spoken by the Buddha on the Prophecy Received by King Yama.* The second scroll—Chang family." The London scroll reads: "*The Scripture Spoken by the Buddha on the Prophecy Received by King Yama.* Scroll three—Chang family" (see fig. 8).

The puzzle of these two texts can be solved by examining the significance of the words in the dedication, *shou-ch'ih* (received and upheld), and by seeking other colophons and covers that mention Tao-chen.

How is the term *shou-ch'ih* best understood? Lionel Giles, who paid

2. The wording is identical in the two colophons, except Pk 6375 omits *chieh*, which was the standard abbreviation for San-chieh ssu.

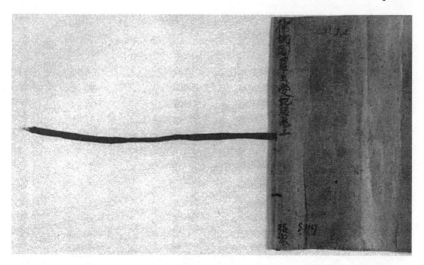

8. Short recension of *The Scripture on the Ten Kings* in scroll format. Cover of scroll, with title and mention of Chang family. S 3147. ©British Library.

special attention to the language of Tun-huang colophons, adopted a flexible attitude toward translation. He renders the term at least three different ways: "acquired," "received and (its precepts) upheld," and "apprehended and borne in mind."[3] The physical dimensions of the term are not insignificant. The second-century dictionary *Shuo-wen* glosses each of the words in very concrete fashion: $shou^b$ is "to receive from another" *(hsiang-fu)*, while *ch'ih* means "to grasp" (wo^b).[4] In colloquial language the term is understood more psychologically as "to believe and hold on to the faith."[5] In addition, *shou-ch'ih* has several

3. See Giles, *Catalogue,* nos. 3438, 2830, 1376. Mair ("Lay Students and the Making of Written Vernacular Narrative," no. 597) renders it "received and retained." It should also be noted that the term *shou-ch'ih* occurs in the text of *The Scripture on the Ten Kings* itself. In all recensions of the text, including the short recension Tao-chen collected, it is part of the clause, "Now if there is a person who cultivates the commissioning of this scripture, or who receives and upholds or reads and intones it . . . ."

4. *Shuo-wen chieh-tzu,* 4:571b–73b, 9:1158b–59a, respectively. Couvreur's interpretation stays close to the *Shuo-wen.* For $shou^b$ Couvreur lists "accipere, obtinere . . . in se recipere"; for *ch'ih* he lists "firmiter tenere; sustinere, adjuvare"; see Couvreur, *Dictionarium Sinicum & Latinum ex Radicum Ordine,* pp. 134b, 408a.

5. Definition from Lin, *Lin Yutang's Chinese-English Dictionary of Modern Usage,* p. 1169b. Similarly, the editors of *Kuo-yü tz'u-tien* provide the gloss: "to accept in one's mind is called 'receiving' [$shou^b$], to recall without forgetting is called 'upholding' [*ch'ih*]"; Wang et al., *Kuo-yü tz'u-tien (Gwoyeu Tsyrdean),* p. 3099a.

technical meanings in Buddhism. Nakamura Hajime distinguishes three senses of the term in Buddhist philosophy:[6]

1. To accept and remember a teaching,
2. To receive as one's own the clothing made according to the rules,
3. One of the ten acts of the Law: to take possession of scriptures of the Great Vehicle with unusual devotion.

While none of these can be ruled out, the last of the Buddhist meanings may prove most helpful in understanding precisely what Tao-chen was up to when he "received and upheld" *The Scripture on the Ten Kings*. Several schools of Buddhist thought advocated "receiving and upholding" as the sixth of ten ways to devote oneself to sacred texts. One of the Yogācāra treatises translated by Hsüan-tsang (602–664) states:[7]

> Within this Great Vehicle there are ten methods. One is to write and copy. Two is to make offerings. Three is to give to others. Four is to listen attentively with a concentrated mind when others intone and read. Five is to unroll scriptures and read them oneself. Six is to receive and uphold [*shou-ch'ih*]. Seven is to explain properly the meaning of the text to others. Eight is to chant and intone. Nine is to think it over. Ten is to cultivate the practice.

This digression into Buddhist scholasticism is not irrelevant, for it seems that as a youth Tao-chen followed a path of devotion very similar to the one demarcated by the ten acts listed above. In the early 1980s there came to light a Tun-huang manuscript entitled *A Catalogue of Scriptures Entered into the Storehouse*, formerly believed to have been lost. In it Tao-chen recorded his motivations for collecting texts, his plan of action, and the benefits he hoped would result. Tao-chen's dedication to the text states:[8]

6. Nakamura, *Daijiten*, p. 638a–b. Sanskrit equivalents include *dhārayati, udrahaṇa, dhāraṇa,* and *uddeśa* for the first meaning; *udgrahaṇa, udgraha, udgṛhīta, upā* plus √*dā (upādāya),* and *grāhaka* for the third meaning; see ibid. De Jong suggests *udgṛhṇāti* for *shou*[b] and *dhārayati* for *ch'ih;* see de Jong, Review of Lionel Giles, *Descriptive Catalogue of the Chinese Manuscripts from Tunhuang in the British Museum*, p. 228.

7. Translation from *Pien chung-pien lun (Madhyāntavibhaṅgaṭīkā)*, Vasubandhu, trans. Hsüan-tsang (602–664), *T* no. 1600, 31:474b. For a similar enumeration in verse, see *Pien chung-pien lun sung (Madhyāntivibhaṅgakārikā)*, Maitreya, trans. Hsüan-tsang, *T* no. 1601, 31:479c. For an explanation, see *Hsien-yang sheng-chiao lun*, Asaṅga, trans. Hsüan-tsang, *T* no. 1602, 31:491a. For Sanskrit reconstructions, see Mochizuki, *Daijiten*, pp. 2272c–73a. For a different enumeration, see *Sheng-t'ien-wang po-jo po-lo-mi ching*, Upaśūnya (fl. 538–565), *T* no. 231, 8:725a.

8. The text is Pk *hsin* 329, transcr. Oda, "Tonkō sangaiji no *gen issai nyozō kyō mokuroku ni tsuite*," pp. 557–66. The text opens with a listing of texts, which on the physical manuscript takes up sixty-two lines in three sheets of paper. Imme-

On the fifteenth day of the sixth month of the fifth year of Ch'ang-hsing, *chia-wu* in the sequence of years [29 July 934], the disciple of San-chieh ssu, *bhikṣu* Tao-chen, having seen that among the contents of the storehouse of his temple the sets[9] of scriptures and commentaries were incomplete, thereupon bowed his forehead to the ground and, with devout sincerity, took an oath and made prayers: I will go carefully through the cartons and storehouses of all the families, seeking after old and decayed scriptural texts. I will gather them in the monastery, repair and patch them from beginning to end, and pass them down to other ages. Their light will beautify the gate of mystery for ten thousand generations and one thousand autumns. Offered fully and forever.

I pray that dragons, gods, and the eight classes of beings might guard and protect our spiritual sands;[10] that Brahmā, Śakra, and the

---

diately after, at the right hand margin of the fourth sheet, begins Tao-chen's dedication. The scroll may have originally begun with Tao-chen's dedication, and the three sheets of the catalogue were later glued to the beginning of the manuscript. My translation of the dedication to the text corresponds to lines 63–75, transcr. ibid., pp. 560–61. Oda notes that the handwriting of Pk *hsin* 329 matches that of S 3624, a descriptive catalogue of scriptures held at San-chieh ssu. Pk *hsin* 329 was first collected in 1911 by the Ōtani expedition, led by Tachibana Zuichō. Since that time it has passed through many hands and has been described, sometimes rather differently, by several scholars. One of the earliest catalogues of the Ōtani collection lists it as no. 333 (originally designated *p'an* in the sequence of the *Ch'ien-tzu wen*). For some time it was kept at the Port Arthur Museum (Liaoning). The manuscript was probably part of the batch that, owing to steep import duties, did not make it back to Japan.

A very similar text is Th Institute 345. After the catalogue on Th 345, there is written "This record is incomplete" *(tz'u-lu pu-ting)*, which suggests that Th 345 was the rough draft and Pk *hsin* 329 the final copy; see Tun-huang yen-chiu-yüan, *Tun-huang*, p. 291. Th 345 was first described in an article published in 1959, which locates a manuscript with a similar title in the private collection of a Mr. Jen in Tun-huang; see Chin, "Tun-huang k'u-k'an ming-shu k'ao." A catalogue published in 1977 shows that the latter manuscript had become part of the collection housed at the Tun-huang yen-chiu-yüan; see Liu and Shih, "Tun-huang wen-wu yen-chiu-so ts'ang tun-huang i-shu mu-lu," no. 345.

9. "Sets" translates *pu-chih*, literally "sets and wrappers" or "sets and cases," similar to *pu-chih*[b], "a case for storing books"; see Morohashi, *Jiten*, no. 39460.48.

10. I am uncertain of my translation of *shen-sha* as "spiritual sands." The term was used in Taoist literature in the sense of "magical sand," but that is not entirely appropriate here; see *P'ei-wen yün-fu*, p. 933b. Perhaps the term is simply an adjective *(shen,* "spiritual") plus the descriptive toponym *(Sha)* that was often used during the T'ang dynasty for the prefecture of Sha-chou in which Tun-huang was located. Less likely, the term could be emended on ortho-

four kings unite their borders in perpetual peace; that the gods of the
walls and moats be prosperous and happy, the gods of soil and grain
extend their glory; that the local rulers and great princes always reach
the precious position; that forebears and descendants soar beyond, to
meet at the Dragon Flower Tree;[11] and that present scions be graced
with emoluments the benefits of which extend to the whole clan.

These lines make it clear that Tao-chen assumed the task of library development quite consciously. Disturbed by the condition of books in his
monastery, he took an oath to collect old texts and repair them.[12] Such an
act would result in great good fortune, which Tao-chen discusses at
length. Beginning with the words "I pray that" *(yüan-shih)*, he seeks the
protection of gods of the Buddhist heavens as well as local deities. He registers his wishes for the prosperity of the state. And he hopes for the well-
being of his family, a goal achieved through rebirth in Maitreya's assembly and measured by salaries lucrative enough to support the whole clan.

Tao-chen introduces the results of his search with the words, "Whatever scriptures and commentaries I acquire will appear in this catalogue. They are enumerated fully as follows." The inventory of over
1,200 scrolls includes scriptures belonging to nearly every category of
Chinese Buddhist text. The catalogue is extremely important in the history of the ten kings because it is one of the clearest external references
to the status and location of *The Scripture on the Ten Kings* in medieval
times. The catalogue lists eight separate scrolls of *The Scripture on the Ten
Kings*, called by its formal title *The Scripture on the Prophecy Given to King
Yama Rāja*.[13] These details do not allow us to decide whether the two
surviving copies with Tao-chen's scribblings were among the eight he

---

graphic grounds to *shen-chou* (the spiritual continent, i.e., China); see Morohashi, *Jiten*, no. 24673.254.

11. "To meet at the Dragon Flower Tree" *(hui yü lung-hua)* is a common
prayer for the salvation of one's family in medieval Chinese Buddhism. Sources
describe how the Buddha of the Future, Maitreya, will descend to Jambudvīpa
and, after achieving enlightenment under a tree called "Dragon Flower," will
preach to three large assemblies there; see *Mi-le hsia-sheng ching*, Dharmarakṣa
(fl. 265–313), *T* no. 453, 14:421c; *Mi-le hsia-sheng ch'eng-fo ching*, Kumārajīva
(350–409), *T* no. 454, 14:424b; and *Mi-le hsia-sheng ch'eng-fo ching*, I-ching (635–
713), *T* no. 455, 14:427b.

12. We do not know how old the library of San-chieh ssu was in 934. Chiang
suggests that San-chieh ssu flourished between 904 and 985; see Chiang,
Mo-kao-k'u nien-piao, pp. 645–66.

13. Tao-chen lists the acquisitions separately: "*The Scripture on the Prophecy Given
to King Yama Rāja* in one scroll," and later "*The Scripture on the Prophecy Given to
King Yama Rāja* in seven scrolls." Could the two surviving copies have been part
of the original batch of seven, all obtained from the Chang family? The rough
draft of the catalogue (Th Institute 345) lists only one scroll of the text.

gathered in the year 934. But they do establish that some copies of the text circulated outside of Buddhist temples, and they document the motivations of one monk whose devotion enriched his monastery's library with eight copies of the scripture.[14]

In addition to the two copies of *The Scripture on the Ten Kings*, over sixty surviving Tun-huang manuscripts passed through Tao-chen's hands (see appendix 13). According to their colophons, some he merely "recited" *(nien)* or "turned" *(chuan)*, some he "upheld and recited" *(ch'ih-nien)*, others he "received and upheld" *(shou-ch'ih)*, and one he "circulated" *(hsing)*. In addition to collecting, repairing, and studying texts, Tao-chen took part in copying: some he "inscribed" *(chi')* himself, some he "recited and inscribed" *(nien-chi)*, while others were "inscribed after Tao-chen's copy" (Tao-chen *pen chi*).[15]

Tao-chen's contributions to San-chieh ssu were not limited to books. In a curiously placed colophon to a handwritten copy of Nāgārjuna's *Chung-lun* (Treatise on the Mean; Skt.: *Mūlamadhyamakakārikā*), a scribe records a long list of items that Tao-chen donated to the monastery. After stating that the treatise was copied and recited by the monk Hui-hai in a *chi-hai* year (939?), it describes Tao-chen's acquisitions, which apparently did not include this particular text. The colophon states:[16]

> On the fifteenth day of the first month of the *i-wei* year [2 February 935?] at San-chieh ssu *The Great Prajñāpāramitā Scripture* was repaired along with a lesson to be read in the inner chapel. The *śramaṇa* Tao-

14. Other sources make reference to hundreds of other scrolls procured by Tao-chen. One brief note, undated and bound in the form of a booklet, is entitled "A Copy of the Record of Assorted Scriptures Acquired by *Bhikṣu* Tao-chen of San-chieh ssu, Who Searched in All Quarters"; S 6225, reprod. Huang, *Pao-tsang*, 45:137b–38b.

15. *Nien:* Pk 5788, P 3917A; *chuan:* S 3452; *ch'ih-nien:* P 2930; *shou-ch'ih:* S 3147, P 2318, Pk 5788, Pk 6375, Pk 8018, Pk 8230; *hsing:* S 4160; *chi':* S 1635, P 2836; *nien-chi:* Tp 4736; . . . *pen chi:* P 2193. For further details, see appendix 13.

16. S 5663, reprod. Huang, *Pao-tsang*, 44:236a–b; transcr. with omissions and trans. Giles, *Catalogue* no. 4298. The manuscript consists of fifty-seven loose strips of rectangular paper, pierced through the middle for binding with a string. The colophon is inscribed in the middle of the text of the treatise, between the second and third chapters. I hypothesize that the *i-wei* year was 935 rather than 995 for two reasons. The earlier date would place Tao-chen's donation of these items at a very reasonable elapse—exactly seven months—after his vow, translated above, to scour the area for books. Secondly, the earliest reference to Tao-chen is dated 934, and the very last surviving mention of him is dated 987 (in S 4915, on which see below). If he was twenty years old in 934, he would have been over eighty in 995, which is possible but not likely. Cf. Vetch, "Liu Sahe: traditions et iconographie," p. 86. For the dating of some items I rely on an unpublished study by Shih P'ing-t'ing, "San-chieh ssu, tao-chen, tun-huang tsang-ching," which she graciously shared with me.

chen also put in order and repaired[17] eleven copies of various scriptures. He also made one copy of *The Scripture on Repaying Kindness* and made one copy of *The Larger Scripture on Names of the Buddhas.* Tao-chen gave rise to the thought [of enlightenment][18] and commissioned sixty wrappers for *The Great Prajñāpāramitā* of brocaded crimson embroidered silk,[19] all complete. He also commissioned fifty silver banners for donation to San-chieh ssu, and one incense burner with bronze bells[20] and one incense bowl[21] for donation to San-chieh ssu. Tao-chen commissioned twenty-seven banners of the priest Liu Sa-ho[22] for donation, one incense burner with silver bells, an incense bowl, incense and flowers, and one carpet. The above were donated to the priests forever as an offering.

Tao-chen repaired one copy of *The Great Prajñāpāramitā.* He repaired thirteen copies of various scriptures. Twenty-seven banners, one incense burner with bronze bells, one incense bowl, one scripture-reading table, one scripture storehouse, one scripture case, incense and flowers, one carpet—the above were donated to the storehouse of scriptures as an offering.

17. For "put in order and repaired" the manuscript clearly reads *t'iao-hsiu,* although Giles, *Catalogue,* no. 4298, leaves the first character in question.

18. "Gave rise to the thought [of enlightenment]" *(fa [p'u-t'i] hsin)* is a standard liturgical description of the intention behind an act of offering; see chapter 9, n. 23.

19. "Brocaded crimson embroidered silk" translates *chin-fei ti-ling.* I am unable to find a specific technical meaning for these terms.

20. "One incense burner with bronze bells" translates *t'ung-ling hsiang-lu i,* emending *ling²* to *ling².* The clause refers to one item because the enumerator comes after both objects; cf. Giles, *Catalogue,* no. 4298, who interprets it as two items ("a bronze bell, one incense-burner").

21. Here and below for "incense bowl" the manuscript is not perfectly clear. I read the two characters as *hsiang-ch'ien* (incense bowl); for this use of *ch'ien,* see Chang, *Ta-tz'u-tien,* no. 15587, definition *ting.* Giles translates it as I do (incense bowl, presumably *hsiang-ch'ien*), but transcribes it incorrectly as *hsiang-lien* (fragrant rice); see Giles, *Catalogue,* no. 4298.

22. Cf. Giles, who makes Liu Sa-ho a contemporary of Tao-chen's: "Tao-chen made for presentation by the priest Liu Sa-ho 27 banners . . . ." (ibid.). The legend of Liu Sa-ho (fl. 343–435) underwent a resurgence in northwestern China in the tenth century. Earlier sources relate that after a youth spent killing deer and committing other sinful acts, Liu Sa-ho was rescued from hell by Kuan-yin. He thereupon became a monk and, under the Buddhist name of Hui-ta, was involved in a long series of miracles associated with statues and Aśokan stupas. He was the subject of both artistic and literary representations in tenth-century Tun-huang. Studies include Ch'en, "Liu Sa-ho yen-chiu"; Shih, "Liu Sa-ho yü tun-huang mo-kao-k'u"; Sun, "Mo-kao-k'u te fo-chiao shih-chi ku-shih," p. 207; idem, "Liu Sa-ho ho-shang shih-chi k'ao"; Vetch, "Lieou Sa-ho et les grottes de Mo-kao"; and idem, "Liu Sahe: traditions et iconographie."

Whatever its status in Yogācāra philosophy, "receiving and uphold-ing" was not restricted to books and teachings. In addition to seeking texts, repairing them, reading them, and commissioning the creation of new copies, Tao-chen returned to San-chieh ssu laden with other trea-sures, some of them quite heavy, necessary for sustaining the Buddhist faith.[23] Here the more literal interpretation of *shou-ch'ih* may help best in understanding how he received donations from local families and managed to carry them securely back to the temple.

Tao-chen probably did not have to call at unfamiliar gates when he went in search of books, bells, and other *sacra*. In an undated colophon to *The Scripture on Names of the Buddhas*, Tao-chen wrote:[24]

The *śramaṇa* Tao-chen repaired this scripture. His age is nineteen. His secular surname is Chang.

Unfortunately it is impossible to know if Tao-chen's family was the same Chang family that originally owned the two (out of an original set of at least three) copies of *The Scripture on the Ten Kings*. It is equally diffi-cult to locate Tao-chen's family with any precision in the history of Tun-huang. The surname Chang plays as frequent and as prominent a role in the political history of Tun-huang as it does in the history of Taoism. Simply in terms of numbers the Changs, comprising several distinct lin-eages, were a powerful force in the region: between the years 775 and 1000, people with the surname Chang amounted to 16 percent of the recorded population of Tun-huang.[25] Chang I-ch'ao (r. 851–872) led an army that overthrew Tibetan rule over Tun-huang in 848. From 851 until about 920 the Chinese court bestowed the formal right to rule the area, by hereditary succession, to three generations of Changs, accord-ing them the title *Kuei-i-chün chieh-tu-shih* (Military Commissioners of the Kuei-i Commandery). Before, during, and after the period of for-mal rule by the Chang family, members of the lineage were active, and at times preeminent, in the cultural life of Tun-huang. They wrote texts, commissioned scriptures, joined the Buddhist order, and paid for the construction of new grottoes.[26]

23. For a study of lists of temple possessions, see Hou, "Trésors du monas-tère Long-hing à Touen-houang: une étude sur le manuscrit P 3432."

24. Pk 5788, reprod. Huang, *Pao-tsang*, 62:80a. According to Ch'en Yüan, who handled the manuscript in the 1920s, the manuscript does indeed show sig-nificant signs of repair: the handwriting and the color of the first two pages are different from that of the other pages; Ch'en, *Tun-huang chieh-yü lu*, p. 57r. Pk 5788 should probably be dated ca. 938 because the information in its colophon matches closely the colophon to Tp 4736, reprod. *(Kuo-li chung-yang t'u-shu-kuan ts'ang) Tun-huang chüan-tzu*, p. 1179b, which is dated *wu-hsü*/V/20 (probably 20 June 938).

25. See Tohi, "Kigigun jidai," pp. 253–55.

26. The detailed history of the Chang clan in Tun-huang has yet to be writ-ten, but even a brief survey finds a pervasive correspondence between the fam-

The possibility that his own family was the original owner of some copies of *The Scripture on the Ten Kings* would cast interesting light on Tao-chen's successful campaign to develop the holdings of San-chieh ssu. One might speculate that many of the texts and antiques he brought to the temple might have come from his old home. The ambitions he entertained for the welfare of his ancestors and the success of his descendants (translated above in the preface to his catalogue of 934) may have had a solid cause in the pious donations of his own family. Just as his family's belongings may have been transferred to the monastery during his lifetime, there is also some marginal evidence that Tao-chen's own manuscripts ended up in the possession of his family.[27]

The texts that Tao-chen copied and collected provide an excellent illustration of the pluralism characteristic of medieval Chinese Buddhism. Just as the works of Hsüan-tsang (602–664) occupied pride of place in the Buddhist canon of the high T'ang, so too were they prominent among the books collected by Tao-chen. Some, like the voluminous *Ta po-jo po-lo-mi-to ching* (Greater Prajñāpāramitā Scripture; Skt.: *Mahāprajñāpāramitāsūtra*), were collections of shorter texts,[28] while others were commentaries on Yogācāra philosophy.[29] Tao-chen did not, how-

---

ily name and the production of manuscripts: Changs either commissioned or copied Buddhist texts in the sixth century (S 6727, reprod. Huang, *Pao-tsang,* 51:45b–51b, copied by Chang A-sheng on Yen-ch'ang 5/IV/12 [21 May 514]); seventh century (S 114, reprod. Huang, *Pao-tsang,* 1:563a–76b, copied for Chang Chün-ch'e in Shang-yüan 2 [676]); eighth century (S 2723, reprod. Huang, *Pao-tsang,* 22:549a–55a, copied by Chang Wan-chi on Ching-yün 2/III/19 [11 April 711]); ninth century (S 4057, reprod. Huang, *Pao-tsang,* 33:428b–29a, copied or owned by a certain Chang, dated Ch'ien-fu 6/I/13 [7 February 879]); and tenth century (S 2073, reprod. Huang, *Pao-tsang,* 15:697a–711b, recorded by Chang Ch'ang-chi in K'ai-pao 5 [972]). For the place of the Chang family in Tun-huang political history, see Čuguevskiĭ, "Touen-houang du VIIIᵉ au Xᵉ siècle," pp. 9–13; Eberhard, "The Leading Families of Ancient Tun-huang," esp. pp. 213–14; Fujieda, "Shashū kigikun setsudoshi shimatsu"; and Tohi, "Kigigun jidai," pp. 233–96. On the role of the Chang family in sponsoring construction and restoration of grottoes, see Fujieda, "Tonkō senbutsudō no chūkō," pp. 45–91. For *The Transformation Text on Chang I-ch'ao (Chang I-ch'ao pien-wen),* see Mair, *Tun-huang Popular Narratives,* pp. 167–71, 305–11.

27. In large characters on the cover of the brief list of scriptures translated above there occurs a phrase the last two characters of which I am uncertain: "This scripture must belong to [?] [?]"; S 6225, reprod. Huang, *Pao-tsang,* 45:138a. The two characters look like *lang-chuan,* which could be a personal name or a simplified form of *lang-chiu,* "uncle." If it is indeed the latter, then one could conjecture that the manuscript was passed down in Tao-chen's sister's household.

28. Copies of *Ta po-jo po-lo-mi-to ching (Mahāprajñāpāramitāsūtra)* collected by Tao-chen include Pk 2318 and Pk 8018. The text, translated by Hsüan-tsang (602–664), is printed as *T* no. 220.

29. See, for example, P 2161, a copy of *Ta-sheng pai-fa ming-men lun k'ai-tsung-i chi* collected by Tao-chen. The text, by T'an-kuang (fl. 700–782), printed as

ever, ignore local schools of thought. He collected copies of the *Wu-liang-shou tsung-yao ching* (Scripture on the Essentials of Infinite Life), a text containing *dhāraṇīs* invoking Amitābha Buddha, which was translated from Tibetan into Chinese by the monk Čhos-grub (Ch.: Fa-ch'eng) (fl. 780–860) and disseminated widely in the northwest—probably because it was copied by order of the state—during the period of Tibetan rule.[30] Other texts in Tao-chen's possession were centrally concerned with the monastic life. Some dealt with techniques of visualization,[31] while others offered summaries of *Vinaya* regulations.[32] Late in his life Tao-chen made a copy of verses that had recently been put together as a legitimating text for the Ch'an school.[33] Tao-chen also possessed a copy of monastic folklore concerning the disciple of the historical Buddha named Mu-lien.[34]

Like the texts he collected, Tao-chen's professional life was not limited to any easily defined sphere. As noted, in 934 Tao-chen went outside the monastery in search of holy objects, collecting items from the homes of private families. Remains from Tun-huang show that seventeen and one-half years later Tao-chen had further significant contact with the lay world. On the seventh night of the twelfth month in a *hsin-hai* year (6 January 952), Tao-chen led a tour of the Caves of Unsurpassed Height (Mo-kao-k'u). Judging from unsigned notes of the pilgrimage, the group, aided by lanterns, made offerings at eleven or more major grottoes.[35] The occasion was the Buddhist holiday known as La-

---

T no. 2810, is a commentary on *Ta-sheng pai-fa ming-men lun (Mahāyānaśatadhar-maprakāśamukhaśāstra)*, Vasubandhu, trans. Hsüan-tsang, *T* no. 1614. On T'an-kuang, see Ueyama, "Donkō to tonkō no bukkyōgaku."

30. For an exemplum, see S 3452. The text is also known under the title *Ta-sheng wu-liang-shou ching*, Čhos-grub (Ch.: Fa-ch'eng) (fl. 780–860), *T* no. 936. It exists in Sanskrit, Tibetan, Khotanese, two Chinese, Hsi-hsia, Uighur, Mongol, and Manchu translations. For studies of the monk Fa-ch'eng and discussions of his works, see Demiéville, "Récents travaux sur Touen-houang," pp. 47–62; Mimaki, "*Daijō muryōju shūyō kyō*," pp. 167–72; Ueyama, "Daiban-koku daitoku sanzō hōshi shamon hōjō no kenkyū"; and Wu, "Daibankoku daitoku sanzō hōshi hōjō den ko."

31. P 2130 contains histories and prayers concerning the Pure Land as well as the visualization text *Kuan-fo san-mei hai ching*. The latter is by Buddhabhadra (359–429), printed as *T* no. 643.

32. S 4160, entitled *Ssu-fen lü lüeh-sung*, is an abstract of the *Ssu-fen lü (Dharma-guptavinaya)* in five-syllable verse. Giles classifies it under "Uncanonical Vinaya Texts"; Giles, *Catalogue*, no. 5495.

33. The manuscript is S 1635, also printed as *T* no. 2861. Entitled *Ch'üan-chou ch'ien-fo hsin-chu chu-tsu-shih sung*, the text was written by Hsing-teng (fl. 951–959). On the authorship of this text, see Yabuki, *Meisha yoin kaisetsu*, 1:249–50, 2:530–33.

34. The manuscript is P 2193, entitled *Mu-lien yüan-ch'i*.

35. The text is Th Institute 322, reprod. and transcr. Wu, "Tun-huang shih-k'u la-pa jan-teng fen-p'ei k'u-k'an ming-shu." Its title is partially effaced; it

pa hui (roughly, "Assembly on the Eighth of the Exorcism Month"), held to commemorate the Buddha's achieving enlightenment. The festival, usually observed on the eighth day of the twelfth month, saw a variety of celebrations across China that brought together monks and lay people.[36] The members of the tour were all members of a local Buddhist "society" *(she)*, a confraternity of lay people drawn from a number of families who convened on a regular schedule, usually under the supervision of a monk.

Tao-chen's leadership of a group of lay persons may have been part of his official duties. In 952 he was Rectifier of the Clergy (Seng-cheng). Beginning in the mid-ninth century in Tun-huang the persons occupying this position in each monastery were responsible for administering the daily life of their temple. They arranged monastic schedules, welcomed visitors, led rituals, and so forth. In 987 Tao-chen had risen to the rank of Chief Recorder of the Clergy (Tu seng-lu), but this position, probably in keeping with his advanced age, was largely ceremonial.[37]

As his seniority increased, Tao-chen's contacts with people outside the monastery did not subside. Tao-chen is identified as the officiating monk, Precept Master (Shou-chieh shih-chu), in over twenty "precept certificates" *(chieh-tieh)* dated between 964 and 987.[38] The certificates

---

reads *Shih-erh yüeh pa-jih . . . she-jen pien-k'u jan-teng fen-p'ei k'u-k'an ming-shu* (A Numerical Listing of the Grottoes and Niches Seen by Members of the Society on Their Tour of the Grottoes with Lamps Distributed . . . on the Eighth Day of the Twelfth Month). At the end the text mentions the date *hsin-hai*/XII/7 and refers to "the *śramaṇa* Tao-chen, Rectifier of the Clergy [*Seng-cheng*]." Chin suggests 1011 for the *hsin-hai* year ("Tun-huang k'u-k'an ming-shu k'ao," p. 54), but unless there were two monks who ranked high in the Tun-huang Saṃgha within a span of sixty years, 952 is a more reasonable date. If Tao-chen was roughly twenty years old in 934, then he would have been close to ninety-seven in 1011. Also, as will be discussed more fully below, Tao-chen appears to have remained Rectifier of the Clergy until 987, when he occupied the higher post of Chief Recorder of the Clergy (Tu seng-lu), and it is extremely unlikely that the lower rank of Rectifier would have been used anachronistically.

36. For a survey of opinions on the date of the festival, see *Ta-sung seng-shih lüeh*, Tsan-ning (919–1001), *T* no. 2126, 54:236a. In some areas movement went in the opposite direction: monks were invited to the homes of lay people, where they engaged in ritual bathing to commemorate Śākyamuni's use of water to vanquish and then purify his enemies; see *Fa-yüan chu-lin*, Tao-shih (d. 683), *T* no. 2122, 53:543a.

37. For the administration of the clergy in tenth-century Tun-huang, I follow Chikusa, "Tonkō no sōkan seido," pp. 156–61, 161–71.

38. The place of precept certificates *(chieh-tieh)* in lay Buddhist practice is still poorly understood. Both traditional accounts and modern scholarship group them together with "ordination certificates" *(tu-tieh)* and treat them largely as a function of the ordination of monks and nuns; see, for example, *Shih-shih chi-ku lüeh*, Chüeh-an (1226–1355), *T* no. 2037, 49:840a; Mochizuki, *Daijiten*, pp. 393b–94a; and Ch'en, "Chiao-ting sung-ch'u sha-chou chieh-tieh san-shih."

mention three grades of religious service. In the first, after coming to San-chieh ssu a lay person would receive the five precepts from Tao-chen. The five precepts (*wu-chieh*[b], Skt. *pañcaśīlāni*) of the *upāsaka* and *upāsikā* prohibit (1) killing, (2) stealing, (3) engaging in sexual misconduct, (4) lying, and (5) consuming liquor.[39] Along with taking refuge in the Three Jewels (the "Three Refuges," *san-kuei*), following the five precepts was one of the simplest forms of religious affiliation for Buddhist householders. After repeating each precept three times, saying prayers, and receiving written certification of the act, the believer was free to put the precepts into practice on his or her own.

The second kind of certificate names eight precepts (*pa-chieh*). The eight precepts added three more abstentions to the five listed above: (6) resting on a high bed or decorated bed, (7) using make-up or hairdressing, or watching music and dance, and (8) eating at the wrong time. Lay people did not undertake this regimen on a daily basis. Rather, they followed the eight precepts for a twenty-four-hour period, on days set aside in the Buddhist calendar for ritual purity. Most commonly such days of *chai*—as much feast as they were fast—were the eighth, fourteenth, fifteenth, twenty-third, twenty-ninth, and thirtieth of each month.[40] Participation in this ceremony marked a more specialized and intensified practice of Buddhism, regularized by the lunar cycle and supervised by a high-ranking monk.

In the third kind of precept certificate Tao-chen administered Bodhi-

---

Several interesting facts emerge from the discussion below and the documentation in appendix 13. Precept certificates were given to lay people as well as to monks. They were often given to the same person more than once, when a ceremony was repeated on the Buddhist feast days. Some certificates must have remained in the possession of the officiating monk, which raises the possibility that the recipients were given their own copy. This hypothesis is strengthened by the appearance on many precept certificates of xylographic seals, which were often used to authenticate multiple copies of official documents. Some of the seals picture Buddhist deities; see Séguy, "Images xylographiques conservées dans les collections de Touen-houang de la Bibliothèque nationale." Some of the seals contain the name and office-title of the officiating monk; see, for example, S 3798, reprod. Huang, *Pao-tsang,* 31:445b.

39. On the five precepts, see *Yu-p'o-sai chieh ching,* Dharmakṣema (385–433), *T* no. 1488, 24:1047a–50b, enumerated on 1048a; *Fa-yüan chu-lin,* Tao-shih (d. 683), *T* no. 2122, 53:926c–31b; and Mochizuki, *Daijiten,* pp. 1118c–20b.

40. The eight precepts (*pa-chieh*) go by several other names, including *pa-chai-chieh* (Skt.: *aṣṭâṅga-samanvāgatôpavāsa*) and *pa-kuan-chai.* My listing of them here follows their enumeration in early sources: *Chai ching,* Chih Ch'ien (fl. 220–252), *T* no. 87; *Ch'ih-chai ching,* in *Chung a-han ching (Madhyamāgama), T* no. 26 (202), 1:770a–73a; *Yu-p'o-i to-she-chia ching,* anon. (ca. 420–479), *T* no. 88; and *Pa-kuan-chai ching,* Chü-ch'ü Ching-sheng (fl. 457–464), *T* no. 89. See also *Fa-yüan chu-lin, T,* 53:931b–35c. For modern studies, see Michihata, *Chūgoku bukkyō shisō shi no kenkyū,* pp. 380–94; Mochizuki, *Daijiten,* pp. 4207b–08c; and Tsuchihashi, "Sutain shūshū no ju hassai kaigi ni tsuite."

sattva precepts *(p'u-sa chieh)* to a recipient. The notion of "Bodhisattva precepts" (or "Mahāyāna precepts," *ta-sheng chieh*) has a long and complicated history in Mahāyāna Buddhism, and in medieval China there were several competing definitions of the idea.[41] The specific Bodhisattva precepts mentioned most commonly in precept certificates from Tun-huang are ten in number.[42] The first five are the abstentions of lay Buddhists noted above. The second five involve abstaining from (6) speaking of others' sins, (7) praising oneself and blaming others, (8) greed, (9) anger, and (10) slandering the Three Jewels. This listing follows precisely the explanation of Bodhisattva precepts contained in one of the most important guides to Chinese Buddhist practice, the apocryphal *Scripture of Brahmā's Net.* That text states explicitly that religious and lay alike should receive the Bodhisattva precepts. Judging from the names of the recipients recorded on the certificates and the absence of monastic titles like *bhikṣu* and *śramaṇa,* Tao-chen probably bestowed the precepts only on lay persons.

This section began with the suggestion that although they may have been created in a Buddhist scriptorium and were ultimately shelved in the library of San-chieh ssu, two copies of *The Scripture on the Ten Kings* may well have been lodged outside the monastery for part of their existence. They made their way into the storehouse of San-chieh ssu because of the quest—undertaken formally, with prayers, as an act of devotion—on the part of a monk named Tao-chen. Early in his monastic career, when his aspirations were still intertwined with the fortunes of his family, Tao-chen frequently left the monastery to search for holy texts in the secular world. When he rose to high position in the Buddhist Order he still maintained close ties with the society outside the temple walls. In addition to regulating the life of monks, he conducted tours of the local sacred places for organized lay groups and initiated lay people into the same elementary system of morality on which *The Scripture on the Ten Kings* was based.

41. My account follows the system described in *Fan-wang ching,* anon. (ca. 431–481), *T* no. 1484, 24:1004a–05a, which lists the ten precepts and stipulates that monks, nuns, and lay people recite them in confession twice monthly. See also de Groot, *Le code du Mahāyāna en Chine,* pp. 32–40, 207–56; and Ishida, *Bommō kyō,* pp. 69–126. Some sources define the Bodhisattva precepts as the ten precepts taken by novices, on which see the discussion in chapter 11, n. 8. Other sources expand greatly on the categorization and theology of the precepts from a Mahāyāna perspective. For a traditional account, see *P'u-sa ti-ch'ih ching (Bodhisattvabhūmi),* Dharmakṣema (385–433), *T* no. 1581, 30:910a–18b. Modern studies include Demiéville, "Bosatsukai"; Michihata, *Chūgoku bukkyō no kenkyū,* pp. 84–166; idem, *Chūgoku bukkyō shisō shi no kenkyū,* pp. 326–80; Mochizuki, *Daijiten,* pp. 3253b–55a, 2218c–21c; Satō, *Chūgoku bukkyō ni okeru kairitsu no kenkyū,* pp. 299–435; Tsuchihashi, "Tonkōbon ju bosatsu kaigi kō"; and idem, "Tonkōbon ni mirareru shuju no bosatsu kaigi: sutain bon o chūshin to shite."

42. See, for example, S 2851, reprod. Huang, *Pao-tsang,* 24:80b; precepts discussed in Giles, "Dated Chinese Manuscripts in the Stein Collection," part 3, p. 20.

14. The Making of The Scripture on the Ten Kings

THE PREVIOUS SECTIONS offer details about the size and shape of surviving manuscripts as well as the lives and motivations of those who commissioned copies. In concluding this part I ask what the study of textual materials can contribute to our knowledge of the religious and cultural background to *The Scripture on the Ten Kings*.

The composition and binding of *The Scripture on the Ten Kings* demonstrate in the first place that the history of the Chinese book followed no single, invariant line of development. In tenth-century Tun-huang the scripture was produced in a variety of formats. *The Scripture on the Ten Kings* was bound as a scroll and as a booklet, it was produced with illustrations and without them, and it came in sizes longer than a table and small enough to fit in a pocket. This finding corroborates a point made recently by other scholars, that although general trends may be identified in the history of Chinese bookmaking, in real life numerous forms of the book—including handwritten paper scrolls, handwritten bound booklets, and even printed booklets—existed in the same time and place.[1]

One might hypothesize that corresponding to a diversity in format was a wide range of settings in which the text was used. Scrolls containing pictures and hymns were most readily used in a congregational setting, perhaps carried by an officiating priest to a mourning family. Their hymns were easily sung in unison. Their pictures supplemented the message of the text with entertainment for all and education for the untutored. The scrolls and booklets containing only prose and chants were probably not intended for viewing by such a broad audience. They served as props for monks who recited the story and chanted the *gāthās* at services. The larger booklets were particularly well suited to this setting; it was convenient to flip their pages while chanting. Like the *Diamond* sūtra with which many were bound, they were "to be held in the hand and chanted Brahmin-style."[2] Owing to its size, the one surviving

1. See Drège, "Les cahiers des manuscrits de Touen-houang"; and Ch'ang, "T'ang-tai t'u-shu hsing-chih te yen-pien." I am grateful to Robert Hymes for bringing this general point to my attention in commenting on an early draft of Teiser, "The Growth of Purgatory."
2. "To be held in the hands and chanted Brahmin-style" *(ch'ih-ching fan-yin)* are the words placed as a title (or stage direction) to a set of five-syllable chants preceding the text of a *Diamond* sūtra bound in booklet format; Cft xi.001–2, reprod. Whitfield, *Art*, 2: fig. 98. The last chant is corrupt, containing only four syllables.

152

example of a tiny booklet of *The Scripture on the Ten Kings* was probably not used as a prop in a public performance. In an earlier section I surmised that it was used by a monk studying in private for memorial rites he performed in public, but it could have also satisfied the needs of a pious lay person and, at the same time, served primarily a talismanic function. Whether or not these hypotheses are accepted, the undeniable variety in format complicates the easy scholarly opinion that assigns a purely collective function to scrolls and an exclusively personal function to booklets.[3]

Related to the coexistence of a range of formats is the flexible relationship between format and text. In scrolls *The Scripture on the Ten Kings* is presented in short, medium, and long recensions, both with and without illustrations. In booklets usually the short recension is copied, but the tiny booklet contains the long recension. There is some consistency —excluding the frontispiece—in the correlation of pictures with hymns. Yet here too there is an exception: in one scroll the illustrations for *The Scripture on the Ten Kings* are placed too close together for any words to be included.[4]

The evidence discussed in Part One of this study proved that the ideas, texts, and images of the ten kings circulated throughout China in the tenth century. The findings of Part Two, however, are rooted in the surviving manuscripts of *The Scripture on the Ten Kings,* all of which come from Tun-huang. Hence although the reign of the ten kings and the importance of holding memorial rituals in medieval China cannot be subject to doubt, it is reasonable to question whether or not the conclusions about the production of *The Scripture on the Ten Kings* are limited to Northwest China.

3. Drège ("Les cahiers des manuscrits," p. 28) summarizes the standard view, which distinguishes sharply between the collective nature of scrolls and the entirely private function of booklets: "The relatively small number of booklets in comparison to that of scrolls in the tenth century indicates that in this period this new form is still far from having eliminated the scroll, at least at Tun-huang: the booklet, an item of personal use, was indispensable at first for the exclusive gain of the individual, serving in reality as a breviary or prompt [*aide-mémoire*], whereas the scroll maintains its collective role as an item of the library."

4. The scroll containing illustrations but not the text of *The Scripture on the Ten Kings* is Cft cii.001, reprod. Whitfield, *Art,* 2: pl. 63; and P 4523, reprod. Huang, *Pao-tsang,* 133:365b–68b. Although none of the *Ten Kings* booklets contains illustrations, other texts bound as booklets do. Some are drawn in ink by hand, some are polychromes, and others are printed monotones. See, for example, S 6983 (Kuan-yin chapter of the *Lotus* sūtra), reprod. Huang, *Pao-tsang,* 54:219b–39b; P 3136 (three texts), reprod. Huang, *Pao-tsang,* 126:381b–85a; P 4098 (*Diamond* sūtra), reprod. Huang, *Pao-tsang,* 133:128a–32a; and P 4578 (*Diamond* sūtra), reprod. Huang, *Pao-tsang,* 133: 518a–31.

In terms of materials the evidence from Tun-huang is largely, but not
entirely, consistent with the rest of China. The paper scroll remained
the dominant form of the book throughout medieval China. Judging
from T'ang dynasty evidence, the catalogues of Japanese monks, and
the accounts of Sung dynasty writers, the booklet style of binding, with
thread or glue, was not limited to Tun-huang.[5] What is unusual about
the Tun-huang specimens is the high proportion of *booklets* of *The Scripture on the Ten Kings* to *scrolls* of *The Scripture on the Ten Kings*.[6] Booklets
constitute about 1 percent (roughly 400/40,000) of all Tun-huang manuscripts, but booklets of *The Scripture on the Ten Kings* comprise over 25
percent (9/32) of all surviving manuscript copies of *The Scripture on the
Ten Kings*. Was the format of the booklet favored for copying the *Ten
Kings* scripture in other parts of China as well, or were there local reasons for the relatively large percentage of *Ten Kings* booklets in Tun-
huang? Was the booklet format used for copying large numbers of other
texts that by historical accident do not survive? The other peculiarity of
the *Ten Kings* manuscripts, like most texts produced in the economically
isolated region of Tun-huang in the tenth century, is that they were written with a wooden pen.

Turning now from the books to the people who produced them, several conclusions of a sociological nature are possible. Here too we must
maintain a critical attitude toward the sources, asking in each case what
they reveal that is general to medieval China and what is particular to
Tun-huang.

The relevant peculiarities may be summarized as follows. As Gernet
and others have shown, the Buddhist temples of Tun-huang were great
centers of commercial activity as well as religious institutions offering a
variety of services. The economic draw upon the surrounding town
exerted by temples, however, was probably stronger in Tun-huang than
in other parts of China. Due to intensive irrigation, frequent division of
lands, higher prices, and the cultivation of corn and hemp, Tun-huang
temples had a relatively large number of grain mills and oil presses. The
ratio of monks and nuns to the general population in Tun-huang was
also greater than that in most Chinese cities. During the period of

5. See Fujieda, *Moji no bunka shi,* pp. 191–92; and Ch'ang, "T'ang-tai t'u-
shu hsing-chih te yen-pien," pp. 215–18.
6. The statistics may be misleading. The number of extant medieval manuscripts produced outside of Tun-huang is relatively small, and we are still
unclear about the proximate origins of the manuscripts sealed behind T(?)h
Cave 17. The Tun-huang manuscripts originated in the libraries of two or more
temples, yet the corpus also contains government documents and many works
that were once privately owned. For an assessment of the constitution of the
"library," see Fujieda, "Une reconstruction de la 'bibliothèque' de Touen-
houang."

Tibetan rule (782–848) there were twelve or thirteen temples in Tun-huang. In the period of rule by military commandery (848–1035) between sixteen and eighteen temples operated at any one time. During these 250 years the number of monks and nuns living in temples ranged between 1,000 and something over 1,400, while the registered population of the region of Sha-chou (present-day Tun-huang) fluctuated between 10,000 and 20,000. Just the bare fact of a relatively large proportion of monks and nuns in Tun-huang does not, however, lead to any definitive conclusions. Associated with the Buddhist temples of Tun-huang were a large number of Buddhist lay groups. These "societies" *(she)* met at temples on a regular schedule. Many, it is interesting to note, were organized specifically for the purpose of helping members defray the cost of funerals for family members. Thus, although the numbers would indicate that monks and nuns exercised a strong influence in Tun-huang religion and society, the flourishing of Buddhist lay societies at Tun-huang suggests that the activities of lay people or common folk were, if not fully independent of monastic control, at least vigorous in their own right.[7]

Evidence about commissioners and collectors suffers from another prejudice, Tun-huang's unusual geographical position.[8] As a portal for trade between China and regions westward, Tun-huang (the very name of which may derive from an Iranian term) had always been home to a colorful array of cultures, Eastern and Western. The Tibetan rule of northwestern China as a whole left a clearly discernible imprint upon social and religious life in Tun-huang, but most scholars view the long period that followed as a renaissance of Chinese practice, especially

7. The generalizations in this paragraph are based on Fujieda's definitive study of registers of monks and nuns at Tun-huang; see Fujieda, "Tonkō no sōni seki." Other important studies of the institutional history of Tun-huang temples during the eighth, ninth, and tenth centuries include Chiang, *T'ang wu-tai tun-huang ssu-hu chih-tu;* Chikusa, "Tonkō no jiko ni tsuite"; idem, "Tonkō no sōkan seido"; Čuguevskiĭ, "Touen-houang du VIIIe au Xe siècle"; Fujieda, "Shashū kigigun setsudoshi shimatsu," part 4, pp. 92–93; idem, "Toban shihaiki no tonkō"; Gernet, *Les aspects économiques du bouddhisme dans la société chinoise du Ve au Xe siècle;* Naba, "Bukkyō shinkō ni motozukite soshiki seraretaru chūbantō godai jidai no shayū ni tsukite"; idem, "Ryōko kō"; idem, "Tōdai no shayū ni tsukite"; Tohi, "Kigigun jidai"; Twitchett, *Financial Administration under the T'ang Dynasty,* esp. pp. 6–9; idem, "The Monasteries and China's Economy in Medieval Times"; idem, "Monastic Estates in T'ang China"; and Yamaguchi, "Toban shihai jidai."

8. Studies on the cultural geography of Tun-huang include Aldrich, "Tun-huang: The Rise of the Kansu Port in The T'ang Dynasty"; Ch'en, "Chung-shih tun-huang yü ch'eng-tu chih chien te chiao-t'ung lu-hsien"; Enoki, *Tonkō no rekishi, passim;* Kanaoka, *Tonkō no bungaku,* pp. 3–7; Mair, "Reflections on the Origins of the Modern Standard Mandarin Place-Name 'Dunhuang' "; and idem, *T'ang Transformation Texts,* esp. pp. 1–8.

in the institutional history of Chinese Buddhism. After 848, writing
brushes from central and southern China may have been hard to obtain
in Tun-huang, but texts and ideas were not. Contacts were especially
strong with Szechwan, which, spurred by the moving of the capital to
Ch'eng-tu between 881 and 885, was never free of influence from the
metropolitan cultures of the central plain.

With these limitations in mind, what can be said about the people
who commissioned and collected *The Scripture on the Ten Kings*? Recog-
nizing that the definition of "class" in premodern China is a notoriously difficult enterprise,[9] I would prefer to employ more concrete categories like wealth, family background, access to government power,
education and literacy, and relationship to organized religion. Because
it cost some money—how much, we do not know—to order the copying
of a book, we may assume that all commissioners of *The Scripture on the
Ten Kings* had at least some cash to spare. The farmer who dedicated
merit to his plowing ox and the ailing but otherwise undistinguished
nun named Miao-fu may have had the least wealth of all the commissioners in our sample. At the high end of the economic scale are the
commissioner Chai Feng-ta, who also ranks highly in the registers of literacy and government power, and the collector Tao-chen, who seems to
have come from one of the older, more powerful families in Tun-huang.

Three people participated actively in Chinese literary culture. Chai
was a student and later a teacher in the local school, he read widely in
secular and Buddhist sources, and he composed poetry and works of
geography and hagiography. The old man of eighty-five copied some
texts himself and was conversant in Buddhist philosophy. Tao-chen was
involved not only in the copying of texts but in the repair of writing
materials and the collection of bookcases.

Sponsors of *The Scripture on the Ten Kings* maintained a variety of affili-
ations with organized religion. Two were unquestionably clerics, Miao-
fu and Tao-chen. Taking the tonsure and vows of celibacy, however, in
no way precluded contact with the world outside the monastery. Com-
ings and goings with the lay world are especially well documented in the
case of Tao-chen. As a young monk he left San-chieh ssu frequently to
canvass the town for donations of books. Evidence shows that when he
rose to ranks of high position within the Saṃgha, members of the community frequently sought his instruction and blessing in Buddhist
morality. Although he was not a monk, Chai Feng-ta was an ardent—
though not necessarily exclusive—supporter of lay Buddhist projects,
including the propagation of the *Diamond* sūtra. We must be frank in

9. On the complications, both evidential and theoretical, of defining social
class in premodern China, see Johnson, "Communication, Class, and Consciousness in Late Imperial China."

admitting that the social position and religious affiliation of the other, anonymous commissioners of *The Scripture on the Ten Kings* are simply beyond our ken. It is true that references to the sickness of mothers and fathers recur in many of these unsigned dedications, but such concerns were shared equally, and acted upon, by clerics and lay people.[10]

Because of the wealth of information preserved in dedications to *The Scripture on the Ten Kings,* it is possible to specify rather precisely the style of Buddhism practiced by commissioners of the text. The prayers and scriptures in the decalogue that Chai Feng-ta dedicated to his wife between 958 and 960 provide the most integrated portrait of medieval Chinese religion. The kind of Buddhism reflected in them provided an analysis of the ills of human existence and a prescription for their cure. Yet this Buddhism was neither abstract nor sectarian, it did not focus on the concepts of emptiness or no-self, and it did not propound meditation. While it did not negate any of these trends in what may be termed "canonical Buddhism," nevertheless its concerns were elsewhere. It was interested in impermanence, a concept most readily taught by equipping people to deal with the passing of loved ones. It provided an all-encompassing world view in which to make sense of death. Its preachers referred often to morality and the workings of retribution and told stories about how Buddhas and other enlightened beings of the past were able to formulate a salvation that accepted human loss. This style of Buddhism enlisted the aid of powerful Bodhisattvas to protect the unsuspecting from danger. It saw potential misfortune everywhere. Its mythology tended to demonize the world by revealing the terrifying names of invading pathogens and the spiritual etiology of common physical complaints. It also attempted to sanctify the world by offering an arsenal of chants and other specialized techniques for getting rid of bad luck.[11] If the texts dedicated to Chai's wife are representative, this version of Buddhism showed a sensitivity to the worries of women in medieval China: successful childbirth, protecting children from illness or possession, and the salvation of mothers. Yet for all of its emphasis on a clear vision of gloom, it still remained hopeful, never failing to hold open the prospect of rebirth in heaven.

Taken as a whole, the prayers of the other commissioners of the *Ten Kings* text seem internally inconsistent: in an altruistic dedication of merit to enemies there is also a desire for one's own long life. Such

10. At least some monks followed closely the example of Mu-lien. Tunhuang manuscripts preserve several prayers for the salvation of mothers: S 1823, reprod. Huang, *Pao-tsang,* 13:636a–38a; S 5565, reprod. Huang, *Pao-tsang,* 43:450a–51b; and P 2697, dated 935, reprod. Huang, *Pao-tsang,* 123:355a–58; the author of the last is identified as the monk Shao-tsung.

11. On the central role of apotropaic techniques in medieval Chinese religion, see Strickmann, "Magical Medicine."

apparently contradictory motivations, however, find a reasonable place within the plural and intellectually rigorous world of medieval Chinese Buddhism. At one end of the continuum of this kind of Buddhism are the wishes expressed most frequently in the anonymous dedications to *The Scripture on the Ten Kings*. The commissioners of these copies prayed for the relief of their ancestors, whose sufferings were brought to life in the scripture. They also sought long life, good health, and money for themselves, great glory, the birth of sons, and wealth for their families, the remission of sins for their enemies, and an equal salvation, without discrimination, for animals. If undertaken with the proper intention— not an easy task in any religious system—these vows were the perfect expression of the formless, selfless, wishless philosophy of Mahāyāna Buddhism. The complementarity of these two kinds of prayer is perhaps most evident in the dedications of the old man of eighty-five. He argued that the doctrine of emptiness makes invalid any attempt to gain enduring advantage for a permanent self. That recognition was expressed, no less rigorously, in the ritual copying of the *Ten Kings* scripture for the benefit of his own impermanent frame.

The word "ritual," used as both noun and adjective, has cropped up numerous times in this study of colophons. In the final paragraphs of this section I will argue that the production of manuscript copies of *The Scripture on the Ten Kings* was a process saturated by ritual. So stated, of course, the argument says both too much and too little. "Ritual" not only is too bulky, but also carries its own set of obfuscations because of its consistently polemical usage in recent Western cultural history. Short of the sustained attention such a subject requires, I will explicate the production of manuscripts not in terms of "ritual" in general—whatever that may be—but in terms of the functions and formal characteristics attributed by various analysts to ritual.[12]

The copying of texts by scribes may be labeled "ritual" in the sense that it was a repetitive activity governed by formal rules, the authority of which could not be questioned. The training of scribes through the writing of copies indoctrinated students into the linguistic system, gov-

12. The term "ritual" has almost always served to mask illicit distinctions between the rational and the irrational or between the sacred and the profane. Aside from a few recent starts, it has never been the subject of systematic comparison to the more sophisticated Chinese tradition, spanning three millennia, of reflection on *li* (loosely, "ritual"). The history of the term "ritual" is ably summarized in Leach, "Ritual"; and Bell, *Ritual Theory, Ritual Practice*. Attempts to examine Chinese thinking about ritual in a comparative perspective include Bell, "Ritualization of Texts and Textualization of Ritual in the Codification of Taoist Liturgy"; Campany, "Xunzi and Durkheim as Theorists of Ritual Practice"; and Radcliffe-Brown, "Religion and Society." In the following paragraphs I use several terms from Hsün-tzu's chapter on ritual, "Li-lun"; see *Hsün-tzu chi-chieh*, pp. 231–51.

erned by calligraphy, grammar, and traditional authority, of literary Chinese.[13]

Instances of commissioning *The Scripture on the Ten Kings* resemble acts of ritual in several ways. Chai Feng-ta's sponsorship of ten scriptures in memory of his deceased wife conforms to the paradigm of a rite of passage. As I argued earlier, the commissioning of the texts was not subsidiary to a more important ritual. Rather, it was the act of dedicating the scriptures that effected the passage of Chai's wife from the threatening condition of the recently deceased to a secure resting place in heaven. The reproduction of the text both honored her elevation to a new status and protected her descendants from any wrath they feared she might inflict if she were abandoned. The act of commissioning a text curbed the unbridled outpouring of emotion at the same time as it enabled mourning. Through it both Mrs. Ma and her descendants were transformed. The surviving manuscript of *The Scripture on the Ten Kings* is an artifact of her family's devotion and a proof of her salvation.

Several people obeyed the sūtra's instructions by ordering copies of the *Ten Kings* scripture in preparation for their own demise. Miao-fu originally commissioned seven copies, Hsüeh followed the directions to hold preparatory sacrifices twice each month, while the old man of eighty-five had at least three copies made over a period of five months late in his life. Such actions can be said to have brought a certain satisfaction, supporting or nourishing their anxieties about death by modulating their lives according to a regular pattern. The sponsoring of services for one's own future salvation was part of standard Buddhist morality, since any action was undertaken in a world governed by the law of cause-and-effect.

Other functions are apparent in other subscriptions to *The Scripture on the Ten Kings*. The man who prayed for the salvation of his plowing ox, for example, acted out of a sense of interspecies harmony. The "social solidarity" posited by functionalist theory was certainly part of many acts of commissioning too. In light of the curing of illness and insuring of longevity mentioned frequently in prayers, many patrons of the *Ten Kings* text sought the defeat of sickness and the explanation of uncertainty.

The Scripture on the Ten Kings was produced within a system of exchange that was not without its own ritual aspects. That system was founded upon the differentiation of Chinese society into a small group of religious virtuosi and a larger world of lay people. In commissioning the copying of a text, lay people contributed material goods, while the

---

13. Studies on the institutions and cultural significance of the production of manuscripts in the west are voluminous. For two rather different approaches, see Bischoff, *Latin Palaeography;* and Goldberg, *Writing Matter.*

monastic institution supplied the literary tools and the spiritual aid. Each class performed its own duties in producing the text, thus maintaining the distinctions so crucial to medieval society. The commissioning and copying of religious texts allowed religious and lay alike to fulfill their socioreligious obligations.

Produced through a multiplication of ritual functions, *The Scripture on the Ten Kings* in turn produced its own rituals. My best guess is that the finished texts were taken from their shelves in monastery libraries to be unrolled by a head priest or chanted by a chorus of monks in funerals and memorial services. The duties of Buddhist monks were defined partly as the performance of useful services for the larger community. Memorial services were assemblies that brought together the kin and friends of the deceased—as well as renouncers and the households those renouncers had left behind—to face a common challenge.

If the production of *The Scripture on the Ten Kings* was characterized by many of the qualities ascribed to ritual—repetition, formality, authority, transition, transformation, solidarity, security, regularity, theodicy, morality, exchange, duty, hierarchy—it remains to see why. After all, the production of Chinese religious texts was hardly ever free of ritual. Many Taoist scriptures during the age of the manuscript were revealed to humans by gods and thereafter remained esoteric, their transmission hedged about by precepts and purity rules. Later, when the Buddhist and Taoist canons were reproduced primarily by wood-block printing, imperial sponsors and private donors often took advantage of the spiritual merit created by the act.[14] Two factors show what was special about the production of *The Scripture on the Ten Kings,* one doctrinal, one institutional.

The doctrines of one of the most influential strands of Mahāyāna thought in India had a profound effect on the dissemination of Buddhist texts and teachings in China. From the earliest layers of Prajñā-pāramitā literature in Sanskrit comes the tenet that copying or worshiping a sūtra is even more important than reading or understanding it. In the *Aṣṭasāhasrikāprajñāpāramitāsūtra* the god Śakra (i.e., Indra) asks the Buddha:[15]

---

14. On the transmission of Taoist manuscripts, see, for example, Ch'en, *Tao-tsang yüan-liu k'ao,* pp. 1–108; Robinet, *La révélation du Shangqing dans l'histoire du taoïsme;* Seidel, "Imperial Treasures and Taoist Sacraments"; Strickmann, "On the Alchemy of T'ao Hung-ching"; idem, "The Mao-shan Revelations"; idem, *Le taoïsme du Mao chan,* pp. 11–27; and Yoshioka, *Dōkyō kyōten shi ron,* pp. 1–180. On the printing of the Buddhist and Taoist canons, see, for example: Ch'en, *Tao-tsang yüan-liu k'ao,* pp. 141–248; Ono, *Bukkyō kyōten sōron,* pp. 674–979; van der Loon, *Taoist Books in the Libraries of the Sung Period,* pp. 29–63; and Yoshioka, *Dōkyō kyōten shi ron,* pp. 1–180.

15. Conze, trans. *The Perfection of Wisdom in Eight Thousand Lines and Its Verse Summary,* pp. 105, 106; translation modified by the addition of diacritical marks, italicization of foreign terms, and Americanization of British spelling.

Suppose that there are two persons. One of the two, a son or daughter of good family, has written down this perfection of wisdom, made a copy of it; he would then put it up, and would honor, revere, worship, and adore it with heavenly flowers, incense, perfumes, wreaths, unguents, aromatic powders, strips of cloth, parasols, banners, bells, flags, with rows of lamps all round, and with manifold kinds of worship. The other would deposit in *stūpas* the relics of the Tathāgata who has gone to *parinirvāṇa;* he would take hold of them and preserve them; he would honor, worship and adore them with heavenly flowers, incense, etc., as before. Which one of the two, O Lord, would beget the greater merit?

The Buddha responds:

The son or daughter of good family who has made a copy of the perfection of wisdom, and who worships it, would beget the greater merit. For by worshiping the perfection of wisdom he worships the cognition of the all-knowing.

The same idea is expressed in a variety of Chinese Buddhist texts: transcendental wisdom is most fully embodied not in the physical person of the Buddha but in texts.[16] What some scholars have called the "cult of the book" was, at least in Chinese practice, valued as highly as the cult of the Buddha, which involved the worship of the Buddha as well as the principle of enlightenment made manifest in the mummies and relics of Buddhist patriarchs.[17]

The superiority of books over bodies—formulated explicitly as a preference for unread scriptures over deceased Buddhas—had important implications for textual practice. Since its inception Mahāyāna Buddhism had always claimed to be a more inclusive, more broadly based movement than its predecessors. Many Mahāyāna sūtras claimed openly to be new revelations, the final and all-encompassing framework intended to complete, and at times to negate, earlier messages. Mahāyāna scriptures also advertised the merit to be gained from reproducing them. But note that the multiplication of a text did not entail the obligation to read it. Literacy was required only of the copyists, not the commissioners.

16. For the earliest Chinese version, see *Tao-hsing po-jo ching (Aṣṭasāhasrikāprajñāpāramitāsūtra)*, Lokakṣema (fl. 167–186), *T* no. 224, 8:430c–38a. For a partial comparison of the relevant Chinese passages with Sanskrit versions, see Lancaster, "An Analysis of the Aṣṭasāhasrikāprajñāpāramitāsūtra from the Chinese Translations," p. 83. For other references, see Mochizuki, *Daijiten,* pp. 2135b–40a.

17. For a recent reassessment of the worship of texts in early Mahāyāna Buddhism, see Schopen, "The Phrase *'sapṛthivīpradeśaś caityabhūto bhavet'* in the *Vajracchedikā.*" On the importance of relics in the Ch'an tradition, see Faure, *The Rhetoric of Immediacy,* pp. 132–78.

The production of texts is rarely free of institutional influence, which brings us to the second factor. As noted in Part One of this study, if a Buddhist text was deemed canonical, its dissemination was nearly assured. According to Fujieda, during the T'ang dynasty canonical texts were copied on a regular basis, in accordance with a clear procedure, with funding from the Buddhist church. When a new temple was established its copyists worked from master copies of canonical texts borrowed from preexisting temples. Some canonical scriptures were copied ad hoc by government order. The canons of many monasteries were refurbished periodically: when the supervision of a temple library changed hands, the old director reviewed the collection and had new copies made of any missing scrolls before retiring from office. In the beginning of the ninth century each major temple at Tun-huang maintained a scriptorium as part of its library. Each copying office employed roughly ten to twenty copyists, who were paid in tea and cloth.[18]

Texts marked as noncanonical were, of necessity, reproduced by other means. There is no evidence suggesting that any copy of *The Scripture on the Ten Kings* was produced for the library of a new temple, under government sponsorship, or as a replacement for a lost classic. *The Scripture on the Ten Kings* was excluded from every Buddhist canon ever compiled in traditional China, but that does not imply that the Buddhist church proscribed the circulation of the text. Classifying a book as apocryphal could further a multitude of interests and hide a number of motivations. The proliferation of the text clearly brought advantage to some quarter of the Buddhist establishment. Lacking the means of reproduction assured by canonical status, the replication of *The Scripture on the Ten Kings* was guaranteed by the centrality of its teachings to the cult of the dead. The rationale is inscribed in the text itself: the ritual of copying the scripture is the best means to insure safety in the realm of the ten kings.

18. I rely in this paragraph on Fujieda's analysis of the relevant documents, most of which come from Tun-huang and date from the period of Tibetan rule; see Fujieda, "Toban shihaiki no tonkō," pp. 270–76.

PART THREE

Text

HAVING EXAMINED the making of purgatory in Part One and the making of books about purgatory in Part Two, I now look more narrowly at the nature of the text of *The Scripture on the Ten Kings*. The notion of "text" as I use it here is somewhat different from "the original words of a literary work." *The Scripture on the Ten Kings* includes far more than just writing, and those portions—including pictures, songs, chants, and prayers—need to be taken just as seriously as the words of the sūtra proper. To understand the techniques employed in *The Scripture on the Ten Kings,* this part attempts to answer questions of genre, language, and vocabulary. What genres of literature and song does the text use? What is its language? From where does its vocabulary derive?

I employ three overlapping styles of analysis to answer these questions. I look first at the language and genres of the text, seeking to locate *The Scripture on the Ten Kings* within the history of Chinese Buddhist literature. Here my emphasis is on genre and grammar. Next I turn to the members of the bureaucracy described in the text, paying special attention to the portrayal of those characters in the illustrations to the scripture. I also offer some historical background to the major figures. In chapter 17 I offer an annotated translation of the long recension of *The Scripture on the Ten Kings.* I have chosen one of the surviving manuscripts as the "basic" text because it contains the fewest errors and exhibits the greatest care in its copying. But I have also gone to some length to document and discuss variants, since they too count as readings—or, since the majority of them are homophonous with the basic text, as hearings —of the text. Rather than treating the scripture genealogically with the goal of restoring it to its original form, I have used a textual (or "distributional") approach and emphasized the diversity of variants. Whenever variants are, in my opinion, meaningful, I provide a translation. The annotation concerns the meaning, diction, grammar, and history of the words of the text. The translation attempts to reflect in English the rather limited lexicon employed in the sūtra, for example, by translating *ssu* by the same root in two different expressions, *ming-ssu*, "dark offices," and *ssu-lu*, "Officer of Records." Translators of Chinese Buddhist literature have many fine examples of translation style from which to choose. My preference in this work is to strive for word-for-word felicity and a sensitivity to literary and vernacular Chinese, combined as much as possible with the demands of fluency in English.

15. Language and Genre

AN ANALYSIS OF the linguistic and generic peculiarities of *The Scripture on the Ten Kings* helps in understanding its status as an indigenous Chinese Buddhist scripture tied closely to the performance of ritual. The language of Chinese Buddhist scriptures has only recently begun to receive the close attention it deserves.[1] Unfortunately, space allows only a brief consideration of the grammatical and lexical aspects of the language of the text and its use of different genres of Buddhist literature.

The medieval text of *The Scripture on the Ten Kings* comes wrapped in liturgical language, which indicates that the story of the scripture could be told only after an audience made the proper prayers and invoked the appropriate deities. Because of their importance to the message and practice of the text, the liturgical prologue and epilogue have in this study been treated as integral elements of the scripture proper. The stage directions at the beginning refer to chanting the words of the scripture and reciting the name of Amitābha Buddha, both of which were common formats for the reading of religious texts in medieval China. Following the ending title comes the conclusion of the service, in which the audience recited four short admonitions to practice in life what the Buddha preaches in the text.

The story within the liturgy—although the "text proper" is also striated with religious songs and chants—may be assigned broadly to the genre of a Buddhist sūtra *(ching)*, and more narrowly to that of a prophecy. Like other Buddhist sūtras, the formal title of *The Scripture on the Ten Kings* includes the words "Spoken by the Buddha" *(Fo-shuo)*. In the opening phrase "Thus have I heard" *(ju-shih wo wen)*, the text rein-

1. See Mair, "Buddhism and the Rise of the Written Vernacular in China"; Ui, *Yakkyō shi kenkyū;* Wang, *Fo-tien han-i chih yen-chiu;* Zürcher, "Late Han Vernacular Elements in the Earliest Buddhist Translations"; and idem, "A New Look at the Earliest Chinese Buddhist Texts."

forces its claim to represent an oral transmission validated by tradition. Although the meaning and punctuation of this standard Buddhist opening are open to some doubt,[2] in China it was usually taken to mean that the discourse can be traced to Śākyamuni's closest disciple, Ānanda, who, after the passing of the Buddha, is supposed to have recited aloud all of the sermons he had heard from the mouth of the founder. The scripture next names the time and place of the sermon and describes the audience. The narrative is a mixture of third-person description and direct speech. Three distinct speakers are represented: the Buddha, Ānanda as interlocutor, and King Yama, who sometimes speaks on behalf of or together with the other administrators of purgatory. The story ends with a variant of the closing of many Mahāyāna sūtras, in which the Buddha reiterates the name of the scripture and entrusts it for safekeeping and propagation to a member of the audience, King Yama.

The other genre of which *The Scripture on the Ten Kings* partakes is that of the prophecy (Skt.: *vyākaraṇa;* Ch.: *shou-chi*), in this case given to King Yama. A prophecy is a prediction by a Buddha that in the future one of his congregation will attain Buddhahood. Such texts often catalogue the conditions under which the enlightenment will occur, including the time, the locale, the name of the Buddha, and lengthy descriptions of his realm and its inhabitants. Prophecies date from some of the earliest layers of Indian Buddhist literature and proliferated greatly with the rise of the Mahāyāna. Thus, although it is difficult to imagine that before the advent of Mahāyāna, Buddhist literature would depict the ruler of the dead as a Buddha-in-training, nevertheless, aside from occasional references to compassion and a minor role (in the written text) assigned to Ti-tsang Bodhisattva, the scripture betrays hardly any concern with polemical justifications of Mahāyāna teachings.

The Scripture on the Ten Kings was probably written in Chinese, but its language successfully mimics the language used in medieval Buddhist scriptures translated from Indian originals. The hallmark of Buddhist scriptural literature being its prosimetric form, we need to examine both the prose and verse portions.

Like most Buddhist texts, especially after the sūtras translated by Kumārajīva (350–409) became popular, the prose of *The Scripture on the Ten Kings* consists mostly of four-character phrases. That pattern persists in the long listing of deities at the beginning of the text and in some of the longer sentences, occasionally necessitating the use of the possessive *chih*[b] or the conjunction *chi* as padding. The language is largely monosyllabic, and there is some parallelism between consecutive phrases. Although the text is basically written in literary Chinese, some

2. See Brough, "Thus Have I Heard . . ."; and Kajiyama, "Thus Spoke the Blessed One . . ."

elements of the vernacular are present. Examples of this "Buddhist Hybrid Chinese"[3] include the use of *shih* as copula and the frequent appearance of binomes, especially verbal compounds (e.g., *shih-hsien,* "to manifest oneself as") but also nominal ones (e.g., *k'u-ch'u,* "suffering").

The specialized terminology employed in the scripture provides other clues to its literary tradition. Like other Chinese Buddhist texts, *The Scripture on the Ten Kings* adopts several different methods for indicating Sanskritic terms and proper nouns. The names for some deities are fully transliterated (e.g., the Bodhisattva named T'o-lo-ni, for Dhāraṇī); some are translated (e.g., P'u-hsien, for Samantabhadra); while others are rendered from the Sanskrit half in sound and half in sense, like Ta-fan (for Mahābrahmā, or "Great Brahmā"). Technical terms are represented both in translation in common usages like the "Three Jewels" (*san-pao,* for *triratna*) and in transliterations like *o-hsiu-lo* (for *asura*) and *hsiu-to-lo* (for *sūtra*). In these respects the language of *The Scripture on the Ten Kings* matches that of most medieval Buddhist texts.

One unusual feature of *The Scripture on the Ten Kings* is the preponderance of legal terminology. The text abounds with terms like "to settle verdicts" *(ch'u-tuan),* "to decide" *(p'an^b),* and "to determine lives and register deaths" *(ting-sheng chu-ssu).* In this respect the *Ten Kings* sūtra resembles an earlier indigenous Chinese Buddhist scripture describing purgatory, the *Ching-tu san-mei ching* (Scripture on [Bodhisattva] Ching-tu's Samādhi). This stylistic feature may have simply been a matter of vocabulary and precedent: in seeking words to describe a newly emerging system of postmortem judgment, the authors of these texts found indigenous forensic and administrative terms to have the greatest explanatory power.

The verse portions of *The Scripture on the Ten Kings* come in two distinct styles. The first is the Chinese version of the Sanskrit metrical form called *gāthā* (rendered in Chinese as *chi^b* or *ch'ieh-t'o*). The *gāthās* in *The Scripture on the Ten Kings* consist of quatrains of five syllables per line. They follow no consistent rhyme scheme, and some have no rhyme at all. Each line was chanted with a pause between the second and third words.

The second verse form, contained only in the long recension of *The Scripture on the Ten Kings,* is called in Chinese *tsan,* which I render as "hymn."[4] Because of its importance in Chinese Buddhism and its piv-

3. See especially Mair ("Buddhism and the Rise of the Written Vernacular in China," p. 3), who describes a "Buddhist Hybrid Sinitic"; and Zürcher, "Late Han Vernacular Elements in the Earliest Buddhist Translations."

4. Studies dealing with hymns as a Buddhist verse form include Bodman, "Poetics and Prosody in Early Medieval China," pp. 99–160; Ch'en, "Ssu-sheng san-wen"; Chou, "Fo-chiao tung-ch'uan tui chung-kuo yin-yün-hsüeh

otal role in this text, its history is worth examining in some detail. The term *tsan* is usually used to translate Sanskrit *stotra,* an early verse form consisting of hymns of praise addressed to deities. In China the word *tsan* included several literary forms. Jao Tsung-i explains:[5]

> The word *tsan* properly speaking means "introduction, celebration, eulogy." In Chinese literature it is applied to considerably different genres: (1) to judgments (appreciations) in prose concerning historical figures, inserted in works of history by their authors; (2) to the eulogies in verse accompanying painted portraits; (3) in religious literature to poetical pieces that are sung, with or without musical accompaniment: it is this last sense which prevails among Buddhists and Taoists.

Although the actual techniques of singing and the specific tunes are largely unknown, some details concerning medieval hymnology are contained in early sources. Hui-chiao (497–554), for instance, includes biographies of hymnodists *(ching-shih)* and preachers *(ch'ang-tao)* in his *Biographies of Eminent Monks.* He comments:[6]

> In the Indian custom, any instance of singing the words of the Law is called *pai* [derived from a Prakrit form of the Skt. root *bhan,* "to say"]. In this country the chanting of scriptures is called "turning and reading" [*chuan-tu*], and singing hymns is termed "Brahmanic *pai*" [*fan-pai*]. Previously, hymns and psalms to the various deities were sung in rhyme and accompanied on string instruments. But since the five orders[7] are different from the profane, it is fitting that a cappella tunes are considered the finest.

Known by the earlier name of *fan-pai,* hymns in the Chinese Buddhist tradition are alleged to have originated with Ts'ao Chih (192–232). Although some do survive from the Six Dynasties period, they proliferated during the T'ang dynasty and, under the names *tsan* (hymns) or *li-tsan-wen* (texts for liturgical hymns), were utilized by a broad range of

---

chih ying-hsiang," pp. 35–42; Demiéville, "Bombai"; Hirokawa, "Raisan"; Hrdličková, "The First Chinese Translations of Buddhist Sūtras and Their Place in the Development of Story-Telling"; Jao, *Airs de Touen-houang (Touen-houang k'iu),* Demiéville's French adaptation, pp. 25–44; Lévi, "Sur la récitation primitive des textes bouddhiques"; Sawada, *Bukkyō to chūgoku bungaku,* pp. 1–66, esp. pp. 2–16; Tu, *Chiao-lu yen-chiu,* pp. 147–51; and Whitaker, "Tsaur Jyr and the Introduction of *Fannbay* into China."

5. Jao, *Airs de Toung-houang,* from Demiéville's French adaptation, p. 26.

6. *Kao-seng chuan,* Hui-chiao (497–554), *T* no. 2059, 50:415b; mostly following Bodman, "Poetics and Prosody in Early Medieval China," p. 479.

7. The "five orders" *(wu-chung)* are the five categories of those who leave the family: *bhikṣu, bhikṣuṇī, śikṣamāna, śrāmaṇera,* and *śrāmaṇerikā;* see Mochizuki, *Daijiten,* p. 1207b.

Buddhist movements. They formed part of repentance liturgies and rites invoking Maitreya, and they were an important technique in the Teaching of the Three Stages *(san-chieh chiao)*. Hymns were a signficant aspect of Pure Land practice—which in T'ang China was not confined to any single Buddhist tradition—and collections of hymns were attributed to major Pure Land figures, including T'an-luan (476–542), Shan-tao (613–681), and Fa-chao (fl. 766–804). Aside from *The Scripture on the Ten Kings*, hymns dealing with purgatory and the hells do not appear to have survived into the modern period. We do, however, have a brief bibliographical note written in 594 describing a text entitled *Ti-yü tsan ching* (A Scripture of Hymns on the Underground Prisons), which was appended to the text of two scriptures. The note reveals that the hymns were written in a style different from that of the two sūtras. It states:[8] "After the scriptures there are added hymns on the underground prisons. They are not the same type as the scriptures."

As a literary genre, religious hymns vary considerably. They consist of quatrains with lines of five syllables or seven syllables, and they employ a variety of rhyme schemes. Some hymns, as do most in *The Scripture on the Ten Kings*, accompany illustrations to a text, a tradition carried on during the Sung dynasty in the genre of "illustrated hymns" *(t'u-tsan,* or "illustrations and hymns").[9] The hymns in *The Scripture on the Ten Kings* all consist of quatrains. Their rhyme scheme is consistently AABA, with varying prosodic patterns. A caesura usually comes after the first four characters in a line. In many of the stanzas about the courts of the ten kings, the first two lines recount the sufferings endured by the deceased, and the last two lines describe the measures that the living can take to alleviate them.

8. *Chung-ching mu-lu* (594), Fa-lu (d.u.) et al., *T* no. 2146, 55:137a. The scriptures placed before the hymns were extracts from *Ch'i-ch'u san-kuan ching,* An Shih-kao (fl. 148–170), *T* no. 150a. This sūtra is a collection of many small texts dealing with basic Buddhist doctrine, covering a variety of topics in epistemology, morality, charity, and meditation. It was translated into Chinese several times; see Ono, *Daijiten,* 4:333b–34d.

9. Tu *(Chiao-lu yen-chiu,* pp. 147–51) traces the connection to *t'u-tsan.* For an example of this genre, see *(Fo-kuo ch'an-shih) Wen-shu chih-nan t'u-tsan,* Wei-po (fl. 1103), Sung xylograph reproduced in Lo, *Lo Hsüeh-t'ang hsien-sheng ch'üan-chi ch'u-pien,* 18:7673–7702.

16. The Bureaucracy

ILLUSTRATED COPIES OF *The Scripture on the Ten Kings* open with the pictorial equivalent of the formula that begins all Buddhist sūtras. The first illustration (see plate 1a, page 180) is placed at the head of the text to introduce the setting in which the scripture was preached, a style of frontispiece that began in T'ang dynasty manuscripts and gained in popularity with the advent of printing. Śākyamuni is seated on a lotus in the center, his hands in the sign of preaching the law (Skt.: *dharmadeśanamudrā;* Ch.: *shuo-fa yin*). The canopy above him is suspended from two Sāla trees, which locate the scene in the city of Kuśinagara as specified in the text. Śākyamuni's two chief disciples sit at his sides, Śāriputra on the left, Maudgalyāyana on the right. To the sides of the altartable in front of Śākyamuni are the monk Tao-ming and a golden lion, both of whom Chinese folklore associated with Ti-tsang Bodhisattva. The ten kings are arrayed in two lines, seated on a low dais. They hold their hands with palms together as a sign of respect (Skt.: *añjali;* Ch.: *ho-chang*). They are undifferentiated except for the fifth, King Yama, seated top left. In the background stand four magistrates *(p'an-kuan)*, whose names are given in other cartouches as Wang, Sung, Ts'ui, and Chao. Other versions of the frontispiece shift the focus from the beginning of the story to its soteriological end, showing Ti-tsang Bodhisattva as the central figure or depicting Ti-tsang together with Kuan-yin Bodhisattva (plate 1b).

The second illustration (plate 2) consists of the six Bodhisattvas who travel from their respective realms to praise Śākyamuni. Although the text names all six of them, only the two most well known ones are easily distinguished in the picture: Ti-tsang (Kṣitigarbha), hooded, carrying a staff at top right, and Kuan-yin (Avalokiteśvara), carrying a fly-whisk at bottom right. The others are a diverse lot. Nāgārjuna (fl. 150–250) was the founder of the Mādhyamika school of philosophy in India. Ch'ang-pei (Sadāprarudita) Bodhisattva is described in early Chinese Buddhist literature as helping to spread the teachings of Prajñāpāramitā in Gandhāra.[1] Dhāraṇī Bodhisattva may have been invoked as a powerful personification of the Sanskrit-sounding syllables that confer great power on those who utter them, which were used throughout medieval Chinese Buddhism, or he may have been modeled on the figure of that

---

1. See *Tao-hsing po-jo ching (Aṣṭasahāsrikāprajñāpāramitāsūtra)*, Lokakṣema (fl. 167–186), *T* no. 224, 8:470c–74a.

name in a fifth-century source.[2] The sixth Bodhisattva, Chin-kang-tsang (Vajragarbha), is mentioned in numerous scriptures, including an important chapter of the *Hua-yen* sūtra.[3]

The Scripture on the Ten Kings is apparently the earliest source in which the six Bodhisattvas are mentioned together as a group.[4] Given their diversity—they range from the well known to the obscure, and some lack any other connections to the afterlife or the dark world—it is difficult to account for their occurrence in the *Ten Kings* sūtra. Evidence from other recensions of *The Scripture on the Ten Kings,* however, may help to place their development in a possible chronological sequence. The medium recension of the scripture contains a listing of only three bodhisattvas. The long recension adds three to that list for a total of six, and the short recension adds five more for a total of eleven (see appendix 14).

The third illustration (plate 3a) depicts the envoy, dressed in black, riding a black horse, and carrying a black banner, whom Yama promises to Śākyamuni that he will send to the home of the deceased to verify that the proper offerings are being made. Two attendants run by the messenger's side. In some versions of the picture the messenger carries a banner the shape and coloring of which are identical to those used in medieval mortuary rituals.[5]

The messenger marks a shift in both the technique and the substance of the narrative. Up until this point the story has been about King Yama and his future life. Except for the arrival of the six Bodhisattvas, the plot contains no action. The dispatch of the messenger is a clue to the audience that a new story is about to begin. The new plot concerns the progress of the dead, which is dependent on the faithfulness of the living in making offerings. The horseman clad in black connects the world of the living and the underground chambers through which the deceased is now beginning to pass. One variant (plate 3b) fills out the scene by depicting the process of verification mentioned in the next hymn: at a table strewn with scrolls, a low-ranking official looks through records—

2. See *Ta-fang-teng ta-chi ching,* Dharmakṣema (385–433), ed. Seng-chiu (fl. 586–594), *T* no. 397, 13:5b–28b.
3. See *Ta-fang-kuang fo hua-yen ching (Avataṃsakasūtra),* Buddhabhadra (359–429), *T* no. 278, 9:542a–78a.
4. Tokushi ("Kōzō," pp. 277–78) traces them to apocryphal texts describing how Ti-tsang manifests himself in each of the six paths of rebirth, but the names in the earlier sources do not match those of the six Bodhisattvas. The portrayal of Ti-tsang in the Garbhadhātu *maṇḍala* is another analogue for six figures, but the names there do not match either; see Mikkyō jiten hensankai, *Mikkyō daijiten,* p. 2314a–b.
5. See Jera-Bezard and Maillard, "Le rôle des bannières et des peintures mobiles dans les rituels du bouddhisme d'Asie centrale," esp. p. 63.

presumably those compiled by the messenger—to confirm that sacrifices have been made.

The fourth illustration (plate 4) portrays the judgment of the deceased in the court of the first king, Ch'in Kuang wang. The king sits behind a desk on which papers are stacked and signals with his right hand to the two clerks in front. To his sides stand the Boys of Good and Evil. Four sinners stand before him, without cangues, crouching out of fear and respect. At bottom right stands a virtuous woman carrying her donation of a scroll.

Ch'in Kuang wang appears for the first time in Chinese history in *The Scripture on the Ten Kings*.[6] The most likely interpretation of his name is that, like the third king, the first character is a place name and the second character functions as a descriptive personal name. In this reading, Ch'in Kuang wang means "The Great [or Extensive] King of Ch'in," or "The King Who Extends Ch'in." Ch'in was the name of a Chinese state as early as the Western Chou dynasty (as well as the name adopted by that state when it established imperial rule in 221 B.C.E.) and the dynastic name chosen by a succession of non-Chinese rulers of northern China during the years 359–394, 384–417, and 385–431.

By the time they reach the second court, shown in the fifth illustration (plates 5a, 5b), the dead entertain no hope of escape. Cangues have been placed around their necks, and they find themselves cut off from the rest of the world by mountains, which in some traditional Buddhist cosmologies were thought to separate the human continent from the regions of hell. At this juncture the dead must also cross the River Nai (Nai-ho). Underground rivers are found in several medieval Chinese accounts of the afterlife.[7] Building on this indigenous background, the River Nai was probably created by someone familiar with early Buddhist descriptions of hell. One such source enumerates ten cold hells, including a "Hell of No Recourse" *(nai-ho ti-yü),* so named because the inmates there, lacking any hope for rescue, constantly yell "No recourse!"[8] Using Nai-ho as a name for a river running through purgatory suggests that at this point in their journey, the dead despair of turn-

6. For brief studies of Ch'in Kuang wang, see Hsiao, *Tun-huang su-wen-hsüeh lun-ts'ung,* p. 191; and Mochizuki, *Daijiten,* pp. 2025c–26a. Hsiao unconvincingly cites the names of two functionaries under Feng-tu, the so-called Taoist hell, as precedents for Ch'in Kuang wang; the names are Ch'in Shih-huang and Ch'in I. Since Kuang was also used as a personal name, it is possible to render the name as "King Kuang of Ch'in."

7. See Hsiao, *Tun-huang su-wen-hsüeh lun-ts'ung,* pp. 223–24; and Lo, *Tun-huang chiang-ching pien-wen yen-chiu,* pp. 262–66.

8. See *Ch'ang a-han ching (Dīrghāgama),* trans. Buddhayaśas (fl. 408–412) and Chu Fo-nien (fl. 365), *T* no. 1, 1:125c.

ing back. The figures at the top of the picture cross at the deepest part, the female donor by bridge, the next three figures at the shallowest section, while the two figures at the bottom may have been allowed to skirt the river altogether. Drawing attention to the watery transition, the name of the second king is Ch'u-chiang wang, which might be rendered literally as "King of the First River."

The sixth illustration (plates 6a, 6b) shows the court of the third king, Sung Ti wang. Since the king himself appears somewhat undistinguished, illustrators seem to have made special efforts to embellish this scene. The fruitless protests of the sinner (plate 6a) may have evoked humor: supporting his cangue with one hand, he holds out a tablet of writing with the other, a gesture that would hardly convince a sword-wielding demon to be more gentle.

The name of the third king does not appear in earlier sources. It should probably be understood along the lines of the name of the first king: Sung was the name of a Chou dynasty state (comprising modern Honan and Kiangsu) and of a dynasty ruling southern China from 420 to 479, while Ti (literally "Imperial") would be an appropriately majestic name for a highly ranking official in purgatory.

The seventh illustration (plate 7a) complements the accompanying hymn by showing the scale of karma, one of the implements that insures the impartial administration of justice. Standing before the king in this, the fourth court, are one sinner, shown begging for mercy, and next to him one donor, carrying a scroll horizontally in his hands. Other versions add details about the process of judgment. One example (plate 7b) shows how the scale is used. Here a scroll donated by a sinner is weighed against the counterbalance. The Boys of Good and Evil stand at each side, and, given that the Boy of Evil displays his record of events to the right, opposite the prisoner's donation, one can guess that the scale will tip in favor of evil.

The name of the fourth king is Wu-kuan wang, literally "King of the Five Offices."[9] He appears as a standard member of the infernal bureaucracy in several indigenous Chinese Buddhist scriptures dating from the fifth century. One text states that he ranks just below King Yama, and that he collates all the reports on evil actions sent by lower-level functionaries.[10] Another source explains his name by specifying the "Five Offices," each supervising a specific infraction of the lay Buddhist precepts: the Officer of Butchering oversees the taking of life, the

9. For studies, see Hsiao, *Tun-huang su-wen-hsüeh lun-ts'ung*, p. 191; Mochizuki, *Daijiten*, pp. 1162–63b; Sakai, "Jūō shinkō," pp. 619–20, and Waley, *Catalogue*, p. xxviii, n. 1.
10. See *Kuan-ting ching*, Hui-chien (fl. 457), *T* no. 1331, 21:535c.

Officer of Water punishes theft, the Officer of Metal deals with fornication; the Officer of Earth administers cases of lying, and the Officer of Heaven adjudicates crimes of drunkenness.[11] Inspiration for Wu-kuan wang can be found both in indigenous Chinese sources, which call the five sense-organs the "Five Offices," and in Indian Buddhist sources.

Another tool of justice is shown in the eighth illustration (plates 8a, 8b), which shows the court of the fifth king, King Yama. A sinner who apparently entered a plea of innocent stands before the infamous karma mirror (yeh-ching, "mirror of deeds"), which displays the sinner in his previous life beating an animal.[12] Perhaps out of fear of the guards who yank on the hair of the deceased as described in the accompanying hymn, three other sinners attempt to flee, clutching at their pigtails.

King Yama may be traced to the beginnings of Indo-European civilization, where he appears with a twin sister.[13] In the earliest hymns of the Ṛg Veda, he is a benign god who cares for the dead. In Indian Buddhism he is often portrayed as a judge of the dead, and many early Chinese translations of Indian texts attempt to explain his ambiguous status as both exalted king and low-ranking being, since he too suffers below the earth. Like the word for "impermanence" (wu-ch'ang), which serves as a euphemism for death in medieval and modern Chinese, merely mentioning King Yama is another way of talking about the undergound prisons through which all people must pass. Yama is the highest ranking of the ten kings; he is often referred to as a "Son of Heaven" (T'ien-tzu) and wears the mien, the cap with jade pieces suspended from silk strings (shown here decorated with the Northern Dipper) appropriate to the rank of emperor.

The illustration of the sixth court (plate 9) proves that, as the hymn states, only an instant separates the destinies of heaven and hell. The donors in this court, whose piety is recorded in the long scroll flopping to the ground, ascend by clouds to paradise, while the evil person, his head visible just inside the walls, enters the prison to witness the punishments inflicted on people reborn there.

The name of the sixth king is Pien-ch'eng wang, which can be ren-

11. *Ching-tu san-mei ching*, translated several times during the fifth century; the version here is cited in *Ching-lü i-hsiang*, Pao-ch'ang (fl. 495–516), *T* no. 2121, 53:259b.

12. The mirror of deeds appears to be a Chinese invention; see Hsiao, *Tun-huang su-wen-hsüeh lun-ts'ung*, pp. 225–27; and Mochizuki, *Daijiten*, p. 1034a–b. It is mentioned in Chinese sources as early as the seventh century; see *Ching-hsin chieh-kuan fa*, Tao-hsüan (d. 667), *T* no. 1893, 45:819c, 823b–c.

13. The literature on Yama is voluminous. For general accounts, see Bhattacharji, *The Indian Theogony*, pp. 48–108; Hsiao, *Tun-huang su-wen-hsüeh lun-ts'ung*, pp. 192–99; Mochizuki, *Daijiten*, pp. 318a–20c; Osabe, "Tōdai mikkyō ni okeru Enma Ō to taisan fukun"; and Seidel, "Danda."

dered literally as "King of Transformations."[14] The name might be based on a hell described as early as the fifth century. Tales collected by Wang Yüan (424–479) note that on a trip to the dark regions one Chao T'ai entered a *shou pien-hsing ch'eng*, or "city where people receive transformed shapes." Those sent there after death are turned into various animals according to their deeds.[15] Manuscript variants and modern accounts of the ten kings often use the homophonous form Pien-ch'eng wang[b], "King of the City of Transformations," and some Sung dynasty sources refer to the king as Pien-ch'eng wang[c], or "King of the City of Pien [i.e., K'ai-feng]." Whatever the geographical implications of the name, the standard form implying simply "change" would be an appropriate description of the afterlife in both Buddhism and Taoism.

The next illustration (plate 10) is the court of T'ai-shan wang, "King of Mount T'ai," who presides over the passage of the deceased forty-nine days after death. The scene is depicted with surprisingly few flourishes, given the significance of the forty-ninth day after death in Buddhism and the importance of Mount T'ai in ancient Chinese religion. T'ai-shan wang is distinguished only by the small canopy floating over his head. Four sinners advance toward him, the second one from the top perhaps waving to his loved ones, as mentioned in the hymn.

The King of Mount T'ai is of unmistakably Chinese origin, since Mount T'ai (in modern Shantung) was recognized as the seat of the administration of the dead even before the Han dynasty.[16] The register of life and death was believed to be kept there, and the *hun* and *p'o* spirits of the deceased gathered there after death. With the translation of Buddhist sūtras into Chinese beginning in the first centuries of the Common Era, "Mount T'ai" (T'ai-shan) was often used to translate the Sanskrit term for hell *(naraka)*.

The eleventh illustration (plate 11a) marks the passage of one hundred days. The scene in this version is relatively spare. At top two donors carry a banner and a statue, a clerk unrolls his records, and three sinners are led—one by his hair—before the king. Other versions (plate 11b) include a sinner wearing a special cangue consisting of a round wooden collar from which hangs a heavy metal ball. The device

14. For brief studies, see Hsiao, *Tun-huang su-wen-hsüeh lun-ts'ung,* pp. 190–91; Mochizuki, *Daijiten,* p. 4534a; and Pelliot, Review of Waley, *Catalogue,* pp. 388–89.

15. See *Ming-hsiang chi,* collated in Lu, *Ku hsiao-shuo kou-ch'en,* pp. 378–79; trans. Kao, ed., *Classical Chinese Tales of the Supernatural and the Fantastic,* pp. 169–70.

16. On Mount T'ai, see Chavannes, *Le T'ai chan;* Hsiao, *Tun-huang su-wen-hsüeh lun-ts'ung,* pp. 195–99; and Sakai, "Taisan shinkō no kenkyū."

is called a *ch'ien^b*, which classical sources prescribe for restraining criminals, animals, and slaves.

The king administering the one-hundred-day mark is P'ing-teng wang, the "Uniform" or "Impartial" King.[17] Medieval sources give P'ing-teng wang a number of identities. The most likely explanation is that P'ing-teng wang in the system of the ten kings was based on an epithet for King Yama, namely, "the impartial one" (Skt.: *samatā*, Ch.: *p'ing-teng*), an apt quality for the foremost judge of the dead.[18] T'ang dynasty Tantric texts identify P'ing-teng wang as a manifestation of Ti-tsang Bodhisattva,[19] while Manichaean texts from the same period place a P'ing-teng wang as one of twelve underworld judges.[20] Although his origin in the mythology of King Yama is the most likely historical scenario, in many contexts, including *The Scripture on the Ten Kings,* he functions as an independent figure in his own right.[21]

The twelfth illustration (plate 12) shows the court of the ninth king, through which the deceased passes one year or thirteen months after death. A sinner, freed from the cangue, clasps his hands in respect before the king. Two donors stand at top left. The streams of clouds appearing here are an allusion to the six paths mentioned in the hymn, although by law they are accessible only from the tenth court.

The ninth king is called Tu-shih wang, literally "King of the Capital" or "King of the Market of the Capital."[22] Pelliot suggests that the market-place of a capital city is a natural location for a prison, since markets were the site for public executions. It is more likely that Tu-shih wang was modeled on older names for underground officials that included the word "capital" *(tu^b)* in their title. One fifth-century Chinese Buddhist apocryphon, for instance, refers to Tu-yang wang and Tu-kuan wang.[23]

17. For studies, see Hsiao, *Tun-huang su-wen-hsüeh lun-ts'ung,* p. 190; Mochizuki, *Daijiten,* pp. 4361c–62a; Sakai, "Jūō shinkō," pp. 620–24; and Waley, *Catalogue,* p. xxviii.

18. See *I-ch'ieh ching yin-i,* Hui-lin (737–820), *T* no. 2128, 54:338c; and Nakamura, *Daijiten,* pp. 1146d–47a.

19. See *Pai-ch'ien-sung ta-chi ching ti-tsang p'u-sa ch'ing-wen fa-shen tsan,* Pu-k'ung chin-kang (705–774), *T* no. 413, 13:792b.

20. See *Mo-ni-chiao hsia-pu tsan, T* no. 2140, 54:1273c; and *Po-ssu-chiao ts'an ching, T* no. 2141b, 54:1285c; trans. Chavannes and Pelliot, "Un traité manichéen retrouvé en Chine," part 1, p. 584.

21. See, for instance, the story of Kuo Shen-liang's after-death encounter with P'ing-teng wang dated to the year 686 in *Ta-fang-kuang fo hua-yen ching kan-ying chuan,* Hui-ying (fl. 687), Hu Yu-cheng (fl. 783), *T* no. 2074, 51:175c.

22. For brief studies, see Sakai, "Jūō shinkō," p. 624; and Pelliot, Review of Waley, *Catalogue,* p. 389.

23. *Ching-tu san-mei ching,* cited in *Ching-lü i-hsiang, T* 53:259a–b. Other kings in the same list include Ch'a-tu wang, Sheng-tu wang, Hsüan-tu wang, Kao-tu wang, and Yüan-tu wang; ibid.

The thirteenth illustration (plate 13a) shows the last court, in which the dead are assigned to their next mode of life. The cloud paths shown here denote the five (sometimes six) paths of rebirth. Other versions portray the paths more clearly, using symbols to indicate gods, *asuras,* humans, beasts, hungry ghosts, and sufferers in hell. Some (plate 13b) also add a rack of animal skins to the left of the king. Presumably the king's assistants would drape the sinner with the hide appropriate to his next rebirth.

Unlike the other nine, the tenth king is a martial figure: he wears a padded military suit and a general's cap, he breathes fire, and he is accompanied by standard-bearers and club-wielding demons.[24] Army officers with similar names (e.g., Wu-tao chiang-chün wang, "General-King of the Five Paths") appear in eighth-century Tantric texts.[25] These accounts might have been building, in turn, on the name of a god mentioned in early biographies of the Buddha, Chu-wu-tao ta-shen (Great Spirit Who Rules the Five Paths) or Wu-tao shen (Spirit of the Five Paths).[26] Whatever his origins, by positioning a figure who sends the deceased back into the world of the living precisely at the end of the tenth court, *The Scripture on the Ten Kings* attempts to bring its narrative full circle.

The fourteenth illustration (plate 14a) raises the prospect of a happy conclusion to the journey through purgatory. The walls define the city of hell, the worst imaginable mode of rebirth. The sinner laid out on the iron bed is probably the person who used goods belonging to the Three Jewels (i.e., Saṃgha property) referred to in the prose portion of the scripture. The two figures without cangues who offer thanks outside the walls are headed toward a happier fate. The cause of their salvation is open to interpretation, depending on how one reads the objects beside the two figures and the identity of the monk at right.[27] The objects

24. For brief treatments, see Hsiao, *Tun-huang su-wen-hsüeh lun-ts'ung,* pp. 212–15; Lo, *Tun-huang chiang-ching pien-wen yen-chiu,* pp. 254–56; Oda, "Godō daishin kō"; and Sakai, "Jūō shinkō," p. 619.

25. See *Yen-lo wang kung-hsing fa tz'u-ti,* Pu-k'ung chin-kang (705–774), *T* no. 1290, 21:374a, 375b.

26. The first is mentioned in *T'ai-tzu jui-ying pen-ch'i ching,* Chih Ch'ien (fl. 220–252), *T* no. 185, 3:475c; the latter in *P'u-yao ching (Lalitavistara),* Chu Fa-hu (fl. 265–313), *T* no. 186, 3:507c.

27. Most iconographical studies agree that the monk in plates 14a and 14b is Tao-ming, but do not provide any details about the rolls tied together (both plates) or the cloth wreath (plate 14a). The only discussion of them I have found is by Tokushi, who describes the wreath as "a cloth tied up with thread" *(kase ito to konpō shita fuhaku)* and refers to the bundle of rolled items as a "gift" *(sokushū,* traditionally the honorarium given to one's teacher at the beginning of a course of study); Tokushi, "Kōzō," pp. 285, 286.

might represent a gift of pieces of cloth sewn together in a wreath by thread (on the left) and a gift of rolled bolts of cloth secured by a strip (on the right). This interpretation is strengthened by the fact that when only one supplicant is shown outside the walls in other versions (plate 14b), only one gift is pictured, too. At any rate the donation of such items by lay people to monks was common in medieval China and would form the perfect contrast to the stealing of Saṃgha property for which the sinner is being punished. If so, the monk is simply generic, placed in this scene to remind us that charity should be directed not to the ten kings, but more immediately to monks. Furthermore, the monk here resembles none of the monks shown in the frontispiece (Śāriputra, Maudgalyāyana, or Tao-ming).

According to another interpretation, the monk outside the city of hell is Tao-ming, who was known for popularizing paintings of Ti-tsang Bodhisattva (perhaps the objects pictured in plate 14b?) and could draw on the Bodhisattva's power to rescue those in need.

In other versions of the illustration it is clear that Ti-tsang himself dispenses aid to the deceased. In plate 14c Ti-tsang, appearing in the guise of a monk, feeds broth to a woman wearing a cangue. Ti-tsang's role as a compassionate monk was well established in medieval times. In addition to his role in the Teaching of the Three Stages *(san-chieh chiao)* as a savior in a degenerate age, he appeared variously as an incarnation of Yama, as a specialist in delivering people from hell, and as master of the six paths of rebirth.[28]

Yet another figure was shown in the pictures, no longer extant, described in the notes to an illustrated copy of *The Scripture on the Ten Kings*. Those notes, perhaps interpreting a picture much like plate 14c, place the Buddha's disciple Maudgalyāyana (Ch.: Mu-lien) at the scene. The notes state,[29] "This is the scene at the Hell of the Iron Bed where the Great Maudgalyāyana converts the prison guard and rescues his mother." Despite different opinions about the identity of the figure here, in its last frame *The Scripture on the Ten Kings* makes it clear that a savior—either a godlike Bodhisattva or a saintly monk—is available to people as they move through the territory of the ten kings.

---

28. Ti-tsang appeared in a variey of guises in medieval China, many of them known only through Tun-huang paintings and manuscripts. His evolution is far too complex to be treated here. For overviews, see Levering, "Kṣiti-garbha"; Manabe, *Jizō bosatsu no kenkyū;* Matsumoto, "Hibō jizō bosatsu no bunpu"; idem, "Jizō jūō zu to inro bosatsu"; idem, *Tonkō ga no kenkyū,* 1:368–401; Sakurai, *Jizō shinkō;* Soymié, "Notes d'iconographie chinoise: les acolytes de Ti-tsang"; de Visser, *The Bodhisattva Ti-tsang (Jizō) in China and Japan;* and Yabuki, *Sangai kyō no kenkyū,* pp. 638–58.

29. Trans. from P 3304v, reprod. Huang, *Pao-tsang,* 127:370b.

1a. First illustration to *The Scripture on the Ten Kings*. Frontispiece. P 2003-1. Photograph courtesy of Bibliothèque nationale, Paris.

1b. First illustration to *The Scripture on the Ten Kings*. Frontispiece. Cft 00404 (L). ©British Museum.

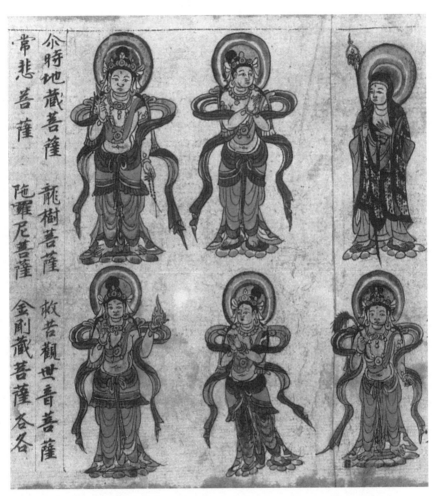

爾時地藏菩薩

龍樹菩薩

救苦觀世音菩薩

金剛藏菩薩

各各

陁羅尼菩薩

常悲菩薩

2. Second illustration to *The Scripture on the Ten Kings*. Six Bodhisattvas.
P 2003–2. Photograph courtesy of Bibliothèque nationale, Paris.

閻羅法王白佛言世尊我等諸王皆當發使乘黑馬把黑幡著黑衣檢云人家造何功德准名放牒抽出罪人不違業碩

3a. Third illustration to *The Scripture on the Ten Kings*. Messenger. P 2003-3. Photograph courtesy of Bibliothèque nationale, Paris.

3b. Third illustration to *The Scripture on the Ten Kings*. Official checking names.
P 4523–2. Photograph courtesy of Bibliothèque nationale, Paris.

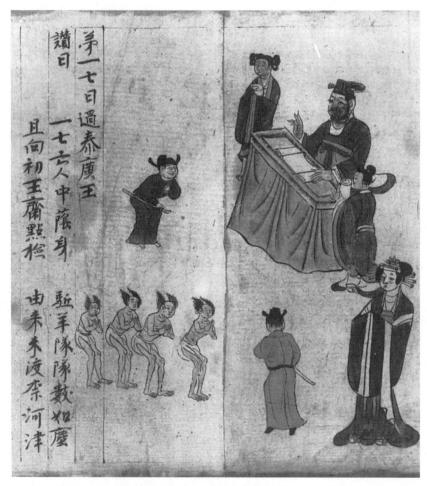

第一七日過秦廣王

讚曰

一七亡人中蔭身

且向初王廳點檢

駈羊隊隊數如麈

由來未渡奈河津

4. Fourth illustration to *The Scripture on the Ten Kings*. First king. P 2003–4. Photograph courtesy of Bibliothèque nationale, Paris.

5b. Fifth illustration to *The Scripture on the Ten Kings*. Second king. P 4523–4. Photograph courtesy of Bibliothèque nationale, Paris.

5a. Fifth illustration to *The Scripture on the Ten Kings*. Second king. P 2003–5. Photograph courtesy of Bibliothèque nationale, Paris.

第三七日過宋帝王

讚曰

亡人三七轉悕惶

各各點名知所在

群群驅送五官王

始覺冥途險路長

6a. Sixth illustration to *The Scripture on the Ten Kings*. Third king. P 2003–6. Photograph courtesy of Bibliothèque nationale, Paris.

6b. Sixth illustration to *The Scripture on the Ten Kings*. Third king. P 2870–6. Photograph courtesy of Bibliothèque nationale, Paris.

7a. Seventh illustration to *The Scripture on the Ten Kings*. Fourth king.
P 2003–7. Photograph courtesy of Bibliothèque nationale, Paris.

7b. Seventh illustration to *The Scripture on the Ten Kings*. Fourth king.
P 4523–6. Photograph courtesy of Bibliothèque nationale, Paris.

8a. Eighth illustration to *The Scripture on the Ten Kings*. Fifth king.
P 2003–8. Photograph courtesy of Bibliothèque nationale, Paris.

9. Ninth illustration to *The Scripture on the Ten Kings*. Sixth king.
P 2003-9. Photograph courtesy of Bibliothèque nationale,
Paris.

8b. Eighth illustration to *The Scripture on the
Ten Kings*. Fifth king. P 4523-7. Photograph
courtesy of Bibliothèque nationale, Paris.

10. Tenth illustration to *The Scripture on the Ten Kings*. Seventh king.
P 2003–10. Photograph courtesy of Bibliothèque nationale, Paris.

11b. Eleventh illustration to *The Scripture on
the Ten Kings*. Eighth king. Satō ms.-11.
Photograph by John Blazejewski of a Japanese collotype in the author's collection.

11a. Eleventh illustration to *The Scripture on the Ten Kings*. Eighth king. P 2003–11. Photograph courtesy of Bibliothèque nationale, Paris.

第九一年過都市王

讚曰

一年過此轉苦辛　男女脩何功德因

六道輪迴仍未之　遺經造像出達津

12. Twelfth illustration to *The Scripture on the Ten Kings*. Ninth king.
P 2003-12. Photograph courtesy of Bibliothèque nationale, Paris.

13a. Thirteenth illustration to *The Scripture on the Ten Kings*. Tenth king. P 2003-13. Photograph courtesy of Bibliothèque nationale, Paris.

13b. Thirteenth illustration to *The Scripture on the Ten Kings*. Tenth king. Satō ms.-13. Photograph by John Blazejewski of a Japanese collotype in the author's collection.

14a. Fourteenth illustration to *The Scripture on the Ten Kings*. Monk and city of hell. P 2003–14. Photograph courtesy of Bibliothèque nationale, Paris.

14b. Fourteenth illustration to *The Scripture on the Ten Kings*. Monk and city of hell. Satō ms.-14. Photograph by John Blazejewski of a Japanese collotype in the author's collection.

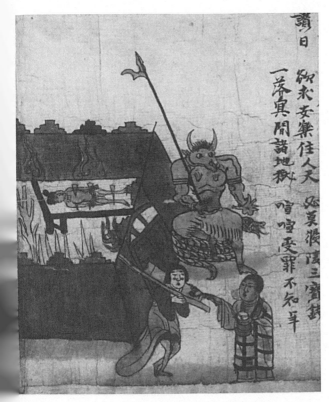

欲求安樂佳人天

必莫浪陳三寶錢

一落真開講地獄

喧喧受罪不知年

前日

14c. Fourteenth illustration to *The Scripture on the Ten Kings*. Monk and city of hell. S 3961-12. ©British Library.

17. Translation

Conventions

The translation establishes a critical edition of the long recension of *The Scripture on the Ten Kings*. It notes all variants in six tenth-century manuscripts, using the first (A) as a basic text:

> **A** = P 2003. Complete text with illustrations.
> **B** = P 2870. Complete text with illustrations.
> **C** = Satō ms. Complete text with illustrations.
> **D** = S 3961. Incomplete text with illustrations.
> **E** = P 3761. Incomplete text.
> **F** = Cft 00212 (L). Incomplete text with illustrations.

Where relevant I refer to related texts:

> **g** = P 3304v. Notes on an illustrated text, incomplete.
> **h** = Pk 8045, middle recension of *The Scripture on the Ten Kings*.
> **i** = Hōjuin ms., based on a Muromachi (1185–1330) copy derived from a Sung dynasty original of the long recension, reproduced as *T* no. 3143.
> **j** = Korean printed edition of the long recension, dated 1469, transcribed in *Z*, 2b, 23.
> **k** = *Jizō bosatsu hosshin innen jūō kyō*, related Japanese apocryphon, ca. 1100; transcribed in *Z*, 2b, 23.
> **l** = S 3147, short recension of *The Scripture on the Ten Kings*.

Where relevant I refer to modern critical editions:

> **V** = Sakai, "Jūō shinkō," which collates **C** with **i**, **j**.
> **W** = Tokushi, "Kōzō," which collates **A** with **C**, **D**, **i**.
> **X** = Hsiao, *Tun-huang su-wen-hsüeh lun-ts'ung*, which collates **A** with **E**, **i**.
> **Y** = Tu, *Chiao-lu yen-chiu*, which collates **A** with **B**, **D**.

Hymns *(tsan)* are prefaced by the words, "the hymn goes . . ."
Chants *(ch'ieh-t'o)* are marked with an asterisk (*).
Illustrations in the original are indicated by reference to [plates].

The Text

[Plate 1a]

We reverently open the chanting of *The Scripture of King Yama Rāja*[1] *Concerning the Sevens of Life*[2] *to Be Cultivated in Preparation for Rebirth in the Pure Land.* May our vows and admonitions be lucky.[3] We open the scripture and begin the hymns with the five assemblies.[4] We recite: "A-mi-tābha Buddha."

Recorded by *śramaṇa* Tsang-ch'uan[5] of Ta-sheng-tz'u ssu in Ch'eng-tu Prefecture.

The Scripture Spoken by the Buddha to the Four Orders[6] *on the Prophecy*[7] *Given to King Yama Rāja Concerning the Sevens of Life to Be Cultivated in Preparation for*[8] *Rebirth in the Pure Land.*

1. **King Yama Rāja (Yen-lo wang).** Yen-lo is an abbreviation of the transliteration Yen-mo lo-she (Skt.: Yama rāja), which means "King Yama." The addition of *wang*, "king," is redundant. The text also uses the name Yen-mo wang, "King Yama," which combines transliteration of the name with translation of the title, and Yen wang, "King Yama."

2. **Sevens of Life** *(sheng-ch'i)* are the feasts cultivated while one is still alive, usually semimonthly, which result in an easier journey through purgatory. Contrast *ch'i-ch'i*, "the seven sevens," which descendants perform after one's death. Var.: *sheng-ch'i chai*, "seven feasts of life" (l); see also practice characters on P 2249v, reprod. Huang, *Pao-tsang*, 118:62b.

3. **Be lucky** *(yu-yüan)*, a colloquialism. *Yüan* in the sense of prior cause was established prior to Buddhist influence in China (see Morohashi, *Jiten*, no. 27656), but the term also has associations with the Buddhist understanding of causality.

4. **The five assemblies** *(wu-hui)* are five different styles of chanting the name of Amitābha Buddha. They apparently originated with a proselytizer named Fa-chao (fl. 766–804), who reports that he learned them directly from Amitābha during the summer meditation retreat in 766. Although early descriptions of the chanting differ, they all agree that chanting should progress through five stages, getting faster and louder each time, and that such chanting results in achieving enlightenment. For Fa-chao's account of his experiences, see *Ching-t'u wu-hui nien-fo sung-ching kuan-hsing i*, Fa-chao, P 2066, transcr. *T* no. 2827, 85:1253b–54a. On the five methods, see Tsukamoto, *Tō chūki no jōdo kyō*, reprint ed., pp. 405–12. On Fa-chao, see Satō, "Tonkō shutsudo hōshō oshō nenbutsu san," pp. 196–222; and Tsukamoto, op. cit., pp. 308–405. The occurrence of the five assemblies establishes 766 as a *terminus ante quem* for this version of *The Scripture on the Ten Kings*.

5. **Tsang-ch'uan** is the reputed author of the text, or, according to some traditions, the creator of the hymns. Ta sheng-tz'u ssu was established in 756. For details, see chapter 5.

6. **Four Orders** *(ssu-chung)*, Skt.: *catasraḥ parṣadaḥ*, are the four divisions of the Buddha's disciples: monks *(bhikṣu)*, nuns *(bhikṣunī)*, lay men *(upāsaka)*, and lay women *(upāsikā)*.

7. **Prophecy** *(shou-chi)*, Skt.: *vyākaraṇa*, a prediction by the Buddha that one of his followers will achieve Buddhahood.

8. **To be cultivated in preparation for** *(yü-hsiu)*. Var. synonym: *ni-hsiu*, "to be cultivated in anticipation of" (D, l).

The hymn goes:
When the Thus Come One approached *parinirvāṇa*,[9]
He widely summoned heavenly dragons[10] and earth spirits.
For King Yama's sake he made a prophecy,
And then handed down this rite for the preparatory cultivation of
the sevens of life.

Thus have I heard. Once, the Buddha was among the pair of Sāla trees on the banks of the Ajitavatī[11] River in the city of Kuśinagara. As he approached *parinirvāṇa* the Buddha lifted himself up and emitted a ray that universally illuminated the great multitude as well as myriad Bodhisattvas and Mahāsattvas;[12] heavenly dragons and spirit kings; Śakra, Emperor and Chief of Heaven;[13] the great kings of the four heavens;[14] Great Brahmā, King of Heaven;[15] the *asura*-kings;[16] the various kings of great empires; Yama, Son of Heaven; the Magistrate of Mount T'ai;[17] the Officer of Life Spans and Officer of Records;[18] the

9. *Parinirvāṇa (po-nieh-p'an)* means "perfect extinction." Var. radical: *po-nieh-p'an*[b] (D).
10. **Heavenly dragons** *(t'ien-lung)* could also be translated as "gods and dragons" (or *nāgas*), the first two of the "eightfold order" *(pa-pu chung)* of spiritual beings: (1.) *deva*, (2.) *nāga*, (3.) *yakṣa*, (4.) *gandharva*, (5.) *asura*, (f.) *garuḍa*, (7.) *kiṃnara*, (8.) *maharoga;* see Mochizuki, *Daijiten*, pp. 4223c–24a; ₁nd Nakamura, *Jiten*, pp. 1105d–06a. See also below, *t'ien-lung shen-wang*, "he ₁venly dragons and spirit kings."
11. **Ajitavatī River (O-wei-pa-t'i ho)**, usually transliterated as O-shih-to-fa-ti ho. Hsüan-tsang (602–664) reports that the river was thirty-four *li* northwest of the city of Kuśinagara, and that the Sāla trees on its western bank were recognized as the site of the Buddha's demise; see *Ta-t'ang hsi-yü chi*, Hsüan-tsang, *T* no. 2087, 51:903b. Var. inversion: O-wei-pa-ho-t'i (C).
12. **Myriad Bodhisattvas and Mahāsattvas** *(chu-p'u-sa mo-ho-sa)*, beings of enlightenment and great beings, respectively.
13. **Śakra, Emperor and Chief of Heaven (T'ien-chu ti Shih)**. Śakra is another name for Indra, the god who rules at the center of the Heaven of Thirty-three.
14. **The great kings of the four heavens** *(ssu-t'ien ta-wang)*, Skt.: *catvāsraḥ mahārajikāḥ*, reside on the four sides of Mount Sumeru and serve as protectors of the Dharma. To the east is Dhṛtarāṣṭra, south Virūḍhaka, west Virūpākṣa, north Vaiśravaṇa. W mistakenly omits *ta*.
15. **Great Brahmā, King of Heaven (Ta-fan t'ien-wang)** resides in a heaven located above the realm of desire but still within the realm of form.
16. *Asura* kings *(o-hsiu-lo wang)*. *Asuras* are large, powerful gods, situated below the gods in heaven but above the earth.
17. **The Magistrate of Mount T'ai (T'ai-shan fu-chün)** administers the realm of the dead located under Mount T'ai (in modern Shantung). Here he is treated as a relatively minor figure in the bureaucracy. Below the text places him as the seventh king.
18. **Officer of Life Spans (Ssu-ming) and Officer of Records (Ssu-lu)** keep records of people's deeds and adjust their date of death accordingly. The first is invoked as a god in pre-Han sources, and the two appear together in Buddhist

Great Spirit of the Five Paths;[19] and the officials of the underground prisons. They all came to the gathering, respectfully reverenced the World Honored One, brought their hands together, and stood [to the side].

> The hymn goes:
> At that time the Buddha extended a ray of light that filled the
>   Great Thousand,[20]
> Reaching everywhere to dragons and ghosts, uniting humans and
>   gods.
> Indra, Brahmā, the various gods,[21] and multitudes from the dark,
>   hidden world
> All came to bow their heads in front of the World Honored One.

The Buddha announced to the entire great multitude[22] that in a world to come, Yama rāja, Son of Heaven, would attain the role of Buddha. He would be named[23] "King P'u-hsien,[24] Thus Come One," and he would fully possess the Ten Titles.[25] His land would be ornamented

---

and Taoist sources in the fourth and fifth centuries; see Harper, "Religious Traditions of the Warring States, Ch'in, and Han"; Hsiao, *Tun-huang su-wen-hsüeh lun-ts'ung,* pp. 199–207; and Soymié, "Notes d'icnonographie chinoise: les acolytes de Ti-tsang," part 1.

19. **Great Spirit of the Five Paths (Wu-tao ta-shen)** oversees the five realms into which sentient beings can be reborn: god (Skt.: *deva;* Ch.: *t'ien*), human being *(manuṣya; jen),* ghost *(preta; o-kuei),* animal *(tiryagoni; ch'u-sheng),* and hell being *(naraka; ti-yü). Asuras (o-hsiu-lo)* are sometimes added to the list to make "six paths" *(ṣadgati; liu-tao);* see Mochizuki, *Daijiten,* pp. 5071c–72a. This spirit may be equivalent to the tenth king of purgatory.

20. **Great Thousand *(ta-ch'ien)*** abbreviates "Three Thousand Great Thousand World Systems" *(san-ch'ien ta-ch'ien shih-chieh),* often translated as "Trichiliocosm," comprising 1,000 small world-systems, 1,000 middle-sized ones, and 1,000 large ones. The term signifies every possible tangible universe. Var.: *ta-chung,* "great multitude" (D).

21. **Various gods *(chu-shen).*** W mistakenly reads *ch'ing-t'ien,* "invited gods."

22. **Entire great multitude *(chu-ta-chung).*** Var.: *chu-ta-ch'en,* "myriad great lords" (D).

23. **Would be named *(ming-yüeh).*** Var.: *hao-yüeh,* "would be titled" (E).

24. **King P'u-hsien (P'u-hsien wang)** is apparently related to P'u-hsien Bodhisattva (Skt.: Samantabhadra Bodhisattva). Among his many manifestations in Buddhism, P'u-hsien plays a major role in the *Hua-yen* sūtra *(Ta-fang-kuang fo hua-yen ching),* acquaintance with which the text seems to assume. W mistakenly omits *wang.*

25. **Ten Titles *(shih-hao).*** All Buddhas are called by ten (actually eleven) honorific appellations: (1.) Tathāgatha, (2.) Arhat, (3.) Samyaksaṃbuddha, (4.) Vidyācaraṇasampanna, (5.) Sugata, (6.) Lokavid, (7.) Anuttara, (8.) Puruṣadamyasārathi, (9.) Śāstādevamanuṣyāṇāṃ, (10.) Buddha, (11.) Bhagavat.

and pure, decorated with a hundred jewels. His country would be named "Flower Ornament,"[26] and it would be completely filled with Bodhisattvas.

> The hymn goes:
> On this day the World Honored One prophesied that Yama rāja
> Would before long realize Buddhahood;
> His country, decorated with jewels, would always be pure,
> With many multitudes cultivating the practice of the Bodhisattva.

At that time Ānanda[27] spoke to the Buddha, saying, "World Honored One, on account of what causes and conditions does Yama rāja, Son of Heaven, settle verdicts in the dark regions? And[28] why, then, in this assembly, has he received a prophecy of the fruits [he will enjoy] in the future?"

The Buddha said, "There are two causes and conditions for serving as the various kings in those dark paths. The first involves[29] Bodhisattvas who dwell[30] on the immovable ground of inconceivable liberation.[31] Desiring to aid in the transformation of all sentient beings in their extreme suffering, they manifest themselves[32] in the role of those like that King Yama.[33] The second involves those who have descended to Yama's heaven[34] to play the role of Great King Māra,[35] because in giving rise to the practice of good they violated the precepts.[36] They keep

26. **Flower Ornament (Hua-yen).** This country would naturally conjure up associations with the sūtra of the same name, but neither Chinese version refers to it; see *Ta-fang-kuang fo hua-yen ching (Avataṃsakasūtra)*, Buddhabhadra (359–429), *T* no. 278; and ibid., Śikṣānanda (652–710), *T* no. 279.

27. **Ānanda (O-nan),** cousin and disciple of the Buddha, is a frequent interlocutor in Buddhist texts. His role as the person who remembered best all of the Buddha's sermons does not seem especially important here.

28. **And *(fu)*.** Var.: *fu*[b] (D).

29. **Involves *(shih)*,** or "is," used here in its colloquial sense as a copula. See also the hymn to the tenth court.

30. **Dwell *(chu)*.** Var. radical: *wang*[b] (B).

31. **Liberation *(chieh-t'o)*.** Var. radical: *chieh-shuo* (D).

32. **Manifest themselves *(shih-hsien)*.** Var. homonym: *shih-hsien*[b] (D).

33. **Those like that King Yama *(pi* Yen-mo wang *teng)*.** Var.: Yen-mo *t'ien-chung teng-wang,* "kings like those in Yama's heaven" (D). Yen-mo *t'ien-chung* is probably reduplicated from the following line.

34. **To Yāma's heaven (Yen-mo *t'ien-chung)*.** This Yāma (more commonly transcribed Yen-mo t'ien), who resides in one of the lower heavens, apparently differs from King Yama. Other texts state that they are two roles played by the same figure; see *Ta p'i-lu-che-na ch'eng-fo ching shu,* I-hsing (683–727), *T* no. 1796; 39:634a–b.

35. **Great King Māra (Ta-mo wang),** the tempter and "Evil One" in Buddhist mythology, could also be understood in a more general sense as "great demon king." Var. radical: Ta-mo-wang[b] (C).

36. **Violated the precepts *(wei fan-chieh)*.** Var.: *fan-chieh* (D).

order over the various ghosts and judge the cases on Jambudvīpa[37] involving the ten evils[38] and the five abominations.[39] For all sinners locked up in prison, day and night undergoing suffering—as the wheel [of rebirth] turns among them and they receive bodily form in accord with their actions—[the kings] determine their lives and register their deaths.[40] Now the causes and conditions of this Yama,[41] Son of Heaven, are already ripe.[42] For this reason I have prophesied a country of jewels[43] and the realization of great *bodhi* in a world to come. All of you, men and gods, should not[44] doubt it."

> The hymn goes:
> Compassionate toward the hated,[45] he transforms all—that is
>   majestic numinosity;
> The wheel turns in the six paths, never delaying or stopping.[46]
> Teaching and transforming, he detests suffering[47] and thinks of
>   joy,
> Hence he manifests himself in the form of Yama rāja, Son of
>   Heaven.

37. **On Jambudvīpa (Yen-fu-t'i *nei*).** Jambudvīpa is the southern continent in Buddhist cosmology. India and China are located on it, and among the four continents only Jambudvīpa can serve as the birthplace of Buddhas. Var.: omitted (D).

38. **Ten evils *(shih-o)*,** Skt.: *daśākuśala,* are 1. killing, 2. stealing, 3. adultery, 4. lying, 5. uttering harsh words, 6. uttering words that cause enmity between others, 7. engaging in idle talk, 8. greed, 9. anger, and 10. perverted views.

39. **Five abominations *(wu-ni)*,** Skt.: *pañcānantarīyāṇi,* are 1. killing one's mother, 2. killing one's father, 3. killing an *arhat;* 4. maliciously shedding the blood of a Buddha; and 5. disrupting the Saṃgha.

40. **Determine their lives and register their deaths *(ting-sheng chu-ssu)*.** Var.: *ting-sheng-ssu,* "determine their lives and deaths" (D), the first of many elisions which breaks the four-character phrasing; and var. transposition: *ting-sheng ssu-chu* (C).

41. **Now . . . this Yama *(chin tz'u* Yen-mo).** Var.: *chin* Yen-mo, "Now . . . Yama" (D).

42. **Already ripe.** The original reads *i-shu.* On grammatical grounds I emend to *i-shu*[b] following D, h, i, j.

43. **A country of jewels.** The original reads *tsun-kuo,* "respected country." Because it matches the language above, I emend to *pao-kuo,* following C, D, E, i, j.

44. **Should not *(ying pu)*.** Var.: *pu ying* (D, E).

45. **Compassionate toward the hated *(pei-tseng)*.** Var. radical: *pei-tseng*[b], "advancing compassion" (C, D), a later Buddhist technical term referring to the Bodhisattva's preference for compassion over wisdom; see *Tsu-t'ing shih-yüan,* Shan-ch'ing (fl. 1108), *Z,* 2b, 18:60vb.

46. **Never delaying or stopping *(pu hsi-t'ing)*.** Var.: *pu chan-t'ing,* "not stopping for a moment" (D, E).

47. **Detests suffering *(yen-k'u)*,** or "turns hateful suffering into thoughts of joy." Var. radical: *yen-k'u*[b], which is synonymous; see Chang, *Ta-tz'u-tien,* no. 20977, def. 6.

Now if there is a person who cultivates the commissioning of[48] this scripture, or who receives and upholds or reads and intones it, then after giving up his life he will not be reborn in the three paths,[49] nor will he enter any of the various[50] great underground prisons.

> The hymn goes:
> If a person believes in the Law and does not doubt it,[51]
> And copies the text of this scripture, obeys it, and upholds it,[52]
> Then upon giving up his life he will instantly pass over the three evil paths,
> And in this body he will always avoid entering Avīci.[53]

For any serious crimes[54] that require serving in the underground prisons for ten *kalpas* or five *kalpas*[55]—killing[56] one's father; injuring one's mother;[57] breaking the fast; breaking the precepts;[58] slaughtering pigs, cattle, sheep, chickens, dogs, or poisonous snakes[59]—a person can during life commission this scripture or the various images of the Honored Ones, and it will be noted in the dark registry.[60] On the day one

48. **Cultivates the commissioning of** *(hsiu-tsao)*. Var.: *tsao*[b], "commissions" (D).

49. **Three paths** *(san-t'u)* are the lower three forms of rebirth: animal, hungry ghost, and hell being. Var.: *t'u*, "paths" (D). Below the text uses the synonym *san-o-t'u*, "three evil paths."

50. **Any of the various** *(i-ch'ieh chu)*. Var.: *i-ch'ieh chih*, "any" (C).

51. **Believes in the Law and does not doubt it** *(hsin-fa pu ssu-i)*. Var.: *pu hsin-fa. . . . ,* "does not believe in the Law" (C), which requires reading the whole line as "does not believe that the Law is not inconceivable." Var. radical: *pu ssu-i* (D).

52. **And copies . . . and upholds it.** This line gives an unusual rhyme structure to the hymn, ABCA. Because the line is repeated in a later hymn, it may have been inserted here in place of an original that preserved the common AABA rhyme.

53. **Avīci** *(o-p'i)* is the lowest of the eight hells. The Sanskrit means "without interval" (usually translated as *wu-chien*), because the pause between rounds of torture allowed in other hells is not practiced there. Var., here and below: *o-pi* (D).

54. **For any serious crimes . . . and wipe away your sins.** Var.: the entire paragraph and following hymn are missing in C.

55. **Five *kalpas*** *(wu-chieh)*. Var.: missing (D).

56. **Killing** *(sha)*, here and below used as a synonym for *sha*[b].

57. **Killing one's father, injuring one's mother** *(sha-fu hai-mu)*. Var.: *sha-hai-mu*, "killing and injuring one's mother" (D).

58. **Breaking the precepts** *(p'o-chieh)*. Var.: omitted in E, which breaks the four-word phrasing.

59. **Chickens, dogs, or poisonous snakes** *(chi kou tu-she)*. W mistakenly reads *chi kou she*.

60. **Dark registry** *(ming-an)*, or "registry of the dark regions," the records of each person's actions maintained by the bureaucracy of the other world. Var.: *yeh-ching*, "mirror of actions" (D).

arrives,[61] King Yama will be delighted and will decide to release the person to be reborn in a rich and noble household, avoiding [punishment for] his crimes and errors.

> The hymn goes:
> Breaking the fast, damaging the precepts, slaughtering chickens
>   and pigs[62]
> Are reflected clearly in the mirror of actions—retribution is
>   never void.[63]
> If one commissions this scripture together with the painting of
>   images,[64]
> King Yama will decide to release you and wipe away your sins.

If there is a good son or good daughter, *bhikṣu* or *bhikṣuṇī, upāsaka,* or *upāsikā*[65] who cultivates in preparation the seven feasts of life, twice each month[66] offering support to the Three Jewels, then whoever provides for[67] the ten kings will have their names revised and reports will be given; memorials will be sent up to the Six Ministries,[68] the Boys of Good and Evil[69] will send memorials to all the officials[70] of heaven's

61. **On the day one arrives** *(shen tao chih jih).* Var.: missing (D).
62. **Chickens and pigs** *(chi chu).* A reads *chu chi* with a transposition sign clearly written between the two words. W, X, Y mistakenly omit the transposition.
63. **Void** *(hsü).* W mistakenly reads *ling.* In Tun-huang manuscripts and some later printed works radical no. 141, *hu,* often looks like radical no. 173, *yü.* For examples see Ōfuchi, *Tonkō dōkyō,* 1:400, radical no. 141; and Chu-lin, *Fo-chiao nan-tzu tzu-tien,* no. 3156. In A *hsü* clearly looks different than *ling,* which occurs in the second hymn before this one.
64. **Painting of images** *(hua-hsiang).* Var.: *shu-hsiang,* "copying of images" (D).
65. ***Upāsikā*** *(yu-p'o-i).* Var.: missing (B); adds *shu,* "etcetera" (D).
66. **Twice each month.** The short recension specifies the days as the fifteenth and thirtieth (l).
67. **Then whoever provides for** *(so-she)* is problematic because it is not an independent clause. The variant makes more sense: *ch'i-she,* "praying to and providing for" (D, E, i, j). The next clause would then be rendered: "Then names will be revised . . . ."
68. **The Six Ministries** *(liu-ts'ao)* are probably the six divisions (usually called *liu-pu*) of the central government beginning in the Sui dynasty: ministries of Personnel, Revenue, Rites, War, Justice, and Works.
69. **The Boys of Good and Evil** *(Shan-o t'ung-tzu)* accompany each person through life. One records all good deeds, the other records all evil deeds, and both carry the records to the courts of purgatory. Below they are referred to as the "Twin Boys." They were sometimes assimilated to the Officer of Life Spans and the Officer of Records. They originated in the Chinese underworld and in medieval Taoism, and made their way into apocryphal Buddhist sources; see Soymié, "Notes d'iconographie chinoise: les acolytes de Ti-tsang," part 1.
70. **All the officials** *(kuan-teng).* Var., here and below: *kuan-tien,* "officials" (D).

ministries and earth's prefects, and it will be noted in the register of
names.[71] On the day one arrives,[72] one will expediently attain assigned
rebirth in a place of happiness. One will not dwell in intermediate darkness[73] for forty-nine days, and one will not have to wait for sons and
daughters to attempt posthumous salvation.[74] As one's life span passes
before the ten kings, if there is one feast missing,[75] then one is detained
before one king, remaining there continuously to undergo suffering,
unable to emerge into birth, detained for the length of one year. For this
reason you are admonished to perform this crucial service[76] and to pray
for[77] the reward of rebirth in the Pure Land.

> The hymn goes:[78]
> The four orders cultivate the feast from time to time:
> Two offerings over three–ten days is the standard rite.
> Don't miss a chance for good karmic conditions or let your merit
>   dwindle,
> For then you'll be caught up in the intermediate darkness,
>   detained by the dark offices.

[Plate 2]

At that time Ti-tsang[79] Bodhisattva, Lung-shu[80] Bodhisattva, Chiu-
k'u[81] kuan-shih-yin Bodhisattva, Ch'ang-pei[82] Bodhisattva, Dhāraṇī

71. **Register of names** *(ming-an^b)*. Var. homophone: *ming-an,* "dark register" (D).
72. **On the day one arrives** *(shen tao chih jih)*. Var.: *hou,* "later," added at
the beginning (D).
73. **Intermediate darkness** *(chung-yin)*, or "intermediate shade." The term
describes the space between death and the next rebirth. A common variant,
chung-yin^b (used in the hymn below in D), clearly means "intermediate darkness." *Yin* is sometimes synonymous with *yün,* "aggregates," which in Buddhist
usage connotes the *skandhas,* the five psycho-physical components of the person.
Thus, *chung-yin* might also refer to "the *skandhas* of the intermediate period."
Other Buddhist sources describe the forty-nine-day period as "the intermediate
state of existence" *(chung-yu;* Skt.: *antarābhava);* see Bareau, "Chūu."
74. **Posthumous salvation** *(chui-chiu)*. W mistakenly reads *chui-fang.*
75. **If there is . . . missing** *(jo ch'üeh)*. Var.: *ming ch'üeh,* "[if] the name is
missing" (C).
76. **Crucial service** *(yao-shih)*. Var.: *o-shih,* "evil matter" (C).
77. **And to pray for** *(chi^d)*. Var. radical: *so,* "of the" (C).
78. **The hymn goes** *(tsan-yüeh)*. Var.: repeated where two sheets of paper
are glued together (B).
79. **Ti-tsang,** Skt.: Kṣitigarbha. W mistakenly reads Ti-yü. The six Bodhisattvas are discussed in chapter 16.
80. **Lung-shu,** Nāgārjuna.
81. **Chiu-k'u** (literally "Who Saves from Suffering") is one of the appellations of Kuan-shih-yin (Avalokiteśvara). W mistakenly reads Kuan-yin.
82. **Ch'ang-pei,** Sadāprarudita.

Bodhisattva, and Chin-kang-tsang[83] Bodhisattva each returned in a ray of light from his home path and arrived at the place of the Thus Come One. From different mouths but with the same voice, they sang hymns praising how the World Honored One grieves for the common person and preaches this wondrous Law, which raises the dead and saves the living. With the crowns of their heads they reverenced the Buddha's feet.

> The hymn goes:
> With legs,[84] body,[85] and head,[86]
> The Bodhisattvas of the six rays set in motion their profound
>   compassion;
> With the same voice each one sang hymns in praise
> Of how he toils diligently and transforms all creatures, never
>   getting weary.

At that time all the wardens of the eighteen[87] prisons,[88] Yama, Son of Heaven, and the dark officers of the six paths paid their respects and made a vow: "If[89] there is a member of the four orders—a *bhikṣu, bhikṣuṇī, upāsaka,* or *upāsikā*[90]—who commissions this scripture or sings a hymn or intones[91] a single verse,[92] then we shall all[93] exempt him from all of his suffering and pain. We shall reverse the decision so that he emerges from the underground prisons and goes to rebirth[94] in the heavenly path. We shall not allow him to be delayed or to undergo suffering even for one night."

83. **Chin-kang-tsang,** Vajragarbha.
84. **Legs** *(tsu-hsi),* literally "feet and knees." W mistakenly reads *shih-sheng.*
85. **Body.** The original reads *ch'i-hsiung.* I emend to *ch'i-hsiung*[b], literally "navel and chest," following D, W, X. *Hsiung* and *hsiung*[b] are common variants of *hsiung*; see Chu-lin, *Fo-chiao nan-tzu tzu-tien,* no. 2912.
86. **Head** *(k'ou chi mei),* literally "mouth and eyebrows."
87. **Eighteen** *(i-shih-pa-chung).* Although eighteen differs from the "standard" number of eight hells, there was an early precedent for this enumeration. The *Shih-pa ni-li ching* (Scripture on the Eighteen Naraka), trans. An Shih-kao (fl. 148–170) *T* no. 731, describes eight hot and ten cold hells; for a rough précis, see Goodrich, *Chinese Hells,* pp. 128–34. The short recension reads twenty-eight (I). Var.: *i-shih-pa-t'ung,* "eighteen boys of the" (C).
88. **Wardens of the . . . prisons** *(yü-chu).* Var.: *ti-yü-chu,* "wardens of the underground prisons" (D).
89. **Made a vow: "If** *(fa-yüan. Jo).* Var. transposition: *fa jo yüan* (B).
90. *Upāsikā (yu-p'o-i).* Var. radical: *yu-p'o-i*[b] (D).
91. **Sings a hymn or intones** *(tsan-sung).* Var.: *tu-sung,* "reads or intones" (B).
92. **A single verse** *(i-chi).* Technically speaking, *chi*[b] is a transliteration of *gāthā,* but I render it here as "verse" to distinguish this word from another transliteration of *gāthā, ch'ieh-t'o,* which occurs below.
93. **We shall all** *(wo chieh).* Var.: *wo tang,* "we should" (D).
94. **Goes to rebirth** *(wang-sheng).* Var.: *te-sheng,* "attains rebirth" (E).

The hymn goes:
The dark officers, the note-takers, as well as King Yama
And all the Buddhas glorified the scripture and reverentially
    offered praise:
If among the four orders someone can uphold a single verse,
We shall all send him off to the halls of heaven.

At that time King Yama, Son of Heaven, spoke to the Buddha, saying a verse:

[∗] "*Namo arhat.*[95]
Many are the evil acts[96] of sentient beings.
The cycle of rebirth has no determinate marks,
Just like waves upon the water."

The hymn goes:
King Yama spoke to the Buddha, saying a *gāthā,*
Reciting with sympathy, "Many are the sins and sufferings of all
    sentient beings.
The cycle of rebirth in the six paths has no determinate marks.
Birth and extinction are still the same as waves upon the water."

[∗] May the breeze of his wisdom
Drift over[97] the river of the wheel of the Law.
May his ray of brightness illuminate worldly realms,
Making a tour of all past experience.[98]

[∗] Universally saving all sentient beings from suffering,
Subduing[99] and gathering together the various demons,
The four kings administer the realm of states,
And transmit the Buddha's *sūtras.*

The hymn goes:
May the Buddha bring forth the rising of the wind of wisdom,
Drifting over the sea of the Law, washing away the dust that
    conceals.
The four kings who protect the world also made a vow
That they would hand down this classic and circulate it
    everywhere.

95. *Namo arhat (nan-wu o-lo-ho),* meaning "homage to the worthy one."
Var. radical: *o-lo-ho*[b], and the whole line is repeated (E).
96. **Evil acts** *(o-yeh).* Var.: *tsui-k'u,* "sins and sufferings" (D), which occurs
in the next hymn.
97. **Drift over** *(p'iao-yü).* Var.: *p'iao-hsing,* "whirl up" (C, D).
98. **Of all past experience** *(hsi ching-kuo).* Var.: *hsi ching-kuo*[b], "and passing
over everything" (D, i, j, V, W, X).
99. **Subduing** *(chiang-fu).* Var.: *chiang-kuei,* "subduing ghosts" (D).

[*] Common people who cultivate goodness are few;
Those who are confused and who believe in depravity[100] are many.
Uphold the scripture and you will avoid the underground prisons;
Copy it and you will be spared calamity and illness.

[*] You will pass over the difficulties of the three worlds
And never see a *yakṣa*.[101]
You will ascend to a high rank in your place of rebirth;
You will be rich, noble, and enjoy a long posterity.[102]

The hymn goes:[103]
Because of evil actions, the power of common people to do good is
    slight;
They believe in falsity, have perverted views,[104] and will enter
    Avīci.
If you wish to seek riches and nobility and a family with a long
    life span,
You should copy the text of this scripture, obey it, and uphold it.

[*] With utmost mind intone this scripture,
And the kings of heaven will constantly note it in their
    registers.[105]
Do not take life in sacrificing to the spirits,
Because for this you will enter the underground prisons.

[*] In reciting the Buddha's [name], you can transgress the
    authentic scripture[106]—
You must admonish and exert[107] yourself.

100. **Believe in falsity *(hsin-hsieh)*.** Var. radical: *hsin-yeh* (E).
101. **A *yakṣa (yao-ch'a)*,** more commonly transcribed *yeh-ch'a*, is a semi-divine spirit in other contexts viewed as benevolent.
102. **Enjoy a long posterity *(shou-chui ch'ang)*.** Var. homophone: *shou-chui ch'ang*[b], "have long life and a long posterity" (C, E).
103. **The hymn goes.** The hymn does not rhyme.
104. **Have perverted views *(tao-chien)*.** Var. radical, here and below: *tao-chien*[b] (E).
105. **Note it in their registers *(chi-lu)*.** Var.: *ssu-lu*[b], "bestow registers"(D). Variants add extra lines. D adds two lines, maintaining some symmetry, while C adds only the first: "If you wish to attain a place without crimes / then do not fail broadly to make blessings."
106. **You can transgress the authentic scriptures *(fan chen-ching)*.** The variant makes more sense: *pa chen-ching*, "and taking up the authentic scriptures" (D, E, X).
107. **Admonish and exert *(chieh-hsü)*,** in the sense of preventing oneself from doing evil and urging oneself to do good; cf. *Wang Fan-chih shih-chi*, in Demiéville, *L'oeuvre de Wang le zélateur*, préface B. *Hsü*[b] is an attested form of *hsü*; see Chu-lin, *Fo-chiao nan-tzu tzu-tien*, no. 336. Var.: *chieh-hsü*[b] (D).

In your hands wield the diamond knife[108]
To wipe out Māra's tribe.[109]

The hymn goes:
Actions of sin and suffering within the three paths are completed
    with ease;
They are all conditioned by[110] taking life while sacrificing to[111]
    spirits.
You should aspire to wield the diamond[112] sword[113] of authentic
    wisdom,
To cut off[114] Māra's tribe, and to awaken to the unborn.

[∗] The Buddha puts into action an impartial mind,
In which sentient beings are insufficiently endowed.
The cultivation of blessings seems like particles of dust,
The commission of sins like mountain peaks.[115]

[∗] You should cultivate the commissioning of this scripture,
And you will be able to endure[116] the sufferings of the
    underground prisons,
Be reborn into a powerful and noble family,
And forever[117] be protected by good spirits.

The hymn goes:
Sins are like mountain peaks, as numerous as sand in the Ganges;
Blessings are few, like particles of dust; they don't amount to
    much.
But still good spirits will forever protect you,
And you can be reborn into a powerful, rich,[118] and devout
    family.

---

108. **Diamond knife** *(chin-kang tao)*. In Mahāyāna Buddhist thought, wisdom (Skt.: *prajñā;* Ch.: *po-jo* or *hui*) is like the hardest known substance, the diamond, in being able to cut through delusion. The metaphor is developed further in the next hymn.

109. **Māra's tribe (Mo-chung-tsu)**, or "tribes of demons."

110. **Conditioned by** *(yüan)*, an unusual verbal usage of *yüan.*

111. **Sacrificing to** *(chi^c)*. Var. radical: *ch'a,* "investigating" (E).

112. **Diamond** *(chin-kang)*. Var.: *chin-kuang,* "metallic and bright," or "flashing" (E).

113. **Sword** *(chien)*. Var.: *jih,* "bluntness" (D); see Chang, *Ta-tz'u-tien,* no. 41082.

114. **To cut off** *(k'an-ch'u)*. Var.: *k'an-tuan ch'u,* "cut off and get rid of" (C), which makes an eight-syllable line.

115. **Like mountain peaks.** Var.: adds another line, making a five-line *gāthā:* "If you wish to attain a life span long and extended" (D).

116. **Endure** *(ch'ih)*. Var.: *ch'u,* "do away with" (C, D, E).

117. **Forever** *(ch'ang)*. Var. synonym: *heng* (D).

118. **Powerful, rich** *(hao fu)*. Var.: *hao kuei,* "powerful, noble" (C, D). *Hao^b* is sometimes used for *hao;* Morohashi, *Jiten,* no. 16831, def. 7.

[*] Those people who commission the scripture or who read and
   intone it—
When Impermanence[119] suddenly[120] arrives,
The kings of heaven will forever guide and introduce them,
And Bodhisattvas will offer[121] flowers to welcome them.

[*] Dedicate your mind[122] to going to the Pure Land
For eighty trillion[123] lifetimes;
The cultivation of practice will be perfected and achieved,
And diamond *samādhi*[124] will be completed.[125]

The hymn goes:
If a person serves the Buddha by commissioning and upholding this
   scripture,
Then as he approaches the end, Bodhisattvas will personally come
   to welcome him.
After the causes[126] of the cultivation of practice in the Pure
   Country are perfected,[127]
He will come to authentic enlightenment and enter the golden
   city.[128]

At that time[129] the Buddha announced[130] to Ānanda and all of the
dragons, gods,[131] and other members of the eight groups; together with

119. **Impermanence** *(wu-ch'ang)*, used here as a euphemism for death.
120. **Suddenly** *(hu-erh)*. Var.: *hu-shih* (C), which is grammatically improbable.
121. **Offer** *(p'eng)*. Var.: *pa*, "carry" (C). W mistakenly reads *feng*.
122. **Dedicate your mind** *(yüan-hsin)* is unusual. *Hsin-yüan*, "Vow in your mind," would be more mellifluous. Var.: *sui-hsin*, "in accordance with your mind" (D).
123. **Eighty trillion** *(pa-pai-i-ch'ien)* is an unusual number in Buddhist sources. The number 84,000 would be more significant, but is unattested.
124. **Diamond** *samādhi (chin-kang san-mei)*, Skt.: *vajrôpamasamādhi*, or *vajrasamādhi*, is an immovable state of absorption near or equivalent to enlightenment. For a discussion of the many meanings of the term in Chinese Buddhist exegesis, see Buswell, *The Formation of Ch'an Ideology in China and Korea*, pp. 104–15.
125. **Will be completed** *(ch'eng)*. X suggests emending to *ch'eng*[b], "City of," by analogy with the next hymn.
126. **Causes** *(yin*[c]*)*. V mistakenly reads *yüan*[b], "full" (attested in i, j), which would make the line read, "With the cultivation of practice in the Pure Country full and perfected."
127. **Are perfected** *(man-i)*. Var. homophone: *man-i*[b] (D).
128. **Enter the golden city** *(ju chin-ch'eng)*. In pre-Buddhist Chinese thought the "golden city" is a metaphor for the solidity of self-cultivation; see Morohashi, *Jiten*, no. 40152.568.
129. **At that time. . . .** This paragraph is included in the middle recension (h).
130. **The Buddha announced** *(fo kao)*. Var.: *chi*[d] (C), which omits *fo* and misreads *kao*.
131. **Dragons, gods** *(t'ien-lung)*. Var.: *lung shen*, "dragons, spirits" (D).

the various great spirits;[132] Yama rāja, Son of Heaven; the Magistrate of Mount T'ai; the Officer of Life Spans and the Officer of Records; the Great Spirit of the Five Paths; all the officials of the underground prisons; and the great kings[133] who traverse the path, that they should give rise to compassion: "The Law is broad and forgiving.[134] I allow you to be lenient with the compassionate and filial sons and daughters of all sinners. When they cultivate merit[135] and perform sacrifices to raise the dead, repaying the kindness shown in giving birth to them and supporting them, or when during the seven sevens they cultivate feasts and commission statues[136] in order to repay their parents' kindness,[137] then you should allow them to attain rebirth in the heavens."[138]

> The hymn goes:
> The Buddha informed Yama rāja and the various great spirits,
> "The actions committed by[139] sentient beings are hard to explain fully.[140]
> You should open up kindness and permit them to make merit,
> And teach the dull how to leave behind suffering and emerge from the stream of delusion."[141]

[Plate 3a]

Yama rāja, the King of the Law, spoke to the Buddha, saying, "World Honored One, we,[142] the various kings, will send out messengers riding

132. **Great spirits** *(ta-shen).* Var.: *ta-ch'en,* "great lords" (D), here and below.

133. **Great kings** *(ta-wang).* Var.: *t'ien-wang,* "heavenly kings" (D, h).

134. **Broad and forgiving** *(k'uan-tsung).* Var.: *Hao-tsung,* "powerful and forgiving" (D).

135. **Cultivate merit** *(hsiu-fu).* Variants restore four-character phrasing: *hsiu-chai tsao-fu,* "cultivate the feasts and make merit" (D); *hsiu-fu chui-chai,* "cultivate merit and hold posthumous feasts" (h).

136. **Commission statues** *(tsao-hsiang).* Var.: *tsao-ching tsao-hsiang,* "commission scriptures and commission statues" (h), which restores four-character phrasing.

137. **In order to repay their parents' kindness** *(i pao fu-mu en).* Variants restore four-character phrasing: *i pao fu-mu,* "in order to repay their parents" (D); *pao fu-mu en,* "to repay their parents' kindness" (h).

138. **You should allow them to attain rebirth in the heavens** *(ling te sheng-t'ien).* Var.: *te-sheng t'ien-shang,* "they will attain rebirth up in heaven" (h).

139. **Actions committed by** *(tsao-yeh),* or "karma created by." Var.: *tsui-yeh,* "sins and actions" (D).

140. **Are hard to explain fully** *(chü nan ch'en).* Var.: *ssu wei-ch'en,* "resemble fine dust" (D).

141. **Stream of delusion** *(mi-chin),* which in its Buddhist-influenced usage connotes the whole world of birth and death. In non-Buddhist contexts the term means to be unable to ford a stream or to have lost one's way; see Morohashi, *Jiten,* no. 38825.40; and Lin, *Lin Yutang's Chinese English Dictionary of Modern Usage,* p. 379. The term occurs again in the hymn to the ninth court. Cf. also *kuan-chin,* "important crossing," in the hymn to the tenth court.

142. **We** *(wo-teng).* Var.: *wo,* "we" (D).

black[143] horses, holding black banners, and wearing[144] black clothes. They will inspect the homes[145] of deceased people to see what merit is being made. We will allow names to be entered, dispose of warrants, and pluck out sinners. May we not go against our vows."

> The hymn goes:
> The various kings dispatch messengers to inspect the deceased
> And see what causes of merit their sons and daughters are
>   cultivating.
> Depending on one's name, one can be released from the prisons of
>   the three paths,
> And be spared passage[146] through the dark regions[147] and any
>   encounters with suffering and grief.

[King Yama said,] "I humbly vow to the World Honored One that I will listen to the preaching and inspect the feasts for the names[148] of the Ten Kings."

> The hymn goes:
> King Yama went to the Buddha and again[149] explained the
>   situation:
> "I humbly vow to be compassionate in carrying out verification.
> After death, when common people cultivate merit,
> I will inspect the feasts and listen for the preaching of the
>   names of the Ten Kings."

[Plate 4]

The first. After seven days they pass before King Kuang of Ch'in.[150]

> The hymn goes:
> During the first seven, dead people with bodies of intermediate
>   darkness[151]

143. **Black *(hei)*.** Var. radical: *li* (C).
144. **Wearing *(cho)*.** Y misreads as synonymous *cho^b*. Var.: *cho^b* (D).
145. **Homes *(chia)*.** Var.: missing (D).
146. **Passage *(li^b)*.** Var. radical: *li^c* (D).
147. **Dark regions *(ming-chien)*.** Var.: *jen-chien,* "human regions" (g).
148. **Names *(ming-tzu)*.** Var.: *ming* (D).
149. **Again *(tsai)*.** Var.: *chih,* "directly" (D).
150. **King Kuang of Ch'in (Ch'in Kuang wang).** The original reads T'ai Kuang wang, which I emend following B, C, D, g, i, j. X and Y mistakenly read Ch'in Kuang wang. The cartouche in the first illustration to B gives the name Ch'en Kuang Wang. For further information on this and the other nine kings, see chapter 16.
151. **Bodies of intermediate darkness *(chung-yin shen)*,** the kind of body one possesses between death and the next life. The phrase recurs in the hymn to the seventh court. Y mistakenly reads *chung-yin shen^b*.

Are herded like sheep, rank after rank,[152] numerous as particles
of dust.
Now they move toward the first king, who inspects each point of
the fast;
Still to come[153] they have not yet crossed the stream of the
River Nai.

[Plate 5a]

The second. After seven days they pass before the King of the First
River.[154]

The hymn goes:
During the second seven, dead people cross the River Nai;
In hordes of a thousand and groups of ten thousand they step
through the river's waves.[155]
The ox heads[156] who guide the way clasp cudgels at their
shoulders;[157]
The ghost soldiers[158] who press people ahead raise[159] pitchforks
in their hands.

[Plate 6a]

The third. After seven days[160] they pass before King Ti of Sung.[161]

The hymn goes:
Dead people during the third seven turn from one annoyance to the
next,

152. **Are herded like sheep, rank after rank** *(ch'ü-yang tui-tui)*. Var.: *ch'ü-chiang sui-yeh*, "are urged on and led in accordance with their actions" (D, g).
153. **Still to come** *(yu-lai)*. Var.: *yu-lai*[b] (D).
154. **The King of the First River (Ch'u-chiang wang)**. The short recension consistently places the King of the First River in the third court and King Ti of Sung in the second court (l).
155. **River's waves** *(chiang-po)*. Var.: *hung-po*, "flooding waves" (D, g).
156. **Ox heads** *(niu-t'ou)*. Together with "horse face" *(ma-mien)*, ox heads are commonly depicted as guards in the underworld in Indian and Chinese sources; see Hsiao, *Tun-huang su-wen-hsüeh lun-ts'ung*, pp. 217–22; Mochizuki, *Daijiten*, pp. 1266c–67a.
157. **Clasp cudgels at their shoulders** *(chien hsieh-pang)*. Var.: *mi shih-pang*, "are confused in using cudgels" (C); *chien shih-pang*, "use cudgels at their shoulders" (D).
158. **Ghost soldiers** *(kuei-tsu)*. Var.: *yü-tsu*, "prison soldiers" (C).
159. **Raise** *(ching*[b]*)*. Var. radical: *ching*[c] (B).
160. **Days** *(jih*[b]*)*. Var.: omitted (D).
161. **King Ti of Sung (Sung Ti wang)**. Var.: Tsung Ti wang, attested in early manuscripts (Pk *hsin* 1537) and in printed sources (k).

And begin to be aware how long is the narrow[162] road that winds
   through the dark paths.
One-by-one [the kings] check off names—they know where everyone is;
Rank-after-rank[163] [the guards] drive them along to the King of
   the Five Offices.

[Plate 7a]

The fourth. After seven days they pass before the King of the Five
Offices.

The hymn goes:
The balance of actions[164] in the five offices is suspended in the air;
To the left and the right the Twin Boys complete the logbook of
   actions.[165]
The lightness and heaviness[166] [of retribution], alas, is due
   to[167] what the feelings desire;
Whether low or high,[168] one is responsible for past[169] causes
   and conditions.

[Plate 8a]

The fifth. After seven days they pass before[170] King Yama rāja.

The hymn goes:
During the fifth seven, Yama rāja[171] puts an end to[172] sounds of
   dispute,

162. **Narrow (hsien).** Var. radical: *hsien^b* (D, g).
163. **Rank-after-rank (tui-tui).** Var.: *chün-chün,* "prefecture-by-prefec-
ture" (D).
164. **Balance of actions (yeh-ch'eng),** or "karma scale." Var.: *yeh-ching,*
"mirror of actions" (C, D, g).
165. **Logbook of actions (yeh-pu).** Var.: *i-pu,* "logbook of intentions" (C).
166. **Lightness and heaviness.** The original reads *chuan-chung,* an easy
orthographic error for *ch'ing-chung,* "lightness and heaviness," or "weight." I
emend to *ch'ing-chung* to maintain the parallel with the next line, following B, C,
D, g, i, j, W, X.
167. **Alas is due to (ch'i yu)** is somewhat strained; cf. the Japanese translation of the hymn in k, which uses *ani,* "unfortunately," or "unexpectedly";
Ishida, *"Bussetsu jizō bosatsu hosshin innen jūō kyō,"* p. 212. The variant makes
more sense: *ch'i-yu^b,* "arise from" (D).
168. **Whether low or high (ti-ang).** W mistakenly reads *chia-ang.* Var.:
ti-yang (D, g).
169. **Past (hsi).** Var.: *hsi^b,* "putting an end to" (D, g).
170. **They pass before (kuo).** The original omits *kuo.* I add it for consistency
with the introductory phrasing in the other nine courts, following B, C,
D, g, i, j.
171. **Yama rāja (Yen-lo).** Var.: Yen-wang, "King Yama" (g); Yen-lo wang,
"King Yama rāja" (D), which makes eight syllables in the line.
172. **Puts an end to (hsi^b).** Var.: *hsi^c* (D, g).

But in their hearts sinners are resentful and unwilling.
With their hair yanked[173] and their heads pulled up to look in
the mirror of actions,[174]
They begin to know that affairs[175] from previous lives are
rendered distinct and clear.

[Plate 9]

The sixth. After seven days they pass before the King of Transformations.

The hymn goes:
Dead people during the sixth seven clog the dark paths,
Mortally afraid that the living will be stupid in holding to their
opinions.
Day in and day out all they see is the power of merit,
How the difference between the halls of heaven and the prisons
underground lies in a *kṣana*.[176]

[Plate 10]

The seventh. After seven days they pass before the King of Mount T'ai.

The hymn goes:
During the seventh seven in the dark paths the bodies of
intermediate darkness
Search for their fathers and mothers, [hoping] to meet with loved
ones and kin.[177]
Fortunate actions at this time have yet to be determined;
They watch again to see what causes [for merit] sons and daughters
will perform.

[Plate 11a]

The eighth. After one hundred days they pass before the Impartial
King.[178]

173. **With their hair yanked** *(ts'e-fa).* Var.: *ts'e-faᵇ,* "yanked and pushed out" (g).
174. **Their heads pulled up** *(yang-t'ou).* Var.: *wang-t'ou,* "their heads turned" (D, g).
175. **Affairs** *(shihᶜ).* Var.: *tsui,* "sins" (g).
176. *Kṣana (hsü-yü),* an instant.
177. **Search for fathers and mothers, [hoping to] meet with loved ones and kin** *(chuan ch'iu fu-mu hui ch'ing-ch'in).* Ishida (*"Bussetsu jizō bosatsu hosshin innen jūō kyō,"* p. 262) renders the line: "Seek only the intimacy and care provided by their parents."
178. **Impartial King (P'ing-teng wang).** The original reads P'ing-cheng wang, literally "King of Equality and Truth." I emend to P'ing-teng wang following h, i, j, W.

The hymn goes:
After one hundred days dead people[179] are subjected to more
   annoyances:
Their bodies meet with[180] cangues and shackles,[181] and they are
   wounded by whips.
If sons and daughters exert themselves in cultivating[182] merit,
Then [the dead] will be spared from dropping into the underground
   prisons, those places of eternal suffering.

[Plate 12]

The ninth. At one year they pass before the King of the Capital.

The hymn goes:
At one year they pass here, turning about in suffering and grief,
   depending on what merit their sons and daughters have
   cultivated.[183]
The wheel of rebirth in the six paths is revolving, still not
   settled;
Commission a scripture or commission an image,[184] and they will
   emerge from the stream of delusion.

[Plate 13a]

The tenth. At three years[185] they pass before the King Who Turns the
Wheel of Rebirth in the Five Paths.

The hymn goes:
For the last three, where they pass[186] is an important
   crossing.[187]

179. **After one hundred days dead people** *(pai-jih wang-jen)*. Var.: *wang-jen pai-jih*, "dead people after one hundred days" (i, j, W, X), which according to X makes a more regular prosodic structure.
180. **Meet with** *(tsao)*. Var. radical, here and below: *ts'ao* (D).
181. **Cangues and shackles** *(chia-ch'ou)*. The *chia*[b] (or "cangue," translating via Portuguese) is placed around the neck. *Ch'ou*, "shackles," are equivalent to *hsieh*, which include both fetters and manacles.
182. **Cultivating** *(hsiu)*. Var.: *tsao*[b], "making" (D, g).
183. **Depending on what merit . . . cultivated** *(hsiu ho kung-te yin)*. Var.: *hsiu-chai fu-yeh yin*, "depending on what fortunate actions and feasts . . . cultivated" (i), which according to X makes a more regular prosodic structure.
184. **Commission an image** *(tsao-hsiang)*. Var.: *tsao-fo*, "commission a Buddha[-image]."
185. **At three years** *(san-nien)*. Var.: *kuo san-nien*, "after three years" (D).
186. **For the last three, where they pass** *(hou-san so-li)*. Var.: *ssu-hou san-li*, "after death, the third passing" (B).
187. **Important crossing** *(kuan-chin)*, a place to ford a stream; see Morohashi, *Jiten*, no. 41470.100. The original uses a cursive form of *kuan* which is easily confused with *k'ai*, "open." The cursive form is attested in Ōfuchi, *Tonkō dōkyō*, 2:401.

Good and evil [rebirth][188] depend only on fortunate actions as a
cause.
If you don't perform good, there will be still more grief,[189] and
within a thousand days
They will be reborn into a womb only to die in birth, or to perish
at a tender age.[190]

[Plate 14a]

[Yama said,] "When the ten feasts are completely fulfilled, we will
spare them from the sins of the ten evils and release them to be reborn
in heaven."

The hymn goes:[191]
One body in the six paths suffers without rest;
The ten evils and the three paths are not easy to bear.
But if you exert yourselves to cultivate the feasts, and your
merit is complete,
Then all sins[192] as numerous as sand in the Ganges will disappear
of themselves.

[Yama continued,] "I will[193] send the four *yakṣa* kings to preserve and
protect this scripture and not let it fall into destruction."[194]

The hymn goes:
King Yama upheld the Law and sang a hymn[195] glorifying and
praising it,
Proclaiming to men and gods and to all fields for the practice of
the Way.
"I will send *yakṣas* to preserve[196] and protect it;

188. **Good and evil [rebirth]** *(hao-o).* Var.: *hao-yeh,* "good actions" (g).
189. **Still more grief** *(shang-yu).* Var.: *shang-yu^b* (D, g).
190. **Or to perish at a tender age.** The wording of the original is difficult: *pa
wang-jen,* which means either "to pluck out a dead person," which is unlikely, or
"and be hurried into death," which is an attested but infrequent usage of *pa^b;*
see Morohashi, *Jiten,* no. 11959, def. 2.3. I emend to *yao-wang-jen* following i, j,
k, W. The orthography of the original is difficult to make out: the hand radical
is clear, but the phonetic is not. Var.: *ao wang-jen,* "measuring the deceased"
(D); *hsien wang-jen,* "pushing along the deceased" (g). Note also that *yao* in Tun-
huang manuscripts is often written with the phonetic component in *pa^b;* see
Ōfuchi, *Tonkō dōkyō,* 2:393; and Chu-shih, *Fo-chiao nan-tzu tzu-tien,* no. 681.
191. **The hymn goes** *(tsan-yüeh).* Var.: omitted (D).
192. **All sins** *(chu-tsui).* W mistakenly reads *chu-tsui^b.*
193. **Will** *(tang).* Var.: *ch'ang,* "will always" (D).
194. **Fall into destruction** *(hsien-mo).* The word recurs in the next hymn.
Orthographically *hsien-mo* is easy to confuse with *yin-mo,* "fade into obscurity,"
but the two are distinct; see Chu-shih, *Fo-chiao nan-tzu tzu-tien,* nos. 3893, 3917.
In the hymn, var: *yin-mo* (j).
195. **Sang a hymn** *(tsan).* Var.: *yüan^c,* "vowed to" (D).
196. **To preserve** *(ch'ï).* Var.: *wang,* "[*yakṣa*-]kings" (D).

I will not let it fall into destruction, and will forever have it
   circulate."

We bow our heads low to the World Honored One. Most of the sinners in the prisons made use of[197] property belonging to the Three Jewels. With loud wrangling they suffer punishment for their sins. People
with awareness and faith can guard against violating[198] the Three Jewels. Retribution for actions[199] is hard to endure. Those who see this
scripture must cultivate and study it.[200]

> The hymn goes:
> If you wish to seek peace and happiness and to dwell among humans
>   and gods,
> Then you must immediately stop[201] appropriating money belonging
>   to the Three Jewels.
> Once you fall into the dark regions and the various underground
>   prisons,
> There will only be crying for the sufferings you endure[202] for I
>   don't know how many years.

At that time Yama, King of the Law, leapt for joy, reverenced the
Buddha's feet with his head, stepped back, and sat to one side. The
Buddha said, "The name of this scripture is *The Scripture to the Four
Orders on the Prophecy Given to King Yama Rāja Concerning the Sevens of Life To
Be Cultivated in Preparation for Rebirth*[203] *in the Pure Land.* You should circu-
late it and transmit it among the states and realms, and uphold practice
according to its teachings."

> The hymn goes:
> King Yama stepped back and sat down and listened with his whole
>   mind.
> Then the Buddha with great care and diligence entrusted him with
>   this scripture:
> "Its name is *The Teaching of the Sevens of Life that Are
>   Cultivated in Preparation.*
> You, together with the four orders, must circulate it widely."

197. **Most . . . made use of.** The original is problematic. It reads *to shih-
yung,* "most . . . used." It is a three-character phrase where two-two would be
the norm, and the use of *shih,* either as copula or affirmative indicator, is
ungrammatical. I emend to *to shih-yung*[b] following C.
   198. **Can guard against violating** *(wu-fan).* Var.: *wu-fan*[b] (D, g).
   199. **Retribution for actions** *(pao-yeh).* Var. transposition: *yeh-pao* (D, g).
   200. **Study it** *(hsüeh).* Var. radical: *chüeh,* "become aware of it" (D).
   201. **Must immediately stop** *(ch'e-mo).* Var.: *pi-mo,* "must not" (D, g).
   202. **Sufferings you endure** *(shou-k'u).* Var.: *shou-tsui,* "sins you endure" (D).
   203. **Rebirth in** *(wang-sheng).* Var.: omitted (D).

The Scripture Spoken by the Buddha to the Four Orders on the Prophecy Given to King Yama Rāja Concerning the Sevens of Life To Be Cultivated in Preparation for Rebirth in the Pure Land. May our universal admonitions be lucky. Cultivate merit in preparation.[204] Give rise to the thought [of enlightenment]. Vow to put an end to the wheel of rebirth.[205]

The hymn has two stanzas:

The first hymn:
A single life is perilously brittle,[206] like a lamp in the wind;
Two rats sneak up,[207] gnawing at a creeper[208] in the well.
If within the sea of suffering you don't cultivate a boat or raft
     for crossing,
Then what can you hope to depend on to attain deliverance?

The second hymn:[209]
Not to build boats or bridges[210]—this[211] is human ignorance;

204. **Cultivate . . . in preparation** *(yü-hsiu)*. Var.: *hsiu,* "cultivate" (D).
205. **Vow to put an end to the wheel of rebirth.** The original reads *chuan yüan hsi lun-hui,* which adds *chuan,* "turn and," to an otherwise consistent four-character phrase. I emend by dropping *chuan,* which leaves four four-character phrases in this liturgical section. Var.: *yüan hsi lun-hui* (D), which drops *chuan* and uses *hsiʰ,* "all," for *hsiʰ,* "put an end to."
206. **Perilously brittle** *(wei-ts'ui).* Var.: *wei-o,* "perilously difficult" (D).
207. **Sneak up** *(ch'in-ling).* Var.: *ch'in-ch'i* (D), which I take to be a homophone for *ch'in-ch'iʰ,* "creep up."
208. **Creeper** *(t'eng).* The original reads *t'engʰ,* "to ascend." I emend to *t'eng* (following i, j, W, X), based on the homophony and because the figure of the creeper in the well being gnawed by rats was a well-known parable in Buddhist literature. The original story relates that a man once tried to escape a rampaging elephant by slipping down a well, where he held on to tree roots to support himself. But once he found haven from the elephant, he was beset by further maladies: two rats began to eat away at the roots, honey from a beehive in a tree overhead started to drip into his mouth and attract bees, poisonous snakes crawled toward him from the sides of the well, dragons awaited him at the bottom, and a fire began to burn in the tree. See *P'in-t'ou-lu-t'o-lo-she wei yu-t'o-yen wang shuo-fa ching,* Guṇabhadra (394–468), *T* no. 1690, 32:787a–b. The story is paraphrased in *Fa-yüan chu-lin,* Tao-shih (d. 683), *T* no. 2122, 53:626a–b. *P'ei-wen yün-fu* (p. 1297a) cites *Fa-yüan chu-lin,* in a passage in the latter work I have not been able to find, "As the honey melts in his mouth, the creeper in the well becomes harder to hold on to." The parable forms the entire text of a brief scripture translated in the eighth century, *P'i-yü ching,* I-ching (635–713), *T* no. 217.
209. **The second hymn** *(ti-erh tsan).* Var.: *ti-erh kuei-fo hsiu-hsin tsan,* "The second, a hymn on taking refuge in the Buddha and cultivating the mind" (D).
210. **Boats or bridges** *(kang-ch'iao).* Var.: *ch'iao-fu,* "bridges or rafts" (D).
211. **This** *(tz'u).* W mistakenly reads *i.*

You will encounter danger and constant annoyance—this, sir, you
   must begin to know.
If you are aware that one hundred years pass in the snap of the
   fingers,
Then you mustn't delay in cultivating the feasts and listening to
   the Law.

Appendixes
Glossary
Bibliography
Indexes

Appendix 1
The Ten Kings

Number of Service	Time after Death	King
1	7 days	Ch'in Kuang wang (King Kuang of Ch'in)
2	14 days	Ch'u-chiang wang (King of the First River)
3	21 days	Sung Ti wang (King Ti of Sung)
4	28 days	Wu-kuan wang (King of the Five Offices)
5	35 days	Yen-lo wang (King Yama rāja)
6	42 days	Pien-ch'eng wang (King of Transformations)
7	49 days	T'ai-shan wang (King of Mount T'ai)
8	100 days	P'ing-teng wang (Impartial King)
9	1 year	Tu-shih wang (King of the Capital)
10	3 years	Wu-tao chuan-lun wang (King Who Turns the Wheel of Rebirth in the Five Paths)

Appendix 2
Invitations to Memorial Rites and
Related Memoranda

1. **1 Sept. 887.** Pk 2126v. Invitation to monks to perform memorial service at home for mother. Signed by monk Shan-hui. Dated Kuang-ch'i 3/ VIII/10.
2. **905–915. P 3405.** "Draft of Prayers for Preparatory Cultivation by Monks and Lay People." Dated in B.N., *Catalogue*.
3. **ca. 7 July 924?** S 5527. Untitled schedule of ten feasts observed on behalf of mother, who died on *chia-shen*/ VI/3. Eight feasts named.
4. **8 Feb. 939.** P 2836v. Invitation to monks to perform memorial service at home for father. Signed by Chia Feng-chiu, Lackey to the Military Commissioner. Dated T'ien-fu^b 4/I/17.
5. **4 July 945.** S 5718. Invitation to perform memorial service for monk. Signed by Ch'ing-sui of Chin-kuang-ming ssu. Dated T'ien-fu^b 10/V/22.
6. **2 April 947.** P 3388. Invitation to monks of Chin-kuang-ming ssu to perform memorial service at home for brother. Signed by Ts'ao Yüan-chung. Dated K'ai-yün 4/III/9.
7. **11 May 960.** Pk 2258v. Invitation to monks of Ch'ien-yüan ssu to perform memorial service at home for mother. Signed by the Area Commander, Lower Class, Acting Magistrate of Shou-ch'ang District. Dated Chien[-lung] 1/IV/13.
8. **968.** Pk 5866v. Invitation to monks to celebrate memorial service at home for mother. Signed by Yin. Dated Ch'ien-te 6/IX.
9. **7 Oct. 969?.** P 3367. Invitation to monks of San-chieh ssu to perform memorial service at home for son, a Lackey. Signed by Sung Tz'u-shun, Chief Lackey. Dated *chi-chi*/VIII/23.
10. **23 July 978.** P 3107. Invitation to [Abbot] Piṇḍola Bhāradvāja of Chi-tsu shan to perform memorial service at Ching-t'u ssu for father. Signed by "Bereft Orphan So-and So" *(ku-tsu mou-mou)*. Dated *wu-yin*/ VI/16.

11. **979.** S 6178. Invitation to monks to perform memorial service for heir apparent. Signed by Great Master Kuang-chi. Dated T'ai-p'ing hsing-kuo 4/VII.

12. **986.** S 5855. Invitation to monks at San-chieh ssu to perform memorial service for father at temple. Signed by Yin Ts'un-li, Area Commander. Dated Yung-hsi 3, *ping-hsü*/VI.

13. **13 June 991.** S 86. "Prayer for Transferring Offerings." On behalf of Ma Ch'ou-nü. Offerings made for first weekly feast and concluding weekly feast. 230 monks in attendance, numerous scriptures chanted. Dated Ch'un-hua 2, *hsin-mao*/IV/28.

14. **992.** S 5696. Invitation to Abbot Piṇḍola Bhāradvāja of Chi-tsu shan to celebrate memorial service at home for father, Chief Lackey. Signed by Ch'en Shou-ting, Area Commander. Dated Ch'un-hua 3/VIII.

15. **26 Sept. 992.** P 3152. Invitation to monks at Lung-hsing ssu to perform memorial service at home for father, Chief Lackey. Signed by Ch'en Shou-ting, Area Commander. Dated Ch'un-hua 3/VIII/27.

16. **993.** S 5941. Invitation to monks of Hsien[-te ssu] to perform memorial service at home. Signed by Ts'ao Ch'ang-ch'ien, Area Commander. Dated Ch'un-hua 4, *kuei-ssu*/V.

Appendix 3
Taoist Memorial Rites

Number of Service	Time after Death	True Lord	Celestial Venerables
1	7 days	T'ai-su miao-kuang chen-chün	Yü-pao-huang-shang t'ien-tsun, Chiu-yu pa-tsui t'ien-tsun
2	14 days	Yin-te ting-hsiu chen-chün	Hsüan-chen wan-fu t'ien-tsun, Shih-fang, chiu-k'u t'ien-tsun
3	21 days	Tung-ming p'u-ching chen-chün	T'ai-miao chih-chi t'ien-tsun, Chu-ling tu-ming t'ien-tsun
4	28 days	Hsüan-te wu-ling chen-chün	Hsüan-shang yü-ch'en t'ien-tsun, Fa-ch'iao ta-tu t'ien-tsun
5	35 days	Tsui-sheng hui-ling chen-chün	Tu-hsien shang-sheng t'ien-tsun, Huo-lien tan-chieh t'ien-tsun
6	42 days	Pao-su chao-ch'eng chen-chün	Hao-sheng tu-ming t'ien-tsun, Chin-ch'üeh hua-shen t'ien-tsun
7	49 days	T'ai-shan hsüan-miao chen-chün	T'ai-ling hsü-huang t'ien-tsun, Hsiao-yao k'uai-le t'ien-tsun

Number of Service	Time after Death	True Lord	Celestial Venerables
8	100 days	Wu-shang cheng-tu chen-chün	Wu-liang t'ai-hua t'ien-tsun, Sui-yüan wang-sheng t'ien-tsun
9	1 year	Fei-mo yen-hua chen-chün	Yü-hsü ming-huang t'ien-tsun, Ch'ui-kung t'o-hua t'ien-tsun
10	3 years	Wu-ling wei-te chen-chün	Chen-huang tung-shen t'ien-tsun, Pao-hua yüan-man t'ien-tsun

Source: *Ti-fu shih-wang pa-tu i,* Sch no. 215, *TT* 84, 4r–11v.

Appendix 4
Illustrations to *The Scripture on the Ten Kings*

Group A

1. **P 2003.** Long recension of *The Scripture on the Ten Kings* with fourteen illustrations. Iconography distinct from others; closest to 2 and 3. Mountains shown in courts two through ten.

Group B

2. **P 2870.** Long recension of *The Scripture on the Ten Kings* with fourteen illustrations. Iconography very close to 3. Composition much poorer than 3 (e.g., in last scene, three figures are crowded together). All kings except two, nine, and ten hold court on raised platform with roof supported by poles.

3. **Satō ms.** Long recension of *The Scripture on the Ten Kings* with fourteen illustrations. Iconography very close to 2, but composed much better. Cylindrical object for interrogation in courts three, six, and seven.

Group C

4. **S 3961.** Long recension of *The Scripture on the Ten Kings*. Originally probably contained thirteen illustrations; contains text for but lacks scene of six Bodhisattvas. Beginning of ms. missing, comprising frontispiece and first eighteen lines. Courts drawn too close together, hymns often squeezed in (especially courts three, seven, and nine). Hair ribbons of attendants curled distinctively. Boys of Good and Evil not placed consistently as pair with each king. Iconography distinct from others, often confused (e.g., no sinners in court six, no donors in court seven, odd listing of six paths in court ten).

Group D

5a, 5b. **Cft 00404 (L), Cft 00212 (L).** Two contiguous fragments of *The Scripture on the Ten Kings* with illustrations. Only frontispiece and fifteen partial lines of text survive. Joining of two portions suggested by Matsumoto, *Tonkō ga no kenkyū*, 1:404.

Group E

6a, 6b. **P 4523, Cft cii.001 (L).** Two contiguous halves of a hand-scroll of illustrations to *The Scripture on the Ten Kings,* totaling thirteen illustrations. Contains no text. Designed as picture-scroll only, without text, since insufficient space is left for hymns between courts (e.g., 1 cm. for court five, 4 cm. for court 9). Other elements suggest use in storytelling or preaching: scenes more complex than other versions (courts two, four, and five); lacks scene of six Bodhisattvas, which is least narrative of all scenes. Sleeves of kings' robes fly distinctively. Scroll unrolled in clerk's hands in courts one, five, and ten.

Joining of portions unmentioned in previous studies, despite stylistic symmetry and demon split in half between two pieces.

Related illustrations

7a-ii. Thirty-five fragments of two copies of a Uighur translation of the long recension of *The Scripture on the Ten Kings.* Details contained in Appendix 8.

8. **P 3304v.** Informal notes concerning the long recension of *The Scripture on the Ten Kings* and its fourteen illustrations. First noted in Soymié, "Un recueil d'inscriptions sur peintures: le manuscrit P. 3304 verso," pp. 170–79.

Appendix 5
Paintings of Ti-tsang and
the Ten Kings

Paintings are grouped roughly following the order of iconographic development suggested in Ledderose, "The Ten Kings and the Bureaucracy of
Hell."

Group A. In two unordered groups.

1. **EO 1173.**

   Reprod. V-N, *Bannières,* 15:pl. 118.

   Top half: Kuan-yin with one thousand arms. Bottom half: Ti-tsang
   accompanied by ten kings.

   Kings kneel facing forward below Ti-tsang in two groups; at each side
   three in front row, two in back row. Kings not iconographically identifiable, although cartouches (some still legible) name them.

   Attendants: lion, four clerks, two boys.

2. **EO 3580.**

   Reprod. V-N, *Bannières,* 15:pl. 120.

   Top half: Paradise scene with Buddha (Amitābha?) and attendants. Bottom half: hooded Ti-tsang, master of six paths, accompanied by ten kings.

   Kings kneel at 3/4 angle below Ti-tsang in two groups; at each side three
   in front row, two in back row. Fifth and tenth kings identifiable.

   Attendants: Tao-ming, lion, two boys.

3. **MG 17793.**

   Reprod. Fig. 1, and V-N, *Bannières,* 15:pl. 115.

   Hooded Ti-tsang, master of six paths, accompanied by ten kings.

   Kings kneel at 3/4 angle below Ti-tsang in two groups; at each side two
   in front row, three in back row. Kings not identifiable.

   Attendants: Tao-ming, four clerks, two boys.

   Donors painted into scene, rather than in separate panel.

4. **Cft lxiii.002 (ND).**

   Reprod. Kawahara, "Tonkō ga jizō zu shiryō," p. 118, pl. 26.

   Hooded Ti-tsang accompanied by ten kings; two seated Buddhas
   descend from each side.

Ten kings stand in two groups below Ti-tsang. Kings not identifiable.
Attendants: Tao-ming, lion, four clerks.

Group B. Kneeling in a line below Ti-tsang.

5. Cft lxi.009 (L).

Reprod. Whitfield, *Art,* 2:pl. 23.

Hooded Ti-tsang, master of six paths, accompanied by ten kings.

Ten kings kneel carrying *hu* in two lines diagonally below Ti-tsang.
Kings not identifiable.

Attendants: Tao-ming, lion, two boys, four clerks.

Group C. Seated separately below Ti-tsang.

6. EO 3644.

Reprod. V-N, *Bannières,* 14:pl. 12.

Kuan-yin with six arms enthroned at left. Hooded Ti-tsang enthroned at
right, accompanied by ten kings.

Ten kings sit on separate platforms below Bodhisattvas, two lines of four
down each side, one on inside of each line. Each king accompanied by two
boys. Fifth king identifiable.

Attendants: Tao-ming, lion, four clerks.

Group D. Seated separately around Ti-tsang in two lines.

7. MG 17795.

Reprod. V-N, *Bannières,* 15:pl. 114.

Hooded Ti-tsang, master of six paths, accompanied by ten kings.

Ten kings sit on separate platforms at 3/4 angle, in two vertical lines.
Each king accompanied by two boys, except for one king in middle, painted
too close to Ti-tsang. Fifth and tenth king identifiable.

Attendants: lion, four clerks.

8. Cft xxviii.003 (ND)

Reprod. Matsumoto, *Tonkō ga no kenkyū,* 2:pl. 109.

Hooded Ti-tsang, master of six paths, accompanied by ten kings.

Ten kings sit behind separate desks at 3/4 angle, in two vertical lines.
Each king accompanied by two boys. Fifth and tenth kings identifiable.

Attendants: Tao-ming, lion.

Group E. Seated separately around Ti-tsang, nearly in circle.

9. Cft 00355 (ND).

Reprod. Matsumoto, *Tonkō ga no kenkyū,* 2:pl. 111a.

Hooded Ti-tsang accompanied by ten kings.

Ten kings sit behind desks at 3/4 angle around two sides. Kings in attitude of prayer; incense burners on some desks. Each king accompanied by
two boys. Fifth and tenth king identifiable.

Attendants: Tao-ming, lion, four clerks.

10. **MG 17662.**

Reprod. V-N, *Bannières*, 15:pl. 116.

Hooded Ti-tsang, master of six paths, accompanied by ten kings.

Ten kings sit behind desks at 3/4 angle around two sides. Each king accompanied by two boys. Fifth and tenth kings identifiable.

Attendants: Tao-ming, lion, four clerks.

Dated T'ai-p'ing hsing-kuo 8/XI/14 (20 Dec. 983).

(?) 11. **Cft 00225 (ND).**

No reproduction. Discussed in Waley, *Catalogue*, no. 361; Stein, *Serindia*, p. 981; Matsumoto, *Tonkō ga no kenkyū*, 1:387-88; idem, "Hibō jizō bosatsu zō no bunpō," p. 159; Kawahara, "Tonkō ga jizō zu shiryō," p. 118.

Hooded Ti-tsang accompanied by ten kings.

Includes scene of judgment with sinner, mirror, and guard, hence probably similar to 12.

12. **Cft 0021 (L).**

Reprod. Fig. 2, and Whitfield, *Art*, 2:pl. 24.

Hooded Ti-tsang accompanied by ten kings.

Ten kings sit behind desks at 3/4 angle around two sides. Each king accompanied by one or two boys. Fifth and tenth kings identifiable.

Scene of judgment at bottom shows sinner in front of mirror.

Attendants: Tao-ming, lion.

F. Later painting

13. **MG 17794.**

Reprod. V-N, *Bannières*, 15:pl. 117.

Hooded Ti-tsang accompanied by ten kings. Southern plant behind Ti-tsang. Architecturally precise balustrade crosses behind him. Two boys descend from right.

Ten kings dressed in late Sung, early Yüan fashion. Kings stand below Ti-tsang in relaxed manner, some conversing, nine at right, one at left.

Attendants: Tao-ming, lion, four clerks, two guards, two boys.

Architectural details, use of space, dress of kings all suggest late Sung or early Yüan dating.

Appendix 6

Taoist Lay Feasts

Number of Feast	Day of Month	Direction	Chief Deity	Assistant
1	1	NW	Pei-tou	Ch'uan-yen shih-che
2	8	N	Pei-tou ssu-sha kuei	Ch'ih-ch'e shih-che
3	14	NE	T'ai-i shih-che	Tien-ssu shih-che
4	15	E	T'ien-ti	T'ien-ti-shui san-kuan and Chien-ssu shih-che
5	18	SE	T'ien-i	Tsei-ts'ao shih-che
6	23	S	T'ai-i pa-shen shih-che	Fu-chang shih-tsung
7	24	SW	Pei-ch'en	Shou-chai san-chiang-chün
8	28	W	Hsia-t'ai-i	T'ien-kung shih-che
9	29	Nadir	Chung-t'ai-i	Chu-kuan chiang-chün
10	30	Zenith	Shang-t'ai-i	T'ien-ti shih-che

Source: *T'ai-shang tung-hsüan ling-pao yeh-pao yin-yüan ching,* Sch no. 336, *TT* 174–75, 4.10r–v.

Appendix 7
Buddhist Lay Feasts

Number of Feast	Day of Month	Chief Deity (Sanskrit)	Assistant
1	1	Ting-kuang ju-lai fo (Dīpaṃkara Tathāgata Buddha)	Shan-o t'ung-tzu
2	8	Yao-shih liu-li-kuang fo (Bhaiṣajyaguru Vaiḍūryaprabha Buddha)	T'ai-tzu
3	14	Hsien-chieh ch'ien-fo	Ch'a-ming ssu-lu
4	15	O-mi-t'o fo (Amitābha Buddha)	Wu-tao ta-chiang-chün
5	18	Kuan-shih-yin p'u-sa (Avalokiteśvara Bodhisattva)	Yen-lo wang (Yama rāja)
6	23	Lu-she-na fo (Vairocana Buddha)	T'ien ta-chiang-chün
7	24	Ti-tsang p'u-sa (Kṣitigarbha Bodhisattva)	T'ai-shan fu-chün
8	28	O-mi-t'o fo (Amitābha)	T'ien-ti Shih (Śakra)
9	29	Yao-wang yao-shang p'u-sa (Bhaiṣajyarāja and Bhaiṣajyasa-mudgata Bodhisattvas)	Ssu-t'ien wang
10	30	Shih-chia-mou-ni fo (Śākyamuni Buddha)	Ta-fan t'ien-wang (Brahmā)

Source: *Ta-sheng ssu-chai jih*, S 1164, transcr. *T* no. 2849, 85:1299c–1300a.

Appendix 8
Uighur Fragments of *The Scripture on the Ten Kings*
Discovered at Qočo (Sinkiang) and
Possible Correspondences to the Chinese Version

a. MIK 3:2, reprod. Gabain, "Kṣitigarbha-Kult in Zentralasien," fig. 55.
b. 3:3, fig. 61.
c. 3:12, fig. 71.
d. 3:4535, fig. 79. Corresponds to last illustration, walled city of hell.
e. 3:4647a, fig. 73. Corresponds to hymn and illustration to eighth court. Line 1: "Lord named . . . ng" may render Chinese p'ing-teng (*b'iwəng-təng). Line 8: "from the hell of suffering."
f. 3:4647b, fig. 59.
g. 3:4647c, fig. 65
h. 3:4690a, fig. 76.
i. 3:4690b, fig. 58.
j. 3:4698a, fig. 74.
k. 3:4951, fig. 53.
l. 3:6167, fig. 50.
m. 3:6266, fig. 75.
n. 3:6281, fig. 70.
o. 3:6327, fig. 57.
p. 3:6331, fig. 80. Corresponds to hymn to last illustration, walled city of hell.
q. 3:6332, fig. 78.
r. 3:6337, fig. 69.
s. 3:6394, fig. 72.
t. 3:6395a and 6443a, fig. 60.
u. 3:6395c, fig. 52.
v. 3:6615, fig. 56.
w. 3:6670, fig. 81.
x. 3:7246, fig. 62. Corresponds to hymn and illustration to tenth court and beginning of next hymn. Line 1: "at the end of the third year." Line 5: "released within a thousand days."

y. 3:7248, fig. 64. Corresponds to hymn and illustration to second court and beginning of third court. Line 2: "cow-headed." Line 4: Uighur *triž-ul* renders Ch.: *ch'a^b*, both usually used for Skt.: *triśūla* ("trident"). Line 5: Uighur *tsung* may transliterate first character in variant of Chinese name of third king, *Tsung (*tsuong);* see Csongor, "Chinese in the Uighur Script of the T'ang Period," no. 160.

z. 3:7256, fig. 77. Corresponds to hymn and illustration to tenth court and beginning of next hymn. Line 4: "released within a thousand days."

aa. 3:7259, fig. 48.

bb. 3:7260, fig. 49.

cc. 3:7272, fig. 68.

dd. 3:7450, fig. 47.

ee. 3:7451, fig. 54. Corresponds to hymn and illustration to eighth court. Line 2: "eighth . . . day." Line 5: "in shackles." Line 7: "hell of suffering."

ff. 3:7573, fig. 51.

gg. 3:7578, fig. 63.

hh. 3:7582, fig. 67.

ii. 3:8734, fig. 66.

Appendix 9

The Thirteen Buddhas (Jūsan butsu) in Japanese Memorial Services

Number of Service	Time after Death	King (Chinese)	Buddhist Deity (Sanskrit)
1	7 days	Shinkō ō (Ch'in Kuang wang)	Fudō myō ō (Acalanātha vidyārāja)
2	14 days	Shokō ō (Ch'u-chiang wang)	Shaka nyorai (Śākyamuni Tathāgata)
3	21 days	Sōtei ō (Sung Ti wang)	Monju bosatsu (Mañjuśrī Bodhisattva)
4	28 days	Gokan ō (Wu-kuan wang)	Fugen bosatsu (Samantabhadra Bodhisattva)
5	35 days	Enma ō (Yen-lo wang)	Jizō bosatsu (Kṣitigarbha Bodhisattva)
6	42 days	Hensei ō (Pien-ch'eng wang)	Miroku bosatsu (Maitreya Bodhisattva)
7	49 days	Taizan ō (T'ai-shan wang)	Yakushi nyorai (Bhaiṣajyarāja Tathāgata)
8	100 days	Byōdō ō (P'ing-teng wang)	Kanzeon bosatsu (Avalokiteśvara Bodhisattva)

Number of Service	Time after Death	King (Chinese)	Buddhist Deity (Sanskrit)
9	1 year	Toshi ō (Tu-shih wang)	Seishi bosatsu (Mahāsthāmaprāpta) [originally Ashuku nyōrai (Akṣobhya Tathāgata)]
10	3 years	Godō tenrin ō (Wu-tao chuan-lun wang)	Amida nyorai (Amitābha Tathāgata)
11	7 years		Ashuku nyorai (Akṣobhya Tathāgata)
12	13 years		Dainichi nyorai (Mahāvairocana Tathāgata)
13	33 years		Kokūzō bosatsu (Ākāśagarbha Bodhisattva)

Source: Mochizuki, *Daijiten,* pp. 2253a–54b.

The first ten (with a variant for number nine) are described in the Japanese apocryphon, *Jizō hosshin innen jūō kyō, Z* 2b, 24:381va–84va.

Appendix 10
Manuscript Copies of *The Scripture on the Ten Kings*

I. Booklets

1. **S 5450.** Glued Booklet. Two texts: 1. *Diamond* sūtra, trans. Kumāra-jīva, 32 sections, based on Hsi-ch'uan printed ed.; 2. *The Scripture on the Ten Kings,* short recension. Colophon: anonymous.
2. **S 5531.** Stitched Booklet. Ten texts, ninth is *The Scripture on the Ten Kings,* short recension. Colophon: dated *keng-ch'en*/XII/20 (31 Jan. 921?).
3. **S 5544.** Glued booklet. Two texts: 1. *Diamond* sūtra, trans. Kumāra-jīva, 32 sections, based on Hsi-ch'uan printed ed.; 2. *The Scripture on the Ten Kings,* short recension. Colophon: anonymous, dated *hsin-wei*/I (911?).
4. **S 5585.** Glued booklet. Two texts: 1. *Diamond* sūtra, incomplete (probably trans. Kumārajīva, 32 sections, based on Hsi-ch'uan printed ed., because *dhāraṇī* match); 2. *The Scripture on the Ten Kings,* short recension.
5. **P 3761.** Tiny booklet. *The Scripture on the Ten Kings,* long recension, no illustrations, incomplete.
6. **P 5580.** Glued booklet. Two texts: 1. *Diamond* sūtra, incomplete (probably trans. Kumārajīva, 32 sections, based on Hsi-ch'uan printed ed., because *dhāraṇī* match); 2. *The Scripture on the Ten Kings,* short recension, incomplete.
7. **Dhk 143** (one sheet only). Booklet. Probably two texts: (1. *Diamond* sūtra); 2. *The Scripture on the Ten Kings,* short recension.
8. **Dhk 931** (one sheet only). Booklet. Probably two texts: (1. *Diamond* sūtra); 2. *The Scripture on the Ten Kings,* short recension.
9. **San 262 (location unknown).** Booklet. Two texts: 1. *Diamond* sūtra, based on Hsi-ch'uan printed ed., 2. *The Scripture on the Ten Kings.*

II. Scrolls

10. **S 2489.** Scroll. *The Scripture on the Ten Kings,* medium recension. Colophon: Miao-fu.

11. **S 2815.** Scroll. *The Scripture on the Ten Kings,* short recension, incomplete.

12. **S 3147.** Scroll. *The Scripture on the Ten Kings,* short recension. Colophon: Tao-chen. Cover: Chang family.

13. **S 3961.** Illustrated scroll. *The Scripture on the Ten Kings,* long recension, incomplete.

14. **S 4530.** Scroll. *The Scripture on the Ten Kings,* short recension, incomplete. Colophon: Old man, dated *wu-ch'en*/XII/14 (8 Jan. 909).

15. **S 4805.** Scroll. *The Scripture on the Ten Kings,* short recension, incomplete.

16. **S 4890.** Scroll. *The Scripture on the Ten Kings,* short recension, incomplete.

17. **S 6230.** Scroll. *The Scripture on the Ten Kings,* short recension, incomplete. Colophon: anonymous, dated T'ung-kuang 4, *ping-hsü*/VI/6 (18 July 926).

18. **S 7598.** Scroll. *The Scripture on the Ten Kings,* short recension, incomplete.

19a, b. **Cft 00404 (L), Cft 00212 (L).** Illustrated scroll. *The Scripture on the Ten Kings,* long recension, incomplete.

20a, b. **Cft cii.001 (L), P 4523.** Illustrated scroll containing no text. Pictures match those of illustrated versions of *The Scripture on the Ten Kings.*

21. **P 2003.** Illustrated scroll. *The Scripture on the Ten Kings,* long recension.

22. **P 2870.** Illustrated scroll. *The Scripture on the Ten Kings,* long recension.

22. **Pk 1226.** Scroll. *The Scripture on the Ten Kings,* short recension, incomplete. Colophon: old man, dated *wu-ch'en*/VIII/1 (30 Aug. 908).

23. **Pk 4544.** Scroll. *The Scripture on the Ten Kings,* short recension, incomplete. Colophon: dedication to wife of Chai Feng-ta, dated IV/19 (10 May 958).

24. **Pk 6375.** Scroll. *The Scripture on the Ten Kings,* short recension, complete but ends after names of ten kings. Colophon: Tao-chen. Cover: Chang family.

25. **Pk 8045.** Scroll. *The Scripture on the Ten Kings,* medium recension, incomplete. Colophon: Miao-fu.

26. **Pk 8066.** Scroll. *The Scripture on the Ten Kings,* short recension, incomplete.

27. **Pk 8237.** Scroll. *The Scripture on the Ten Kings,* short recension, incomplete.

28. **Pk *hsin* 1537.** Scroll. *The Scripture on the Ten Kings,* short recension. Colophon: Chai Ting-yu, Chang Yü-chien.

29. **Satō ms.** Illustrated scroll. *The Scripture on the Ten Kings,* long recension. Colophon: Tung Wen-yüan, dated *hsin-wei*/XII/10 (2 Jan. 912?).

30. **Nakamura ms.** Scroll. *The Scripture on the Ten Kings,* short recension. Colophon: Hsüeh Yen-ch'ang, dated Ch'ing-t'ai 3, *ping-shen*/XII/[29] (12 Feb. 937).

31. **Dhk 803.** Scroll. *The Scripture on the Ten Kings,* short recension, incomplete.
32. *San 535* **(location unknown).** Probably scroll. *The Scripture on the Ten Kings,* probably short recension. Colophon: old man, dated *wu-ch'en/* VII/28 (27 Aug. 908).

III. Related Texts and Later Copies

1. **P 3304v.** Notes on illustrations to *The Scripture on the Ten Kings,* long recension.
2a–j. **MIK III:4607a, 4607f, 4693a, 4693b, 4693b bis, 4693c, 4693d, 4693e, 6321, 7473.** Fragments of an illustrated scroll. *The Scripture on the Ten Kings,* long recension, incomplete. Dated ca. 1050–1250. Discovered at Qočo.
3. **Hōjuin ms.** Illustrated scroll. *The Scripture on the Ten Kings,* long recension. Japanese copy perhaps based on Sung dynasty Chinese original. Reprod. *T* no. 3143.
4. **Korean printed ed.** *The Scripture on the Ten Kings,* long recension. Dated 1469. Transcr. *Z,* 2b, 23.
5. **Related Japanese apocryphon.** *Jizō bosatsu hosshin innen jūō kyō.* Dated ca. 1100. Transcr. *Z,* 2b, 23.

Appendix 11
A Chronology of the Life of
Chai Feng-ta

(ca. 883)   Born. Date is deduced from note stating that he was twenty years old when he wrote poems in T'ien-fu 2 (902). Pk *hsin* 836.

8 June 902   1. Copied *Ni-ts'e chan*. Colophon: dated T'ien-fu 2/IV/ *ting-ch'ou*, inscribed by Chai Tsai-wen, identified as Chai Feng-ta, "a capable student in the prefectural school in the Tun-huang commandery of Ho-hsi."
                 2. Wrote poems. Pk *hsin* 836.

31 March 904   1. Copied *Wu-chao yao-chüeh lüeh*.
                 2. Copied *Ni-ts'e chan*.
                 3. Copied *Chan shih-erh-shih lai fa*. Colophon: dated T'ien-fu 4, *chia-tzu*/intercalary III/12, signed "a student of *yin-yang* studies in the prefectural school."[1] P 2859.

11 May 908   1. Wrote *Ch'ih-sung chin-kang ching ling-yen kung-te chi*.
                 2. Copied *K'ai-yüan huang-ti tsan chin-kang ching kung-te*. Colophon: dated T'ien-fu 8, *wu-ch'en*/V/8, written by Chai Feng-ta, "wearer of the common cloth."
                 3. Copied *Chin-kang po-jo po-lo-mi ching*. Colophon: copied by Chai Feng-ta, "a disciple of the common cloth." P 2094.

24 May 915   Copied *Hsin p'u-sa ching*. Colophon: dated *i-hai*/IV/8 (probably 915 because it is followed by prayer to Maitreya on occasion of rebuilding of grottoes in T'ung-kuang 4 [926]), written by Chai Feng-ta, "wearer of the common cloth." P 2668.

ca. 924   Wrote calendar for Cheng-ming 10 (i.e., T'ung-kuang 2) (924). Composed by Chai Feng-ta, "Lackey, Acting Attendant Officer and Counselor." S 2404.

1. Fujieda ("Tonkō rekijitsu fu," p. 406) conjectures that the author is Chai. The date is problematic because in that year there was an intercalary fourth month, not third month. If "intercalary" *(jun)* is incorrect, the date would be T'ien-fu 4/III/12 (31 March 904). If the intercalary fourth month were intended, the date would be T'ien-fu 4/intercalary IV/12 (29 May 904).

242

ca. 926	Wrote calendar for T'ung-kuang 4 (926). Composed by Chai Feng-ta, "Attendant Officer and Counselor." Colophon: dated *ping-hsü*/III/14 (29 April 926), copied by unidentified scribe. P 3247 verso, *san* 673.
ca. 928	1. Wrote preface to calendar for T'ien-ch'eng 3 (928). Composed by Chai Feng-ta, "Attendant Officer and Counselor."
	2. Probably added note to poems written in 902 on recto.
	3. Probably copied *Mao-shih.* Pk *hsin* 836v.
ca. 940	Commissioned cave painting. Offered by Chai Feng-ta, "Lackey to the Military Commissioner, Acting Attendant Officer and Counselor, Grand Master of Imperial Entertainments with Silver Seal and Blue Ribbbon, Chancellor of the Directorate of Education, Concurrently Vice Censor-in-Chief, Supreme Pillar of State."[2] Th Cave 98.
20 July 945	Wrote *Shou Ch'ang hsien ti-ching.* Colophon: dated T'ien-fu[b] 10, *i-ssu*/VI/9, submitted by Chai, "Erudite in the Prefectural School." *San* 1700.
ca. 956	Wrote calendar for Hsien-te 3 (956). Composed by Chai Feng-ta, "Court Gentleman for Promoted Service, Acting Erudite in the Prefectural School." Colophon: "checked and corrected by Wen [i.e. Tsai-wen, original name of Chai Feng-ta]. Copied by Chai Wen-chin." S 95.
958–960	Commissioned copying of ten scriptures on three scrolls in memory of wife. Colophons: dated beginning Hsien-te 5, *wu-wu*/III/7 (29 March 958), offered by Chai Feng-ta, "the disciple, Gentleman for Court Discussion, Acting Vice Director of the Ministry of Public Works in the Department of State Affairs." Tts 175, Pk 4544, P 2055.
ca. 959	Wrote calendar for Hsien-te 6 (959). Composed by Chai Feng-ta, "Gentleman for Court Discussion, Acting Vice Director of the Ministry of Public Works in the Department of State Affairs, Acting Erudite of the Classics in Sha Prefecture, Concurrently Palace Censor, Awarded the Crimson Fish Pouch." P 2623.
7 July 966	Mentioned in note dated *ping-yin*/VI/17.[3] P 3197.
ca. 966–982	Died. After 966 there are no known texts written by Chai and no known references to him. The next surviving annotated calendar (S 1473) covers T'ai-p'ing hsing-kuo 7 (982) and was completed by Chai Wen-chin, a student of Chai Feng-ta's.

2. Fujieda ("Tonkō rekijitsu fu," pp. 435–36) suggests ca. 940 for the date.
3. See BN, *Catalogue.*

Appendix 12
Texts Copied by a Man in
His Eighties

8 April 905	*Diamond* sūtra.[1] Colophon: dated T'ien-fu 5,[2] *i-ch'ou*/III/1, eighty-two years old. S 5534.
29 May 905	*Diamond* sūtra. Colophon: dated T'ien-yu 2, *i-ch'ou*/IV/23, eighty-two years old. S 5444.
17 Jan. 906	*Diamond* sūtra. Colophon: dated T'ien-fu 2 [*sic*],[3] *i-ch'ou*/XII/20, eighty-two years old. S 5965.
22 Feb. 906	*Diamond* sūtra. Colophon: dated T'ien-yu 3, *ping-yin*/I/26, eighty-[three years old]. Th Museum 53.
27 Feb. 906	*Diamond* sūtra. Colophon: dated T'ien-yu 3, *ping-yin*/II/2, eighty-three years old. S 5451.
28 Feb. 906	*Diamond* sūtra. Colophon: dated T'ien-yu 3, *ping-yin*/II/3, eighty-three years old. S 5669.
30 April 906	*Diamond* sūtra. Colophon: dated T'ien-yu 3, *ping-yin*/IV/5, eighty-three years old. P 2876.
27 April 907	*Diamond* sūtra. Colophon: dated *ting-mao*/III/12, eighty-four years old. Pk 8909.
27 Aug. 908	*Scripture on the Ten Kings.* Colophon: dated *wu-ch'en*/VII/28, eighty-five years old. *San* 535.
30 Aug. 908	*Scripture on the Ten Kings.* Colophon: dated *wu-ch'en*/VIII/1, eighty-five years old. Pk 1226.
8 Jan. 909	*Scripture on the Ten Kings.* Colophon: dated *wu-ch'en*/XII/14, eighty-five years old. S 4530.

1. All eight copies of the *Diamond* sūtra present the translation by Kumārajīva (350–409) entitled *Chin-kang po-jo po-lo-mi ching.* They are all divided into thirty-two sections, based on a printed edition from Szechwan, and bound as a booklet.
2. Although the reign-period T'ien-fu was changed to T'ien-yu the year before, T'ien-fu was used anachronistically as late as 910; see p. 119, n. 50.
3. Following the sexagenary cycle and the man's age, the reign-name should be T'ien-yu.

Appendix 13
Texts and Inscriptions Mentioning
Tao-chen

I. Dated Manuscripts and Inscriptions Mentioning Tao-chen

29 July 934. Pk *hsin* 329. *Chien i-ch'ieh ju-tsang ching mu-lu.* Dated Ch'ang-hsing 5, *chia-wu*/VI/15.

29 July 934. Th Institute 345. *San-chieh ssu chien i-ch'ieh ju-tsang ching mu-lu.* Dated Ch'ang-hsing 5, *chia-wu*/VI/15.

2 Feb. 935. S 5663. *Chung-lun.* Colophon: record of texts and objects collected and repaired by Tao-chen. Dated *i-wei*/I/15.

20 June 938. Tp 4736. *Ching-ming ching kuan-chung shih-ch'ao.* Colophon: "Recited and inscribed on the twentieth day of the fifth month in the summer of *wu-hsü* by *śramaṇa* Tao-chen of San-chieh ssu. His secular surname is Chang."

27 May 950. Th Cave 108. Tao-chen mentioned. Dated T'ien-fu[b] 15/V/8.

6 Jan. 952. Th Institute 322. *Shih-erh yüeh pa-jih . . . she-jen pien-k'u jan-teng fen-p'ei k'u-k'an ming-shu.* Text mentions "*śramaṇa* Tao-chen, Rectifier of the Clergy," dated *hsin-hai*/XII/7.

II. Precept Certificates Bestowed by Tao-chen

4 March 964. P 2994. Eight Precepts. Recipient: Li Han-erh. Dated *chia-tzu*/I/15. Officiant: "Śramaṇa Tao-chen, Precept Master, Rectifier of the Buddhist Clergy, Great Lecture Master, Recipient of the Purple Robe."

14 March 964. P 3392. Eight Precepts. Recipient: P'u-t'i Tsui. Dated *chia-tzu*/I/28. Officiant: "Tao-chen, Precept Master, Rectifier of the Buddhist Clergy, Great Lecture Master, Recipient of the Purple Robe."

14 March 964. P 3414. Eight Precepts. Recipient: Li Han-erh. Dated *chia-tzu*/I/28. Officiant: "Tao-chen, Precept Master, Rectifier of the Buddhist Clergy, Great Lecture Master, Recipient of the Purple Robe."

26 June 964. S 532 (1). Eight Precepts. Recipient: Li Han-erh. Dated

Ch'ien-te 2/V/14. Officiant: "Tao-chen, Precept Master, Rectifier of the Buddhist Clergy, Recipient of the Purple Robe."

27 June 964. P 3482. Eight Precepts. Recipient: T'ang P'u-t'i Fa. Dated Ch'ien-te 2/V/15. Officiant: "Tao-chen, Precept Master, Rectifier of the Buddhist Clergy, Recipient of the Purple Robe."

5 July 964. S 532 (2). Five Precepts. Recipient: Woman Chang. Dated Ch'ien-te 2/V/23. Officiant: "Tao-chen, Precept Master, Rectifier of the Buddhist Clergy, Recipient of the Purple Robe."

22 Oct. 964. P 3238. Recipient: Woman Chang. Dated Ch'ien-te 2/IX/ 14. Officiant: "Tao-chen, Precept Master, Rectifier of the Buddhist Clergy, Recipient of the Purple Robe."

23 Oct. 964. P 3320. Five Precepts. Recipient: Woman Chang. Dated Ch'ien-te 2/IX/15. Officiant: "Tao-chen, Precept Master, Rectifier of the Buddhist Clergy, Recipient of the Purple Robe."

19 Feb. 965. S 532 (3). Five Precepts. Recipient: Woman Chang. Dated Ch'ien-te 3/I/15. Officiant: "Śramaṇa Tao-chen, Precept Master, Rectifier of the Buddhist Clergy, Recipient of the Purple Robe."

19 Feb. 965. P 3455. Five Precepts. Recipient: Li Han-erh. Dated Ch'ien-te 3/I/15. Officiant: "Śramaṇa Tao-chen, Precept Master, Rectifier of the Buddhist Clergy, [Recipient of] the Purple Robe."

4 March 965. S 347. Eight Precepts. Recipient: Woman Chang. Dated Ch'ien-te 3/I/28. Officiant: "Śramaṇa Tao-chen, Precept Master, Rectifier of the Buddhist Clergy, Ordination Preceptor, Recipient of the Purple Robe."

4 March 965. P 3143. Great Precepts of the Thousand Buddhas. Recipient: P'u-t'i Tsui. Dated Ch'ien-te 3/I/28. Officiant: "Tao-chen, Precept Master, Recipient of the Purple Robe, Member of the Buddhist Clergy."

965. S 5313. Five Precepts. Recipient: Woman Li. Dated *i-ch'ou*/IX/ . . . . Officiant: "Śramaṇa Tao-chen, Precept Master, Rectifier of the Buddhist Clergy, Recipient of the Purple Robe."

8 Feb. 966. S 4844. Five Precepts. Recipient: P'u-t'i Tsui. Dated Ch'ien-te 4/I/15. Officiant: "Śramaṇa Tao-chen, Precept Master, Rectifier of the Buddhist Clergy, Recipient of the Purple Robe."

8 Feb. 966. P 3140. Eight Precepts. Recipient: Li Han-erh. Dated Ch'ien-te 4/I/15. Officiant: ". . . Precept Master and . . . of the Buddhist Clergy."

4 Feb. 982. S 330 (4). Eight Precepts. Recipient: Ch'eng Hui-i. Dated T'ai-p'ing hsing-kuo 7/I/8. Officiant: "Tao-chen, Precept Master, Member of the Buddhist Clergy."

4 Feb. 982. S 330 (6). Eight Precepts. Recipient: Hui-hung. Dated T'ai-p'ing hsing-kuo 7/I/8. Officiant: "Śramaṇa Tao-chen, Precept Master, Member of the Buddhist Clergy."

9 June 982. P 3203. Recipient: Teng Hui-chi. Dated T'ai-p'ing hsing-kuo 7/V/15. Officiant: "Śramaṇa Tao-chen, Precept Master."

18 June 982. S 330 (3). Eight Precepts. Recipient: Woman Ch'eng. Dated T'ai-p'ing hsing-kuo 7/V/24. Officiant: "Śramaṇa Tao-chen, Precept Master."

23 Feb. 983. P 3207. Eight Precepts. Recipient: Li Han-erh. Dated T'ai-p'ing hsing-kuo 8/I/8. Officiant: "Tao-chen, Precept Master, Member of the Buddhist Clergy."

23 Feb. 983. P 3439 (1). Eight Precepts. Recipient: Li Hsin-chu. Dated T'ai-p'ing hsing-kuo 8/I/8. Officiant: "Tao-chen, Precept Master, Member of the Buddhist Clergy."

12 March 983. P 3439 (3). Eight Precepts. Recipient: Li Sheng-chu. Dated T'ai-p'ing hsing-kuo [8?]/I/25. Officiant: "Śramaṇa . . . , Precept Master."

13 March 983. P 3439 (2). Eight Precepts. Recipient: Li Sheng-chu. Dated [T'ai-p'ing hsing-kuo 8?]/I/26. Officiant: "Śramaṇa Tao-chen, Precept Master."

976-983. P 4959. Eight Precepts. Recipient: Li Han-erh. Dated T'ai-ping hsing-kuo . . . . Officiant: "Precept . . . Tao-chen."

12 Feb. 984. S 2448. Eight Precepts. Recipient: P'u-t'i Ai. Dated T'ai-p'ing hsing-kuo 9/I/8. Officiant: "Śramaṇa Tao-chen, Precept Master."

19 Feb. 984. S 330 (2). Eight Precepts. Recipient: Female disciple Ch'eng Hui-i. Dated T'ai-p'ing hsing-kuo 9/I/15. Officiant: "Śramaṇa Tao-chen, Precept Master."

19 Feb. 984. P 3206. Eight Precepts. Recipient: Teng Chu-nu. Dated T'ai-p'ing hsing-kuo 9/I/15. Officiant: . . . .

3 March 984. S 330 (5). Eight Precepts. Recipient: Ch'eng Hui-i. Dated T'ai-p'ing hsing-kuo 9/I/28. Officiant: "Śramaṇa Tao-chen, Precept Master."

3 March 984. S 1183. Eight Precepts. Recipient: Chu-nu. Dated T'ai-p'ing hsing-kuo 9/I/28. Officiant: "Śramaṇa Tao-chen, Precept Master."

5 June 985. S 330 (1). Eight Precepts. Recipient: Ch'eng Hui-i. Dated Yung-hsi 2/V/14. Officiant: "Śramaṇa Tao-chen, Precept Master."

6 June 985. S 4115. Eight Precepts. Recipient: Fa-ch'ing. Dated Yung-hsi 2/V/15. Officiant: "Śramaṇa Tao-chen, Precept Master."

6 June 985. P 3483. Eight Precepts. Recipient: Chang Fa-man. Dated Yung-hsi 2/V/15. Officiant: "Śramaṇa Tao-chen, Precept Master."

987. S 4915. Bodhisattva Precepts. Recipient: Chih-hui Hua. Dated Yung-hsi 4/V/ . . . . Officiant: "Śramaṇa Tao-chen, Precept Master, Chief Recorder of the Clergy, Great Master, Recipient of the Purple Robe."

III. Undated Manuscripts Mentioning Tao-chen

S 1635. *Ch'üan-chou ch'ien-fo hsin-chu chu-tsu-shih sung.* Verso: "Recorded by śramaṇa Tao-chen of San-chieh ssu in Sha-chou."

S 2635. *Chin-kang po-jo po-lo-mi ching.* Colophon in large writing: "Inscribed with his own hand by the *bhikṣu* monk Tao-chen."

S 3147. *Yen-lo wang shou-chi ssu-chung ni-hsiu sheng-ch'i chai wang-sheng ching-*

t'u ching. Colophon: "Received and upheld by *bhikṣu* Tao-chen of [San-]chieh [ssu]."

S 3452. *Wu-liang-shou tsung-yao ching.* Verso: "Turned by *śramaṇa* Tao-chen, of San-chieh-ssu."

S 4160. *Ssu-fen lü lüeh-sung.* Colophon: "Circulated by *bhikṣu* Tao-chen of San-chieh ssu."

S 5448. *Tun-huang lu.* Cover: Tao-chen's name appears.

S 6225. *San-chieh ssu pi-ch'iu Tao-chen chu-fang ch'iu-mi chu-ching sui-te tsa-ching lu-chi.* Cover: "This scripture must belong to Uncle . . . ."

P 2130. (1) Untitled histories and prayers connected with Pure Land. (2) *Kuan-fo san-mei hai ching.* Colophon: "Scriptures belonging to Tao-chen of San-chieh ssu do not leave the temple."

P 2161. *Ta-sheng pai-fa ming-men lun k'ai-tsung-i chi.* Colophon: ". . . and recorded by *śramaṇa* Tao-chen of San-chieh ssu."

P 2193. *Mu-lien yüan-ch'i.* Colophon: "Original recording of Tao-chen of [San-]chieh [ssu]." Strips glued to verso to repair holes.

P 2270. (1) *Ta-sheng wu-fang-pien pei-tsung.* (2) *Wu-keng chuan-sung.* Colophon: "Tao-chen of San-chieh ssu."

P 2340. *Chiu-hu shen-ming ching.* Verso: "*Bhikṣu* Tao-chen of San-chieh ssu."

P 2641v. Notes on commissioning of repairs to Mo-kao-k'u. Includes "Monk Tao-chen and ten others."

P 2836. Informal commentary on unnamed text. Colophon: "Recorded by *śramaṇa* Tao-chen of San-chieh ssu."

P 2930. Unidentified notes. Colophon: "Received and recited by *bhikṣu* Tao-chen of San-chieh ssu."

P 3917A, B. *Chung-lun.* Colophon in middle of text: "Reciting completed by *śramaṇa* Tao-chen, Vinaya Monk of Great Virtue of San-chieh ssu." On cover: "Donated and entered into the catalogue by Tao-chen."

P tib. 1261v (= P 3301v). Tao-chen's name is seventh in a list of twelve monks given gifts during a feast.[1]

Pk 1362. *Ta po-jo po-lo-mi-to ching.* Colophon: "*Bhikṣu* Tao-chen of [San-] chieh [ssu]."

Pk 2318. *Ta po-jo po-lo-mi-to ching.* Colophon: "Received and upheld by *bhikṣu* Tao-chen."

Pk 5788. *Fo-ming ching.* Colophon: "*Śramaṇa* Tao-chen repaired this scripture at the age of nineteen. His secular surname is Chang." Verso: "Recited by Tao-chen of San-chieh ssu. Received and upheld by *śramaṇa* Tao-chen of San-chieh ssu." Tao-chen wrote his name on the verso side along most joints where sheets of paper are glued together.

Pk 6375. *Yen-lo wang shou-chi ch'üan-hsiu sheng-ch'i chai kung-te ching.* Colophon: "Received and upheld by *bhikṣu* Tao-chen."

Pk 8230. *Ho shih-chieh wen.* Verso: *Chin-kuang-ming tsui-sheng-wang ching.* Colophon: "Received and upheld by Tao-chen of [San-]chieh [ssu]."

---

1. See BN, *Catalogue.*

Appendix 14

A Comparison of the Bodhisattvas
Listed in Different Recensions of
The Scripture on the Ten Kings

Medium	Long	Short	Sanskrit Equivalent
(e.g., S 2489)	(e.g., P 2003)	(e.g., S 3147)	
1. Ti-tsang	1. Ti-tsang	1. Ti-tsang	Kṣitigarbha
	2. Lung-shu	2. Lung-shu	Nāgārjuna
	3. Chiu-k'u kuan-shih-yin	3. Chiu-k'u kuan-shih yin	Avalokiteśvara
		4. P'u-kuang	
	4. Ch'ang-pei	5. Ch'ang-pei	Sadāprarudita
		6. Ch'ang-ts'an	
2. T'o-lo-ni	5. T'o-lo-ni	7. T'o-lo-ni	Dhāraṇī
3. Chin-kang tsang	6. Chin-kang tsang	8. Chin-kang-tsang	Vajragarbha
		9. Wen-shu shih-li	Mañjuśrī
		10. Mi-le	Maitreya
		11. P'u-hsien	Samantabhadra

In the short recension numbers five and six may have been paired, thus making ten bodhisattvas to match the number of kings. Those ten Buddhas and bodhisattvas do not match the names of those in the Japanese apocryphon, *Jizō bosatsu hosshin innen juō kyō*.

249

Glossary

a-niang 阿娘
a-niang^b 阿孃
a-p'o 阿婆
Amida nyorai 阿彌陀如來
An 安
An-kuo ssu 安國寺
Ashuku nyorai 阿閦如來
ao wang-jen 扶亡人
ch'a 察
ch'a^b 叉
Ch'a-ming ssu-lu 察命司錄
Ch'a-tu wang 茶都王
Chai Feng-ta 翟奉達
chai-jih 齋日
Chai Ting-yu 翟定友
Chai Tsai-wen 翟再溫
Chai Wen-chin 翟文進
ch'an 禪
Chang 張
Chang A-sheng 張阿勝
Chang Ch'ang-chi 張長繼
Chang Chün-ch'e 張君徹
Chang I-ch'ao 張議潮
Chang Kuo 張果
Chang Kuo-lao 張果老

Chang-shih 長史
Chang-shih ssu-ma 長史司馬
Chang Tu 張讀
Chang T'u 張圖
Chang Wan-chi 張萬及
Chang Yü-chien 張玉件
ch'ang 常
Ch'ang-an 長安
Ch'ang-chin 常謹
Ch'ang-hsing 長興
Ch'ang-pei 常悲
Ch'ang-pi 常祕
ch'ang-tao 唱導
Ch'ang-ts'an 常慘
Chao 趙
ch'ao-ching 抄經
ch'e-mo 輒莫
Chen-chün 真君
Chen-chün^b 真峻
Chen-huang tung-shen t'ien-tsun
  真皇洞神天尊
Chen-ming 貞明
Ch'en Chen 陳鍼
Ch'en Kuang wang 陳廣王
Cheng Ch'u-hui 鄭處誨

251

cheng-i 證義

cheng-ming 證明

cheng-ming[b] 證盟

Cheng-yen 正演

ch'eng 成

ch'eng[b] 城

Ch'eng Ching 成景

Ch'eng-tu 成都

chi 及

chi[b] 偈

chi[c] 祭

chi[d] 吉

chi[e] 記

chi chu 鷄猪

chi-hai 己亥

Chi-hsien yüan 集賢院

chi kou she 鷄狗蛇

chi-kou tu-she 鷄狗毒蛇

chi-lu 記錄

ch'i 豈

ch'i[b] 起

ch'i[c] 齊

ch'i[d] 祈

ch'i[e] 妻

ch'i-ch'i 七七

ch'i-ch'i chai 七七齋

Ch'i-chou 齊州

Ch'i-chüeh 氣訣

ch'i-hsiung 齊兇

ch'i-hsiung[b] 臍肓

ch'i-nien 祈念

ch'i-she 祈設

ch'i-yu 豈由

ch'i-yu[b] 起由

chia 家

chia[b] 枷

chia-ang 假昂

chia-ch'ou 枷杻

chia-mu 家母

chia-tzu 甲子

chia-wu 甲午

Chiang 絳

chiang-fu 降伏

chiang-kuei 降鬼

chiang-po 江波

ch'iao-fu 橋筏

chieh 界

Chieh 嘆

chieh-hui 戒惠

chieh-hui[b] 戒慧

chieh-hsü 誡勗

chieh-hsü[b] 戒勗

chieh-shuo 解說

chieh-tieh 戒牒

chieh-ting-hui 戒定慧

chieh-t'o 解脫

ch'ieh-lan 伽藍

ch'ieh-t'o 伽陀

chien 劍

chien[b] 漸

Chien-chiao shang-shu kung-pu
    yüan-wai-lang 檢校尚書工部員
    外郎

chien hsieh-pang 肩挟棒

Chien-ssu shih-che 監司使者

chien shih-pang 肩使棒

ch'ien 襟

ch'ien[b] 鉗

Ch'ien-fo-tung 千佛洞

Ch'ien-fu 乾符

Ch'ien-ning 乾寧

Ch'ien-tzu wen 千字文

chih 直

chih[b] 帙

chih[c] 炙

Chih-chin-kang shen 執金剛神

Chih-i 智顗

Chih-p'an 志磐

Chih-sheng 智昇

Chih-te 至德

chih tzu 之子

Chih-yu 智祐

ch'ih 持

ch'ih-chai ch'u-tsui 持齋除罪

Ch'ih-ch'e shih-che 持車使者

ch'ih-ching fan-yin 持經梵音

ch'ih-nien 持念

Ch'ih-sung chin-kang ching ling-yen kung-te chi 持誦金剛經靈驗功德記

Chin 晉

Chin ching 金經

Chin-ch'üeh hua-shen t'ien-tsun 金闕化身天尊

chin-fei ti-ling 錦緋締綾

chin-kang 金剛

Chin-kang ching 金剛經

chin-kang san-mei 金剛三昧

chin-kang tao 金剛刀

Chin-kang-tsang 金剛藏

chin-kuang 金光

chin tz'u Yen-mo 今此琰魔

chin Yen-mo 今琰魔

Ch'in 秦

ch'in-ch'i 侵期

ch'in-ch'i[b] 侵欺

Ch'in Kuang ta-wang 秦廣大王

Ch'in Kuang wang 秦廣王

ch'in-ling 侵凌

ching 經

ching[b] 擎

ching[c] 敬

ching-che-chuang 經折裝

ching-chin 精進

ching-mo 兢模

ching-shih 經師

Ching-tu san-mei ching 淨度三昧經

ching-t'u 淨土

ching-tsang 經藏

Ching-yün 景雲

ch'ing-chung 輕重

Ch'ing-t'ai 清泰

Ch'ing-t'ai ssu 清泰寺

ch'ing-t'ien 請天

Chiu-hua shan 九華山

Chiu-k'u 救苦

chiu sha-mi 蔓沙彌

Chiu-yu pa-tsui t'ien-tsun 九幽拔罪天尊

cho 著

cho[b] 着

Cho 綽

Chou 周

Chou Fang 周昉

Chou-hsüeh po-shih 州學博士

ch'ou 杻

ch'ou[b] 雔

ch'ou[c] 讎

chu 住

chu chi 猪鷄

Chu Ch'ien 竹庋

chu-chih 諸志

Chu-kuan chiang-chün 諸官將君

Chu-ling tu-ming t'ien-tsun 朱陵度命天尊

chu-p'u-sa mo-ho-sa 諸菩薩摩訶薩

chu-ta-ch'en 諸大臣

chu-ta-chung 諸大眾

chu-t'ien 諸天

chu-tsui 諸罪

chu-tsui[b] 渚罪

Chu-wu-tao ta-shen 主五道大神

ch'u 除

ch'u-chai ch'u-tsui 除齋除罪

Ch'u-chiang wang 初江王

ch'u-sheng 畜生

ch'u-tuan 處斷

chuan 轉

chuan[b] 撰

chuan ch'iu fu-mu hui ch'ing-
ch'in 專求父母會情親

chuan-chung 轉重

chuan-tu 轉讀

chuan yüan hsi lun-hui 轉願息
輪廻

Ch'uan-yen shih-che 傳言使者

chui-chiu 追救

chui-fang 追放

chui-nien 追念

Ch'ui-kung t'o-hua t'ien-tsun
垂功託化天尊

Chung t'ai-i 中太一

Chung-t'iao shan 中條山

chung-yin 中蔭

chung-yin[b] 中陰

chung-yin shen 中蔭身

chung-yin shen[b] 中陰身

chung-yu 中有

chü nan-ch'en 具難陳

ch'ü-chiang sui-yeh 驅將隨業

"Ch'ü fo-chai lun" 去佛齋論

ch'ü-yang tui-tui 驅羊隊隊

chüan-chieh 詮嗟

chüan-chieh[b] 痊瘥

chüan-chou 卷軸

chüan-tzu 卷子

chüeh 覺

chün-chün 郡郡

Dainichi nyorai 大日如來

Datsueba 奪衣婆

Eigenji 永源寺

erh-shih 二時

Fa-chao 法照

Fa-ch'eng 法成

Fa-ch'iao ta-tu t'ien-tsun 法橋
大度天尊

fa-hsiang 法相

fa-hsin 發心

fa jo yüan 發若願

fa p'u-t'i hsin 發菩提心

fa yüan jo 發願若

Fa-yün 法雲

fan chen-ching 犯真經

fan-chia 梵夾

fan-chieh 犯戒

fan-pai 梵唄

Fang-shan 房山

fang-sheng 放生

"Fang-sheng pu" 放生部

Fei-mo yen-hua chen-chün 飛魔
演化真君

fen-ts'ao 粉草

feng 俸

Feng-ta 奉達

Feng-t'ai hsien 鳳臺縣

fo 佛

fo kao 佛告

Fo-mu ching 佛母經

fo-shuo 佛説

*Fo-shuo yen-lo wang shou-chi ssu-
chung yü-hsiu sheng-ch'i wang-
sheng ching-t'u ching* 佛説閻羅
王授記四眾預修生七往生淨
土經

fu 復

fu[b] 伏

fu[c] 福

Fu-chang shih-tsung 符章侍從

Fu-chou 福州

fu-chün 府君

fu-t'ien 福田

Fudō myō ō 不動明王

Fugen bosatsu 普賢菩薩

Hai-yen 海晏

hao 豪

hao[b] 毫

hao-fu 豪富

hao-kuei 毫貴

Hao-li 蒿里

hao-o 好惡

Hao-sheng tu-ming t'ien-tsun
　　好生度命天尊

hao-tsung 毫縱

hao-yeh 好業

hao-yüeh 號曰

hei 黑

heng 恆

Heng-shan 恆山

ho-chang 合掌

Ho-hsi tun-huang chün chou-
　　hsüeh shang-tsu tzu-ti 河西敦
　　煌郡州學上足子弟

ho-shan 和善

Ho Shih-k'ai 和士開

Hōfukuzenji 寶福禪寺

Hōnenji 法然寺

honji suijaku 本地垂迹

hou 後

hou-san so-li 後三所歷

hu 虎

hu-erh 忽爾

Hu Kuo-chen 胡國珍

hu-shih 忽是

hua-hsiang 畫像

Hua-yen 華嚴

huan 患

huan-ni 患尼

Huang-ch'üan 黃泉

hui 慧

hui[b] 回

Hui-ch'ang 會昌

Hui-hai 惠海

Hui-neng 慧能

Hui-ta 慧達

hui yü lung-hua 會於龍華

Hui-yüan 慧遠

hun 魂

hun-chia 渾家

hung-po 洪波

Huo-lien tan-chieh t'ien-tsun
　　火鍊丹界天尊

hsi 昔

hsi[b] 息

hsi[c] 悉

hsi-chang 錫杖

hsi ching-kuo 昔經過

hsi ching-kuo[b] 悉經過

Hsi-ch'uan 西川

Hsi-ch'uan Kuo-chia chen yin-pen
　　西川過家真印本

Hsi-huang shang-jen 義皇上人

Hsi-ming ssu 西明寺

Hsi-ning 熙寧

Hsi-tsung 僖宗

Hsia t'ai-i 下太一

hsiang-chiao 象教

hsiang-ch'ien 香櫬

hsiang-fu 相付

hsiang-hao 相好

hsiang-lien 香櫬

Hsiang-mo pien-wen 降魔變文

hsiao 孝

Hsiao 蕭

hsiao-hsiang 小祥
Hsiao-yao k'uai-le t'ien-tsun 逍遙
　快樂天尊
hsieh 械
hsieh[b] 邪
hsien 嶮
hsien[b] 險
Hsien-chieh ch'ien-fo 賢劫千佛
hsin-fa pu ssu-i 信法不思議
hsin-hsieh 信邪
hsien-mo 陷沒
hsien-shih yüeh 見世曰
Hsien-te 顯德
hsien wang-jen 狀亡人
hsin-hai 辛亥
hsin sha-mi 新沙彌
hsin-wei 辛未
hsin-yeh 信耶
hsin-yüan 心願
hsing 行
hsing-che 行者
hsing-chuang 行狀
Hsing sha-chou ching-hsüeh po-
　shih 行沙州經學博士
hsiu 修
hsiu-chai fu-yeh yin 修齋福業因
hsiu-chai tsao-fu 修齋造福
hsiu-fu 修福
hsiu-fu chui-chai 修福追齋
hsiu ho kung-te yin 修何功德因
hsiu-tsao 修造
hsiung 兇
hsiung[b] 肖
hsiung[c] 胸
hsü 虛
hsü[b] 勗
hsü[c] 勖

hsü[d] 戌
hsü-yü 須臾
Hsüan-chen wan-fu t'ien-tsun
　玄真萬福天尊
Hsüan-hsü 玄緒
Hsüan-kuai lu 玄怪錄
Hsüan-lang 玄郎
Hsüan-shang yü-ch'en t'ien-tsun
　玄上玉晨天尊
Hsüan-shih chih 宣室志
Hsüan-te wu-ling chen-chün 玄德
　五靈真君
Hsüan-tu wang 玄都王
Hsüan-tsang 玄奘
Hsüan-tsung 玄宗
hsüeh 學
Hsüeh Yen-ch'ang 薛延唱
i 以
i-chi 一偈
i-ch'ieh 一切
i-ch'ieh chih 一切之
i-ch'ieh chu 一切諸
i-ching yüan 譯經院
I-ch'u 義楚
i-huo 疑惑
I-hsing 一行
I-ming chi 一鳴集
i pao fu-mu 以報父母
i pao fu-mu en 以報父母恩
i-pu 意薄
i-p'u 一鋪
i-shih-pa-chung 一十八種
i-shih-pa-t'ung 一十八童
i-shu 以熟
i-shu[b] 已熟
i-wei 已未
jen 人

Jen 任

jen-chien 人間

jih 釰

jih^b 日

Jizō 地藏

Jizō jūō kyō or *gyō* 地藏十王經

Jizō jūō kyō senchū 地藏十王經
撰注

jo ch'üeh 若闕

Jōdoji 淨土寺

jōdo shinshū 淨土真宗

jōdo shū 淨土宗

Jōjin 成尋

ju 儒

ju chin-ch'eng 入金城

ju-i pao-chu 如意寶珠

ju-shih wo wen 如是我聞

ju-tsang 入藏

jun 閏

k'ai 開

K'ai-feng 開封

K'ai-pao 開寶

K'ai-p'ing 開平

K'ai-yüan 開元

*K'ai-yüan huang-ti tsan chin-kang
ching kung-te* 開元皇帝讚金剛
經功德

K'ai-yüan ssu 開元寺

K'ai-yüan shih-chiao lu 開元釋教錄

K'ai-yüan t'ien-pao i-shih 開元天寶
遺事

kami 神

k'an-ch'u 斬除

k'an-tuan ch'u 斬斷除

kanbun 漢文

kang-ch'iao 舡橋

Kanzeon bosatsu 觀世音菩薩

Kao-ch'ang 高昌

Kao-tao chuan 高道傳

Kao-tu wang 高都王

Kao-tsu 高祖

kase ito to kenpō shita fuhaku
かせ系と梱包した布帛

Ken'eō 懸衣翁

keng-ch'en 庚辰

Kokūzō bosatsu 虛空藏菩薩

Kōtoin 高桐院

k'ou chi mei 口及眉

k'u-ch'u 苦楚

kuan 關

kuan-chin 關津

Kuan-shih-yin 觀世音

Kuan-shih-yin p'u-sa 觀世音菩薩

kuan-teng 官等

kuan-tien 官典

Kuan-yin 觀音

k'uan-tsung 寬縱

Kuang-fu ssu 廣福寺

Kuang-t'ien wen-wu ta-sheng
hsiao-kan huang-ti 光天文武大
聖孝感皇帝

Kuei-i-chün chieh-tu-shih 歸義軍
節度使

kuei-tsu 鬼卒

kung-te 功德

k'ung 空

kuo 過

Kuo 過

Kuo Jo-hsü 郭若虛

Kuo-lao hsien-jen 果老仙人

kuo san-nien 過三年

Kuo Shen-liang 郭神亮

La-pa hui 臘八會

lang-chiu 郎舅

lang-chuan 郎專

lao-jen 老人

lao-jen shou-hsieh liu-ch'uan
老人手寫流傳

lao-weng 老翁

li 里

li[b] 曆

li[c] 歷

li[d] 禮

Li Ao 李翱

Li Nu-tzu 李奴子

li-sheng 利生

Li Sheng-to 李盛鐸

Li T'ung-hsüan 李通玄

li-tsan-wen 禮讚文

Li Tsung-ta 李宗大

Liang-chu 良渚

lieh-chuan 列傳

"Lin-chung fang-chüeh" 臨終
方訣

Lin-huai 臨淮

ling 靈

ling[b] 令

ling[c] 鈴

Ling-chou lung-hsing pai-ts'ao-
yüan ho-shang su-hsing shih fa-
hao tseng-jen 靈州龍興白草院
和尚俗性史法號增忍

Ling-hsiu ssu 靈修寺

ling jen pu-huan shao pu 令人不
患少不

Ling-lu 令錄

ling te sheng-t'ien 令得生天

liu-i 六藝

liu-pu 六部

Liu Sa-ho 劉薩何

liu-tao 六道

Liu Tao-ch'un 劉道醇

liu-ts'ao 六曹

Lo-yang 洛陽

lu 錄

Lu-she-na fo 盧舍耶佛

Lu wu-tao ta-shen 錄五道大神

Lung-hsing ssu 龍興寺

lung-shen 龍神

Lung-shu 龍樹

lung-t'ien pa-pu 龍天八部

lung-wang pa-pu 龍王八部

lü 律

Ma 馬

ma-mien 馬面

man-i 滿己

man-i[b] 滿以

mappō 末法

mei-ku 魅蠱

Meng Luan 孟欒

mi 密

mi-chin 迷津

Mi-le 彌勒

mi shih-pang 迷使棒

Miao 妙

Miao-fu 妙福

Miao-shan 妙善

mien 覓

ming 名

Ming 明

ming-an 冥案

ming-an[b] 名案

ming-chien 冥間

ming ch'üeh 名闕

ming-fu shih-wang 冥府十王

Ming-huang tsa-lu 明皇雜錄

ming-ssu 冥司

ming-ssu chi 冥司偈

ming-tzu 名字

Ming-wang 明王

ming-yüeh 名日

Miroku bosatsu 彌勒菩薩

Mo-chung-tsu 魔種族

Mo-kao-k'u 莫高窟

Mo-yeh 摩耶

Monju bosatsu 文殊菩薩

Morimura Yoshiyuki 森村義行

Mu Jen-ch'ien 睦仁蒨

Mu-lien 目蓮

mu-lu 目錄

Nai-ho 奈河

nai-ho ti-yü 奈何地獄

Nan-p'ing ssu 南平寺

nan-wu o-lo-ho 南無阿羅訶

nan-wu Ti-tsang p'u-sa 南無地藏
    菩薩

Nan-yang 南陽

nei-ch'in 內親

nei-wai ch'in-yin 內外親因

nei-wai ch'in-yin[b] 內外親姻

ni-hsiu 逆修

Ni-ts'e chan 逆策占

Nichiren 日蓮

nien 念

nien-chi 念記

nien pien-hsiang 念變像

Ning-po 寧波

ning-shang 寧上

Niu Seng-ju 牛僧孺

niu-t'ou 牛頭

o-hsiu-lo 阿修羅

o-hsiu-lo wang 阿修羅王

o-kuei 餓鬼

o-lo-ho 阿羅訶

o-lo-ho[b] 阿羅河

O-mi-t'o 阿彌陀

O-nan 阿難

o-pi 阿鼻

o-p'i 阿毗

o-shih 惡事

O-shih-to-fa-ti ho 阿恃多伐底河

O-wei-pa-ho-t'i 阿維跋河提

O-wei-pa-t'i ho 阿維跋提河

o-yeh 惡業

Ou-yang Hsiu 歐陽修

pa 把

pa[b] 拔

pa-chai-chieh 八齋戒

pa chen-ching 把真經

pa-chieh 八戒

pa-pai-i-ch'ien 八百億千

pa-pu chung 八部眾

pa-shih-wu lao-jen 八十五老人

pa-ta-wang 八大王

pa wang-jen 拔亡人

pai 唄

Pai (or Po) Chü-i 白居易

pai-jih chai 百日齋

pai-jih wang-jen 百日亡人

p'an 盤

p'an[b] 判

p'an-kuan 判官

Pao-chi 寶誓

Pao-chi p'u-sa hui 寶誓菩薩會

pao fu-mu en 報父母恩

Pao-hua yüan-man t'ien-tsun
    寶華圓滿天尊

pao-hsi 寶錫

Pao-kuang 寶光

pao-kuo 寶國

Pao-lin ssu 寶林寺

Pao-su chao-ch'eng chen-chün
    寶肅昭成真君

Pao-tsang 寶藏

pao-yeh 報業

Pei-ch'en 北辰

Pei-tou 北斗

Pei-tou ssu-sha kuei 北斗司殺鬼

pei-tseng 悲憎

pei-tseng[b] 悲增

P'ei 裴

pen-chi 本紀

pen-hsing k'ung 本性空

pen-hsing shih k'ung 本性實空

"Pen-lun" 本論

p'eng 捧

pi-ch'iu 比丘

pi-ch'iu-ni 比丘尼

pi-mo 必莫

Pi-shu-sheng 祕書省

pi Yen-mo wang teng 彼琰魔王等

p'iao-hsing 飄興

p'iao-yü 漂輿

pien 變

Pien-ch'eng wang 變成王

Pien-ch'eng wang[b] 變城王

Pien-ch'eng wang[c] 汴城王

ping-hsü 丙戌

ping-shen 丙申

ping-yin 丙寅

P'ing-cheng wang 平正王

p'ing-teng 平等

P'ing-teng wang 平等王

po-jo 波若

po-nieh-p'an 般涅槃

po-nieh-p'an[b] 般涅盤

"Po-wu hui-pien" 博物彙編

p'o 魄

p'o-chieh 破戒

p'o-mo 潑墨

pu chan-t'ing 不暫停

pu-chih 部袟

pu-chih[b] 部帙

pu hsi-t'ing 不繫停

pu hsin-fa 不信法

pu-sa 布薩

pu ssu-i 不思議

pu ying 不應

P'u-hsien 普賢

P'u-hsien wang 普賢主

P'u-kuang 普廣

p'u-sa 菩薩

p'u-sa chieh 菩薩戒

p'u-t'i hsin 菩提心

Ryōchū 良忠

san 讚

san[b] 三

san-chieh chiao 三階教

San-chieh ssu 三界寺

san-ch'ien ta-ch'ien shih-chieh
    三千大千世界

san-chüan 三卷

san-hui 三回

san-hun ch'i-p'o 三魂七魄

san-hsieh liu-ch'uan 三寫流傳

san-kuei 三歸

san-nien 三年

san-o-t'u 三惡塗

san-pao 三寶

san-t'u 三塗

san-t'u chih tsai tsai[b] 三塗之哉災

san-tuan 三端

sankon shichihaku 三魂七魄

Seiganji 誓願寺

Seishi bosatsu 勢至菩薩

Seng-cheng 僧正

seng-ch'ieh-lan-mo 僧伽藍摩

so 所

so-she 所設

so-yu 所有

sokushō 束脩

ssu 司

ssu-chung 四眾

ssu-hou san-li 死後三曆

Ssu-k'ung T'u 司空圖

Ssu-lu 司錄

ssu-lu[b] 賜錄

Ssu-ming 司命

ssu-nang 私囊

ssu-ta t'ien-wang 四大天王

ssu-t'ien ta-wang 四天大王

ssu wei-ch'en 似微塵

su 俗

sui-hsin 隨心

Sui-yüan wang-sheng shih-fang ching-t'u ching 隨願往生十方淨土經

Sui-yüan wang-sheng t'ien-tsun 隨願往生天尊

Sung 宋

Sung Ti wang 宋帝王

sha 煞

sha[b] 殺

Sha 沙

Sha-chou 沙州

sha-fu hai-mu 殺父害母

sha-hai-mu 殺害母

sha-mi 沙彌

sha-t'u 殺土

sha-t'u[b] 沙土

Shaka nyorai 釋迦如來

shan-ho 善和

Shan-o t'ung-tzu 善惡童子

Shan-tao 善導

Shang-shu 尚書

Shang-shu ling 尚書令

Shang-shu ling-lu 尚書令錄

Shang t'ai-i 上太一

shang-tso 上座

Shang-yüan 上元

she 社

shen 神

shen-chou 神州

Shen-fu-shan ssu 神福山寺

"Shen-fu-shan ssu ling-chi chi" 神福山寺靈蹟記

Shen-hsien t'i-tao ling-yao ching 神仙體道靈要經

"Shen-i tien" 神異典

shen-Sha 神沙

shen tao chih jih 身到之日

sheng-ch'i 生七

sheng-ch'i chai 生七齋

Sheng-shou ssu 聖壽寺

Sheng-tu wang 聖都王

Sheng-tz'u ssu 聖慈寺

shih 是

shih[b] 使

shih[c] 事

shih[d] 時

Shih 史

shih-ch'a-mo-na 式叉摩那

shih-ch'a-ni 式叉尼

shih-chai 十齋

shih-chia 世家

Shih-chia-mou-ni fo 釋迦牟尼佛

shih-chieh 十戒

shih-chih-chai 十直齋

Shih-fang chiu-k'u t'ien-tsun 十方救苦天尊

shih-hao 十號

Shih-ho-shang 史和尚

"Shih-hui chai wen" 十會齋文

shih-hsien 示現

shih-hsien[b] 是現

shih-i 失譯

shih-jen so-wei 世人所謂

shih-lo-mo-na-li-chia 室羅摩孥
　理迦

Shih-men cheng-t'ung 釋門正統

shih-o 十惡

shih-ssu jih pa-shih-wu ch'uan
　十四日八十五傳

shih-sheng 是勝

shih-shu 世術

shih-t'ien ta-wang 十天大王

Shih-tsung 世宗

shih-wang ch'eng 十王城

Shih-wang ching 十王經

shih-wang hsiang 十王像

shinbutsu shūgō 神佛習合

Shingon 真言

shinjin 信心

shou 手

shou[b] 受

Shou-chai san-chiang-chün 守宅三
　將軍

Shou Ch'ang hsien ti-ching 壽昌縣
　地境

shou-chi 授記

Shou-chieh shih-chu 授戒師主

shou-ch'ih 受持

shou-chui ch'ang 受追長

shou-chui ch'ang[b] 壽追長

shou-hsieh liu-ch'uan 手寫流傳

shou-k'u 受苦

shou pien-hsing ch'eng 受變形城

shou-tsui 受罪

shù 屬

shu[b] 述

Shu 蜀

shu-hsiang 書像

Shuang-wang 雙王

Shūei 宗叡

Shui-lu chai i-wen 水陸齋儀文

"Shui-lu chai i-wen hou-hsü" 水陸
　齋儀文後序

Shui-lu i 水陸儀

Shui-lu ta-chai ling-chi chi 水陸大
　齋靈跡記

shuo-fa yin 說法印

ta 大

Ta-ai-tao 大愛道

"Ta-ai-tao po-nieh-p'an p'in" 大愛
　道般涅槃品

ta-chang-fu 大丈夫

ta-ch'en 大臣

ta-chieh-ni 大戒尼

ta-ch'ien 大千

ta-chung 大眾

Ta-fan 大梵

Ta-fan t'ien-wang 大梵天王

ta-hsiang 大祥

Ta-li 大力

Ta-mo wang 大魔王

Ta-mo wang[b] 大磨王

Ta-po-nieh-p'an ching 大般涅槃經

ta-shen 大神

Ta-sheng 大聖

ta-sheng chieh 大乘戒

Ta-sheng-tz'u ssu 大聖慈寺

ta-wang 大王

Tachibana Zuichō 橘瑞超

t'ai-hsi 胎息

T'ai-i 太乙

T'ai-i pa-shen shih-che 太一八神
　使者

T'ai-i shih-che 太一使者

T'ai Kuang wang 泰廣王

T'ai-ling hsü-huang t'ien-tsun
太靈虛皇天尊

T'ai-miao chih-chi t'ien-tsun 太妙
至極天尊

T'ai-p'ing hsing-kuo 太平興國

T'ai-su miao-kuang chen-chün
泰素妙廣真君

T'ai-shan fu-chün 泰山府君

T'ai-shan hsüan-miao chen-chün
泰山玄妙真君

T'ai-shan wang 泰(or 太)山王

T'ai-shang tao-chün 太上道君

T'ai-tsung 太宗

T'ai-tzu 太子

T'ai-tz'u ssu 太慈寺

T'an-luan 曇鸞

tang 當

t'ang-t'ang 堂堂

T'ang-yün 唐韻

tao-ch'ang ssu 道場司

Tao-chen 道真

Tao-chen pen chi 道真本記

tao-chien 倒見

tao-chien[b] 到見

Tao-hsüan 道宣

Tao-ming 道明

Tao-ming[b] 導冥

Tao-shih 道世

"Tao-t'i lun hsü" 道體論序

Tao-yin 道氤

te-sheng 得生

te-sheng t'ien-shang 得生天上

t'eng 藤

t'eng[b] 騰

Ti 帝

ti-ang 低昂

ti-ch'i chai 第七齋

ti-erh tsan 第二讚

ti-mou-ch'i chai 第某七齋

Ti-tsang 地藏

Ti-tsang pen-yüan kung-te ching
地藏本願功德經

Ti-tsang p'u-sa 地藏菩薩

Ti-tsang shih-wang ching 地藏十
王經

ti-ying 低迎

ti-yü 地獄

Ti-yü 地獄

Ti-yü ching 地獄經

ti-yü chu 地獄主

ti-yü pien-hsiang 地獄變相

Ti-yü tsan ching 地獄讚經

"T'i teng chen-tung" 題登真洞

t'iao-hsiu 條修

Tien-ssu shih-che 典司使者

t'ien 天

T'ien-ch'eng 天成

T'ien-chu ti Shih 天主帝釋

T'ien-fu 天復

T'ien-fu[b] 天福

T'ien-hsi-tsai 天息災

T'ien-i 天一

T'ien-kung shih-che 天公使者

t'ien-lung 天龍

t'ien-lung shen-wang 天龍神王

T'ien-pao 天寶

T'ien-sheng 天聖

T'ien ta-chiang-chün 天大將軍

T'ien-t'ai 天台

T'ien-ti 天帝

T'ien-ti Shih 天帝釋

T'ien-ti shih-che 天帝使者

T'ien-ti-shui san-kuan 天地水
三官

T'ien-tsun 天尊

T'ien-tzu 天子

t'ien-wang 天王

T'ien-yu 天祐

Ting-kuang fo 定光佛

Ting-kuang ju-lai 定光如來

Ting-kuang ju-lai fo 定光如來佛

ting-sheng chu-ssu 定生注死

ting-sheng-ssu 定生死

ting-sheng ssu-chu 定生死注

To-pao t'a 多寶塔

to shih-yung 多是用

to shih-yung[b] 多使用

t'o-ling shen-hsien 託靈神仙

T'o-lo-ni 陀羅尼

t'o-t'i t'ai-yang 託體太陽

t'o-ying 託影

tu 度

tu[b] 都

Tu-hsien shang-sheng t'ien-tsun 度仙上聖天尊

Tu-kuan wang 都官王

Tu Liang 杜良

Tu seng-lu 都僧錄

tu-sung 讀誦

Tu-shih wang 都市王

tu-tieh 度牒

Tu-yang wang 都陽王

t'u 塗

T'u-lu-fan 吐魯蕃

t'u-tsan 圖讚

t'u-wang hsiang 土王像

tui-tui 隊隊

tun 頓

Tun-huang 敦煌

Tung-ch'an ssu 東禪寺

Tung-ch'uan 東川

Tung-ming p'u-ching chen-chün 洞明普靜真君

Tung Wen-yüan 董文員

Tung-yang chün 東陽郡

t'ung-hsing 童行

T'ung-hsüan hsien-sheng 通玄先生

T'ung-kuang 同光

t'ung-ling hsiang-lu i 銅鈴香盧臺

t'ung-tzu 童子

tsai 再

tsai[b] 哉

tsai[c] 災

tsai-chi 載記

Tsai-wen 再溫

tsan 讚

tsan-sung 讚誦

tsan-shu 讚述

tsan-yüeh 讚曰

Tsang-ch'uan 藏川

tsang-tien 藏殿

tsao 遭

tsao[b] 造

tsao-ching tsao-hsiang 造經造像

tsao-fo 造佛

tsao-hsiang 造像

tsao-yeh 造業

ts'ao 槽

ts'e-fa 策髮

ts'e-fa[b] 策發

ts'e-tzu 策子

ts'e-tzu[b] 冊子

ts'e-yeh 冊葉

Tsei-ts'ao shih-che 賊曹使者

Tseng-jen 增忍

Tso Ch'üan 左全

tsu-hsi 足膝

tsui 罪

tsui-k'u 罪苦

Tsui-sheng hui-ling chen-chün
　最聖耀靈真君

tsui-yeh 罪業

Ts'ui 崔

Ts'ui I-ch'i 崔義起

tsun-kuo 尊國

Tsung 宗

Tsung-chien 宗鑑

Tsung Ti wang 宗帝王

Tzu-chou 資州

tz'u 此

tz'u^b 次

tz'u chi tu p'u-sa yeh 此即度菩
　薩也

tz'u yin-tu p'u-sa yeh 此印度菩薩也

wai-yin 外姻

wang 王

wang^b 往

Wang 王

Wang Chang 王長

Wang Ch'iao-shih 王喬士

Wang Ch'iao *tao-shih* 王僑道士

Wang Ch'ung-yü 王崇裕

Wang Chü-jen 王居仁

Wang-hsiang ch'eng-ming t'u 圖象
　成名圖

wang-jen pai-jih 亡人百日

Wang Jen-yü 王仁裕

Wang Jih-hsiu 王日休

wang-kuo ch'i 亡過妻

wang-sheng 往生

wang-t'ou 往頭

Wang Yüan-ch'i 王元戚

Wang Yüan-lu 王圓錄

wasan 和讚

wei 偽

Wei-chou 維州

wei fan-chieh 為犯戒

wei-miu 偽謬

wei-o 危厄

wei-ts'ui 危脆

wei-wang 偽妄

wei-wang luan-chen 偽妄亂真

Wen-shu-shih-li 文殊師利

wo 我

wo^b 握

wo chieh 我皆

wo tang 我當

wo-teng 我等

Wu 武

wu-ch'ang 無常

wu-ch'en 戊辰

Wu-ch'eng 武成

wu-chieh 五刧

wu-chieh^b 五戒

wu-chien 無間

wu-chung 五眾

Wu Ch'ung 吳充

wu-fan 勿犯

wu-fan^b 物犯

wu-hui 五會

wu-hsing 五行

wu-hsü 戊戌

Wu K'o-chi 吳克己

Wu-kuan wang 五官王

Wu-liang t'ai-hua t'ien-tsun 無量
　太華天尊

Wu-ling wei-te chen-chün 五靈威
　德真君

wu-ni 五逆

Wu-shang cheng-tu chen-chün
　無上正度真君

Wu-tao chiang-chün wang 五道將
軍王
Wu-tao chuan-lun wang 五道轉
輪王
Wu-tao shen 五道神
Wu-tao ta-chiang-chün 五道大
將軍
Wu Tsung-yüan 武宗元
wu-wu 戊午
Yakushi nyorai 藥師如來
yang 陽
Yang Ch'ui 楊垂
Yang O 楊鍔
yang-t'ou 仰頭
Yang Tung-ch'ien 楊洞潛
yao 夭
yao-ch'a 藥叉
yao-ch'en 謠讖
Yao Ch'ung 姚崇
yao-shih 要事
Yao-shih liu-li-kuang 藥師琉璃光
Yao-shih liu-li-kuang fo 藥師琉璃
光佛
yao-wang-jen 夭亡人
Yao-wang yao-shang p'u-sa 藥王
藥上菩薩
yeh 業
yeh-ch'a 夜叉
yeh-ch'eng 業秤
yeh-ching 業鏡
yeh-pao 業報
yeh-pu 業薄
Yen-ch'ang 延昌
Yen-fu-t'i nei 閻浮提內
Yen-ho 延和
yen-k'u 猒苦
yen-k'u[b] 厭苦

Yen-lo 閻羅
Yen-lo *chih tzu* 閻羅之子
Yen-lo shou-chi 閻羅授記
Yen-lo wang 閻羅王
Yen-lo wang shou-chi ching 閻羅王
授記經
Yen-lo wang shuo mien ti-yü ching
閻羅王說免地獄經
Yen-lo wang tung t'ai-shan ching
閻羅王東泰山經
Yen-mo lo-she 閻摩羅闍
Yen-mo t'ien 焰摩天
Yen-mo t'ien-chung 琰魔天中
Yen-mo t'ien-chung teng-wang
琰魔天中等王
Yen-mo wang 琰魔王
Yen wang 閻王
yin 蔭
yin[b] 陰
yin[c] 因
yin[d] 印
yin-mo 隱沒
Yin-te ting-hsiu chen-chün 陰德
定休真君
ying pu 應不
Yomi no kuni 預彌國
yu-lai 由來
yu-lai[b] 猶來
yu-ming kuei-shen 幽冥鬼神
yu-p'o-i 優婆夷
yu-p'o-i[b] 優婆姨
yu-yüan 有緣
Yung-shu 永叔
yü 雨
Yü-chen 玉真
yü-chu 獄主
Yü-hsiang 虞鄉

yü-hsiu 預修

Yü-hsü ming-huang t'ien-tsun
　玉虛明皇天尊

yü-lan-p'en hui 盂蘭盆會

Yü-pao huang-shang t'ien-tsun
　玉寶皇上天尊

Yü-p'ien 玉篇

yü-tsu 獄卒

yüan 緣

yüan[b] 圓

yüan[c] 願

yüan hsi lun-hui 願悉輪迴

yüan-hsin 願心

yüan-shih 願使

Yüan-shih t'ien-tsun 元始天尊

Yüan-tu wang 原都王

yün 蘊

Zenshin 禪珍

Zonkaku 存覺

Bibliography

Primary Sources: Manuscripts

Stein Collection. See Giles, *Catalogue;* and Giles, "Dated Manuscripts in the Stein Collection."

S 86. Prayer for deceased woman Ma 馬. Dated Ch'un-hua 淳化 2, *hsin-mao* 辛卯/IV/8 (13 June 991). Reprod. Huang, *Pao-tsang,* 1:457b. Transcr.Wang, *So-yin,* pp. 109b–10a. Study: TB, *Mokuroku,* 2:72.

S 95. *Hsien-te san-nien ping-ch'en sui chü-chu li-jih* 顯德三年丙辰歲具注曆日. Complete calendar for Hsien-te 顯德 2 (956). Authored and read by Chai Feng-ta 翟奉達. Copied by Chai Wen-chin 翟文進. Reprod. Huang, *Pao-tsang,* 1:486a–88a. Studies: Fujieda, "Tonkō rekijitsu fu," p. 422; Hsiang, "Chi tun-huang shih-shih ch'u chin t'ien-fu shih-nien hsieh-pen *Shou Ch'ang hsien ti-ching,*" p. 438; Ikeda, *Shikigo,* no. 2349; Ogawa, "Tonkō butsuji no gakushirō," p. 501.

S 114. *Miao-fa lien-hua ching* 妙法蓮華經. Copied to benefit deceased sister of Chang Chün-ch'e 張君徹. Dated Shang-yüan 上元 3 (676). Reprod. Huang, *Pao-tsang,* 1:563a–76a.

S 330. Six precept certificates. All bestowed by Tao-chen 道真. 1. Recipient: Ch'eng Hui-i 程惠意. Dated Yung-hsi 雍熙 2/V/14 (5 June 985). 2. Recipient: Ch'eng Hui-i 程惠意. Dated T'ai-ping hsing-kuo 太平興國 9/I/15 (19 Feb. 984). 3. Recipient: Woman Ch'eng 程. Dated T'ai-p'ing hsing-kuo 太平興國 7/V/24 (18 June 982). 4. Recipient: Ch'eng Hui-i 程惠意. Dated T'ai-p'ing hsing-kuo 太平興國 7/I/8 (4 Feb. 982). 5. Recipient: Ch'eng Hui-i 程惠意. Dated T'ai-p'ing hsing-kuo 太平興國 9/I/28 (3 March 984). 6. Recipient: Hui-hung 惠弘. Dated T'ai-p'ing kuo 太平國 [sic] 7/I/8 (4 Feb. 982). Reprod. Huang, *Pao-tsang,* 3:137a–40a. Studies: Drège, "Papiers de Dunhung"; Shih, "San-chieh ssu, Tao-chen, tun-huang tsang-ching"; T'ang and T'ao, *Tun-huang she-hui ching-chi wen-hsien chen-chi shih-lu,* 4:97, 93, 84, 94, 85; and TB, *Mokuroku,* 2:11–12.

S 347. Precept certificate. From Tao-chen 道真. Recipient: Woman
Chang 張. Dated Ch'ien-te 乾德 3/I/28 (4 March 965). Reprod.
Huang, *Pao-tsang*, 3:193b–94a. Studies: Shih, "San-chieh ssu, Tao-
chen, tun-huang tsang-ching"; T'ang and T'ao, *Tun-huang she-hui
ching-chi wen-hsien chen-chi shih-lu*, 4:80; and TB, *Mokuroku*, 2:10.

S 532. 3 Precept certificates. All bestowed by Tao-chen 道真 1. Recipient:
Li Han-erh 李憨兒. Dated Ch'ien-te 乾德 2/V/14 (26 June 964). 2.
Recipient: Woman Chang 張. Dated Ch'ien-te 乾德 2/V/23 (5 July
964). 3. Recipient: Woman Chang 張. Dated Ch'ien-te 乾德 3/I/15
(19 Feb. 965). Reprod. Huang, *Pao-tsang*, 4:327a–29b. Studies:
Drège, "Papiers de Dunhuang"; Shih, "San-chieh ssu, Tao-chen,
tun-huang tsang-ching"; T'ang and T'ao, *Tun-huang she-hui ching-
chi wen-hsien chen-chi shih-lu*, 4:72, 72, 77; TB, *Mokuroku*, 2:10;
and Tsuchihashi, "Tonkō bon ni mirareru shuju no bosatsu kaigi,"
pp. 166b–67a.

S 1183. Precept certificate. From Tao-chen 道真. Recipient: Chu-nu 住奴.
Dated T'ai-p'ing hsing-kuo 太平興國 9/I/28 (3 March 984). Reprod. Huang, *Pao-tsang*, 9:164b–65a. Studies: Drège, "Papiers de
Dunhuang"; Shih, "San-chieh ssu, Tao-chen, tun-huang tsang-
ching"; T'ang and T'ao, *Tun-huang she-hui ching-chi wen-hsien chen-chi
shih-lu*, 4:95; and TB, *Mokuroku*, 2:12–13.

S 1473. *T'ai-p'ing hsing-kuo ch'i-nien jen-wu sui chü-chu li-jih* 太平興國七年
壬午歲具注曆日. Calendar for T'ai-p'ing hsing-kuo 太平興國 7
(982). By Chai Wen-chin 翟文進. Reprod. Huang, *Pao-tsang*,
11:143a–45a.

S 1635. *Ch'üan-chou ch'ien-fo hsin-chu chu-tsu-shih sung* 泉州千佛新著諸祖
師頌 Recorded by Tao-chen 道真. Reprod. Huang, *Pao-tsang*,
12:335a–37a. Transcr. *T* no. 2861. Studies: Shih, "San-chieh ssu,
Tao-chen, tun-huang tsang-ching"; and Yabuki, *Meisha yoin kaisetsu*,
part 2, pp. 530–33.

S 1823. Untitled prayer for mother. Reprod. Huang, *Pao-tsang*, 13:636a–
38a.

S 2073. *Lu-shan yüan-kung hua* 廬山遠公話. Recorded by Chang Ch'ang-
chi 張長繼. Dated K'ai-pao 開寶 5 (972). Reprod. Huang, *Pao-
tsang*, 15:697a–711b. Transcr. *T* no. 2859. Studies: Mair, "Inventory"; TB, *Mokuroku*, 4:28-29; and Yabuki, *Meisha yoin kaisetsu*, part 1,
pp. 238–40.

S 2404. Partial calendar for T'ung-kuang 同光 2 (924). Written by Chai
Feng-ta 翟奉達. Reprod. Huang, *Pao-tsang*, 19:188a–b. Study:
Fujieda, "Tonkō rekijitsu fu," pp. 411–12.

S 2448. Precept certificate. Bestowed by Tao-chen 道真. Recipient:
Woman P'u-t'i Ai 菩提愛. Dated T'ai-p'ing hsing-kuo 太平興國9/I/8
(12 Feb. 984). Reprod. Huang, *Pao-tsang*, 19:540b–41a. Studies:
Drège, "Papiers de Dunhuang"; Shih, "San-chieh ssu, Tao-chen, tun-

huang tsang-ching"; T'ang and T'ao, *Tun-huang she-hui ching-chi wen-hsien chen-chi shih-lu*, 4:91; and TB, *Mokuroku*, 2:12.

S 2489. *Yen-lo wang shou-chi ssu-chung ni-hsiu sheng-ch'i* . . . 閻羅王授記四眾逆修生七. Dedication: Miao-fu 妙福 of An-kuo ssu 安國寺. Reprod. Huang, *Pao-tsang*, 20:175a–76b. Studies: Ikeda, *Shikigo*, no. 2483; and Kanaoka, "Tonkō bon jigoku bunken kanki," p. 38 (colophon transcr. incorrectly).

S 2575. Correspondence to and from Saṃgha official Hai-yen 海晏. Dates from 905–929. Reprod. Huang, *Pao-tsang*, 21:203a–12b. Study: TB, *Mokuroku*, 2:17–18.

S 2614v. Untitled list of temples and names. Colophon recto dated Cheng-ming 貞明 7, *hsin-ssu* 辛巳/IV/16 (26 May 921). Reprod. Huang, *Pao-tsang*, 21:496b–505a. Studies: Fujieda, "Tonkō no sōni seki," pp. 297–302; Ikeda, *Chūgoku kodai sekichō kenkyū*, pp. 592–97; Mair, "Inventory"; and TB, *Mokuroku*, 2:27.

S 2635. *Chin-kang po-jo po-lo-mi ching* 金剛般若波羅密經. Recorded by Tao-chen 道真. Reprod. Huang, *Pao-tsang*, 21:603a–11a. Study: Shih, "San-chieh-ssu, Tao-chen, tun-huang tsang-ching."

S 2669. Untitled registry of nunneries. Fujieda ("Tonkō no sōni seki," pp. 305–12) dates it to ca. 865. Reprod. Huang, *Pao-tsang* 22:145b–49b. Studies: Fujieda, "Tonkō no sōni seki," pp. 305–12; Ikeda, *Chūgoku kodai sekichō kenkyū*, pp. 573–79; and TB, *Mokuroku*, 2:24.

S 2723. *Tsan o-mi-t'o fo ping lun* 讚阿彌陀佛并論. Copied by Chang Wan-chi 張萬及. Dated Ching-yün 景雲 2/III/19 (11 April 711). Reprod. Huang, *Pao-tsang*, 22:549a–55a.

S 2815. *Yen-lo wang shou-chi ching* 閻羅王受記經 (title at end). Reprod. Huang, *Pao-tsang*, 23:573b–74b.

S 2851. Precept certificate. Bestowed by Chih-kuang 智廣. Recipient: Woman Miao-te 妙德. Reprod. Huang, *Pao-tsang*, 24:80b.

S 2926. *Wu-ch'ang ching* 無常經. Verso: 1. *Chiao-liang shu-chu kung-te ching* 校量數珠功德經. Includes date Yen-ho 延和 1/VI/20 (28 July 712). 2. *Yao-hsing she-shen ching* 要行捨身經. Reprod. Huang, *Pao-tsang*, 24:485a–91a.

S 3092. 1. Prayer. 2. *Huan-hun chi* 還魂記. Reprod. Huang, *Pao-tsang*, 25:667b–68a. Transcr. incorrectly Wang, *So-yin*, p. 173b. Studies: Soymié, "Jizō no shishi ni tsuite," pp. 49–51.

S 3147. *Yen-lo wang shou-chi ssu-chung ni-hsiu sheng-ch'i chai wang-sheng ching-t'u ching* 閻羅王授記四眾逆脩生七齋往生淨土經. Colophon: Tao-chen 道真. Reprod. Huang, *Pao-tsang*, 26:244a–46b. Studies: Ikeda, *Shikigo*, no. 2499.

S 3452. *Wu-liang shou tsung-yao ching* 無量壽宗要經. Colophon and verso: Tao-chen 道真. Reprod. Huang, *Pao-tsang*, 28:503a–5b. Studies: Ikeda, *Shikigo*, no. 2497; Shih, "San-chieh ssu, Tao-chen, tun-huang tsang-ching."

S 3798. Precept certificate. Seal of Ho-hsi tu-seng-t'ung 河西都僧統. Recipient: Woman Ch'ing-ching I 清淨意. Dated Yung-hsi 雍熙 4/V/26 (24 June 987). Reprod. Huang, *Pao-tsang*, 31:445b. Study: TB, *Mokuroku*, 2:13.

S 3961. *Shih-wang ching* 十王經 (title at end). Includes illustrations. Reprod. Huang, *Pao-tsang*, 32:569b–76b.

S 4057. *Ta po-jo po-lo-mi-to ching* 大般若波羅密多經. Lay student Chang 張. Dated Ch'ien-fu 乾符 6/I/13 (7 Feb. 879). Reprod. Huang, *Pao-tsang*, 33:428b–29a.

S 4115. Precept certificate. From Tao-chen 道真. Recipient: Woman Fa-ch'ing 法清. Dated Yung-hsi 雍熙 2/V/15 (6 June 985). Reprod. Huang, *Pao-tsang*, 34:63b. Studies: Drège, "Papiers de Dunhuang"; Shih, "San-chieh ssu,Tao-chen, tun-huang tsang-ching"; T'ang and T'ao, *Tun-huang she-hui ching-chi wen-hsien chen-chi shih-lu*, 4:99; and TB, *Mokuroku*, 2:13.

S 4160. *Ssu-fen lü lüeh-sung* 四分律略頌. Circulated by Tao-chen 道真. Reprod. Huang, *Pao-tsang*, 34:265a–68b. Studies: Ikeda, *Shikigo*, no. 2496 (colophon transcr. incorrectly); Shih, "San-chieh ssu, Tao-chen, tun-huang tsang-ching."

S 4530. *Yen-lo wang shou-chi ching* 閻羅王授記經 (title at end). Transmitted by old man on *wu-ch'en* 戊辰/XII/14 (8 Jan. 909). Reprod. Huang, *Pao-tsang*, 36:474–75. Studies: Ikeda, *Shikigo*, no. 2148; and Kanaoka, "Tonkō bon jigoku bunken kanki," p. 38 (colophon transcr. incorrectly).

S 4805. *Yen-lo wang ching* 閻羅王經 (title at end). Reprod. Huang, *Pao-tsang*, 38:81b–83a.

S 4844. Precept certificate. Bestowed by Tao-chen 道真. Recipient: P'u-t'i Tsui 菩提最. Dated Ch'ien-te 乾德 4/I/15 (8 Feb. 966). Reprod. Huang, *Pao-tsang*, 38:217a. Studies: Drège, "Papiers de Dunhuang"; Shih, "San-chieh ssu, Tao-chen, tun-huang tsang-ching"; T'ang and T'ao, *Tun-huang she-hui ching-chi wen-hsien chen-chi shih-lu*, 4:83; and TB, *Mokuroku*, 2:11.

S 4890. *Yen-lo wang shou-chi ch'üan-hsiu sheng-ch'i chai kung-te ching* 閻羅王受記勸修生七齋功德經. Reprod. Huang, *Pao-tsang*, 38:436b–37a.

S 4915. Precept certificate. Bestowed by Tao-chen 道真. Recipient: Chih-hui Hua 智惠花. Dated Yung-hsi 雍熙 4/V/ . . . (987). Reprod. Huang, *Pao-tsang*, 38:542b–43a. Studies: Drège, "Papiers de Dunhuang"; Shih, "San-chieh ssu, Tao-chen, tun-huang tsang-ching"; T'ang and T'ao, *Tun-huang she-hui ching-chi wen-hsien chen-chi shih-lu*, 4:101; and TB, *Mokuroku*, 2:13–14.

S 5313. Precept certificate. Bestowed by Tao-chen 道真. Recipient: Woman Li 李. Dated *i-ch'ou* 乙丑/IX (965). Reprod. Huang, *Pao-tsang*, 41:604. Studies: Shih, "San-chieh ssu, Tao-chen, tun-huang tsang-ching"; T'ang and T'ao, *Tun-huang she-hui ching-chi wen-hsien chen-chi shih-lu*, 4:81; and TB, *Mokuroku*, 2:11.

S 5444. Booklet. *Chin-kang po-jo po-lo-mi ching* 金剛般若波羅密經. Colophon: Old man. Dated T'ien-yu 天祐, *i-ch'ou* 乙丑/IV/23 (29 May 905). Reprod. Huang, *Pao-tsang*, 42:548a–62a. Study: Ikeda, *Shikigo*, no. 2127.

S 5447. Booklet. 1. *Wu-ch'ang ching* 無常經. 2. *Po-jo po-lo-mi-to hsin ching* 般若波羅密多心經. Reprod. Huang, *Pao-tsang*, 42:600a–03a.

S 5448. Booket. *Tun-huang lu* 敦煌錄. Cover: Tao-chen 道真. Reprod. Huang, *Pao-tsang*, 42:603b–7a. Studies: Giles, "Tun Huang Lu"; and Shih, "San-chieh ssu, Tao-chen, tun-huang tsang-ching."

S 5450. Booklet. 1. *Chin-kang po-jo po-lo-mi ching* 金剛般若波羅密經. 2. *Yen-lo wang shou-chi ho-ssu-chung ni-hsiu sheng-ch'i chai kung-te wang-sheng ching-t'u ching* 閻羅王授記合四眾逆脩生七齋功德往生淨土經. Anonymous dedication. Reprod. Huang, *Pao-tsang*, 42:610b–22a. Studies: Ch'en, "Chung-shih tun-huang yü ch'eng-tu chih chien te chiao-t'ung lu-hsien," p. 81; and Ikeda, *Shikigo*, no. 2481.

S 5451. Booklet. *Chin-kang po-jo po-lo-mi ching* 金剛般若波羅密經. Colophon: Old man. Dated T'ien-yu 天祐 3, *ping-yin* 丙寅/II/2 (26 Feb. 906). Reprod. Huang, *Pao-tsang*, 42:622b–30a. Studies: Ch'en, "Chung-shih tun-huang yü ch'eng-tu chih chien te chiao-t'ung lu-hsien," p. 81; and Ikeda, *Shikigo*, no. 2133.

S 5458. Booklet. 1. *Kuan-yin ching* 観音經 2. *Shan-o yin-kuo ching* 善惡因果經. 3. *Po-jo po-lo-mi-to hsin ching* 般若波羅密多心經. 4. *Ti-tsang p'u-sa ching* 地藏菩薩經. 5. *T'ien ch'ing-wen ching* 天請問經. Reprod. Huang, *Pao-tsang*, 42:653a–79a.

S 5527. Untitled schedule of feasts for departed mother. *Chia-shen* 甲申 year (924?). Reprod. Huang, *Pao-tsang*, 43:213b–c.

S 5531. Booklet. 1. *Miao-fa lien-hua ching* 妙法蓮華經. 2. *Chieh pai-sheng yüan-chia t'o-lo-ni ching* 解百生怨家陀羅尼經. 3. *Ti-tsang p'u-sa ching* 地藏菩薩經. 4. *T'ien ch'ing-wen ching* 天請問經. 5. *Hsü-ming ching* 續命經. 6. *Mo-li-chih t'ien ching* 摩利支天經. 7. *Yen-shou-ming ching* 延壽命經. 8. Questions and answers. 9. *Yen-lo wang shou-chi ssu-chung ni-hsiu sheng-ch'i chai kung-te wang-sheng ching-t'u ching* 閻羅王授記四眾逆脩往七齋功德往生淨土經. 10. *Po-jo po-lo-mi-to hsin ching* 般若波羅密多心經. Dated *keng-ch'en* 庚辰/XII/20 (31 Jan. 921?). Reprod. Huang, *Pao-tsang*, 43:218b–50b.

S 5534. Booklet. *Chin-kang po-jo po-lo-mi ching* 金剛般若波羅密經. Colophon: Old man. Dated T'ien-fu 天復 5, *i-ch'ou* 乙丑/III/1 (8 April 905). Reprod. Huang, *Pao-tsang*, 43:265b–72b. Studies: Ch'en, "Chung-shih tun-huang yü ch'eng-tu chih chien te chiao-t'ung lu-hsien," p. 81; and Ikeda, *Shikigo*, no. 2126.

S 5544. Booklet. *Chin-kang po-jo po-lo-mi ching* 金剛般若波羅密經. 2. *Yen-lo wang shou-chi ho-ssu-chung ni-hsiu sheng-ch'i chai kung-te wang-sheng ching-t'u ching* 閻羅王授記合四眾逆修生七齋功德往生淨土經. Dedication. Dated *hsin-wei* 辛未/I (911?). Reprod. Huang, *Pao-tsang*, 43:356b–64a. Studies: Ch'en, "Chung-shih tun-huang yü ch'eng-tu chih chien te chiao-t'ung lu-hsien," p. 82; Ikeda, *Shikigo*, nos. 2154, 2155; and Kanaoka, "Tonkō bon jigoku bunken kanki," p. 38   (colophon transcr. incorrectly).

S 5565. Booklet. Untitled prayer for deceased mother. Reprod. Huang, *Pao-tsang*, 43:450a–51b.

S 5581. Booklet. 1. *Po-jo po-lo-mi-to hsin ching* 般若波羅密多心經. 2. *Hsü-ming ching* 續命經. 3. *Yen-shou-ming ching* 延壽命經. 4. *Fo-mu ching* 佛母經. 5. *Miao-fa lien-hua ching* 妙法蓮華經. 6. Prayers. 7. *Chin-kang po-jo po-lo-mi ching* 金剛般若波羅密經. Reprod. Huang, *Pao-tsang*, 43:505b–20b.

S 5585. Booklet. 1. *Chin-kang po-jo po-lo-mi ching* 金剛般若波羅密經. 2. *Yen-lo wang shou-chi ho-ssu-chung ni-hsiu sheng-ch'i chai kung-te wang-sheng ching-t'u ching* 閻羅王授記合四眾逆脩生七齋功德往生淨土經. Reprod. Huang, *Pao-tsang*, 43:538a–41a.

S 5646. Booklet. 1. *Chin-kang po-jo po-lo-mi-to ching* 金剛般若波羅密經. 2. *Mo-li-chih t'ien p'u-sa t'o-lo-ni ching* 摩利支天菩薩陀羅尼經. 3. *Chai-fa ch'ing-ching ching* 齋法清淨經. Dated Ch'ien-te 乾德 7, *chi-ssu* 己巳/ IV/15 (4 May 969). Reprod. Huang, *Pao-tsang*, 44:133b–59a.

S 5663. 57 loose strips of paper pierced for stringing. *Chung-lun* 中論. Two long colophons. 1. Copying by Hui-hai 惠海. Dated *chi-hai* 己亥 (939)? 2. Books and items collected by Tao-chen 道真. Dated *i-wei* 乙未   (935). Reprod. Huang, *Pao-tsang*, 44:235b–64a. Transcr. Wang, *So-yin*, p. 225. Studies: Chikusa, "Tonkō no sōkan seido," p. 193, n. 81; Shih, "San-chieh ssu, Tao-chen, tun-huang tsang-ching"; and TB, *Mokuroku*, 2:69.

S 5669. *Chin-kang po-jo po-lo-mi ching* 金剛般若波羅密經. Colophon: old man. Dated T'ien-yu 天祐 3, *ping-yin* 丙寅/II/3 (28 Feb. 906). Reprod. Huang, *Pao-tsang*, 44:298b–300b. Studies: Ch'en, "Chung-shih tun-huang yü ch'eng-tu chih chien te chiao-t'ung lu-hsien," p. 82; and Ikeda, *Shikigo*, no. 2134.

S 5676v. Untitled tally of clerics at 15 temples. Reprod. Huang, *Pao-tsang*, 44:323b. Studies: Fujieda, "Tonkō no sōni seki," p. 314; and TB, *Mokuroku*, 2:26–27, 39.

S 5696. Invitation to funeral for deceased father. Dated Ch'un-hua 淳化 3 /VIII (992). Reprod. Huang, *Pao-tsang*, 44:362b–63a. Study: T'ang and T'ao, *Tun-huang she-hui ching-chi wen-hsien chen-chi shih-lu*, 4:184.

S 5718. Letter concerning memorial service for monk. Dated T'ien-fu[b] 天福 10/V/22 (4 July 945). Reprod. Huang, *Pao-tsang*, 44:399b. Studies: T'ang and T'ao, *Tun-huang she-hui ching-chi wen-hsien chen-chi shih-lu*, 4:174; and TB, *Mokuroku*, 2:56.

S 5855. Invitation to monks at San-chieh ssu 三界寺 to perform memorial service. Dated Yung-hsi 雍熙 3, *ping-hsü* 丙戌 VI (986). Reprod. Huang, *Pao-tsang*, 44:514a. Studies: T'ang and T'ao, *Tun-huang she-hui ching-chi wen-hsien chen-chi shih-lu*, 4:181; and TB, *Mokuroku*, 2:56.

S 5924. Accordion booklet. Questions about monastic behavior. Reprod. Huang, *Pao-tsang*, 44:574a.

S 5941. Invitation to monks at Hsien-te ssu 顯德寺 to perform memorial service at home. Dated Ch'un-hua 淳化 4, *kuei-ssu* 癸巳/V (993). Reprod. Huang, *Pao-tsang*, 44:584a. Study: TB, *Mokuroku*, 2:57.

S 5965. Booklet. *Chin-kang po-jo po-lo-mi ching* 金剛般若波羅密經. Dedication by old man. Dated T'ien-fu 天復 2, *i-ch'ou* 乙丑/XII/20 (17 Jan. 906). Reprod. Huang, *Pao-tsang*, 44:619b–17b (photos in reverse order). Studies: Ch'en, "Chung-shih tun-huang yü ch'eng-tu chih chien te chiao-t'ung lu-hsien," p. 82; and Ikeda, *Shikigo*, no. 2129 (colophon transcr. incorrectly).

S 6178. Invitation to monks to perform memorial service for heir apparent. Dated T'ai-p'ing hsing-kuo 太平興國 4/VII (979). Reprod. Huang, *Pao-tsang*, 45:93a. Studies: T'ang and T'ao, *Tun-huang she-hui ching-chi wen-hsien chen-chi shih-lu*, 4:180; and TB, *Mokuroku*, 2:56.

S 6225. *San-chieh ssu pi-ch'iu Tao-chen chu-fang ch'iu-mi chu-ching sui-te tsa-ching lu-chi* 三界寺比丘道真諸方求覓諸經隨得雜經錄記. Short list of texts Tao-chen 道真 collected. Reprod. Huang, *Pao-tsang*, 45:137b–38b. Studies; Shih, "San-chieh ssu, Tao-chen, tun-huang tsang-ching"; and TB, *Mokuroku*, 2:45.

S 6230. *Yen-lo wang shou-chi ching* 閻羅王授記經. Anonymous dedication. Dated T'ung-kuang 同光 4, *ping-hsü* 丙戌/VI/6 (18 July 926). Reprod. Huang, *Pao-tsang*, 45:142b–44a. Studies: Ikeda, *Shikigo*, no. 2228; Kanaoka, "Tonkō bon jigoku bunken kanki," p. 38 (colophon transcr. incorrectly).

S 6726. *Chin-kang po-jo po-lo-mi ching* 金剛般若波羅密經. Reprod. Huang, *Pao-tsang*, 51:37a–45a. Study: Ch'en, "Chung-shin tun-huang yü ch'eng-tu chih chien te chiao-t'ung lu-hsien," p. 82.

S 6727. *Ta fang-teng t'o-lo-ni ching* 大方等陀羅尼經. Copied by Chang A-sheng 張阿勝. Dated Yen-ch'ang 延昌 3, *chia-wu* 甲午/IV/12 (21 May 514). Reprod. Huang, *Pao-tsang*, 51:45b–51b.

S 6983. Illustrated booklet. 1. *Miao-fa lien-hua ching, kuan-shih-yin p'u-sa p'u-men p'in* 妙法蓮華經，觀世音菩薩普門品. 2. *Ti-tsang p'u-sa ching* 地藏菩薩經. Reprod. Huang, *Pao-tsang*, 54:219b–39b. Study and reprod.: Fujieda, "Sutain tonkō shūshū e'iri *kannon gyō* sasshi."

S 7598. Fragment of short recension of *Yen-lo wang shou-chi ching* 閻羅王授記經. Reprod. Huang, *Pao-tsang*, 55:260a.

Cft xi.001–2 (L). Booklet. *Chin-kang po-jo po-lo-mi ching* 金剛般若波羅密經. Reprod. Whitfield, *Art*, 2:pl. 67, fig. 98. Studies: Waley, *Catalogue*, no. 212; Whitfield, *Art*, 2:341.

Cft xxii.0026 (L). Booklet. 1. *Hui-hsiang lun ching* 迴向輪經. 2. *Fu-mu en-chung ching* 父母恩重經. 3. *Wu-ch'ang ching* 無常經. Reprod. Whitfield, *Art*, 2: pl. 69, fig. 96.

Cft cii.001 (L). Scroll of illustrations to *Yen-lo wang shou-chi ching* 閻羅王授記經. Second half of P 4523. Reprod. Whitfield, *Art*, 2: pl. 63. Studies: Matsumoto, *Tonkō ga no kenkyū*, 1:402–4; Stein, *Serindia*, p. 1087; Tokushi, "Kōzō," pp. 274–87; Waley, *Catalogue*, no. 80; and Whitfield, *Art*, 2:339.

Cft 00212 (L). Partial frontispiece and beginning of text to *Yen-lo wang shou-chi ching* 閻羅王授記經. Second half of Cft 00404 (L). Reprod. Whitfield, *Art*, 2: figs. 91a, 91b. Studies: Matsumoto, *Tonkō ga no kenkyū*, 1:374–75, 404–5; Stein, *Serindia*, p. 976; and Whitfield, *Art*, 2:338.

Cft 00213 (L). Tiny booklet. *Hsü-ming ching* 續命經. Reprod. Whitfield, *Art*, 2: fig. 99.

Cft 00404 (L). Partial frontispiece to *Yen-lo wang shou-chi ching* 閻羅王授記經. First half of Cft 00212 (L). Reprod. Whitfield, *Art*, 2: figs. 91a, 91c. Studies: Matsumoto, *Tonkō ga no kenkyū*, 1:374–75, 404–5; Stein, *Serindia*, pp. 997–98; Waley, *Catalogue*, no. 78; and Whitfield, *Art*, 2:338.

Pelliot collection. See BN, *Catalogue;* and Pelliot/Lu, "Shu-mu."

P 2003. *Yen-lo wang shou-chi ssu-chung yü-hsiu sheng-ch'i wang-sheng ching-t'u ching* 閻羅王授記四眾預修生七往生淨土經. 14 illustrations. Reprod. Huang, *Pao-tsang*, 112:24b–34a.

P 2055. 1. *Yü-lan-p'en ching* 盂蘭盆經. 2. *Ta-po-nieh-p'an mo-yeh fu-jen p'in ching* 大般涅槃摩耶夫人品經. 3. *Shan-o yin-kuo ching* 善惡因果經. Third scroll commissioned in a series of three; see Tts 4532 and Pk 4544. Colophons to each text contain schedule of services for wife of Chai Feng-ta 翟奉達. Copied Hsien-te 顯德 5–7 (958–960). Reprod. Huang, *Pao-tsang*, 113:278a–88a. Study: Ikeda, *Shikigo*, nos. 2357–59.

P 2094. 1. *Ch'ih-sung chin-kang ching ling-yen kung-te chi* 持誦金剛經靈驗功德記. 2. *K'ai-yüan huang-ti tsan chin-kang ching kung-te* 開元皇帝讚金剛經功德. 3. *Chin-kang po-jo po-lo-mi ching* 金剛般若波羅蜜經. Colophons: copied by Chai Feng-ta 翟奉達. Dated T'ien-fu 天復 8, *wu-ch'en* 戊辰/IV/9 (11 May 908). Reprod. Huang, *Pao-tsang*, 114:122b–33b. 1. and 2. transcr. *T* no. 2743. Studies: Fujieda, "Tonkō rekijitsu fu," p. 435 (colophon transcr. incorrectly); Ikeda, *Shikigo*, nos. 2145, 2146 (colophon transcr. incorrectly); Wang, *Tun-huang ku-chi hsü-lu hsin-pien*, 14:218–70.

P 2130. 1. Untitled histories and prayers on Pure Land. 2. *Kuan-fo san-mei hai ching* 觀佛三昧海經. Colophon mentions Tao-chen 道真. Reprod. Huang, *Pao-tsang*, 115:187b–96b. Study: Shih, "San-chieh ssu, Tao-chen, tun-huang tsang-ching."

P 2161. *Ta-sheng pai-fa ming-men lun k'ai tsung-i chi* 大乘百法明門論開宗義記. Colophon mentions Tao-chen 道真. Dated a *ssu* 巳 year/XI/19. Reprod. Huang, *Pao-tsang*, 116:1a–47. Studies: Ikeda, *Shikigo*, no. 1846; Shih, "San-chieh-ssu, Tao-chen, tun-huang tsang-ching"; and Yabuki, *Meisha yoin kaisetsu*, part 1, pp. 165–69.

P 2193. *Mu-lien yüan-ch'i* 目蓮緣起. Colophon mentions Tao-chen 道真. Reprod. Huang, *Pao-tsang*, 116:500a–5b. Transcr. Wang, *Tun-huang pien-wen chi*, pp. 701–12. Studies: Mair, "Inventory"; Ikeda, *Shikigo*, no. 2502; Shih, "San-chieh ssu, Tao-chen, tun-huang tsang-ching"; and TB, *Mokuroku*, 4:20.

P 2249v. Writing exercises. Includes beginning of *Yen-lo wang shou-chi ching* 閻羅王授記經. Reprod. Huang, *Pao-tsang*, 118:62b–64b. Study: Mair, "Inventory."

P 2270. 1. *Ta-sheng wu-fang-pien pei-tsung* 大乘五方便北宗. 2. *Wu-keng chuan-sung* 五更轉頌. Colophon mentions Tao-chen 道真. Reprod. Huang, *Pao-tsang*, 118:312a–20. Studies: Ikeda, *Shikigo*, no. 2493; and Shih, "San-chieh ssu, Tao-chen, tun-huang tsang-ching."

P 2292. 1. Letter from Ching-t'ung 靖通. 2. Explanation of *Wei-mo-chieh so-shuo ching* 維摩詰所說經. Dated Kuang-cheng 廣政 10/VIII/9 (25 Sept. 947). Reprod. Huang, *Pao-tsang*, 118:554a–62b. Transcr. Wang, *Tun-huang pien-wen chi*, pp. 592–618. Study: Mair, "Inventory."

P 2305v. Explanations of *Wu-ch'ang ching* 無常經. Reprod. Huang, *Pao-tsang*, 119:32b–38a. Transcr. Wang, *Tun-huang pien-wen chi*, pp. 656–71. Study: Mair, "Inventory."

P 2340. *Chiu-hu shen-ming ching* 救護身命經. Colophon mentions Tao-chen 道真. Reprod. Huang, *Pao-tsang*, 119:370a–74. Studies: Ikeda, *Shikigo*, no. 2498; Shih, "San-chieh ssu, Tao-chen, tun-huang tsang-ching."

P 2623. *Hsien-te liu-nien chi-wei sui chü-chu li-jih ping-hsü* 顯德六年己未歲具注曆日並序. Calendar for Hsien-te 顯德 6 (959). By Chai Feng-ta 翟奉達. Reprod. Huang, *Pao-tsang*, 122:586a. Studies: Fujieda, "Tonkō rekijitsu fu," pp. 423–24; Hsiang, "Chi tun-huang shih-shih ch'u chin t'ien-fu shih-nien hsieh-pen *Shou-Ch'ang hsien ti-ching*," p. 438; Mair, "Inventory"; Makita, *Gikyō kenkyū*, p. 339; and Wang, *So-yin*, p. 268.

P 2641v. Notes on repairs to Mo-kao-k'u 莫高窟. Tao-chen 道真 mentioned. Reprod. Huang, *Pao-tsang*, 123:97b–99a. Study: Shih, "San-chieh ssu, Tao-chen, tun-huang tsang-ching."

P 2668. Several texts, including *Hsin p'u-sa ching* 新菩薩經. Commissioned by Chai Feng-ta 翟奉達. Dated *i-hai* 乙亥/IV/8 (24 May 915). Reprod. Huang, *Pao-tsang*, 123:210a–11b. Study: Li, "T'ang sung shih-tai te tun-huang hsüeh-hsiao."

P 2680. Biographies, including *Ling-chou lung-hsing pai-ts'ao yüan ho-shang su-hsing shih, fa-hao tseng-jen* 靈州龍興白草院和尚俗姓史法號增忍. Reprod. Huang, *Pao-tsang*, 123:279a–84b. Study: Mair, "Inventory."

P 2697. Prayer for deceased mother by monk Shao-tsung 紹宗. Dated Ch'ing-t'ai 清泰 2/IX/14. Reprod. Huang, *Pao-tsang*, 123:355a–58.

P 2836. Selections from scriptures. Colophon mentions Tao-chen 道真. Verso: invitation to monks to perform memorial service. Dated

T'ien-fu[b] 天福 4/I/17 (8 Feb. 939). Signed by Chia Feng-chiu 賈
奉玖. Reprod. Huang, *Pao-tsang*, 124:417b–20b. Studies: Gernet, *Les
aspects économiques du bouddhisme dans la société chinoise*, p. 201; Ikeda,
Shikigo, no. 2494; Shih, "San-chieh ssu, Tao-chen, tun-huang tsang-
ching"; T'ang and T'ao, *Tun-huang she-hui ching-chi wen-hsien chen-chi
shih-lu*, 4:172; and TB, *Mokuroku*, 1:103, 367.

P 2859. Booklet. 1. *Wu-chao yao-chüeh lüeh* 五兆要決略. 2. *Ni-ts'e chan* 逆策
占 3. *Chan shih-erh shih lai fa* 占十二時來法. Colophon at end sounds
like Chai Feng-ta 翟奉達, "a student of *yin-yang* studies in the prefectural school." Dated T'ien-fu 天復 4, *chia-tzu* 甲子/intercalary III
[*sic*]/12 (31 March 904) (on the dating, see appendix 11, n. 1).
Reprod. Huang, *Pao-tsang*, 124:510a–21a. Study: Ikeda, *Shikigo*, no
2124.

P 2870. *Yen-lo wang shou-chi ssu-chung yü-hsiu sheng-ch'i wang-sheng ching-
t'u ching* 閻羅王授記四眾預修生七往生淨土經. 14 illustrations. Re-
prod. Huang, *Pao-tsang*, 124:585b–93b.

P 2876. Booklet. *Chin-kang po-jo po-lo-mi ching* 金剛般若波羅蜜經. Anonymous colophon dated T'ien-yu 天祐 3, *ping-yin* 丙寅/IV/5 (30 April
906). Reprod. Huang, *Pao-tsang*, 124:608b–22a. Studies: Ch'en,
"Chung-shih tun-huang yü ch'eng-tu chih chien te chiao-t'ung lu-
hsien," p. 81; and Ikeda, *Shikigo*, no. 2135.

P 2930. Questions on Buddhist texts. Colophon mentions Tao-chen 道真.
Reprod. Huang, *Pao-tsang*, 125:313a–21b. Studies: Ikeda, *Shikigo*,
no. 2501; and Shih, "San-chieh ssu, Tao-chen, tun-huang tsang-
ching."

P 2994. Precept certificate. Recipient: Li Han-erh 李憨兒. Bestowed by
Tao-chen 道真. Dated *chia-tzu* 甲子/I/15 (4 March 964). Reprod.
Huang, *Pao-tsang*, 125:550b. Studies: Shih, "San-chieh ssu, Tao-chen,
tun-huang tsang-ching"; and T'ang and T'ao, *Tun-huang she-hui
ching-chi wen-hsien chen-chi shih-lu*, 4:69.

P 3107v. Invitation to memorial service. Dated *wu-yin* 戊寅/VI/16 (23
July 978). Reprod. Huang, *Pao-tsang*, 126:320a. Studies: Gernet, *Les
aspects économiques du bouddhisme dans la société chinoise*, p. 201; Mair,
"Inventory"; T'ang and T'ao, *Tun-huang she-hui ching-chi wen-hsien
chen-chi shih-lu*, 4:171; and TB, *Mokuroku*, 2:57–58.

P 3136. Booklet. 1. *Fo-mu ching* 佛母經. 2. *Po-jo po-lo-mi-to hsin ching* 般若波
羅蜜多心經. 3. *Mo-li-chih t'ien ching* 摩利支天經. Reprod. Huang,
Pao-tsang, 126:381b–85a.

P 3140. Precept certificate. Recipient: Li Han-erh 李憨兒. Bestowed by
Tao-chen 道真. Dated Ch'ien-te 乾德 4/I/15 (8 Feb. 966). Reprod.
Huang, *Pao-tsang*, 126:412a. Studies: Drège, "Papiers de Dunhuang";
Shih, "San-chieh ssu, Tao-chen, tun-huang tsang-ching"; and T'ang
and T'ao, *Tun-huang she-hui ching-chi wen-hsien chen-chi shih-lu*, 4:82.

P 3143. Precept certificate. Recipient: P'u-t'i Tsui 菩提最. Bestowed by
Tao-chen 道真. Dated Ch'ien-te 乾德 3/I/28 (4 March 965). Re-

prod. Huang, *Pao-tsang*, 126:416a–b. Studies: Drège, "Papiers de Dunhuang"; Shih, "San-chieh ssu, Tao-chen, tun-huang tsang-ching"; and T'ang and T'ao, *Tun-huang she-hui ching-chi wen-hsien chen-chi shih-lu*, 4:79.

P 3152. Invitation to memorial service. Dated Ch'un-hua 淳化 3/VIII/27 (26 Sept. 992). Reprod. Huang, *Pao-tsang*, 126:430b. Studies: Gernet, *Les aspects économiques du bouddhisme dans la société chinoise*, p. 201; and T'ang and T'ao, *Tun-huang she-hui ching-chi wen-hsien chen-chi shih-lu*, 4:183.

P 3167v. Memorandum concerning nuns. Dated Ch'ien-ning 乾寧 2/III (895). Reprod. Huang, *Pao-tsang*, 126:480a–b. Studies: Fujieda, "Tonkō no sōni seki," pp. 319–21; Naba, "Tōdai no shayū ni tsukite," part 3, pp. 118–20; and TB, *Mokuroku*, 2:15.

P 3197v. Writing exercieses. Mentions Chai Feng-ta 翟奉達 and date of *ping-yin* 丙寅/VI/17 (7 July 966). Reprod. Huang, *Pao-tsang*, 126:557b–61b. Study: Mair, "Inventory."

P 3203. Precept certificate. Recipient: Teng Hui-chi 鄧惠集. Bestowed by Tao-chen 道真. Dated T'ai-p'ing hsing-kuo 太平興國 7/V/15 (9 June 982). Reprod. Huang, *Pao-tsang*, 126:574a–b. Studies: Drège, "Papiers de Dunhuang"; Shih, "San-chieh ssu, Tao-chen, tun-huang tsang-ching"; and T'ang and T'ao, *Tun-huang she-hui ching-chi wen-hsien chen-chi shih-lu*, 4:86.

P 3206. Precept certificate. Recipient: Teng Chu-nu 鄧住奴. Dated T'ai-p'ing hsing-kuo 太平興國 9/I/15 (19 Feb. 984). Reprod. Huang, *Pao-tsang*, 126:576b. Studies: Drège, "Papiers de Dunhuang"; Shih, "San-chieh ssu, Tao-chen, tun-huang tsang-ching"; and T'ang and T'ao, *Tun-huang she-hui ching-chi wen-hsien chen-chi shih-lu*, 4:92.

P 3207. Precept certificate. Recipient: Li Han-erh 李憨兒. Bestowed by Tao-chen 道真. Dated T'ai-ping hsing-kuo 太平興國 8/I/8 (23 Feb. 983). Reprod. Huang, *Pao-tsang*, 126:577a–b. Studies: Drège, "Papiers de Dunhuang"; Shih, "San-chieh ssu, Tao-chen, tun-huang tsang-ching"; T'ang and T'ao, *Tun-huang she-hui ching-chi wen-hsien chen-chi shih-lu*, 4:87; and TB, *Mokuroku*, 2:14.

P 3238. Precept certificate. Recipient: Woman Chang 張. Bestowed by Tao-chen 道真. Dated Ch'ien-te 乾德 2/IX/14 (22 Oct. 964). Studies: Drège, "Papiers de Dunhuang"; Shih, "San-chieh ssu, Tao-chen, tun-huang tsang-ching"; and T'ang and T'ao, *Tun-huang she-hui ching-chi wen-hsien chen-chi shih-lu*, 4:75.

P 3247v. *Ta-t'ang t'ung-kuang ssu-nien chü-li* 大唐同光四年具曆. Written by Chai Feng-ta 翟奉達. Dated *ping-hsü* 丙戌/III/14 (29 April 926). First part of *san* 673. Reprod. Huang, *Pao-tsang*, 127:169b–72a. Transcr. Tung, "Ta-t'ang t'ung-kuang ssu-nien chü-chu li ho-pi," pp. 1049–58. Studies: Fujieda, "Tonkō rekijitsu fu," pp. 413–14; Hsiang, "Chi tun-huang shih-shih ch'u chin t'ien-fu shih-nien hsieh-pen

Shou Ch'ang hsien ti-ching, p. 438; and Wang, *Tun-huang ku-chi hsü-lu hsin-pien*, 8:201–21.

P 3304v. Untitled notes describing illustrations to *Yen-lo wang shou-chi ching* 閻羅王授記經. Reprod. Huang, *Pao-tsang*, 127:367a–78. Transcr. Soymié, "Un recueil d'inscriptions sur peintures." Study: Soymié, "Un recueil d'inscriptions sur peintures."

P 3320. Precept certificate. Recipient: Woman Chang 張. Bestowed by Tao-chen 道真. Dated Ch'ien-te 乾德 2/IX/15 (23 Oct. 964). Reprod. Huang, *Pao-tsang*, 127:440a. Studies: Drège, "Papiers de Dunhuang"; Shih, "San-chieh ssu, Tao-chen, tun-huang tsang-ching"; and T'ang and T'ao, *Tun-huang she-hui ching-chi wen-hsien chen-chi shih-lu*, 4:76.

P 3367. Invitation to memorial service. Signed by Sung Tz'u-hsün 宋慈順. Dated *chi-ssu* 己巳/VII/3 (7 Oct. 969?). Reprod. Huang, *Pao-tsang*, 128:36a. Studies: Gernet, *Les aspects économiques du bouddhisme dans la société chinoise*, p. 201; and TB, *Mokuroku*, 2:57.

P 3388. Invitation to memorial service. Signed by Ts'ao Yüan-chung 曹元忠. Dated K'ai-yün 開運 4/III/9 (2 April 947). Reprod. Huang, *Paotsang*, 128:127b. Study: T'ang and T'ao, *Tun-huang she-hui ching-chi wen-hsien chen-chi shih-lu*, 4:173.

P 3392. Precept certificate. Recipient: P'u-t'i Tsui 菩提最. Bestowed by Tao-chen 道真. Dated *chia-tzu* 甲子/I/28 (14 March 964). Reprod. Huang, *Pao-tsang*, 128:150a-b. Studies: Drège, "Papiers de Dunhuang"; Shih, "San-chieh ssu, Tao-chen, tun-huang tsang-ching"; and T'ang and T'ao, *Tun-huang she-hui ching-chi wen-hsien chen-chi shih-lu*, 4:70.

P 3398-1. Booklet. *Chin-kang po-jo po-lo-mi ching* 金剛般若波羅密經. Copied by Yin Yen-ch'ing 陰彥清. Dated T'ien-fu[b] 天福 8/XI/11 (10 Dec. 943). Same ms. redundantly designated P 3493. Reprod. Huang, *Pao-tsang*, 128:157a–66b. Studies: Ikeda, *Shikigo*, no. 2307; and Mair, "Inventory."

P 3405. Collection of prayers, including "Seng-su ni-hsiu kao" 僧俗逆修稾. Reprod. Huang, *Pao-tsang*, 128:220b–24a. Study: Mair, "Inventory."

P 3414. Precept certificate. Recipient: Li Han-erh 李憨兒. Bestowed by Tao-chen 道真. Dated *chia-tzu* 甲子/I/28 (14 March 964). Reprod. Huang, *Pao-tsang*, 128: 244b. Studies: Shih, "San-chieh ssu, Tao-chen, tun-huang tsang-ching"; and T'ang and T'ao, *Tun-huang she-hui ching-chi wen-hsien chen-chi shih-lu*, 4:71.

P 3439. 3 Precept certificates. All bestowed by Tao-chen 道真. 1. Recipient: Li Hsin-chu 李新住. Dated T'ai-p'ing hsing-kuo 太平興國 8/I/8 (23 Feb. 983) 2. Recipient: Li Sheng-chu 李盛住. Dated . . . . /26. 3. Recipient: Li sheng-chu 李盛住. Dated T'ai-p'ing hsing-kuo 太平興國 . . . /I/25 (12 March 983). Reprod. Huang, *Pao-tsang*,

128:325a–27b. Studies: Drège, "Papiers de Dunhuang"; Shih, "San-chieh ssu, Tao-chen, tun-huang tsang-ching"; and T'ang and T'ao, *Tun-huang she-hui ching-chi wen-hsien chen-chi shih-lu*, 4:88, 89, 90.

P 3455. Precept certificate. Recipient: Li Han-erh 李憨兒. Bestowed by Tao-chen 道真. Dated Ch'ien-te 乾德 3/I/15 (19 Feb. 965). Reprod. Huang, *Pao-tsang*, 128:387b. Studies: Drège, "Papiers de Dunhuang"; Shih, "San-chieh ssu, Tao-chen, tun-huang tsang-ching"; and T'ang and T'ao, *Tun-huang she-hui ching-chi wen-hsien chen-chi shih-lu*, 4:78.

P 3482. Precept certificate. Recipient: P'u-t'i Fa 菩提法. Bestowed by Tao-chen 道真. Dated Ch'ien-te 乾德 2/V/15 (27 June 964). Reprod. Huang, *Pao-tsang*, 128:437a–b. Studies: Drège, "Papiers de Dunhuang"; Shih, "San-chieh ssu, Tao-chen, tun-huang tsang-ching"; and T'ang and T'ao, *Tun-huang she-hui ching-chi wen-hsien chen-chi shih-lu*, 4:74

P 3483. Precept certificate. Recipient: Chang Fa-man 張法滿. Bestowed by Tao-chen 道真. Dated Yung-hsi 雍熙 2/V/15 (6 June 985). Reprod. Huang, *Pao-tsang*, 128:438a. Studies: Drège, "Papiers de Dunhuang"; Shih, "San-chieh ssu, Tao-chen, tun-huang tsang-ching"; T'ang and T'ao, *Tun-huang she-hui ching-chi wen-hsien chen-chi shih-lu*, 4:98; and TB, *Mokuroku*, 2:14.

P 3493. See P 3398–1.

P 3600v. List of nuns at P'u-kuang ssu 普光寺. Dated a *hsü* 戌 year (926? 938?). Reprod. Huang, *Pao-tsang*, 129:236a–41. Studies: Fujieda, "Tonkō no sōni seki," pp. 303–4; Naba, "Tōdai no shayū ni tsukite," part 3, pp. 120–22; and TB, *Mokuroku*, 2:28–29.

P 3759. Tiny bound booklet. 1. *Pa-yang shen-chou ching* 八陽神咒經. 2. *Mo-li-chih t'ien p'u-sa t'o-lo-ni ching* 摩利支天菩薩陀羅尼經. Reprod. Huang, *Pao-tsang*, 130:372a–441b.

P 3760. Tiny accordion. 1. *Miao-fa lien-hua ching kuan-shih-yin p'u-sa p'u-men p'in* 妙法蓮華經觀世音菩薩普門品. 2. *Ti-tsang p'u-sa ching* 地藏菩薩經. 3. *Hsü-ming ching* 續命經. Reprod. Huang, *Pao-tsang*, 130:442a–56b.

P 3761. Tiny booklet. *Yen-lo wang yü-hsiu sheng-ch'i wang-sheng ching-t'u ching* 閻羅王預修生七往生淨土經. Reprod. Huang, *Pao-tsang*, 130:457a–79a.

P 3915. Booklet. 1. *Chin-kang po-jo po-lo-mi ching* 金剛般若波羅密經. 2. *Miao-fa lien-hua ching, kuan-shih-yin p'u-sa p'u-men p'in* 妙法蓮華經觀世音菩薩普門品. 3. *O-mi-t'o ching* 阿彌陀經. 4. *An-chai shen-chou ching* 安宅神咒經. 5. *Pa-yang shen-chou ching* 八陽神咒經 6. *Pa-ming p'u-mi t'o-lo-ni ching* 八名普密陀羅尼經. Reprod. Huang, *Pao-tsang*, 132:16a–41a.

P 3916. Booklet. 1. *Ch'i-chü-chih fo mu chun-ni ta ming t'o-lo-ni nien-sung fa-men* 七俱胝佛母准泥大明陀羅尼念誦法門. 2. *Ta t'o-lo-ni mo-fa-chung i-tzu hsin chou ching* 大陀羅尼末法中一字心咒經. 3. *Ch'i-chü-chih fo mu hsin ta chun-t'i t'o-lo-ni ching* 七俱胝佛母心大准提陀羅尼經. 4. *Pu-k'ung chüan-so shen-chou hsin ching* 不空羂索神咒心經. 5. *Fo-ting-hsin kuan-shih-yin p'u-sa ta t'o-lo-ni ching* 佛頂心觀世音菩薩大陀羅尼經. 6. *Chu-hsing-mu t'o-lo-ni ching* 諸星母陀羅尼經. 7. *Wu-k'an ching-kuang ta t'o-lo-ni ching* 無垢淨光大陀羅尼經. 8. *Ta-fo-ting ru-lai ting-chi pai-kai t'o-lo-ni shen-chou ching* 大佛頂如來頂髻白蓋陀羅尼神咒經. 9. *Nien-fo shou-yin chi chen-yen* 念佛手印及真言. 10. *Kuan-tzu-tsai ju-i-lun p'u-sa yü-ch'ieh fa-yao* 觀自在如意輪菩薩瑜伽法要. Reprod. Huang, *Pao-tsang*, 132:41b–105b.

P 3917A, B. *Chung-lun* 中論. Colophon mentions Tao-chen 道真. Transcr. Huang, *Pao-tsang*, 132:106a–28b. Study: Shih, "San-chieh ssu, Tao-chen, tun-huang tsang-ching."

P 3920. Booklet. 1. *Ch'ien-pei ch'ien-yen t'o-lo-ni ching* 千臂千眼陀羅尼經. 2. *Ju-i-lun t'o-lo-ni ching* 如意輪陀羅尼經. 3. *Ta-lun chin-kang tsung-ch'ih t'o-lo-ni shen-chou ching* 大輪金剛總持陀羅尼神咒經. 4. *Chin-kang-ting ching i-ch'ieh ju-lai shen-miao mi-mi chin-kang-chieh ta san-mei-yeh hsiu-hsi yü-ch'ieh ying-ch'ing i* 金剛頂經一切如來深妙祕密金剛界大三昧耶修習瑜伽迎請儀. 5. *Chin-kang-ting ching i-ch'ieh ju-lai chen-shih she ta-sheng hsien-cheng ta-chiao wang ching shen-miao mi-mi chin-kang-chieh ta san-mei-yeh hsiu-hsi yü-ch'ieh i* 金剛頂經一切如來真實攝大乘現證大教王經深妙祕密金剛界大三昧耶修習瑜伽儀. 6. *Chiu-pa yen-k'ou o-kuei t'o-lo-ni ching* 救拔焰口餓鬼陀羅尼經. 7. *Kao-wang kuan-shih-yin ching* 高王觀世音經. Reprod. Huang, *Pao-tsang*, 132:156b–66b.

P 4098. Illustrated booklet. *Chin-kang po-jo po-lo-mi ching* 金剛般若波羅密經. Reprod. Huang, *Pao-tsang*, 133:128a–32a.

P 4523. Scroll of illustrations to *Yen-lo wang shou-chi ching* 閻羅王授記經. First half of Cft cii. 001. Reprod. Huang, *Pao-tsang*, 133:365b–68b. Studies: Matsumoto, *Tonkō ga no kenkyū*, 1:402–4; and Tokushi, "Kōzō," pp. 274–87.

P 4524. *Hsiang-mo pien-wen* 降魔變文. Reprod. Vandier-Nicolas, *Śāriputra et les six maîtres d'erreur*. Study: Mair, "Inventory."

P 4578. Booklet with printed illustrations. *Chin-kang po-jo po-lo-mi ching* 金剛般若波羅密經. Reprod. Huang, *Pao-tsang*, 133:518a–31.

P 4959. Precept certificate. Recipient: Li Han-erh 李憨兒. Bestowed by Tao-chen 道真. Studies: Drège, "Papiers de Dunhuang"; Shih, "San-chieh ssu, Tao-chen, tun-huang tsang-ching"; and T'ang and T'ao, *Tun-huang she-hui ching-chi wen-hsien chen-chi shih-lu*, 4:96.

P 5580. Booklet. 1. *Chin-kang po-jo po-lo-mi ching* 金剛般若波羅密經. 2. *Yen-lo wang shou-chi ling ssu-chung ni-hsiu sheng-ch'i chai kung-te wang-sheng ching-t'u ching* 閻羅王受記令四眾逆修生七齋功德往生淨土經. Reprod. Huang, *Pao-tsang*, 135:556a–58a.

P tib. 1261 (= P 3301). Chinese-Tibetan glossary of *Yü-ch'ieh-shih ti lun* 瑜

伽師地論. Verso: List of monks and nuns given gifts during feast, includes Tao-chen 道真. Studies: Lalou, *Inventaire des manuscrits tibétain de Touen-houang conservées á la Bibliothèque nationale*; Li, "A Sino-Tibetan Glossary from Tun-huang."

Peking Collection. See Ch'en, *Tun-huang chieh-yü lu*; Hsü, *Tun-huang shih-shih hsieh-ching t'i-chi*; and Pei-ching t'u-shu-kuan shan-pen-pu, *Tun-huang chieh-yü lu hsü-pien*. First number and parenthetical designation refer to order in *Ch'ien-tzu wen* 千文字. Second number in parentheses refers to call number used in the National Library.

Pk 1226 (*lieh* 列 26) (8258). *Yen-lo shou-chi ching* 閻羅受記經 (title at end). Commissioned by old man. Dated *wu-ch'en* 戊辰/VIII/1 (30 Aug. 908). Reprod. Huang, *Pao-tsang*, 109:432b–35a.

Pk 1362 (*chang* 張 66) (3066). *Ta-po-jo po-lo-mi-to ching* 大般若波羅密多經. Colophon mentions Tao-chen 道真. Reprod. Huang, *Pao-tsang*, 75:509b–19a. Studies: Ikeda, *Shikigo*, no. 2491; and Shih, "San-chieh ssu, Tao-chen, tun-huang tsang-ching."

Pk 2126v (*tsang* 藏 26) (7133). Invitation to monks to perform memorial services. Dated Kuang-ch'i 光啟 3/VIII/10 (1 Sept. 887). Reprod. Huang, *Pao-tsang*, 104:270b–73a. Study: Gernet, *Les aspects économiques du bouddhisme dans la société chinoise*, p. 201.

Pk 2258v (*jun* 閏 58) (6718). Invitation to monks to perform memorial services. Reprod. Huang, *Pao-tsang*, 101:329a–30b. Studies: Gernet, *Les aspects économiques du bouddhisme dans la société chinoise*, p. 261; and Kao, "Lun tun-huang min-chien ch'i-ch'i chai sang-su," p. 115.

Pk 2318 (*yü* 餘 18) (2211). *Ta po-jo po-lo-mi to ching* 大般若波羅密多經. Colophon mentions Tao-chen 道真. Reprod. Huang, *Pao-tsang*, 72:278a–88b. Studies: Ikeda, *Shikigo*, no. 2490; and Shih, "San-chieh ssu, Tao-chen, tun-huang tsang-ching."

Pk 4544 (*kang* 岡 44) (8259). 1. *Yen-lo wang shou-chi ching* 閻羅王受記經 (title at end). 2. *Hu chu-t'ung-tzu t'o-lo-ni ching* 護諸童子陀羅尼經. 3. *Po-jo po-lo-mi-to hsin ching* 般若波羅密多心經. Second scroll commissioned in a series of three; see P 2055 and Pk 4544. Colophons to each text contain schedule of services for wife of Chai Feng-ta 翟奉達. Dated Hsien-te 顯德 5 (958). Reprod. Huang, *Pao-tsang*, 109:435b–38a. Study: Ikeda, *Shikigo*, nos. 2354–56.

Pk 5788 (*nai* 奈 88) (747). *Fo-ming ching* 佛名經. Colophon on repair of text mentions Tao-chen 道真. Reprod. Huang, *Pao-tsang*, 62:65a–81b. Studies: Ikeda, *Shikigo*, no. 2495; and Shih, "San-chieh ssu, Tao-chen, tun-huang tsang-ching."

Pk 5866 (*ts'ai* 菜 66) (5957). *Miao-fa lien-hua ching* 妙法蓮華經. Dated Ch'ien-te 乾德 6/IX (968?). Verso: Invitation to monks to perform memorial service. Reprod. Huang, *Pao-tsang*, 96:205b–8a; Kao, "Lun tun-huang min-chien ch'i-ch'i chai sang-su," p. 115.

Pk 6375 (*yen* 鹹 75) (8254). *Yen-lo wang shou-chi ch'üan-hsiu sheng-ch'i chai kung-te ching* 閻羅王受記勸修生七齋功德經. Colophon mentions Tao-chen 道真. Reprod. Huang, *Pao-tsang*, 109:422a–24a. Study: Ikeda, *Shikigo*, no. 2500.

Pk 8045 (*tzu* 字 45) (8257). *Yen-lo wang ching* 閻羅王經 (title at end). Colophon mentions Miao-fu 妙福 of An Kuo ssu 安國寺. Reprod. Huang, *Pao-tsang* 109:430b–31b. Studies: Ikeda, *Shikigo*, no. 2484; Kanaoka, "Tonkō bon jigoku bunken kanki," p. 38 (colophon transcr. incorrectly).

Pk 8066 (*tzu* 字 66) (8256). *Yen-lo wang shou-chi ho ssu-chung ni-hsiu sheng-ch'i chai kung-te* 閻羅王受記合四眾逆修生七齋功德. Reprod. Huang, *Pao-tsang*, 109:428b–29b.

Pk 8230 (*fu* 服 30) (7177). *Ho shih-chieh wen* 和十戒文. Cover mentions Tao-chen 道真. Reprod. Huang, *Pao-tsang*, 104:380b–81b. Study: Chin, "Tun-huang k'u-k'an ming-shu k'ao," p. 54; Ikeda, *Shikigo*, no. 2492; and Shih, "San-chieh-ssu, Tao-chen, tun-huang tsang-ching."

Pk 8237 (*fu* 服 37) (8355). *Yen-lo wang shou-chi ho ssu-chung ni-hsiu sheng-ch'i chai wang-sheng ching-t'u ching* 閻羅王受記合四眾逆修生七齋往生淨土經. Reprod. Huang, *Pao-tsang*, 109:424b–26a.

Pk 8909 (*yu* 有 09) (?). *Chin-kang po-jo po-lo-mi ching* 金剛般若波羅密經. Colophon mentions old man. Dated *ting-mao* 丁卯/III/12 (27 April 907). Condition too poor to allow inspection at Peking Library. Studies: Ch'en, "Chung-shih tun-huang yü ch'eng-tu chih chien te chiao-t'ung lu-hsien," p. 80; and Ikeda, *Shikigo*, no. 2142.

Pk *hsin* 329. Originally Ōtani ms. no. 333 (*p'an* 盤). *Chien i-ch'ieh ju-tsang-ching mu-lu* 見一切入藏經目錄. Written by Tao-chen 道真. Dated Ch'ang-hsing 長興 5, *chia-wu* 甲午/VI/15 (29 July 934). Transcr. Oda, "Tonkō sangaiji no *gen issai nyuzōkyō mokuroku* ni tsuite," pp. 557–66. Studies: Ikeda, *Shikigo*, no. 2261; "Kantōchō haku-butsukan Ōtani ke shuppin mokuroku"; Lo, "Jih-pen Chü-shih tun-huang chiang-lai tsang-ching mu-lu"; Oda, "Tonkō sangaiji no *gen issai nyuzōkyō mokuroku* ni tsuite"; and Shih, "San-chieh ssu, Tao-chen, tun-huang tsang-ching."

Pk *hsin* 836. Originally in the possession of a Mr. Han 韓. 1. *Ni-ts'e chan* 逆刺占. Copied by Chai Feng-ta 翟奉達. Colophon dated T'ien-fu 天復 2, *jen-hsü* 壬戌/IV/*ting-ch'ou* 丁丑 (2 June 902). 2. Poems. Verso: 1. Preface to calendar for T'ien-ch'eng 天成 3 (928). Composed by Chai Feng-ta 翟奉達. 2. *Mao-shih* 毛詩. Studies: Hsiang, "Chi tun-huang shih-shih ch'u chin t'ien-fu shih-nien hsieh-pen *Shou Ch'ang hsien ti-ching*," p. 439; Hsiang, "Hsi-cheng hsiao-chi," p. 370; and Ikeda, *Shikigo*, no. 2119.

Pk *hsin* 1537. *Yen-lo wang ching* 閻羅王經 (title at end). Colophon: com-missioned by Chai Ting-yu 翟定友 and Chang Wang-ch'u 張王仵. Study: Ikeda, *Shikigo*, no. 2482.

Tientsin collection. See Liu and Li, "T'ien-chin-shih i-shu po-wu-kuan ts'ang tun-huang i-shu mu-lu fu ch'uan-shih pen hsieh-ching."

Tts 175 (Museum no. 4532). 1. *Wu-ch'ang ching* 無常經. 2. *Shui-yüeh kuan-yin ching* 水月觀音經. 3. *Chou-kuei ching* 咒鬼經. 4. *T'ien ch'ing-wen ching* 天請問經. First scroll commissioned in a series of three; see P 2055 and Pk 4544. Colophons to each text contain schedule of services for wife of Chai Feng-ta 翟奉經. Dated Hsien-te 顯德 5 (958). Study: Ikeda, *Shikigo*, no. 2353.

Tun-huang County Museum. See Jung, "Tun-huang-hsien po-wu-kuan ts'ang tun-huang i-shu mu-lu."

Th Museum 53. *Chin-kang po-jo po-lo-mi ching* 金剛般若波羅密經. Colophon: Commissioned by eighty [-three-year old man]. Dated T'ien-yu 天祐 3, *ping-yin* 丙寅 /II/2 (22 Feb. 906). Study: Ikeda, *Shikigo*, no. 2132.

Th Museum 77. Booklet. 1. *P'u-t'i-ta-mo nan-tsung ting shih-fei lun* 菩提達摩南宗定是非論. 2. *Nan-yang ho-shang tun-chiao chieh-t'o ch'an-men chih-liao hsing t'an-yü* 南陽和上頓教解脫禪門直了性壇語. 3. *Nan-tsung ting hsieh-cheng wu-keng chuan* 南宗定邪正五更轉. 4. *Nan-tsung tun-chiao tsui-shang ta-sheng mo-ho po-jo po-lo-mi ching* 南宗頓教最上大乘摩訶般若波羅密經. 5. *Chu po-jo po-lo-mi-to hsin ching* 注般若波羅多心經.

Tun-huang Institute. See Liu and Shih, "Tun-huang wen-wu yen-chiu-so ts'ang tun-huang i-shu mu-lu."

Th Institute 322. Originally in the possession of a Mr. Wu 吳. *Shih-erh yüeh pa-jih . . . she-jen pien-k'u jan-teng fen-p'ei k'u-k'an ming-shu* 十二月八日···社人遍窟燃燈分配窟龕名數. Mentions Tao-chen 道真. Dated *hsin-hai* 辛亥 /XII/7 (6 Jan. 952). Transcr. Tun-huang yen-chiu-yüan, *Tun-huang*, p. 291. Studies: Chikusa, "Tonkō no sōkan seido," pp. 158–59; Chin, "Tun-huang k'u-k'an ming-shu k'ao," p. 54; Shih, "San-chieh ssu, Tao-chen, tun-huang tsang-ching"; and Wu, "Tun-huang shih-k'u la-pa jan-teng fen-p'ei k'u-k'an ming-shu," p. 49.

Th Institute 345. Originally in the possession of a Mr. Jen 任. *San-chieh ssu tsang-nei ching-lun mu-lu* 三界寺藏內經論目錄. Written by Tao-chen 道真. Dated Ch'ang-hsing 長興 5, *chia-wu* 甲午 /VI/15 (29 July 934). Incomplete version of Pk *hsin* 329. Partial reprod.: Tun-huang yen-chiu-yüan, *Tun-huang*, p. 284. Studies: Chin, "Tun-huang k'u-k'an ming-shu k'ao," p. 54; Ikeda, *Shikigo*, supplemental no. 31; Shih, "San-chieh ssu, Tao-chen, tun-huang tsang-ching"; and Tun-huang yen-chiu-yüan, *Tun-huang*, p. 291.

Satō Collection. Collection of Satō Han'ai 佐藤汎愛, originally held in

Nihon Nagao bijutsukan 日本長尾美術館. Now held in Kubosō kinen bijutsukan 久保惣記念美術館. See *Kubosō korekushon.*

Satō ms. *Yen-lo wang shou-chi ssu-chung yü-hsiu sheng-ch'i wang-sheng ching-t'u ching* 閻羅王受記四眾預修生七往生淨土經. 14 illustrations. Colophon: commissioned by Tung Wen-yüan 董文員. Dated *hsin-wei* 辛未/XII/10 (2 Jan. 912? 30 Dec. 971?). Reprod. *Kubosō korekushon,* item no. 15. Studies: Ikeda, *Shikigo,* no. 2160, supplemental no. 34; Matsumoto, "Tonkō bon *juō kyō* zuken zakkō," pp. 227–32; and Matsumoto, *Tonkō ga no kenkyū,* 1:405–12.

Nakamura Collection. Collection of Nakamura Fusetsu 中村不折, kept in Nakamura shodō hakubutsukan 中村書道博物館, in Tokyo. See Nakamura, *Uiki shutsudo bokuhō shohō genryū kō.*

Nakamura ms. *San* 799. *Yen-lo wang shou-chi ssu-chung ni-hsiu sheng-ch'i chai wang-sheng ching-t'u ching* 閻羅王受記四眾逆修生七齋往生淨土經. Colophon: Commissioned by Hsüeh Yen-ch'ang 薛延唱. Dated Ch'ing-t'ai 清泰 3, *ping-shen* 丙申/XII/ . . . . Transcr. Tokushi, "Kōzō," pp. 259–67. Studies: Ikeda, *Shikigo,* no. 2276; and Nakamura, *Uiki shutsudo bokuhō shohō genryū kō,* 3:19v.

Hōjuin Collection. Held in Hōjuin 寶壽院, Kōyasan 高山野.

Hōjuin ms. *Yen-lo wang shou-chi ssu-chung ni-hsiu sheng-ch'i wang-sheng ching-t'u ching* 閻羅王授記四眾逆修生七往生淨土經. 11 illustrations. Dated Kan'ei 寬永 4/IV/15 (29 May 1627). Based on a Moromachi copy derived from a Sung dynasty original. Reprod. *T* no. 3143.

Museum für Indische Kunst, Berlin.

Ten fragments of a copy of *Yen-lo wang shou-chi ching.*
Contains illustrations. 1. MIK III: 4607a, reprod. Gabain, "Kṣiti-garbha-Kult in Zentralasien," fig. 82. 2. MIK III: 4607f; reprod. fig. 83. 3. MIK 4693a; reprod. fig. 84. 4. MIK III: 4693b; reprod. fig. 85. 5. MIK III: 4693b bis; reprod. fig. 86. 6. MIK III: 4693c; reprod. fig. 87. 7. MIK III: 4693d; reprod. fig. 88. 8. MIK III: 4693e, reprod. fig. 89. 9. MIK III: 6321; reprod. fig. 90. 10. MIK III: 7473; reprod. fig. 91.

Taipei Collection, held in Kuo-li chung-yang t'u-shu-kuan 國立中央圖書館. See P'an, "Kuo-li chung-yang t'u-shu-kuan so-ts'ang tun-huang chüan-tzu t'i-chi."

Tp 4736. *Ching-ming ching kuan-chung shih ch'ao* 淨名經關中釋抄. Colophon mentions Tao-chen 道真. Dated *wu-hsü* 戊戌/V/20 (20 June 938). Reprod. *Tun-huang chüan-tzu,* pp. 1171a–79b. Studies: Ikeda, *Shikigo,* no. 2279; and Shih, "San-chieh ssu, Tao-chen, tun-huang tsang-ching."

St. Petersburg Collection. See Menshikov, *Opisanie.*

Dkh 143 (Menshikov, *Opisanie*, no. 1304). Page from booklet. Text matches short recension of *Yen-lo wang shou-chi ching* 閻羅王授記經.

Dkh 295a (Menshikov, *Opisanie*, no. 1463). Prayer. Dated T'ien-fu 天復 10, *keng-wu* 庚午/III/15 (27 April 910).

Dkh 803 (Menshikov, *Opisanie*, no. 1303). Fragment of scroll. Title at end: *Yen-lo* . . . 閻羅. Text matches short recension of *Yen-lo wang shou-chi ching* 閻羅王授記經.

Dkh 931 (Menshikov, *Opisanie*, no. 1302). Page from booklet. *Yen-lo wang ching* 閻羅王經 (title at end).

Location unknown.

San 262. Now lost. Originally in the collection of Li Sheng-to 李盛鐸. Booklet. 1. *Chin-kang po-jo po-lo-mi-to ching* 金剛般若波羅密多經. 2. *Yen-lo wang shou-chi ching* 閻羅王授記經. Studies: Ch'en "Chung-shih tun-huang yü ch'eng-tu chih chien te chiao-t'ung lu-hsien," p. 80; Wang, *So-yin.*

San 535. Now lost. Originally in the collection of Li Sheng-to 李盛鐸. *Yen-lo wang shou-chi ching* 閻羅王授記經. Colophon: commissioned by old man. Dated *wu-ch'en* 戊辰/VII/28 (27 Aug. 908). Study: Wang, *So-yin.*

San 673. *Ta-t'ang t'ung-kuang ssu-nien chü-li* 大唐同光四年具曆. Written by Chai Feng-ta 翟奉達. Dated *ping-hsü* 丙戌/III/14 (29 April 926). Second part of P 3247v. Now lost. Originally in the collection of Mr. Lo 羅. Studies: Fujieda, "Tonkō rekijitsu fu," pp. 413–14; Hsiang, "Chi tun-huang shih-shih ch'u chin t'ien-fu shih-nien hsieh-pen *Shou Ch'ang hsien ti-ching*, p. 438; and Lo, *Tun-huang shih-shih sui-chin*, entitled "T'ang t'ien-ch'eng yüan-nien ts'an-li" 唐天成元年殘曆.

San 1700. Now lost. *Shou Ch'ang hsien ti-ching* 壽昌縣地境. Written by Chai Feng-ta 翟奉達. Dated T'ien-fu[b] 天福 10, *i-ssu* 乙巳/VI/9 (20 July 945). Studies: Hsiang, "Chi tun-huang shih-shih ch'u chin t'ien-fu shih-nien hsieh-pen *Shou-Ch'ang hsien ti-ching*," p. 437; Mori, "Shinshutsu tonkō sekishitsu isho"; and Wang, *Tun-huang ku-chi hsü-lu hsin-pien*, 7:13–17.

Primary Sources: Cave Inscriptions

Th Cave 98. Commissioned by Chai Feng-ta 翟奉達. Transcr. Tun-huang yen-chiu-yüan, *Tun-huang mo-kao-k'u kung-yang-jen t'i-chi*, p. 45. Studies: Hsiang, "Chi tun-huang shih-shih ch'u chin t'ien-fu shih-nien hsieh-pen *Shou Ch'ang hsien ti-ching*," p. 438; Fujieda, "Tonkō reki-jitsu fu," pp. 435–46; and Tun-huang wen-wu yen-chiu-so, *Tun-huang mo-kao-k'u nei-jung tsung-lu*, pp. 31–32.

Th Cave 108. Mentions Tao-chen 道真. Transcr. Tun-huang yen-chiu-yuan, *Tun-huang mo-kao-k'u kung-yang-jen t'i-chi*, p. 54. Studies: Chikusa, "Tonkō no sōkan seido," pp. 158-59; Chin, "Tun-huang k'u-k'an ming-shu k'ao," p. 54; Shih, "San-chieh ssu, Tao-chen, tun-huang tsang-chin"; and Tun-huang wen-wu yen-chiu-so, *Tun-huang mo-kao-k'u nei-jung tsung-lu*, pp.34–35.

Primary Sources: Texts

Besson zakki 別尊雜記. Shinkaku 心覺 (fl. 1117–1180). *T* no. 3007.

Chai-chieh lu 齋戒錄. Anon. Ca. late seventh century. Sch no. 464. *TT* 207.

Chai ching 齋經. Chih Ch'ien 支謙 (fl. 220–252). *T* no. 87.

Ch'ang a-han ching 長阿含經 (*Dīrghāgama*). Buddhayaśas (Fo-t'o-yeh-she 佛陀耶舍) (fl. 408–412) and Chu Fo-nien 竺佛念 (fl. 365). *T* no. 1.

Chen-yüan hsin-ting shih-chiao mu-lu 真元新定釋教目錄. Yüan-chao 圓照 (fl. 778). *T* no. 2157.

Cheng-fa nien-ch'u ching 正法念處經 (*Saddharmasmṛtyupasthānasūtra*). Gautama Prajñāruci (Ch'ü-t'an Po-jo-liu-chih 瞿曇般若流支) (fl. 538–543). *T* no. 721.

Ch'eng-tu fu-chih, hsin-hsiu (新修) 成都府志. Feng Jen 馮任 (Ming) and Chang Shih-yung 張世雍 (Ming). Printed ed. dated 1621. 58 *chüan*. Microfilm of original held at University of Chicago.

Ch'i-ch'u san-kuan ching 七處三觀經. An Shih-kao 安世高 (fl. 148–170). *T* no. 1509.

Ch'ien-shou ch'ien-yen kuan-shih-yin p'u-sa kuang-ta yüan-man wu-ai ta-pei hsin t'o-lo-ni ching 千手千眼觀世音菩薩廣大圓滿無礙大悲心陀羅尼經. Bhagavaddharma (Ch'ieh-fan-ta-mo 伽梵達摩) (fl. 650–660). *T* no. 1060.

Ch'ien-shou ch'ien-yen kuan-shih-yin p'u-sa ta-pei hsin t'o-lo-ni 千手千眼觀世音菩薩大悲心陀羅尼. Pu-k'ung chin-kang 不空金剛 (Amogha-vajra) (705–774). *T* no. 1064.

Chin-kang po-jo po-lo-mi ching 金剛般若波羅密經 (*Vajracchedikā*). Ku-mārajīva (Chiu-mo-lo-shih 鳩摩羅什) (350–409). *T* no. 235.

Ching-hsin chieh-kuan fa 淨心戒觀法. Tao-hsüan 道宣 (d. 667). *T* no. 1893.

Ching-lü i-hsiang 經律異相. Pao-ch'ang 寶唱 (fl. 516). *T* no. 2121.

Ching-tu san-mei ching 淨度三昧經. Not extant. Perhaps four transla-tions: 1. Chih-yen 智嚴 (fl. 427) and Pao-yün 寶雲 (376–449). 2. Guṇabhadra (Ch'iu-na-pa-t'o-lo 求那跋陀羅) (394–468). 3. T'an-yao 曇曜 (fl. 462). 4. Hsiao Tzu-liang 蕭子良 (fl. 490). Some portions from Tun-huang transcr. Makita, *Gikyō kenkyū*, pp. 254–71.

Ching-t'u wu-hui nien-fo sung-ching kuan-hsing i 淨土五會念佛誦經觀行儀. Fa-chao 法照 (fl. 766–804). P 2066, transcr. *T* no. 2827.

Chiu t'ang shu 舊唐書. Liu Hsü 劉煦 (887–946). 16 vols. Peking: Chung-hua shu-chü, 1975.

Chou-mei ching 咒魅經. Anon. Numerous Tun-huang mss. S 418 and S 2517 transcr. *T* no. 2882.

Chu-tsa lüeh-te-yao ch'ao-tzu 諸雜略得要抄子. Anon. P 2661. Reprod. Huang, *Pao-tsang*, 123:172b–75b.

Ch'u san-tsang chi chi 出三藏記集. Seng-yu 僧祐 (445–518). *T* no. 2145.

Chuan-chi pai-yüan ching 撰集百緣經 (*Avadānaśataka*). Chih Ch'ien 支謙 (fl. 220–252). *T* no. 200.

Chuan-ching hsing-tao yüan wang-sheng ching-t'u fa-shih tsan 轉經行道願往生淨土法事讚. Shan-tao 善導 (d. 662). *T* no. 1979.

Chung a-han ching 中阿含經 (*Madhyamāgama*). Gautama Saṃghadeva (Ch'ü-t'an Seng-ch'ieh-t'i-p'o 瞿曇僧伽提婆) (fl. 383–398). *T* no. 26.

Chung-ching mu-lu 眾經目錄. 594. Fa-ching 法經 (d.u.) et al. *T* no. 2146.

Chung-ching mu-lu 眾經目錄. 602. Yen-tsung 彥悰 (557–610) et al. *T* no. 2147.

Ch'üan t'ang shih 全唐詩. P'eng Ting-ch'iu 彭定求 (1645–1719). 12 vols. Peking: Chung-hua shu-chü, 1960.

Ch'üan t'ang wen, ch'in-ting (欽定)全唐文. Tung Kao 董誥 (1740–1818). 20 vols. Taipei: Ching-wei shu-chü, 1965.

Ch'ün-shu i-pien 群書疑辨. Wan Ssu-t'ung 萬斯同 (1638–1702). Taipei: Kuang-wen shu-chü, 1972.

Dainihon bukkyō zensho 大日本佛教全書. 100 vols. Tokyo: Suzuki gakujutsu zaidan, 1970–1973.

Dainihon zokuzōkyō 大日本續藏經. 150 cases. 1905–1912; reprint ed. Shanghai: Commercial Press, 1923.

Fa-hua chuan-chi 法華傳記. Seng-hsiang 僧詳, a. k. a. Hui-hsiang 慧祥 (fl. 667). *T* no. 2068.

Fa-yüan chu-lin 法苑珠林. Tao-shih 道世 (d. 683). *T* no. 2122.

Fan-i ming-i chi 翻譯名義集. Fa-yün 法雲 (1088–1158). *T* no. 2131.

Fan-wang ching 梵網經. Anon. (ca. 431–481). *T* no. 1484.

Feng-fa yao 奉法要. Hsi Ch'ao 郗超 (336–377). In *Hung-ming chi* 弘明集. Seng-yu 僧祐 (445–518). *T* no. 2102.

Fo lin nieh-p'an chi fa-chu ching 佛臨涅槃記法住經 (*Mahāparinir-vāṇasūtra*). Hsüan-tsang 玄奘 (602–664). *T* no. 390.

Fo-mu po-ni-huan ching 佛母般泥洹經. Hui-chien 慧簡 (fl. 457). *T* no. 145.

Fo po-ni-huan ching 佛般泥洹經 (*Mahāparinirvāṇasūtra*). Po Fa-tsu 白法祖 (fl. 290–306). *T* no. 5.

Fo sheng tao-li-t'ien wei mu shuo-fa ching 佛昇忉利天為母說法經. Chu Fa-hu 竺法護 (Dharmarakṣa) (fl. 265–310). *T* no. 815.

Fo-tsu li-tai t'ung-tsai 佛祖曆代通載. Nien-ch'ang 念常 (d. 1341). *T* no. 2036.

Fo-tsu t'ung-chi 佛祖統紀. Chih-p'an 志磐 (fl. 1258–1269). *T* no. 2035.

Han shih wai-chuan 韓詩外傳. Han Ying 韓嬰 (fl. 2d cent. B.C.E.). Ssu-pu ts'ung-k'an hsin-pien so-pen 四部叢刊新編縮本, vol. 4. 1936; reprint ed. Taipei: Shang-wu yin-ying, 1967.

Heng-yen 恆言. Ch'ien Ta-hsin 錢大昕 (1728–1804). In *Heng-yen, Heng-yen kuang-cheng* 恆言，恆言廣證. Peking: Shang-wu yin-shu-kuan, 1959.

Heng-yen kuang-cheng 恆言廣證. Ch'en Chan 陳鱣 (1753–1817). In *Heng-yen, Heng-yen kuang-cheng* 恆言，恆言廣證. Peking: Shang-wu yin-shu-kuan, 1959.

Hōji san shiki 法事讚私記. Ryōchū 良忠 (1199–1287). In *Jōdoshū zensho* 淨土宗全書, vol. 4. 23 vols. Comp. Jōdoshū kaishū happyakunen kinen keisan jumbikyoku 淨土宗開宗八百年記念慶讚準備局. Tokyo: Sankibō busshorin, 1970–1972.

Hu chu-t'ung-tzu t'o-lo-ni ching 護諸童子陀羅尼經. Bodhiruci (P'u-t'i-liu-chih 菩提流支) (fl. 508–537). *T* no. 1028a.

Hung-tsan fa-hua chuan 弘讚法華傳. Hui-hsiang 慧祥 (fl. 667). *T* no. 2067.

Hsi-fang yao-chüeh shih-i t'ung-kuei 西方要決釋疑通規. K'uei-chi 窺基 (632–682). *T* no. 1964.

Hsiao-ch'u i-ch'ieh tsai-chang pao-chi t'o-lo-ni ching 消除一切災障寶髻陀羅尼經. T'ien-hsi-tsai 天息災 (Devaśānti?), later called Fa-hsien 法賢 (d. 1000). *T* no. 1400.

Hsien-yang sheng-chiao lun 顯揚聖教論. Hsüan-tsang 玄奘 (602–664). *T* no. 1602.

Hsien-yü ching 賢愚經. Attrib. Hui-chüeh 慧覺 (fl. 445). *T* no. 202.

Hsien-yüan pien-chu 仙苑編珠. Wang Sung-nien 王松年 (fl. 10th cent.). Sch no. 596. *TT* 329–30.

Hsin t'ang shu 新唐書. Ou-yang Hsiu 歐陽修 (1007–1072). 20 vols. Peking: Chung-hua shu-chü, 1975.

Hsü hsien chuan 續仙傳. Shen Fen 沈汾 (late T'ang). Sch no. 295. *TT* 138.

Hsüan-p'in lu 玄品錄. 1335. Chang T'ien-yü 張天雨 (Yüan). Sch no. 781. *TT* 558–59.

Hsün-tzu chi-chieh 荀子集解. Ed. Wang Hsien-ch'ien 王先謙 (20th cent.). In *Chu-tzu chi-ch'eng* 諸子集成, vol. 2. Shanghai: Shih-chieh shu-chü, 1935.

I-ch'ieh ching yin-i 一切經音義. Hui-lin 慧林 (737–820). *T* no. 2128.

I-chien chih 夷堅志. Hung Mai 洪邁 (1123–1202). 4 vols. Peking: Chung-hua shu-chü, 1981.

I-chou ming-hua lu 益州名畫錄. 1006. Huang Hsiu-fu 黃休復 (Sung). In *Hua-shih ts'ung-shu* 畫史叢書. 4 vols. Shanghai: Shang-hai jen-min mei-shu ch'u-pan-she, 1963.

I-feng-t'ang chin-shih wen-tzu mu 藝風堂金石文字目. Miao Ch'üan-sun 繆荃孫 (1844–1919). In *Shih-k'o shih-liao hsin-pien* 石刻史料新編, vol. 26. Taipei: Hsin-wen-feng ch'u-pan kung-ssu, 1977.

I-li cheng-i 儀禮正義. Annot. Cheng Hsüan 鄭玄 (127–200). Ed. Hu P'ei-hui 胡培翬 (1782–1849). Kuo-hsüeh chi-pen ts'ung-shu 國學基本叢書, vols. 99-100. Taipei: T'ai-wan shang-wu yin-shu-kuan, 1968.

I-tzu chi-t'e fo-ting ching 一字寄特佛頂經. Pu-k'ung chin-kang 不空金剛 (Amoghavajra) (705–774). *T* no. 953.

Jizō bosatsu hosshin innen jūō kyō 地藏菩薩發心因緣十王經. Attrib. Tsang-ch'uan 藏川. *Z*, 2b, 23.

Jōdo kemmon shū 淨土見聞集. Zonkaku 存覺 (1290–1373). In *Shinshū zensho* 真宗全書, vol. 48. 74 vols. Comp. Tsumaki Naoyoshi 妻木直良. Kyoto: Zōkyō shoen, 1913–1916.

Jūō sandan shō 十王讚嘆鈔. Nichiren 日蓮 (1222–1282). In *Shinshū shiryō shūsei* 真宗史料集成, vol. 5. 13 vols. Comp. Ishida Mitsuyuki 石田充之 and Chiba Jōryō 千葉乘隆. Kyoto: Dohōsha, 1974–1983.

K'ai-yüan shih-chiao lu 開元釋教錄. 730. Chih-sheng 智昇 (fl. 669–740). *T* no. 2154.

Kao-seng chuan 高僧傳. Hui-chiao 慧皎 (497–554). *T* no. 2059.

Ku-chin t'u-shu chi-ch'eng, ch'in-ting (欽定)古今圖書集成. Ch'en Meng-lei 陳夢雷 (1651–ca. 1723) et al. 100 vols. Taipei: Wen-hsing shu-tien, 1964.

Kuan-fo san-mei hai ching 觀佛三昧海經. Buddhabhadra (Fo-t'o-pa-t'o-lo 佛陀跋陀羅) (359–429). *T* no. 643.

Kuan-ting ching 灌頂經. Attrib. Śrīmitra (Po Shih-li-mi-to-lo 帛尸梨密多羅) (fl. 307–355), probably written by Hui-chien 慧簡 (fl. 457). *T* no. 1331.

Le-pang wen-lei 樂邦文類. Tsung-hsiao 宗曉 (d. 1214). *T* no. 1969a.

Li-shih chen-hsien t'i-tao t'ung-chien 歷世真仙體道通鑑. Chao Tao-i 趙道一 (Yüan). Sch no. 296. *TT* 139–48.

Li-tai ming-hua chi 歷代名畫記. 847. Chang Yen-yüan 張彥遠 (fl. 847–874). In *Hua-shih ts'ung-shu* 畫史叢書, vol. 1. 4 vols. Shanghai: Shang-hai jen-min mei-shu ch'u-pan-she, 1963.

Ling-chou lung-hsing ssu pai-ts'ao yüan Shih ho-shang yin-yüan chi 靈州龍興寺白草院史和尚因緣記. S 528. Reprod. Huang, *Pao-tsang*, 4:301a–b.

Ling-pao ling-chiao chi-tu chin-shu 靈寶領教濟度金書. Lin Wei-fu 林偉夫 (1237–1303). Sch no. 466. *TT* 208–63.

Liu-tu chi ching 六度集經. K'ang Seng-hui 康僧會 (d. 280). *T* no. 152.

Lun-yü cheng-i 論語正義. Annot. Liu Pao-nan 劉寶楠 (1791–1855). In *Chu-tzu chi-ch'eng* 諸子集成, vol. 2. Shanghai: Shih-chieh shu-chü, 1936.

Lung-she tseng-kuang ching-t'u wen 龍舒增廣淨土文. Wang Jih-hsiu 王日休 (d. 1173). *T* no. 1970.

Meng-tzu cheng-i 孟子正義. Annot. Chiao Hsün 焦循 (1763–1823). In *Chu-tzu chi-ch'eng* 諸子集成, vol. 2. Shanghai: Shih-chieh shu-chü, 1936.

Mi-le hsia-sheng ch'eng-fo ching 彌勒下生成佛經. Kumārajīva (Chiu-mo-lo-she 鳩摩羅什) (350–409). *T* no. 454.

Mi-le hsia-sheng ch'eng-fo ching 彌勒下生成佛經. I-ching 義淨 (635–713). *T* no. 455.

Mi-le hsia-sheng ching 彌勒下生經. Chu Fa-hu 竺法護 (Dharamrakṣa) (fl. 265–313). *T* no. 453.

Ming-hsiang chi 冥祥記. Wang Yüan 王琰 (fl. 424–479). Not extant. Cited in *Fa-yüan chu-lin* and *T'ai-p'ing kuang-chi*. Collated in Lu, *Ku hsiao-shuo kou-ch'en*, pp. 373–458.

Ming-pao chi 冥報記. T'ang Lin 唐臨 (fl. 600–659). *T* no. 2082.

Mo-ho mo-yeh ching 摩訶摩耶經. T'an-ching 曇景 (fl. 479–502). *T* no. 383.

Mo-ni-chiao hsia-pu tsan 摩尼教下部讚. P 3377, P 3884. Transcr. *T* no. 2140.

O-p'i-ta-mo chü-she lun 阿毘達摩俱舍論 (*Abhidharmakośaśāstra*). Hsüan-tsang 玄奘 (602–664). *T* no. 1558.

O-p'i-ta-mo ta p'i-p'o-sha lun 阿毘達摩大毘婆沙論 (*Mahāvibhāṣā*). Hsüan-tsang 玄奘 (602–664). *T* no. 1545.

Pa-kuan-chai ching 八關齋經. Chü-ch'ü Ching-sheng 沮渠京聲 (fl. 457–464). *T* no. 89.

Pai-ch'ien sung ta-chi ching Ti-tsang p'u-sa ch'ing-wen fa-shen tsan 百千頌大集經地藏菩薩請問法身讚. Pu-k'ung chin-kang 不空金剛 (Amogha-vajra) (705–774). *T* no. 413.

Pao-chi ching ssu-fa Yu-p'o-t'i-she 寶髻經四法憂波提舍. Vimokṣaprajñārṣi (P'i-mu chih-hsien 毘目智仙) (fl. 516–541). *T* no. 1526.

Pei-shan lu 北山錄. Shen-ch'ing 神清 (d. ca. 806–820). *T* no. 2113.

P'ei-wen-chai shu-hua p'u 佩文齋書畫譜. Sun Yüeh-pan 孫岳頒 (1639–1708) et al. 4 vols. Taipei: Hsin-hsing shu-chü, 1972.

P'ei-wen yün-fu 佩文韻府. Chang Yü-shu 張玉書 (1642–1711). 7 vols. Taipei: Shang-wu yin-shu-kuan, 1966.

P'i-yü ching 譬喻經. I-ching 義淨 (635–713). *T* no. 217.

Pien chung-pien lun 辯中邊論 (*Madhyāntivibhaṇgaṭīkā*). Hsüan-tsang 玄奘 (602–664). *T* no. 1600.

Pien chung-pien lun sung 辯中邊論頌 (*Madhyāntivibhangakārikā*). Hsüan-tsang 玄奘 (602–664). *T* no. 1601.

P'in-t'ou-lu-t'o-lo-she wei yu-t'o-yen wang shuo-fa ching 賓頭盧突羅闍為優陀延王說法經. Guṇabhadra (Ch'iu-na-pa-t'o-lo 求那跋陀羅) (394–468). *T* no. 1690.

Po-jo po-lo-mi-to hsin ching 般若波羅密多心經. Hsüan-tsang 玄奘 (602–664). *T* no. 251.

Po-ni-huan ching 般泥洹經 (*Mahāparinirvāṇasūtra*). Ca. 317–420. Anon. *T* no. 6.

Po-ssu-chiao ts'an ching 波斯教殘經. Anon. *T* no. 2141b.

Pu-k'ung chüan-so shen-pien chen-yen ching 不空羂索神變真言經. Bodhi-ruci (P'u-t'i-liu-chih 菩提流志) (fl. 693–727). *T* no. 1092.

P'u-sa pen-hsing ching 菩薩本行經. Ca. 317–420. Anon. *T* no. 155.

P'u-sa ti-ch'ih ching 菩薩地持經 (*Bodhisattvabhūmi*). Dharmakṣema (T'an-wu-ch'en 曇無讖) (385–433). *T* no. 1581.

P'u-yao ching 普曜經 (*Lalitavistara*). Chu Fa-hu 竺法護 (Dharmarakṣa) (fl. 265–313). *T* no. 186.

San tendai godaisan ki 參天台五台山記. Jōjin 成尋 (1011–1081). *DBZ* no. 577a.

Sou-shen chi 搜神記. Chang Kuo-hsiang 張國祥 (Ming). Sch no. 1476. *TT* 1105–06.

Ssu-fen lü 四分律 (*Dharmaguptavinaya*). Buddhayaśas (Fo-t'o-yeh-she 佛陀耶舍) (fl. 408–412) and Chu Fo-nien 竺佛念 (fl. 365). *T* no. 1428.

Ssu-fen lü lüeh-sung 四分律略頌. Anon. S 4160. Reprod. Huang, *Pao-tsang*, 34:265a–68b.

Ssu-t'ien-wang ching 四天王經. Chih-yen 智嚴 (fl. 394–427) and Pao-yün 寶雲 (376–449). *T* no. 590.

Sui t'ien-t'ai chih-che ta-shih pieh-chuan 隋天台智者大師別傳. Kuan-ting 灌頂 (561–632). *T* no. 2050.

Sung hui-yao chi-kao 宋會要輯稿. Hsü Sung 徐松 (1781–1848). Ed. Ch'en Yüan 陳垣. 8 vols. Taipei: Hsin-wen-feng, 1976.

Sung kao-seng chuan 宋高僧傳. Tsan-ning 贊寧 (919–1001). *T* no. 2061.

Sung yüan hsüeh-an pu-i 宋元學案補遺. Huang Tsung-hsi 黃宗羲 (1610–1695). Ed. Wang Tzu-ts'ai 王梓材 (1791–1851) and Feng Yün-hao 馮雲濠 (Ch'ing). 8 vols. Taipei: Shih-chieh shu-chü, 1962.

Sha-mi-ni chieh ching 沙彌尼戒經. Ca. 25–220. Anon. *T* no. 1474.

Shan-o yin-kuo ching 善惡因果經. Anon. *T* no. 2881.

Shan-yu shih-k'o ts'ung-pien 山右石刻叢編. Hu P'in-chih 胡聘之 (fl. 1898). 40 *chüan* in 24 *ts'e*. N.p.: Shan-yu shih-k'o ts'ung-pien pien-tsuan-chü, 1899–1901.

Sheng-t'ien wang po-jo po-lo-mi ching 勝天王般若波羅密經. Upaśūnya (Yüeh-p'o-shou-na 月婆首那) (fl. 538–565). *T* no. 231.

Shih-kuo ch'un-ch'iu 十國春秋. Wu Jen-ch'en 吳任臣 (1628?–1689?). 4 vols. Peking: Chung-hua shu-chü, 1983.

Shih-men cheng-t'ung 釋門正統. Tsung-chien 宗鑑 (fl. 1237). *Z*, 2b, 3.

Shih-men tzu-ching lu 釋門自鏡錄. Huai-hsin 懷信 (fl. 843). *T* no. 2083.

Shih-sung lü 十誦律 (*Sarvāstivādavinaya*). Kumārajīva (Chiu-mo-lo-shih 鳩摩羅什) (350–409), Punyatara (Fu-jo-to-lo 弗若多羅) (fl. 399–415) et al. *T* no. 1435.

Shih-shih chi-ku lüeh 釋氏稽古錄. Chüeh-an 覺岸 (1266–1355). *T* no. 2037.

Shih-shih liu-t'ieh 釋氏六帖. I-ch'u 義楚 (fl. 945–954). In Makita, *Giso rokujō*.

Shih-shih t'ung-lan 施食通覽. 1204. Tsung-hsiao 宗曉 (1151–1214). *Z*, 2a, 6.

Shih-shih yao-lan 釋氏要覽. Tao-ch'eng 道誠 (fl. 1019). *T* no. 2127.

Shin shosha shōrai hōmontō mokuroku 新書寫請來法門等目錄. Shūei 宗叡 (fl. 809–884). *T* no. 2174.

Shinsen jōwa bunrui kokon sonshuku geju shū 新撰真和分類古今尊宿偈頌集. Gidō Shūshin 義堂周信 (1325–1388). *DBZ* no. 819.

Shuo-wen chieh-tzu 説文解字. Hsü Shen 許慎 (d. 120). In *Shuo-wen chieh-tzu ku-lin cheng-pu ho-pien* 説文解字詁林正補合編. Ed. Tuan Yü-ts'ai 段玉裁 (1735–1815) and Ting Fu-pao 丁福保. 12 vols. Taipei: Ting-wen shu-chü, 1977.

Ta-ai-tao po-ni-huan ching 大愛道般泥洹經. Po Fa-tsu 白法祖 (fl. 290–306). *T* no. 144.

Ta chih-tu lun 大智度論 (*Mahāprajñāpāramitāśāstra*). Kumārajīva (Chiu-mo-lo-shih 鳩摩羅什) (350–409). *T* no. 1509.

Ta-chou k'an-ting chung-ching mu-lu 大周刊定眾經目錄. 695. Ming-ch'üan 明佺 (d.u.) et al. *T* no. 2153.

Ta fang-kuang fo hua-yen ching 大方廣佛華嚴經 (*Avataṃsakasūtra*). Buddhabhadra (Fo-t'o-pa-t'o-lo 佛陀跋陀羅) (359–429). *T* no. 278.

Ta fang-kuang fo hua-yen ching 大方廣佛華嚴經 (*Avataṃsakasūtra*). Śikṣānanda (Shih-ch'a-nan-t'o 實叉難陀) (652–710). *T* no. 279.

Ta fang-kuang fo hua-yen ching kan-ying chuan 大方廣佛華嚴經感應傳. Hui-ying 惠英 (fl. 687). Ed. Hu Yu-cheng 胡幽貞 (fl. 783). *T* no. 2074.

Ta fang-teng ta-chi ching 大方等大集經. Seng-chiu 僧就 (fl. 586–594). *T* no. 397.

Ta pao-chi ching 大寶積經. Bodhiruci (P'u-t'i-liu-chih 菩提流支) (fl. 693–729). *T* no. 310.

Ta p'i-lu-che-na ch'eng-fo ching shu 大毘盧遮那成佛經疏. I-hsing 義行 (683–727). *T* no. 1796.

Ta po-jo po-lo-mi-to ching 大般若波羅密多經 (*Mahāprajñāpāramitāsūtra*). Hsüan-tsang 玄奘 (602–664). *T* no. 220.

Ta po-ni-huan ching 大般泥洹經 (*Mahāparinirvāṇasūtra*). Fa-hsien 法顯 (fl. 399–416). *T* no. 376.

Ta po-nieh-p'an ching 大般涅槃經 (*Mahāparinirvāṇasūtra*). Fa-hsien 法顯 (fl. 399–416). *T* no. 7.

Ta po-nieh-p'an ching 大般涅槃經 (*Mahāparinirvāṇasūtra*). Dharmakṣema (T'an-wu-ch'en 曇無讖) (385–433). *T* no. 374.

Ta po-nieh-p'an ching 大般涅槃經 (*Mahāparinirvāṇasūtra*). Hui-yen 慧嚴 (363–443). *T* no. 375.

Ta-sung seng-shih lüeh 大宋僧史略. Tsan-ning 贊寧 (919–1001). *T* no. 2126.

Ta-sheng pai-fa ming-men lun 大乘百法明門論. Hsüan-tsang 玄奘 (602–664). *T* no. 1614.

Ta-sheng pai-fa ming-men lun k'ai tsung-i chi 大乘百法明門論開宗義記. T'an-kuang 曇曠 (fl. 700–782). *T* no. 2810.

Ta-sheng ssu-chai jih 大乘四齋日. Anon. S 2567. Transcr. *T* no. 2849.

Ta-sheng ta-chi ti-tsang shih-lun ching 大乘大集地藏十輪經. Hsüan-tsang 玄奘 (602–664). *T* no. 411.

Ta-sheng wu-liang-shou ching 大乘無量壽經 (*Aparimitāyurdhāraṇīsūtra*). Čhos-grub (Fa-ch'eng 法成) (fl.780–860). *T* no. 936.

Ta-t'ang hsi-yü chi 大唐西域記. Hsüan-tsang 玄奘 (602–664) and Pien-chi 辯機 (fl. 645). *T* no. 2087.

Ta-t'ang nei-tien lu 大唐內典錄. 664. Tao-hsüan 道宣 (596–667). *T* no. 2149.

T'ai-p'ing huan-yü chi 太平寰宇記. Yüeh Shih 樂史 (930–1007). 2 vols. Sung-tai ti-li shu ssu-chung 宋代地埋書四種, no. 1. Taipei: Wen-hai ch'u-pan-she, 1963.

T'ai-p'ing kuang-chi 太平廣記. Li Fang 李昉 (fl. 978). 5 vols. Peking: Jen-min wen-hsüeh ch'u-pan-she, 1959.

T'ai-shang chiu-yao hsin-yin miao ching 太上九要心印妙經. Chang Kuo 張果 (fl. 690–756). Sch 225. *TT* 112.

T'ai-shang tz'u-pei tao-ch'ang hsiao-tsai chiu-yu ch'an 太上慈悲道場消災九幽懺. Ko Hsüan 葛玄 (fl. 221–277). Ed. Li Han-kuang 李含光 (d. 769). Sch no. 543. *TT* 297–99.

T'ai-shang tung-hsüan ling-pao yeh-pao yin-kuo ching 太上洞玄靈寶業報因果經. Ca. mid-6th century. Anon. Sch no. 336. *TT* 174–75.

T'ai-tzu jui-ying pen-ch'i ching 太子瑞應本起經. Chih Ch'ien 支謙 (fl. 220–252). *T* no. 185.

Taishō shinshū daizōkyō 大正新修大藏經. Ed. Takakusu Junjirō 高楠順次郎 and Watanabe Kaigyoku 渡辺海旭. 100 vols. Tokyo: Taishō issaikyō kankōkai, 1924–1935.

T'an-chin wen-chi 鐔津文集. Ch'i-sung 契嵩 (1007–1072), *T* no. 2115.

T'an-we-te lü-pu tsa chieh-mo 曇無德律部雜羯磨. K'ang Seng-k'ai 康僧鎧 (fl. 252). *T* no. 1432.

T'ang hui-yao 唐會要. Wang P'u 王溥 (922–982). 3 vols. Shanghai: Chung-hua shu-chü, 1955.

Tao-hsing po-jo ching 道行般若經 (*Aṣṭasāhasrikāprajñāpāramitāsūtra*). Lokakṣema (Chih Lou-chia-ch'en 支婁迦讖) (fl. 167–186). *T* no. 224.

Tao shen-tsu wu-chi pien-hua ching 道神足無極變化經. An Fa-ch'in 安法欽 (fl.281–306). *T* no. 816.

Tao-tsang, cheng-t'ung (正統) 道藏. Orig. *Ta-ming tao-tsang-ching* 大明道藏經, 1445. 1,120 vols. Shanghai: Commercial Press, 1923–1926.

Ti-fu shih-wang pa-tu i 地府十王拔度儀. Ca. 12th cent. Anon. Sch no. 215. *TT* 84.

Ti-tsang p'u-sa hsiang ling-yen chi 地藏菩薩像靈驗記. 989. Ch'ang-chin 常謹 (Sung). *Z*, 2b, 22.

Ti-tsang p'u-sa pen-yüan ching 地藏菩薩本願經. Attrib. Śikṣānanda (Shih-ch'a-nan-t'o 實叉難陀) (652–710). *T* no. 412.

Ti-tsang p'u-sa shih-chai jih 地藏菩薩十齋日. Anon. S 2568. Transcr. *T* no. 2850.

T'ien ch'ing-wen ching 天請問經 (*Devatāsūtra*), Hsüan-tsang 玄奘 (602–664). *T* no. 592.

T'ien ch'ing-wen ching shu 天請問經疏. Anon. *T* no. 2786.

T'o-lo-ni tsa-chi 陀羅尼雜集. Ca. 502-557. Anon. *T* no. 1336.

T'u-hua chien-wen chih 圖畫見聞誌. Kuo Jo-hsü 郭若虛 (fl. 1010–1074). In *Hua-shih ts'ung-shu* 畫史叢書. 4 vols. Shanghai: Shang-hai jen-min mei-shu ch'u-pan-she, 1963.

Tun-huang chüan-tzu, Kuo-li chung-yang t'u-shu-kuan ts'ang （國立中央圖書館藏）敦煌卷子. 6 vols. Taipei: Shih-men t'u-shu, 1976.

Tung-hsüan ling-pao liu-chai shih-chih sheng-chi ching 洞玄靈寶六齋十直聖紀經. Ca. 11th cent. Anon. Sch no. 1200. *TT* 875.

Tsa a-han ching 雜阿含經 (*Saṃyuktāgama*). Guṇabhadra (Ch'iu-na-pa-t'o-lo 求那跋陀羅) (394–468). *T* no. 99.

Tsa-ch'ao 雜抄. Anon. S 5755. Reprod. Huang, *Pao-tsang*, 44:430b–33b.

Ts'e-fu yüan-kuei 冊府元龜. Wang Ch'in-jo 王欽若 (962–1025) et al. 12 vols. Peking: Chung-hua shu-chü, 1960.

Tseng-i a-han ching 增一阿含經 (*Ekottarāgama*). Gautama Saṃghadeva (Ch'ü-yün Seng-ch'ieh-t'i-p'o 瞿曇僧伽提婆) (fl. 383–398). *T* no. 125.

Tsu-t'ing shih-yüan 祖庭事苑. Shan-ch'ing 善卿 (fl. 1098–1100). *Z* , 2a, 18.

Tzu-chih t'ung-chien 資治通鑑. Ssu-ma Kuang 司馬光 (1019–1086). 20 vols. Peking: Chung-hua shu-chü, 1956.

Wang Fan-chih shih-chi 王梵志詩集. Ca. 750. Critical editions in Demiéville, *L'oeuvre de Wang le zélateur;* and Hsiang, *Wang Fan-chih shih chiao-chu.*

Wen-shu chih-nan t'u, Fo-kuo ch'an-shih （佛國禪師）文殊指南圖. Wei-po 惟白 (fl. 1103). Sung xylograph in Lo, *Lo Hsüeh-t'ang hsien-sheng ch'üan-chi ch'u-pien*, 18:7673–7702. Transcr. *T* no. 1891.

Wu-ch'ang ching 無常經 (*Anityatāsūtra*). I-ching 義淨 (635–713). *T* no. 801.

Wu-fo-ting san-mei t'o-lo-ni ching 五佛頂三昧陀羅尼經. Bodhiruci (P'u-t'i-liu-chih 菩提流支) (fl. 693–727). *T* no. 952.

Wu-shang pi-yao 無上秘要. 577. Anon. Sch no. 1138. *TT* 768–79.

Wu-tai ming-hua pu-i 五代名畫補遺. Liu Tao-ch'un 劉道醇 (fl. 1060). In *Wen-yüan-ko ssu-k'u ch'üan-shu, ying-yin* （影印）文淵閣四庫全書 vol. 812. Taipei: T'ai-wan shang-wu yin-shu-kuan, 1983–1986.

Yen-lo wang kung-hsing fa tz'u-ti 閻羅王供行法次第. Pu-k'ung chin-kang 不空金剛 (Amoghavajra) (705–774). *T* no. 1290.

Yen-lo wang shou-chi ssu-chung ni-hsiu sheng-ch'i wang-sheng ching-t'u ching 閻羅王授記四眾逆修生七往生淨土經. Attrib. Tsang-ch'uan 藏川. Korean ed. dated 1469. *Z*, 2b, 23.

Yen-shih chia-hsün 顏氏家訓. Yen Chih-t'ui 顏之推 (531–591). In *Yen-shih chia-hsün hui-chu* 顏氏家訓彙註. Ed. Chou Fa-kao 周法高. 4 vols. in one. Taipei: Chung-yang yen-chiu-yüan li-shih yü-yen yen-chiu-so, 1960.

Yu-p'o-i to-she-chia ching 優婆夷墮舍迦經. Ca. 420–479. Anon. *T* no. 88.

Yu-p'o-sai chieh ching 優婆塞戒經. Dharmakṣema (T'an-wu-ch'en 曇無讖) (385–433). *T* no. 1488.

Yü-ch'ieh-shih ti lun 瑜伽師地論. Hsüan-tsang 玄奘 (602–664). *T* no. 1579.

Yü-chu chin-kang po-jo po-lo-mi ching hsüan-yen 御注金剛般若波羅密經宣演. Tao-yin 道氤 (d. 740). P 2173. Transcr. *T* no. 2733.

Yü-lan-p'en ching 盂蘭盆經. Chu Fa-hu 竺法護 (Dharmarakṣa) (fl. 265–313). *T* no. 685.

Yü-lan-p'en ching shu 盂蘭盆經疏. Tsung-mi 宗密 (780–841). *T* no. 1792.

Yü-tung ta-shen tan-sha chen-yao chüeh 玉洞大神丹砂真要訣. Chang Kuo 張果 (fl. 690–756). Sch no. 896. *TT* 587.

Yüan-shih t'ien-tsun shuo feng-tu mieh-tsui ching 元始天尊說酆都滅罪經. Ca. 12th–13th cent. Anon. Sch no. 73. *TT* 32.

Yüan-shih wu-lao ch'ih-shu yü-p'ien chen-wen t'ien-shu ching 元始五老赤書玉篇真文天書經. Anon. Sch no. 22. *TT* 26.

Yün-chi ch'i-ch'ien 雲笈七籤. Chang Chün-fang 張君房 (fl. 1008–1029). Sch no. 1032. *TT* 677–702.

Secondary Sources

Akanuma, Chizen 赤沼智善. *Indo bukkyō koyū meishi jiten* 印度佛教固有名詞辭典. 1931; reprint ed. Kyoto: Hōzōkan, 1967.

Aldrich, Richard L. "Tun-huang: The Rise of the Kansu Port in the T'ang Dynasty." Ph.D. dissertation, University of Michigan, 1942.

Bang, W., and R. Rachmati. "Uigurische Bruchstücke über verschiedene Höllen aus der Berliner Turfansammlung." *Ungarische Jahrbücher* 15 (1935):389–402.

Bareau, André. *Les sectes bouddhiques du petit véhicule.* Publications de l'École Française d'Extrême-Orient, vol. 28. Paris: École Française d'Extrême-Orient, 1955.

Bazin, Louis. "Les noms turcs et mongols de la constellation des Pléiades." *Acta Orientalia Academiae Scientiarum Hungaricae* 10.3 (1960):295–97.

———. "Über die Sternkunde in alttürkischer Zeit." *Abhandlungen der Akadamie der Wissenschaften und der Literatur, Geistes- und Sozial wissenschaftlichen Klasse* (Mainz), no. 5 (1963):571–82.

Bell, Catherine. *Ritual Theory, Ritual Practice.* New York: Oxford University Press, 1992.

———. "Ritualization of Texts and Textualization of Ritual in the Codification of Taoist Liturgy." *History of Religions* 27.4 (May 1988):366–92.

Bhattacharji, Sukumari. *The Indian Theogony: A Comparative Study of Indian Mythology from the Vedas to the Purāṇas.* Cambridge: Cambridge University Press, 1970.

Bibliothèque nationale (Paris), Département des Manuscrits. *Catalogue des manuscrits chinois de Touen-houang (Fonds Pelliot chinois)*. Vol. 1: Nos. 2001–2500. Ed. Jacques Gernet et al. Paris: Bibliothèque nationale, 1970. Vol. 3: Nos. 3001–3500. Ed. Michel Soymié et al. Paris: Fondation Singer-Polignac, 1983.

Bischoff, Bernhard. "Kreuz und Buch im Frühmittelalter und in der ersten Jahrhunderten der spanischen Reconquista." 1963. Repr. Bernhard Bischoff. *Mittelalterliche Studien: Ausgewählte Aufsätze zur Schriftkunde und Literaturgeschichte*. 3 vols. Stuttgart: Anton Hiersemann, 1966–1981. 2:284–303.

————. *Latin Palaeography: Antiquity and the Middle Ages*. Rev. ed. Trans. Dáibhí ÓCróinín and David Ganz. Cambridge: Cambridge University Press, 1990.

Bodiford, William M. *Sōtō Zen in Medieval Japan*. Kuroda Institute, Studies in East Asian Buddhism no. 8. Honolulu: University of Hawaii Press, 1993.

Bodman, Richard W. "Poetics and Prosody in Early Mediaeval China: A Study and Translation of Kūkai's *Bunkyō Hifuron*." Ph.D. dissertation, Cornell University, 1978.

Brough, John. "Thus Have I Heard . . . " *BSOAS* 13.2 (1950): 416–26.

Bryder, Peter. *The Chinese Transformation of Manichaeism: A Study of Chinese Manichaean Terminology*. Tryck: Bokförlaget Plus Ultra, 1985.

Buswell, Robert E., Jr. *The Formation of Ch'an Ideology in China and Korea: The Vajrasamādhi-Sūtra, A Buddhist Apocryphon*. Princeton: Princeton University Press, 1989.

————. "Introduction: Prolegomenon to the Study of Buddhist Apocryphal Scriptures." In *Chinese Buddhist Apocrypha*. Ed. Robert E. Buswell, Jr. Honolulu: University of Hawaii Press, 1990. Pp. 1–30.

Cahiers d'Extrême-Asie. No. 3 (1987). *Numéro spécial: Études de Dunhuang*. Ed. Jean-Pierre Drège.

Campany, Robert F. "Xunzi and Durkheim as Theorists of Ritual Practice." In *Discourse and Practice*. Ed. Frank Reynolds and David Tracy. Albany, NY: SUNY Press, 1992. Pp. 197–231.

Chang, Ch'i-yün 張其昀. *Chung-wen ta-tz'u-tien* 中文大辭典. Rev. ed. 10 vols. Taipei: Hua-kang ch'u-pan yu-hsien kung-ssu, 1979.

Chang, Hsi-hou 張錫厚. *Wang Fan-chih shih chiao-chi* 王梵志詩校輯. Peking: Chung-hua shu-chü, 1983.

Chang, Yü-fan 張玉範, ed. *Mu-hsi-hsüan ts'ang-shu t'i-chi chi shu-lu* 木犀軒藏書題記及書錄. Peking: Pei-ching ta-hsüeh ch'u-pan-she, 1985.

Ch'ang, Pi-te 昌彼德. "T'ang-tai t'u-shu hsing-chih te yen-pien" 唐代圖書形制的演變. 1964. Repr. *Chung-kuo t'u-shu shih tzu-liao chi* 中國圖書史資料集. Ed. Liu Chia-pi 劉家璧. Hong Kong: Lung-men shu-tien, 1974. Pp. 209–20.

Chavannes, Édouard. *Le T'ai chan: essai de monographie d'un culte chinois.* Annales du Musée Guimet, vol. 21. Paris: Ernest Leroux, 1910.

Chavannes, Édouard, and Paul Pelliot. "Un traité Manichéen retrouvé en Chine." Part I: *JA*, series 10, 18 (November–December 1911): 499–617; Part II: *JA*, series 11, 1 (January–February 1913):99–199; 1 (March–April 1913):261–383.

Ch'en, Kenneth K. S. *Buddhism in China: A Historical Survey.* Princeton: Princeton University Press, 1964.

Ch'en, Kuo-fu 陳國符. *Tao-tsang yüan-liu k'ao* 道藏源流考. Peking: Chung-hua shu-chü, 1949.

Ch'en, Tso-lung 陳祚龍. "Chung-shih tun-huang yü ch'eng-tu chih chien te chiao-t'ung lu-hsien: tun-huang-hsüeh san-ts'e chih i" 中世敦煌與成都之間的交通路線—敦煌學散策之一. *Tun-huang hsüeh* 敦煌學 1(1974):79–86.

——. "Chiao-ting sung-ch'u sha-chou chieh-tieh san-shih" 校訂宋初沙州戒牒三式. 1973. Repr. Ch'en Tso-lung. *Tun-huang hsüeh-hai t'an-chu* 敦煌學海探珠. 2 vols. Hsiu-lu wen-k'u 岫盧文庫, vol. 55. Taipei: T'ai-wan shang-wu yin-shu-kuan, 1979. Pp. 379–82.

——. "Liu Sa-ho yen-chiu" 劉薩訶研究. In Ch'en Tso-lung. *Tun-huang tzu-liao k'ao-hsieh* 敦煌資料考屑. 2 vols. Hsiu-lu wen-k'u 岫盧文庫, vol. 57. Taipei: T'ai-wan shang-wu yin-shu-kuan, 1979. Pp. 212–52.

Ch'en, Yin-k'o 陳寅恪. "Ssu-sheng san-wen" 四聲三問. *Ch'ing-hua hsüeh-pao* 清華學報 9.2 (April 1934):275–87.

Ch'en, Yüan 陳垣. *Tun-huang chieh-yü lu* 敦煌劫餘綠. Chung-yang yen-chiu-yüan chuan-k'an 中央研究院專刊, no. 4. Peking: Chung-yang yen-chiu-yüan, 1931.

——. *Shih-shih i-nien lu* 釋氏疑年錄. Peking: Chung-hua shu-chü, 1964.

Chiang, Liang-fu 姜亮夫. "Tun-huang ching-chüan t'i-ming lu" 敦煌經卷題名錄. In Chiang Liang-fu. *Tun-huang-hsüeh lun-wen chi* 敦煌學論文集. Shanghai: Shang-hai ku-chi ch'u-pan-she, 1987. Pp. 1047–72.

——. *Mo-kao-k'u nien-piao* 莫高窟年表. Shanghai: Shang-hai ku-chi ch'u-pan-she, 1985.

Chiang, Po-ch'in 姜伯勤. *T'ang wu-tai tun-huang ssu-hu chih-tu* 唐五代敦煌寺戶制度. Chung-hua li-shih ts'ung-shu 中華歷史從書. Peking: Chung-hua shu-chü, 1987.

Chikusa, Masaaki 竺沙雅章. "Tonkō no jiko ni tsuite" 敦煌の寺戶について. *Shirin* 史林 44.5 (September 1961):40–73.

——. "Tonkō no sōkan seido" 敦煌の僧官制度. *TG* 31 (March 1961): 117–98.

Chin, Wei-no 金維諾. "Tun-huang k'u-k'an ming-shu k'ao" 敦煌窟龕名數考. *WW* 1959.5 (cum . no. 105) (May 1959): 50–54, 61.

Chou, Fa-kao 周法高. "Fo-chiao tung-ch'uan tui chung-kuo yin-yün-hsüeh chih ying-hsiang" 佛教東傳對中國音韻學之影響. In Chou

Fa-kao. *Chung-kuo yü-yen lun-ts'ung* 中國語言論叢. Taipei: Cheng-chung shu-chü, 1963. Pp. 21–51.

Chu, Chu-yü 朱鑄禹, and Li Shih-sun 李石孫. *T'ang sung hua-chia jen-ming tz'u-tien* 唐宋畫家人名辭典. Peking: Chung-kuo ku-tien i-shu ch'u-pan-she, 1958.

Chu, Feng-yü 朱鳳玉. *Wang Fan-chih shih yen-chiu* 王梵志詩研究, vol. 1. Taipei: Hsüeh-sheng shu-chü, 1986.

Chu-lin, chü-shih 竹林居士. *Fo-chiao nan-tzu tzu-tien* 佛教難字字典. Hsin-tien: Ch'ang-ch'un-shu shu-fang, 1988.

Clapperton, Robert H. *Paper: An Historical Account of Its Making by Hand From the Earliest Times Down to the Present Day.* Oxford: Shakespeare Head Press, 1934.

Clauson, Sir Gerard. "Early Turkish Astronomical Terms." *Ural-Altaische Jahrbücher* 35 (1964):350–68.

Collins, Steven. *Selfless Persons: Imagery and Thought in Theravada Buddhism.* Cambridge: Cambridge University Press, 1982.

Conze, Edward, trans. *The Perfection of Wisdom in Eight Thousand Lines and Its Verse Summary,* second printing, with corrections. Wheel Series, no. 1. Bolinas, CA: Four Seasons Foundation, 1975.

————. *Vajracchedikā prajñāpāramitā.* Serie Orientale Roma, vol. 13. Rome: Istituto Italiano per il ed Estremo Oriente.

Couvreur, Séraphin, S. J. *Dictionarium Sinicum & Latinum ex Radicum Ordine,* rev. ed. Ho-hsien fu: Missione catholica, 1907.

Csongor, B. "Chinese in the Uighur Script of the T'ang Period." *Acta Orientalia Academiae Scientiarum Hungaricae* 2.1 (1952):73–121.

Čuguevskiĭ, L. I. "Touen-houang du VIIIᵉ au Xᵉ siècle." In *Nouvelles contributions aux études de Touen-houang.* Ed. Michel Soymié. Centre de Recherches d'Histoire et de Philologie de la IVᵉ Section de l'École pratique des Hautes Études, Hautes Études Orientales, 2:17. Geneva: Librairie Droz, 1981. Pp. 1–56.

Dalia, Albert A. "The Political 'Career' of the Buddhist Historian Tsanning." In *Buddhist and Taoist Practice in Medieval Chinese Society.* Buddhist and Taoist Studies, vol. 2. Asian Studies at Hawaii, no. 34. Ed. David W. Chappell. Honolulu: University of Hawaii Press, 1987. Pp. 146–80.

De Bary, William Theodore, et al., eds. *Sources of Chinese Tradition.* 2 vols. New York: Columbia University Press, 1964.

Demiéville, Paul. "Bombai" 梵唄. In Demiéville, *Hōbōgirin,* pp. 93–113.

————. *L'oeuvre de Wang le zélateur (Wang Fan-tche) suivie des Instructions domestiques de l'aïeul (T'ai-kong kia-kiao): poèmes populaires des T'ang (VIIIᵉ-Xᵉ siècles).* Bibliothèque de l'Institut des Hautes Études Chinoises, vol. 26. Paris: Collège de France, Institut des Hautes Études Chinoises, 1982.

————. "Bosatsukai." In Demiéville, *Hōbōgirin,* Pp. 142–46.

———. "Récents travaux sur Touen-houang." *TP* 56.1–3 (1970): 1–95.

———. "Les sources chinoises." In *L'Inde classique.* Ed. Louis Renou and Jean Filliozat. Vol. 2. Paris: Imprimerie nationale, 1953. Pp. 398–463.

———. "La Yogācārabhūmi de Saṅgharakṣa." *BEFEO* 44.2 (1954): 339–436.

Demiéville, Paul, Hubert Durt, and Anna Seidel, eds. *Hōbōgirin: diction-naire encyclopédique du bouddhisme d'après les sources chinoises et japo-naises.* 6 vols. to date. Tokyo: Maison Franco-Japonaise, 1927–.

———. *Répertoire du canon bouddhique sino-japonais,* rev. ed. Supplementary fascicle to *Hōbōgirin.* Tokyo: Maison Franco-Japonaise, 1978.

Drège, Jean-Pierre. "Les accordéons de Dunhuang." In *Contributions aux études de Touen-houang,* vol. 3. Publications de l'École Française d'Ex-trême-Orient, vol. 135. Paris: École Française d'Extrême-Orient, 1984. Pp. 195–211.

———. "Les bibliothèques en Chine aux temps des manuscrits (jusqu'au Xᵉ siècle)." D. Litt. thesis (Doctorat de l'État), Université de Paris VII, 1988.

———. "Les cahiers des manuscrits de Touen-houang." In *Contributions aux études sur Touen-houang,* vol. 1. Ed. Michel Soymié. Centre de Re-cherches d'Historie et de Philologie de la IVᵉ Section de l'École pra-tique des Hautes Études, Hautes Études Orientales, vol. 10. Geneva: Librairie Droz, 1979. Pp. 17–28.

———. "Étude formelle des manuscrits de Dunhuang conservés à Taipei: datation et authenticité." *BEFEO* 74 (1985):477–84.

———. "Le livre manuscrit et les débuts de la xylographie." *Revue française d'histoire du livre,* n. s., no. 42 (January–March 1984): 19–39.

———. "Notes codicologiques sur les manuscrits de Dunhaung et de Turfan." *BEFEO* 74 (1985):485–504.

———. "Papiers de Dunhuang: essai d'analyse morphologique des ma-nuscrits chinois datés." *TP* 67.3–5 (1981):305–60.

———. "À propos de quelques collections 'nouvelles' des manuscrits de Touen-houang." *Cahiers d'Extrême-Asie* 3 (1987):113–29.

Dudbridge, Glen. "Yü-ch'ih Chiung at An-yang: An Eighth-Century Cult and Its Myths." *AM,* third series, 3.1 (1990):27–50.

Eberhard, Wolfram. "The Leading Families of Ancient Tun-huang." *Sinologica* 4.4 (1956):209–32.

Ebrey, Patricia B. *Confucianism and Family Rituals in Imperial China: A So-cial History of Writing about Rites.* Princeton: Princeton University Press, 1991.

———. "Cremation in Sung China." *American Historical Review* 95. 2 (April 1990):406–28.

Enoki, Kazuo 榎一雄, ed. *Tonkō no rekishi* 敦煌の歴史. *Kōza tonkō* 講座 敦煌, vol. 2. Tokyo: Daizō shuppansha, 1980.

Fang, Hao 方豪. "Sung-tai fo-chiao tui chung-kuo yin-shua chi tsao-chih

chih kung-hsien" 宋代佛教對中國印刷及造紙之貢獻. 1970. Repr.
Chung-kuo t'u-shu shih tzu-liao chi 中國圖書史資料集. Ed. Liu Chia-pi
劉家璧. Hong Kong: Lung-men shu-tien, 1974. Pp. 435–61.

Fang, Kuang-ch'ang 方廣錩. *Fo-chiao ta-tsang-ching shih: pa shih shih-chi* 佛
教大藏經史: 八一十世紀. Peking: Chung-kuo she-hui k'o-hsüeh
ch'u-pan-she, 1991.

———. "Han-wen ta-tsang-ching chih-hao t'an-yüan" 漢文大藏經帙號探
源. *Shih-chieh tsung-chiao yen-chiu* 世界宗教研究 1990.1 (cum. no. 39)
(March 1990): 134–44.

———. "Tu tun-huang fo-tien ching-lu cha-chi" 讀敦煌佛典經錄札記.
Tun-huang-hsüeh chi-k'an 敦煌學輯刊, no. 9 (June 1986): 105–18.

Faure, Bernard. *The Rhetoric of Immediacy: A Cultural Critique of Chan/Zen
Buddhism.*. Princeton: Princeton University Press, 1991.

Filliozat, Jean. "Sur le domaine sémantique de *punya*." In *Indianisme et
Bouddhisme: mélanges offerts à Mgr. Étienne Lamotte*. Publications de
l'Institut Orientalist de Louvain, no. 23. Louvain: Institut Orientaliste de l'Université Catholique de Louvain, 1980. Pp. 101–16.

Forte, Antonino. "Daiji (Chine)." In Demiéville, *Hōbōgirin*, 682–704.

———. "The Relativity of the Concept of Orthodoxy in Chinese Buddhism: Chih-sheng's Indictment of Shih-li and the Proscription of
the *Dharma Mirror Sūtra*." In *Chinese Buddhist Apocrypha*. Ed. Robert E.
Buswell, Jr. Honolulu: University of Hawaii Press, 1990. Pp. 239–50.

Franke, Herbert. "Some Aspects of Chinese Private Historiography in
the Thirteenth and Fourteenth Centuries." In *Historians of China and
Japan*. Ed. W. G. Beasley and E. G. Pulleyblank. London: Oxford
University Press, 1961. Pp. 115–34.

———. "The Taoist Elements in the Buddhist *Great Bear Sūtra (Pei-tou
ching).*" *AM*, third series, 3.1 (1990): 75–112.

Fujieda, Akira 藤枝晃. *Moji no bunka shi* 文字の文化史. Tokyo: Iwanami
shoten, 1971.

———. "Une reconstruction de la 'bibliothèque' de Touen-houang." *JA*
269.1–2 (1981): 65–68.

———. "Shashū kigigun setsudoshi shimatsu" 沙州歸義軍節度使始末.
TG 12.3 (December 1941): 58–98; 12.4 (March 1942): 42–75; 13.1
(June 1942): 63–95; 13.2 (January 1943): 46–98.

———. "Sutain tonkō shūshū e'iri *kannon kyō* sasshi–tonkō ni okeru
mokuhitsu no shiyō" スタイン敦煌蒐集繪入り「觀音經」冊子:
敦煌における木筆の使用. *Bokubi* 墨美 no. 177 (March 1968): 3–8.

———. "Toban shihaiki no tonkō" 吐蕃支配期の敦煌. *TG* 31 (March
1961): 199–292.

———. "Tokka rishi hanshōkaku chinzō in ni tsuite" 德化李氏凡將閣珍
藏印について. *Kyōto kokuritsu hakubutsukan gakusō* 京都國立博物館
學叢, no. 7 (1985): 153–73.

———. "Tonkō no sōni seki" 敦煌の僧尼籍. *TG* 29 (March 1959): 285–
338.

_____. "Tonkō rekijitsu fu" 敦煌曆日譜. *TG* 45 (September 1973): 377–441.

_____. "Tonkō senbutsudō no chūkō" 敦煌千佛洞の中興. *TG* 35 (March 1964): 9–139.

_____. "Tonkō shutsudo no chōan kyūtei shakyō" 敦煌出土の長安宮廷寫經. In *Tsukamoto Zenryū hakase shōju kinen bukkyō shigaku ronshū* 塚本善隆博士頌壽記念佛教史學論集. Ed. Tsukamoto hakase shōju kinenkai 塚本博士頌壽記念會. Kyoto: Tsukamoto hakase shōju kinenkai, 1961. Pp. 647–67.

_____. "The Tun-huang Manuscripts: A General Description." *Zinbun: Memoirs of the Research Institute for Humanistic Studies, Kyoto University* 9 (1966): 1–32; 10 (1969): 17–39.

Fujii, Masao 藤井正雄, ed. *Jōdoshū* 淨土宗. Nihon bukkyō kiso kōza 日本仏教基礎講座, vol. 4. Tokyo: Yūzankaku shuppan, 1979.

Fukui, Fumimasa 福井文雅. "*Hannya shin gyō*" 般若心經. In *Tonkō to chūgoku bukkyō* 敦煌と中國仏教. Ed. Makita Tairyō 牧田諦亮 and Fukui Fumimasa 福井文雅. Kōza tonkō 講座敦煌, vol. 7. Tokyo: Daitō shuppansha, 1984. Pp. 35–80.

Gabain, Annemarie von. "Das Alttürkische." In *Philologiae Turcicae Fundamenta*, vol. 1. Ed. Jean Deny et al. Wiesbaden: Franz Steiner Verlag, 1959. Pp. 21–45.

_____. *Alttürkische Grammatik*, 2d ed. Porta Linguarum Orientalium, vol. 23. Leipzig: Harrassowitz, 1950.

_____. "Die alttürkische Literatur." In *Philologiae Turcicae Fundamenta*, vol. 2. Ed. Louis Bazin et al. Wiesbaden: Franz Steiner Verlag, 1965. Pp. 211–43.

_____. "Kṣitigarbha-Kult in Zentralasien, Buchillustrationen aus den Turfan-Funden." In *Indologen-Tagung: Verhandlungen der Indologischen Arbeitstagung im Museum für Indische Kunst Berlin 7. –9. Oktober 1971*. Ed. Herbert Härtel and Volker Moeller. Wiesbaden: Franz Steiner Verlag, 1973. Pp. 47–71.

_____. *Das Leben im uigurischen Königsreich von Qočo (850–1250)*. 2 vols. Veröffentlichungen der Societas Uralo-Altaica, vol. 6. Wiesbaden: Otto Harrassowitz, 1973.

_____. "The Purgatory of the Buddhist Uighurs: Book Illustrations from Turfan." In *Mahayanist Art after A. D. 900*. Ed. William Watson. Colloquies on Art and Archaeology in Asia, no. 2. London: University of London, School of Oriental and African Studies, and the Percival David Foundation of Chinese Art, 1972. Pp. 25–35.

Gernet, Jacques. *Les aspects économiques du bouddhisme dans la société chinoise du V⁻ au X⁻ siècle*. Saigon: Ecole Française d'Extrême-Orient, 1956.

Giles, Lionel. "Dated Chinese Manuscripts in the Stein Collection." *BSOAS* 7.4 (1935):809–36; 8.1 (1935):1–26; 9.1 (1937):1–26; 9.4 (1939):1023–46; 10.2 (1940):317–44; 11.1 (1943):148–73.

_____. *Descriptive Catalogue of the Chinese Manuscripts from Tunhuang in the British Museum*. London: The British Museum, 1937.

_____. "Tun Huang Lu: Notes on the District of Tun-huang." *Journal of the Royal Asiatic Society of Great Britain and Ireland* (July 1914): 703–28; (January 1915):41–47.

Goldberg, Jonathan. *Writing Matter: From the Hands of the English Renaissance*. Stanford: Stanford University Press, 1990.

Goodwin, Janet R. "Shooing the Dead to Paradise." *Japanese Journal of Religious Studies* 16.1 (March 1989):63–80.

Grapard, Allan G. *The Protocol of the Gods: A Study of the Kasuga Cult in Japanese History*. Berkeley: University of California Press, 1992.

Groot, Jan J. M de. "Le code du Mahāyāna en Chine: son influence sur la vie monacale et sur le monde laïque." *Verhandelingen der Koninklijke Akademie van Wetenschappen te Amsterdam, Afdeeling Letterkunde*, 1.2. Amsterdam: Johannes Müller, 1893.

_____. *Les fêtes annuellement célébrées à Émoui*. Trans. C. G. Chavannes. 2 vols. Annales du Musée Guimet, vols. 11, 12. Paris: Ernest Leroux, 1886.

_____. "Miséricorde envers les animaux dans le bouddhisme chinois." *TP* 3 (1892):466–89.

Hamilton, James R. *Les Ouïghours à l'époque des Cinq Dynasties d'après les documents chinois*. Bibliothèque de l'Institut des Hautes Études Chinoises, vol. 10. Paris: Presses Universitaires de France, 1955.

Harders-Steinhaüser, Marianne. "Mikroskopische Untersuchung einiger früher, ostasiatischer Tun-huang-Papiere." *Das Papier* 23.4 (April 1969):210–12.

Harper, Donald. "Religious Traditions of the Warring States, Ch'in, and Han." In "Chinese Religions: The State of the Field." Forthcoming in *Journal of Asian Studies*.

Hayami, Tasuku 速水侑. *Miroku shinkō: mō hitotsu no jōdo shinkō* 彌勒信仰：もう一つの淨土信仰. Nihonjin no kōdō to shisō 日本人の行動と思想, vol. 12. Tokyo: Hyōronsha, 1971.

Hayashiya, Tomojirō 林屋友次郎. *Kyōroku kenkyū* 經錄研究. Tokyo: Iwanami shoten, 1941.

Heng-ching, Bhikṣu, et al., trans. *Sūtra of the Past Vows of Earth Store Bodhisattva*. The Collected Lectures of Tripitaka Master Hsüan Hua. New York: The Institute for Advanced Studies of World Religions, 1974.

Hirai, Yūkei 平井宥慶. "*Kongō hannya kyō*" 金剛般若經. In *Tonkō to chūgoku bukkyō* 敦煌と中國仏教. Ed. Makita Tairyō 牧田諦亮 and Fukui Fumimasa 福井文雅. Kōza tonkō 講座敦煌, vol. 7. Tokyo: Daitō shuppansha, 1984. Pp. 17–34.

_____. "Tonkō bunsho ni okeru *kongō kyō sho*" 敦煌文書における金剛經疏. In *Shiragi bukkyō kenkyū* 新羅佛教研究. Ed. Kim Chi-gyŏn 金知

見 and Ch'ae In-hwan 蔡印幻. Tokyo: Sankibō busshorin, 1973. Pp. 505–73.

Hirakawa, Akira 平川彰. *Abidatsuma kusharon sakuin* 阿毘達磨倶舍論索引. 3 vols. Tokyo: Daizō shuppan, 1973–1978.

————. *Ritsuzō no kenkyū* 律藏の研究. Tokyo: Sankibō busshorin, 1960.

Hiraoka, Gyōbin 廣川堯敏. "Raisan" 禮讚. In *Tonkō to chūgoku bukkyō* 敦煌と中國仏教. Ed. Makita Tairyō 牧田諦亮 and Fukui Fumimasa 福井文雅. Kōza tonkō 講座敦煌, vol. 7. Tokyo: Daitō shuppansha, 1984. Pp. 425–70.

Hiraoka, Takeo 平岡武夫. *Tōdai no koyomi* 唐代の曆. T'ang Civilization Reference Series, no. 1. Kyoto: Kyōto daigaku jinbun kagaku kenkyūjo, 1954.

Ho, Wai-kam. "Aspects of Chinese Painting from 1100 to 1350." In *Eight Dynasties of Chinese Painting: The Collections of the Nelson Gallery-Atkins Museum, Kansas City, and the Cleveland Museum of Art*. Wai-kam Ho, Sherman E. Lee, Laurence Sickman, and Marc F. Wilson. Cleveland: The Cleveland Museum of Art, 1980. Pp. xxv–xxxiv.

Hou, Ching-lang. "Recherches sur la peinture du portrait en Chine, au début de la dynastie Han." *Arts Asiatiques* 36 (1981): 37–58.

————. "Trésors du monastère Long-hing à Touen-houang: une étude sur le manuscrit P. 3432." In *Nouvelles contributions aux études de Touen-houang*. Ed. Michel Soymié. Centre de Recherches d'Histoire et de Philologie de la IVᶜ Section de l'École pratique des Hautes Études, Hautes Études Orientales, 2:17. Geneva: Librairie Droz, 1981. Pp. 149–68.

Howard, Angela F. "Tang and Song Images of Guanyin from Sichuan." *Orientations* 21.1 (January 1990): 49–57.

Hrdličková, V. "The First Translations of Buddhist Sūtras in Chinese Literature and Their Place in the Development of Story-telling." *Archiv Orientální* 26.1 (1958): 114–44.

Hsiang, Ch'u 項楚. *Wang Fan-chih shih chiao-chu* 王梵志詩校注. Shang-hai: Shang-hai ku-chi ch'u-pan-she,. 1991.

Hsiang, Ta 向達. "Chi tun-huang shih-shih ch'u chin t'ien-fu shih-nien hsieh-pen *Shou Ch'ang hsien ti-ching*" 記敦煌石室出晉天福十年寫本壽昌縣地境. 1944. Repr. Hsiang Ta. *T'ang-tai ch'ang-an yü hsi-yü wen-ming* 唐代長安與西域文明. Peking: Sheng-huo tu-shu hsin-chih san-lien shu-tien, 1957. Pp. 429–42.

————. "Hsi-cheng hsiao-chi: kua sha t'an-wang chih i" 西征小記：瓜沙談往之一. 1950. Repr. Hsiang Ta. *T'ang-tai ch'ang-an yü hsi-yü wen-ming* 唐代長安與西域文明. Peking: Sheng-huo tu-shu hsin-chih san-lien shu-tien, 1957. Pp. 337–72.

————. "T'ang-tai k'an-shu k'ao" 唐代刊書考. 1928. Repr. Hsiang Ta. *T'ang-tai ch'ang-an yü hsi-yü wen-ming* 唐代長安與西域文明. Peking: Sheng-huo tu-shu hsin-chih san-lien shu-tien, 1957. Pp. 117–35.

Hsiao, Teng-fu 蕭登福. *Tun-huang su-wen-hsüeh lun-ts'ung* 敦煌俗文學論叢. Taipei: T'ai-wan shang-wu yin-shu-kuan, 1988.

Hsü, Kuo-lin 許國林. *Tun-huang shih-shih hsieh-ching t'i-chi yü tun-huang tsa-lu* 敦煌石室寫經題記與敦煌雜錄 Shanghai: Commercial Press, 1937.

Hu, Wen-ho 胡文和. "Lun ti-yü pien-hsiang t'u" 論地獄變相圖. *Ssu-ch'uan wen-wu* 四川文物 1988. 2 (cum. no. 18) (1988):20–26.

Huang, Min-chih 黃敏枝. *Sung-tai fo-chiao she-hui ching-chi shih lun-chi* 宋代佛教社會經濟史論集. Shih-hsüeh ts'ung-shu 史學叢書. Taipei: Hsüeh-sheng shu-chü, 1989.

Huang, Yung-wu 黃永武. *Tun-huang pao-tsang* 敦煌寶藏. 140 vols. Taipei: Hsin-wen-feng ch'u-pan-she, 1981–1986.

Hucker, Charles O. *A Dictionary of Official Titles in Imperial China*. Stanford: Stanford University Press, 1985.

Ikeda, On 池田溫. *Chūgoku kodai sekichō kenkyū* 中國古代籍帳研究. Tokyo: Tōkyō daigaku tōyō bunka kenkyūjo, 1979.

_____. *Chūgoku kodai shahon shikigo shūroku* 中國古代寫本識語集錄. Tōyō bunka kenkyūjo sōkan, 東洋文化研究所叢刊, no. 11. Tokyo: Tōkyō daigaku tōyō bunka kenkyūjo, 1990.

Iriya, Yoshitaka 入矢義高. "Ō Bonji ni tsuite" 王梵志について. *Chūgoku bungaku hō* 中國文學報 3 (October 1955): 50–60; 4 (April 1956):19–56.

_____. "Ō Bonji shishū kō" 王梵志詩集考. In *Kanda hakase kanreki kinen: shoshigaku ronshū* 神田博士還曆記念:書誌學論集. Ed. Kanda hakase kanreki kinenkai 神田博士還曆記念會. Kyoto: Nihon shashin yinsatsu kabushiki kaisha, 1957. Pp. 491–501.

Ishida, Mizumaro 石田瑞麿. *Bommō kyō* 梵網經. Butten kōza 佛典講座, vol. 14. Tokyo. Daizō shuppansha, 1971.

_____, trans. "*Bussetsu jizō bosatsu hosshin innen jūō kyō*" 佛説地藏菩薩發心因緣十王經. In Ishida Mizumaro. *Minshū kyōten* 民眾經典. Bukkyō kyōten sen 仏教經典選, vol. 12. Tokyo: Tsukuma shobō, 1986. Pp. 183–277, 337–41.

Ishida, Mosaku 石田茂作. *Shakyō yori mitaru nara chō bukkyō no kenkyū* 寫經より見たる奈良朝佛教の研究. Tōyō bunko ronsō 東洋文庫論叢, vol. 11. Tokyo: Tōyō bunko kankō, 1930.

Izumi, Hōkei 泉芳璟. "*Jūō kyō* no kenkyū" 十王經の研究. *Ōtani gakuhō* 大谷學報 22.4 (December 1941):295–318.

Jan, Yün-hua. "Buddhist Historiography in Sung China." *Zeitschrift der Deutschen Morgenländischen Gesellschaft* 114.2 (1964):360–81.

_____. "Buddhist Relations between India and Sung China." *History of Religions* 6.1 (August 1966):24–42; 6.2 (November 1966):135–68.

_____. "The Chinese Understanding and Assimilation of Karma Doctrine." In *Karma and Rebirth: Post Classical Developments*. Ed. Ronald W. Neufeldt. Albany, NY: SUNY Press, 1986. Pp. 145–68.

_____. *A Chronicle of Buddhism in China: 581–906 A.D.; Translations from*

Monk Chih-p'an's "Fo-tsu t'ung-chi." Santiniketan: Sri Gouranga Press Private, Ltd., 1966.

Jao, Tsung-i. *Airs de Touen-houang (Touen-houang k'iu): textes à chanter des VIIIᵉ–Xᵉ siècles.* Trans. and adapted by Paul Demiéville. Mission Paul Pelliot, Documents Conservées à la Bibliothèque nationale. Paris: Éditions du Centre National de la Recherche Scientifique, 1971.

Jera-Bezard, Robert and Monique Maillard. "Le rôle des bannières et des peintures mobiles dans les rituels du bouddhisme d'Asie centrale." *Arts Asiatiques* 44 (1989):57–67.

Johnson, David. "Communication, Class, and Consciousness in Late Imperial China." In *Popular Culture in Late Imperial China.* Ed. David Johnson, Andrew Nathan, and Evelyn Rawski. Berkeley: University of California Press, 1985. Pp. 34–72.

Jong, J. W. de. Review of Giles, *Descriptive Catalogue of the Chinese Manuscripts from Tunhuang in the British Museum. AM*, n.s., 7.1–2 (1959):228–30.

Jung, Ssu-ch'i 榮思奇. "Tun-huang-hsien po-wu-kuan ts'ang tun-huang i-shu mu-lu" 敦煌縣博物館藏敦煌遺書目錄. In *Tun-huang t'u-lu-fan wen-hsien yen-chiu lun-chi* 敦煌吐魯番文獻研究論集. Ed. Pei-ching ta-hsüeh chung-kuo chung-ku-shih yen-chiu chung-hsin 北京大學中國中古史研究中心. Peking: Pei-ching ta-hsüeh ch'u-pan-she, 1986. Pp. 541–84.

Kajitani, Ryōji 梶谷亮治. "Nihon ni okeru jūō zu no seiritsu to tenkai" 日本における十王圖の成立と展開. *Bukkyō geijutsu* 佛教藝術, no. 97 (July 1974):84–98.

Kajiyama, Yūichi. "Thus Spoke the Blessed One . . ." In *Prajñāpāramitā and Related Systems: Studies in Honour of Edward Conze.* Ed. Lewis Lancaster. Berkeley: University of California Press, 1977. Pp. 93–99.

Kajiyoshi, Kōun 梶芳光運. *Kongō hannya kyō* 金剛般若經. Butten kōza 佛典講座, vol. 6. Tokyo: Daizō shuppan, 1972.

Kamata, Shigeo 鎌田茂雄. *Chūgoku bukkyō shi* 中國仏教史. Tokyo: Iwanami shoten, 1978.

Kanaoka, Shōkō 金岡照光. "Kuan-yü tun-huang pien-wen yü t'ang-tai fo-chiao i-shih chih kuan-hsi: i mu-lien pien-wen yü yü-lan-p'en hui wei chung-hsin" 關於敦煌變文與唐代佛教儀式之關係：以目連變文與盂蘭盆會為中心. Paper delivered at International Symposium on Dunhuang and Turfan Studies, Kuo-chi tun-huang t'u-lu-fan hsüeh-shu hui-i. Hong Kong, June 1987.

_____. "Tonkō bon jigoku bunken kanki—awasete bakukōkutsu no seikaku o ronzu" 敦煌本地獄文獻管窺—併莫高窟の性格を論ず. *Komazawa daigaku bukkyō gakubu ronshū* 駒澤大學佛教學部論集, no. 13 (October 1982), 31–53. Abridged version entitled "Tonkō ni okeru jigoku bunken: tonkō shomin shinkō no ichi yōsō" 敦煌における地獄文獻—敦煌庶民信仰の一樣相. In *Tonkō to chūgokū bukkyō* 敦煌と中國仏教. Ed. Makita Tairyō 牧田諦亮 and Fukui

Fumimasa 福井文雅. Kōza tonkō 講座敦煌, vol. 7. Tokyo: Daitō shuppansha, 1984. Pp. 565–87.

_____. "Tonkō bunken ni mirareru shoshin shobosatsu shinkō no ichi yōsō" 敦煌文獻に見られる諸神諸菩薩信仰の一様相. In *Yoshioka hakase kanreki kinen, dōkyō kenkyū ronshū: dōkyō no shisō to bunka* 吉岡博士還暦記念道教研究論集—道教の思想と文化. Ed. Yoshioka hakase kanreki kinen ronshū kankōkai 吉岡博士還暦記念論集刊行會. Tokyo: Kokusho kankōkai, 1977. Pp. 429–56.

_____. *Tonkō no bungaku* 敦煌の文學. Tokyo: Daizō shuppansha, 1971.

Kanda, Kiichirō 神田喜一郎. *Tonkōgaku gojūnen* 敦煌學五十年. Tokyo: Kyōseisha, 1960.

"Kantōchō hakubutsukan Ōtani ke shuppin mokuroku" 關東廳博物館大谷家出品目錄. In *Shin seiiki ki* 新西域記. Ed. Uehara Yoshitarō 上原芳太郎. 2 vols. Tokyo: Yūkōsha, 1937. Appendix 2b.

Kao, Karl S. Y., ed. *Classical Chinese Tales of the Supernatural and the Fantastic: Selections from the Third to the Tenth Century.* Bloomington, IN: Indiana University Press, 1985.

Kao, Kuo-fan 高國藩. "Lun tun-huang min-chien ch'i-ch'i chai sang-su" 論敦煌民間七七齋喪俗. *Tung-fang wen-hua* 東方文化 25.1 (1987): 106–17.

_____. *Tun-huang min-su-hsüeh* 敦煌民俗學. Chung-kuo min-su wen-hua yen-chiu ts'ung-shu 中國民俗文化研究叢書. Shanghai: Shanghai wen-i ch'u-pan-she, 1989.

Kao, Ming-shih 高明士. "T'ang-tai tun-huang te chiao-yü" 唐代敦煌的教育. *Han-hsüeh yen-chiu* 漢學研究 4.2 (December 1986):231–70.

Karlgren, Bernhard. "Grammata Serica Recensa." *Bulletin of the Museum of Far Eastern Antiquities* 32 (1957):1–332.

Kawahara, Yoshio 河原由雄. "Tonkō ga jizō zu shiryō" 敦煌畫地藏圖資料. *Bukkyō geijutsu* 佛教藝術, no. 97 (July 1974):99–123.

Kobayashi, Taichirō 小林太市郎. "Tōdai no daihi kannon narabi ni honchō ni okeru senju shinkō no kigen ni tsuite" 唐代の大悲觀音ならびに本朝における千手信仰の起源について. In *Kannon shinkō* 觀音信仰. Ed. Hayami Tasuku 速水侑. Minshū shūkyō shi sōsho 民眾宗教史叢書, vol. 7. Tokyo: Yūzankaku shuppan, 1982. Pp. 39–136.

Komazawa daigaku zengaku daijiten hensanjo 駒澤大學禪學大辭典編纂所. *Zengaku daijiten* 禪學大辭典. 3 vols. Tokyo: Taishūkan shoten, 1978.

Kubosō korekushon: tōyō kobijutsu ten 久保惣コレクシヨン：東洋古美術展. Tokyo: Nihon keizai shinbunsha, 1982.

Kwon, Chee-yun. "Ten Kings of Hell." Unpublished paper, December 1988.

Kyōdo, Jikō. "A Study of the Buddhist Manuscripts of Dunhuang: Classification and Method." In *Mibu Taishun Hakase shōju kinen: bukkyō no rekishi to shisō* 壬生台舜博士頌壽記念：仏教の歴史と思想. Ed.

Mibu Taishun Hakase shōju kinen ronbunshū kankōkai 壬生台舜博士頌壽記念論文集刊行會. Tokyo: Daizō shuppansha, 1985.

Lalou, Marcelle. *Inventaire des manuscrits tibétains de Touen-houang conservées à la Bibliothèque nationale (Fonds Pelliot tibétain)*. Vol. 1. Paris: Adrien-Maisonneuve, 1939. Vols. 2–3. Paris: Bibliothèque nationale, 1950, 1961.

Lamotte, Étienne, trans. *Le traité de la grande vertu de sagesse de Nāgārjuna (Mahāprajñāpāramitāśāstra)*. 5 vols. Bibliothèque du Muséon, vol. 18. Publications de l'Institut Orientaliste de Louvain, vols. 2, 12, 24. Louvain-la-Neuve: Institut Orientaliste, 1949–1980.

Lancaster, Lewis R. "An Analysis of the Aṣṭasahāsrikāprajñāpāramitā-sūtra from the Chinese Translations." Ph. D. Dissertation, University of Wisconsin, 1968.

Leach, Edmund R. "Ritual." In *International Encyclopedia of the Social Sciences*. Ed. David L. Sills. 18 vols. New York: Macmillan, 1968–1979.13:520–26.

Ledderose, Lothar. "A King of Hell." In *Suzuki Kei sensei kanreki kinen chūgoku kaiga shi ronshū* 鈴木敬先生還曆記念中國繪畫史論集. Tokyo: Yoshikawa kōbunkan, 1981. Pp. 33–42.

———. "Kings of Hell." *Proceedings of the International Conference on Sinology, Section of History of Arts. Chung-yang yen-chiu-yüan kuo-chi han-hsüeh hui-i lun-wen chi, i-shu shih-tsu* 中央研究院國際漢學會議論文集，藝術史組. Taipei: Academia Sinica, 1981. Pp. 191–97.

———. "The Ten Kings and the Bureaucracy of Hell." Paper presented at the Cleveland International Symposium on Chinese Painting, March 1981. Rev. August 1984.

Legge, James, trans. *Confucian Analects*. In *The Chinese Classics, with a Translation, Critical and Exegetical Notes, Prolegomena, and Copious Indexes*, vol. 1. Hong Kong: London Missionary Society's Printing Office, 1861.

———. *The Works of Mencius*. In *The Chinese Classics, with a Translation, Critical and Exegetical Notes, Prolegomena, and Copious Indexes*, vol. 2. Hong Kong: London Missionary Society's Printing Office, 1861.

Levering, Miriam. "Kṣitigarbha." In *The Encyclopedia of Religion*. Ed. Mircea Eliade. New York: Macmillan, 1987. 8:392–93.

Lévi, Sylvain. "Sur la récitation primitive des textes bouddhiques." *JA*, series 11, 5 (May–June 1915):401–47.

Li, Cheng-yü 李正宇. "T'ang sung shih-tai te tun-huang hsüeh-hsiao" 唐宋時代的敦煌學校. *Tun-huang yen-chiu* 敦煌研究 1986.1 (cum. no. 6) (Febuary 1986):39–47.

Li, Chih-chung 李致忠. "Ku-shu hsüan-feng-chuang k'ao-pien" 古書「旋風裝」考辨. *WW* 1981. 2 (cum. no. 297) (Febuary 1981):75–78.

Li, Fang-kuei. "A Sino-Tibetan Glossary from Tun-huang." *TP* 49.4–5(1962):233–356.

Li, Yü-an 李玉安 and Ch'en Ch'uan-i 陳傳藝. *Chung-kuo ts'ang-shu-chia tz'u-tien* 中國藏書家辭典. Wu-han: Hu-pei chiao-yü ch'u-pan-she, 1989.

Lin, Ts'ung-ming 林聰明. *Tun-huang wen-shu-hsüeh* 敦煌文書學. Tun-huang-hsüeh tao-lun ts'ung-k'an 敦煌學導論叢刊, vol. 1. Taipei: Hsin-wen-feng, 1991.

Lin, Yü-t'ang. *Lin Yutang's Chinese-English Dictionary of Modern Usage.* Hong Kong: The Chinese University of Hong Kong, 1972.

Liu, Chung-kuei 劉忠貴 and Shih P'ing-t'ing 施萍亭. "Tun-huang wen-wu yen-chiu-so ts'ang tun-huang i-shu mu-lu" 敦煌文物研究所藏敦煌遺書目錄. *Wen-wu tzu-liao ts'ung-k'an* 文物資料叢刊 1 (1977): 54–67.

Liu, James T. C. *Ou-yang Hsiu: An Eleventh-Century Neo-Confucianist.* Stanford: Stanford University Press, 1967.

Liu, Kuo-chan 劉國展 and Li Kuei-ying 李桂英. "T'ien-chin-shih i-shu po-wu-kuan ts'ang tun-huang i-shu mu-lu fu ch'uan-shih pen hsieh-ching" 天津市藝術博物館藏敦煌遺書目錄附傳世本寫經. *Tun-huang yen-chiu* 敦煌研究 1987.2 (cum. no. 11) (May 1987): 74–95.

Lo, Chen-yü 羅振玉. "Jih-pen Chü-shih tun-huang chiang-lai tsang-ching mu-lu" 日本橘氏敦煌將來藏經目錄. In Lo Chen-yü. *Hsüeh-t'ang ts'ung-k'o* 學堂叢刻, vol. 10. Chekiang, 1915.

_____. *Lo Hsüeh-t'ang hsien-sheng ch'üan-chi ch'u-pien* 羅雪堂先生全集初編. 20 vols. Taipei: Wen-hua ch'u-pan kung-ssu, 1968.

_____. *Tun-huang shih-shih sui-chin* 敦煌石室碎金. Shanghai: Tung-fang hsüeh-hui, 1925.

Lo, Tsung-t'ao 羅宗濤. *Tun-huang chiang-ching pien-wen yen-chiu* 敦煌講經變文研究. Taipei: Wen shih che ch'u-pan-she, 1972.

_____. *Tun-huang pien-wen she-hui feng-su shih-wu k'ao* 敦煌變文社會風俗事物考. Taipei: Wen shih che ch'u-pan-she, 1974.

Lu, Hsün 魯迅. *Ku hsiao-shuo kou-ch'en* 古小說鉤沈. Peking: Jen-min wen-hsüeh ch'u-pan-she, 1951.

Ma, Heng 馬衡. "Chung-kuo shu-chi chih-tu pien-ch'ien chih yen-chiu" 中國書籍制度變遷之研究. 1926. Repr. *Chung-kuo t'u-shu shih tzu-liao chi* 中國圖書史資料集. Ed. Liu Chia-pi 劉家璧. Hong Kong: Lung-men shu-tien, 1974. Pp. 195–208.

Magnin, Paul. "Pratique religieuse et manuscrits datés." *Cahiers d'Extrême-Asie* 3 (1987):131–41.

Mair, Victor H. "Buddhism and the Rise of the Written Vernacular in China:. The Making of a National Language." Unpublished paper, 1992.

_____. "Lay Students and the Making of Written Vernacular Narrative: An Inventory of Tun-huang Manuscripts." *CHINOPERL Papers*, no. 10 (1981):5–96.

_____. "Oral and Written Aspects of Chinese Sutra Lectures (*Chiang-ching-wen*)." *Han-hsüeh yen-chiu* 漢學研究 4.2 (December 1986): 311–34.

_____. "Records of Transformation Tableaux." *TP* 72.1–3 (1986): 3–43.

_____. "Reflections on the Origins of the Modern Standard Mandarin Place-Name 'Dunhuang'—With an Added Note on the Identity of the Modern Uighur Place-Name 'Turpan.'" In *Chi Hsien-lin chiao-shou pa-shih hua-tan chi-nien lun-wen-chi* 季羨林教授八十華誕紀念論文集. Ed. Li Ching 李錚 and Chiang Chung-hsin 蔣忠信. Nan-ch'ang: Chiang-hsi jen-min ch'u-pan-she, 1991. Pp. 901–54.

_____. *T'ang Transformation Texts: A Study of the Buddhist Contribution to the Rise of Vernacular Fiction and Drama in China.* Harvard-Yenching Institute Monograph Series, no. 28. Cambridge, MA: Harvard University Press, 1989.

_____, trans. *Tun-huang Popular Narratives.* Cambridge: Cambridge University Press, 1983.

Makita, Tairyō 牧田諦亮. "The *Ching-tu san-mei ching* and the Tun-huang Manuscripts." Trans. Antonino Forte. *East and West* 21.3–4 (September–December 1971):351–61.

_____. *Gikyō kenkyū* 疑經研究. Kyoto: Kyōto daigaku jinbun kagaku kenkyūjo, 1976.

_____. "Giso *rokujō* ni tsuite" 義楚六帖について. In Makita Tairyō, ed. *Giso rokujō* 義楚六帖. Koten sōkan 古典叢刊, vol. 2. Kyoto: Hōyū shoten, 1979. Pp. 1–5.

_____. "Kan'yaku butten denshōjō no ichi mondai: *Kongō hannya kyō* no meishi ge ni tsuite" 漢訳仏典伝承上の一問題—金剛般若經の冥司偈について. 1966. Repr. Makita Tairyō, *Chūgoku bukkyō shi kenkyū* 中國仏教史研究, vol. 2. Tokyo: Daitō shuppansha, 1984. Pp. 85–98.

_____. "Sannei to sono jidai" 賛寧とその時代. 1953. Repr. Makita Tairyo. *Chūgoku bukkyō shi kenkyū* 中國仏教史研究, vol. 2. Tokyo: Daitō shuppansha, 1984. Pp. 111–45.

_____. "Sōdai ni okeru bukkyō shigaku no hatten" 宋代における佛教史學の發展. *IBK* 3.2 (March 1955): 631–33.

_____. ed. *Giso rokujō* 義楚六帖. Koten sōkan 古典叢刊, vol. 2. Kyoto: Hōyū shoten, 1979.

Makita, Tairyō 牧田諦亮, and Fukui Fumimasa 福井文雅, eds. *Tonkō to chūgoku bukkyō* 敦煌と中國仏教. Kōza tonkō 講座敦煌, vol. 7. Tokyo: Daito shuppansha, 1984.

Manabe, Kosai 真鍋廣濟. *Jizō bosatsu no kenkyū* 地藏菩薩の研究. Kyoto: Sanmitsudō, 1960.

Matsumoto, Eiichi 松本榮一. "Hibō jizō zō no bunpu" 被帽地藏像の分布. *Tōhō gakuhō* 東方學報 (Tokyo) 3 (December 1932): 141–69.

_____. "Jizō jūō zu to inro bosatsu" 地藏十王圖と引路菩薩. *Kokka* 國華, no. 515 (October 1933): 265–70.

_____. "Tonkō bon *jūō kyō* zuken zakkō" 敦煌本十王經圖卷雜考. *Kokka* 國華, no. 621 (August 1942): 227–35.

_____. *Tonkō ga no kenkyū* 敦煌畫の研究. 2 vols. Tokyo: Tōhō bunka gakuin, 1937.

Matsunaga, Alicia. *The Buddhist Philosophy of Assimilation: The Historical Development of the Honji-Suijaku Theory.* Tokyo: Sophia University, 1969.

Matsunaga, Daigan, and Alicia Matsunaga. *The Buddhist Concept of Hell.* New York: Philosophical Library, 1972.

Matsuura, Shūkō 松浦秀光. *Zenke no sōhō to tsuizen kuyō no kenkyū* 禪家の葬法と追善供養の研究. Tokyo: Sankibō busshorin, 1968.

Men'shikov, Lev N., with M. I. Vorob'eva-Desyatovskaya et al. *Opisanie Kitaiskikh Rukopisei.* 2 vols. Dun'-khuanskogo Fonda Instituta Narodov Azii, Akademiya nauk SSSR. Moscow: Izdatel'stvo Vostochnoi Literatury, 1963, 1967.

Michihata, Ryōshū 道端良秀. *Chūgoku bukkyō shisō shi no kenkyū: chūgoku minshū no bukkyō juyō* 中國仏教思想史の研究：中國民眾の仏教受容. Kyoto: Heiryakuji shoten, 1979.

_____. *Tōdai bukkyō shi no kenkyū* 唐代仏教史の研究. Kyoto: Hōzōkan, 1957.

_____. *Chūgoku bukkyō to shakai fukushi jigyō* 中國仏教と社會福祉事業. 1967. Repr. Michihata Ryōshū. *Michihata Ryōshū chūgoku bukkyō shi zenshū* 道端良秀中國仏教史全集, vol. 11. Tokyo: Shoen, 1985.

Mikkyō jiten hensankai 密教辭典編纂會. *Mikkyō daijiten* 密教大辭典 rev. ed. 6 vols. 1968. Reprint ed., Kyoto: Hōzōkan, 1979.

Mimaki, Katsumi 御牧克巳. "*Daijō muryōju shūyō kyō*" 大乘無量壽宗要經. In *Tonkō to chūgoku bukkyō* 敦煌と中國仏教. Ed. Makita Tairyō 牧田諦亮 and Fukui Fumimasa 福井文雅. *Kōza tonkō* 講座敦煌, vol. 7. Tokyo: Daitō shuppansha, 1984. Pp. 167–72.

Mochizuki, Shinkō 望月信亨. *Bukkyō daijiten* 佛教大辭典, 3d ed. 10 vols. Tokyo: Sekai seiten kankō kyōkai, 1958–1963.

Mori, Shikazō 森鹿三. "Shinshutsu tonkō sekishitsu isho toku ni *su shō ken chikyō* ni tsuite" 新出敦煌石室遺書特に壽昌縣地境について. *Tōyō shi kenkyū* 東洋史研究 10.2 (May 1948):1–15.

Moriyasu, Takao 森安孝夫. "Uiguru to tonkō" ウイグルと敦煌. In *Tonkō no rekishi* 敦煌の歷史. Ed. Enoki Kazuo 榎一雄. *Kōza tonkō* 講座敦煌, vol. 2. Tokyo: Daitō shuppansha, 1980. Pp. 299–338.

Morohashi, Tetsuji 諸橋轍次. *Dai kanwa jiten* 大漢和辭典. 13 vols. Tokyo: Taishūkan shoten, 1957–1960.

Mote, Frederick, and Hung-lam Chu. *Calligraphy and the East Asian Book.* Ed. Howard L. Goodman. Special issue, *Gest Library Journal* 2.2 (Spring 1988).

Murayama, Shūichi 村山修一. *Honji suijaku* 本地垂跡. Tokyo: Yoshikawa kōbunkan, 1974.

_____. *Shinbutsu shūgō shichō* 神仏習合思潮. Tokyo: Heiryakuji shoten, 1957.

Mus, Paul. *La lumière sur les six voies: tableau de la transmigration bouddhique d'après des sources sanskrites, pāli, tibétaines et chinoises en majeure partie inédites*. Travaux et Mémoires de l'Institut d'Ethnologie, Université de Paris, vol. 35. Paris: Institut d'Ethnologie, 1939.

Naba, Toshisada 那波利貞. "Bukkyō shinkō ni motozukite soshiki serare-taru chūbantō godai jidai no shayū ni tsukite" 佛教信仰に基きて組織せられたる中晩唐五代時代の社邑に就きて. 1939. Repr. Naba Toshisada. *Tōdai shakai bunka shi kenkyū* 唐代社會文化史研究. Tokyo: Sōbunsha, 1974. Pp. 575–678.

_____. "Ryōko kō" 梁戸玫. 1938. Repr. Naba Toshisada. *Tōdai shakai bunka shi kenkyū* 唐代社會文化史研究. Tokyo: Sōbunsha, 1974. Pp. 169–94.

_____. "Tōdai no shayū ni tsukite" 唐代の社邑に就きて. 1938. Repr. Naba Toshisada. *Tōdai shakai bunka shi kenkyū* 唐代社會文化史研究. Tokyo: Sōbunsha, 1974. Pp. 459–574.

Nakamura, Fusetsu 中村不折. *Uiki shutsudo bokuhō shohō genryū kō* 禹域出土墨寶書法源流考. Tokyo: Seitō shobō, 1927.

Nakamura, Hajime 中村元. *Bukkyō go daijiten* 佛教語大辭典. 3 vols. Tokyo: Tōkyō shoseki kabushiki kaisha, 1975.

Nakamura, Matae 中村又衛. "Nichiren shōnin no *jūō sandan shō* o yo-mite" 日蓮聖人の十王讃歎鈔を讀みて. *Hokke* 法華 11 (1929): 11–26.

Nakano, Teruo 中野照男. "Chōsen no jizō jūō zu ni tsuite: nihon denrai hon o chūshin to shite" 朝鮮の地蔵十王圖について―日本傳來品を中心として. *Bukkyō geijutsu* 佛教藝術 no. 97 (July 1974):124–39.

Niida, Noboru 仁井田陞. "Tonkō hakken *jūō kyō* zuken ni mietaru keihō shiryō" 敦煌發見十王經圖卷に見えたる刑法史料. *TG* 25.3 (May 1938):63–78.

O, Kwang-kyŏk 吳光燨. "*Kongō hannya kyō shū genki* kenkyū" 金剛般若經集驗記研究. In *Shiragi bukkyō kenkyū* 新羅佛教研究. Ed. Kim Chigyŏn 金知見 and Ch'ae In-hwan 蔡印幻. Tokyo: Sankibō bu-sshorin, 1973. Pp. 471–503.

Oda, Yoshihisa 小田義久. "Godō daishin kō" 五道大神玫. *Tōhō shūkyō* 東方宗教, no. 48 (Oct. 1976): 14–29.

_____. "Tonkō sangaiji no *gen issai nyūzōkyō mokuroku* ni tsuite" 敦煌三界寺の「見一切入藏經目錄」について. *Ryūkoku daigaku ronshū* 龍谷大學論集 nos. 434, 435 (1989): 555–76.

Ōfuchi, Ninji 大淵忍爾. *Tonkō dōkyō* 敦煌道教. Vol. 1: *Mokuroku hen* 目錄編. Vol. 2: *Zuroku hen* 圖錄篇. Tokyo: Fukutake shoten, 1978, 1979.

Ogawa, Kan'ichi 小川貫弌. "*Enraō juki kyō*" 閻羅王授記經. In *Tonkō to chūgoku bukkyō* 敦煌と中國仏教. Ed. Makita Tairyō 牧田諦亮 and Fukui Fumimasa 福井文雅. Kōza tonkō 講座敦煌, vol. 7. Tokyo: Daitō shuppansha, 1984. Pp. 223–39.

_____. "Myōshinji shunkōen shozō sō Hongaku *rekidai hennen shakushi tsugan*" 妙心寺春光院所藏宋本覺[歴代編年釋氏通鑑] In *Tsuka-moto Zenryū hakase shōju kinen bukkyō shigaku ronshū* 塚本善隆博士頌

壽記念佛教史學論集. Ed. Tsukamoto hakase shōju kinenkai 塚本博
士頌壽記念會. Kyoto: Tsukamoto hakase shōju kinenkai, 1961.
Pp. 148–62.

_____. "Shūkan *shakumon shōtō* no seiritsu" 宗鑑釋門正統の成立. *Ryū-
koku shidan* 龍谷史壇 no. 43 (June 1958): 8–24.

_____. "Tonkō butsuji no gakushirō" 敦煌佛寺の學士郎. *Ryūkoku dai-
gaku ronshū* 龍谷大學論集 nos. 400, 401 (March 1973):488–506.

Ogiwara, Unrai 荻原雲來. *Bon kan taiyaku bukkyō jiten: hon'yaku myōgi
taishū* 梵漢對譯佛教辭典:翻譯名義大集. Tokyo: Sankibō, 1959.

_____, and Tsuji Naoshirō 辻直四郎. *Kan'yaku taishō bon wa daijiten* 漢訳
對照梵和大字典, rev. ed. Tokyo: Suzuki gakujutsu zaidan, 1979.

Okabe, Kazuo 岡部和雄. "Tonkō zōkyō mokuroku" 敦煌藏經目錄. In
Tonkō to chūgoku bukkyō 敦煌と中國仏教 Ed. Makita Tairyō 牧田諦
亮 and Fukui Fumimasa 福井文雅. *Kōza tonkō* 講座敦煌, vol. 7.
Tokyo: Daitō shuppansha, 1984. Pp. 297–317.

Ono, Gemmyō 小野玄妙. *Bukkyō kyōten sōron* 佛教經典總論. 1936.
Repr. Ono, *Daijiten*, supplementary volume (vol. 14).

_____. *Bukkyō no bijutsu to rekishi* 佛教の美術と歷史. Tokyo: Kaneo
bun'endō, 1943.

_____. *Bussho kaisetsu daijiten* 佛書解説大辭典. 13 vols. Tokyo: Daitō
shuppansha, 1933–1936.

Osabe, Kazuo 長部和雄. "Tōdai mikkyō ni okeru enra ō to taisan
fukun" 唐代密教における閻羅王と太山府君. In *Dōkyō kenkyū* 道教
研究/*Études Taoïstes*, vol. 4. Ed. Yoshioka Yoshitoyo 吉岡義豐 and
Michel Soymié. Tokyo: Henkyōsha, 1971. Pp. 1–28.

Overmyer, Daniel L. "Buddhism in the Trenches: Attitudes toward Popular Religion in Chinese Scriptures Found at Tun-huang." *HJAS* 50.1
(June 1990):197–222.

Pak, Young-sook. *The Cult of Kṣitigarbha: An Aspect of Korean Buddhist
Painting.* Inaugural dissertation, University of Heidelburg, 1981.

P'an, Chi-hsing 潘吉星. *Chung-kuo tsao-chih chi-shu shih-kao* 中國造紙技
術史稿. Peking: Wen-wu ch'u-pan-she, 1979.

_____. "Tun-huang shih-shih hsieh-ching chih te yen-chiu" 敦煌石室寫
經紙的研究. *WW* 1966.3 (cum. no. 185) (March 1966):39–47.

P'an, Chung-kuei 潘重規. "Kuo-li chung-yang t'u-shu-kuan so-ts'ang
tun-huang chüan-tzu t'i-chi" 國立中央圖書館所藏敦煌卷子題記.
Hsin-ya hsüeh-pao 新亞學報 8.2 (1968):321–73.

Pei-ching t'u-shu-kuan shan-pen-pu 北京圖書館善本部. *Tun-huang chieh-
yü lu hsü-pien* 敦煌劫餘錄續編. Mimeograph, 1981.

Pelliot, Paul. "Pa-li t'u-shu-kuan Tun-huang hsieh-pen shu-mu" 巴黎圖書
館敦煌寫本書目. Trans. Lu Hsiang 陸翔. *Kuo-li pei-p'ing t'u-shu-kuan
kuan-k'an* 國立北平圖書館館刊 7.6 (November–December 1933):
21–72; 8.1 (January–Febuary 1934):37–87.

_____. Review of Waley, *A Catalogue of Paintings Recovered from Tun-huang by Sir Aurel Stein. TP* 28.3–5 (1931):383–413.

Peschard-Erlih, Erika. "Les mondes infernaux et les peintures des six voies dans le Japon bouddhique." 3 vols. Ph.D. dissertation, Institut National des Langues et Civilisations Orientales, Université de la Sorbonne Nouvelle, Paris III, 1991.

Petrucci, Raphael. "Essai sur les peintures bouddhiques de Touen-houang: les maṇḍalas." Part 3 of Appendix E, "Essays on the Buddhist Paintings from the Caves of the Thousand Buddhas, Tun-huang." In Aurel Stein. *Serindia: Detailed Report of Explorations in Central Asia and Westernmost China Carried out under the Orders of H.M. Indian Government.* 5 vols. London: Oxford University Press, 1921. Pp. 1400–28.

Pokorny, Julius. *Indogermanisches etymologisches Wörterbuch.* 2 vols. Bern: Francke Verlag, 1959.

Radcliffe-Brown, A. R. "Religion and Society." In A. R. Radcliffe-Brown. *Structure and Function in Primitive Society.* New York: The Free Press, 1965. Pp. 153–77.

Riboud, Krishna and Gabriel Vial. *Tissus de Touen-houang conservés au Musée Guimet et à la Bibliothèque nationale.* Mission Paul Pelliot, Documents Archéologiques publiés sous les Auspices de l'Académie des Inscriptions et Belles-lettres, vol. 13. Paris: Librairie Adrien-Maisonneuve, 1970.

Roberts, Colin H., and T. C. Skeat. *The Birth of the Codex.* London: Oxford University Press, for the British Academy, 1983.

Robinet, Isabelle. *La révélation du Shangqing dans l'histoire du taoïsme.* 2 vols. Publications de l'Ecole Française d'Extrême-Orient, vol. 137. Paris: École Française d'Extrême-Orient, 1984.

Sakai, Tadao 酒井忠夫. "Jūō shinkō ni kan suru shomondai oyobi *enraō juki kyō*" 十王信仰に關する諸問題及び閻羅王受記經. In *Saitō sensei koki shukuga kinen ronbunshū* 齋藤先生古稀祝賀記念論文集. Ed. Saitō sensei koki shukugakai 齋藤先生古稀祝賀會. Tokyo: Katanae shoin, 1937. Pp. 611–56.

_____. "Taisan shinkō no kenkyū" 太山信仰の研究. *Shichō* 史潮 7.2 (1937):70–118.

Sakurai, Tokutarō 桜井德太郎. *Shinbutsu kōshō shi kenkyū: minzoku ni okeru bunka sesshoku no mondai* 神仏交渉史研究―民俗における文化接觸の問題. Tokyo: Ishikawa Kōbunkan, 1968.

_____. ed. *Jizō shinkō* 地藏信仰. Minshū shūkyō shi sōsho 民眾宗教史叢書, vol. 10. Tokyo: Yūzankaku shuppan, 1983.

Satō, Mitsuo 佐藤密雄. *Ritsuzō* 津藏. Butten kōza·佛典講座, vol. 14. Tokyo: Daizō shuppan, 1972.

Satō, Seijun 佐藤成順. "Chūgoku bukkyō ni okeru rinjū ni matsumeru gyōgi" 中國佛教における臨終にまつめる行儀. In *Tōdō Kyōshun hakase koki kinen jōdoshū tenseki kenkyū* 藤堂恭俊博士古稀記念淨土宗典籍研究. Vol. 1: *Kenkyū hen* 研究篇. Ed. Tōdō Kyōshun hakase koki kinenkai 藤堂恭俊博士古稀記念會. Kyoto: Dōbōsha shuppan, 1988. Pp. 141–75.

Satō, Taishun 佐藤泰舜. "Rikuchō jidai no kannon shinkō" 六朝時代の觀音信仰. In *Kannon shinkō* 觀音信仰. Ed. Hayami Tasuki 速水侑. Minshū shūkyō shi sōsho 民眾宗教史叢書, vol. 7. Tokyo: Yūzankaku shuppan, 1982.

Satō, Tatsugen 佐藤達玄. *Chūgoku bukkyō ni okeru kairitsu no kenkyū* 中國佛教における戒律の研究. Tokyo: Mokujisha, 1986.

Satō, Tetsuei 佐藤哲英. "Tonkō shutsudo Hōshō oshō nembutsu san" 敦煌出土法照和尚念佛讚. In *Rekishi to bijutsu no shomondai* 歷史と美術の諸問題. Ed. Seiiki bunka kenkyūkai 西域文化研究會. Seiiki bunka kenkyū 西域文化研究, vol. 6. Kyoto: Hōzōkan, 1963. Pp. 196–222.

Sawada, Mizuho 沢田瑞穂. *Bukkyō to chūgoku bungaku* 佛教と中國文學. Tokyo: Kokusho kankōkai, 1975.

_____. *Jigoku hen: chūgoku no meikai setsu* 地獄變：中國の冥界説. Kyoto: Hōzōkan, 1968.

Schipper, Kristofer M. *Concordance du Tao-tsang, titres des ouvrages*. Publications de l'École Française d'Extrême-Orient, vol. 102. Paris: École Française d'Extrême-Orient, 1975.

_____. "Taoist Ordination Ranks in the Tun-huang Manuscripts." In *Religion und Philosophie in Ostasien: Festschrift für Hans Steininger zum 65. Geburtstag*. Ed. Gert Naundorf, Karl-Heinz Pohl, and Hans-Hermann Schmidt. Königshausen: Neumann, 1985. Pp. 127–48.

Schmidt-Glintzer, Helwig. *Die Identität der buddhistischen Schule und die Kompilation buddhistischer Universalgeschichten in China*. Münchener Ostasiatische Studien, vol. 26. Wiesbaden: Franz Steiner Verlag, 1982.

Schopen, Gregory. "The Phrase '*sa pṛthivīpradeśaś caityabhūto bhavet*' in the *Vajracchedikā*: Notes on the Cult of the Book in Mahāyāna." *Indo-Iranian Journal* 17.3, 4 (November–December 1975): 147–81.

Séguy, Marie-Rose. "Images xylographiques conservées dans les collections de Touen-houang de la Bibliothèque nationale." In *Contributions aux études sur Touen-houang*, vol. 1. Ed. Michel Soymié. Centre de Recherches d'Histoire et de Philologie de la IVᵉ Section de l'École pratique des Hautes Études, Hautes Études Orientales, vol. 10. Geneva: Librairie Droz, 1979. Pp. 119–34.

Seidel, Anna. "Danda." Forthcoming in Demiéville, ed. *Hōbōgirin*.

_____. "Datsueba." Forthcoming in Demiéville, ed. *Hōbōgirin*.

_____. "Imperial Treasures and Taoist Sacraments: Taoist Roots in the Apocrypha." In *Tantric and Taoist Studies in Honour of R. A. Stein*, vol.2. Ed. Michel Strickmann. *Mélanges chinois et bouddhiques*, vol. 21. Brussells: Institut Belge des Hautes Études Chinoises, 1983. Pp. 291–371.

———. "Traces of Han Religion in Funeral Texts Found in Tombs." In *Dōkyō to shūkyō bunka* 道教と宗教文化. Ed. Akizuki Kan'ei 秋月觀. Tokyo: Hirakawa shuppansha, 1987. Pp. 21–57.

Shiga, Takayoshi 滋賀高義. "Kuyō no tame no tonkō shakyō" 供養のための敦煌寫經 In *Ōtani daigaku shozō tonkō ko shakyō* 大谷大學所藏敦煌古寫經, vol. 2. Ed. Nogami Shunjō 野上俊静. Kyoto: Ōtani daigaku tōyōgaku kenkyūshitsu, 1972. Pp. 77–84.

———. "Tonkō shakyō batsubun yori mita bukkyō shinkō" 敦煌寫經跋文より見た佛教信仰. In *Ōtani daigaku shozō tonkō ko shakyō* 大谷大學所藏敦煌古寫經, vol. 1. Ed. Nogami Shunjō 野上俊静. Kyoto: Ōtani daigaku tōyōgaku kenkyūshitsu, 1965. Pp. 151–56.

Shih, P'ing-t'ing 施萍亭. "I-chien wan-cheng te she-hui feng-su shih tzu-liao: tun-huang sui-pi chih san" 一件完整的社會風俗史資料—敦煌隨筆之三. *Tun-huang yen-chiu* 敦煌研究 1987.2 (cum. no. 11) (May 1987):34–37.

———. "San-chieh ssu, Tao-chen, tun-huang tsang-ching" 三界寺道真敦煌藏經. Unpublished paper, 1991.

Shih-tien yen-wang: Wei-po-ju chüan-tseng 十殿閻王：魏伯儒捐贈. *Ten Kings of Hades: The Vidor Collection.* Taipei: Kuo-li li-shih po-wu-kuan, 1984.

Shih, Wei-hsiang 史葦湘. "Liu Sa-ho yü tun-huang mo-kao-k'u" 劉薩訶與敦煌莫高窟. *WW* 1983.6 (cum. no. 325) (June 1983):5–13.

Shinohara, Hisao 篠原壽雄 and Tanaka Ryōshō 田中良昭, eds. *Tonkō butten to zen*, 敦煌仏典と禪. *Kōza tonkō* 講座敦煌, vol. 8. Tokyo: Daitō shuppansha, 1980.

Soothill, William Edward and Lewis Hodous. *A Dictionary of Chinese Buddhist Terms with Sanskrit and English Equivalents and a Sanskrit-Pali Index.* 1937. Reprint ed. Taipei: Ch'eng-wen Publishing Co., 1976.

Soper, Alexander C., trans. *Kuo Jo-Hsü's Experiences in Painting (T'u-hua Chien-Wen Chih): An Eleventh Century History of Chinese Painting Together with the Chinese Text in Facsimile.* American Council of Learned Societies, Studies in Chinese and Related Civilizations, no. 6. Washington: American Council of Learned Societies, 1951.

Soymié, Michel. "Un calendrier de douze jours par an dans les manuscrits de Touen-houang." *BEFEO* 69 (1981):209–28.

———. "Les dix jours de jeûne de Kṣitigarbha." In *Contributions aux études sur Touen-houang*, vol. 1. Ed. Michel Soymié. Centre de Recherches d'Histoire et de Philologie de la IVᵉ Section de l'École pratique des Hautes Études, Hautes Études Orientales, vol. 10. Geneva: Librairie Droz, 1979. Pp. 135–59.

———. "Les dix jours de jeûne du taoïsme." In *Dōkyō kenkyū ronshū:*

dōkyō no shisō to bunka, Yoshioka hakase kanreki kinen 道教研究論集：道教の思想と文化，吉岡博士還暦記念. Tokyo: Kokusho kankōkai, 1977. Pp. 1–21.

―――. "Jizō no shishi ni tsuite" 地藏の獅子について. *Tōhō shūkyō* 東方宗教 no. 19 (August. 1962):37–52.

―――. "Notes d'iconographie bouddhique: des Vidyārāja et Vajradhara de Touen-houang." *Cahiers d'Extrême-Asie* 3 (1987):9–26.

―――. "Notes d'iconographie chinoise: les acolytes de Ti-tsang." *Arts Asiatiques* 14 (1966):45–78; 16 (1967):141–70.

―――. "Un recueil d'inscriptions sur peintures: le manuscrit P. 3304 verso." In *Nouvelles contributions aux études de Touen-houang*. Ed. Michel Soymié. Centre de Recherches d'Histoire et de Philologie de la IVᵉ Section de l'École pratique des Hautes Études, Hautes Études Orientales, 2:17. Geneva: Librairie Droz, 1981. Pp. 169–204.

―――, ed. *Contributions aux études de Touen-houang*, vol. 3. Publications de l'École Française d'Extrême-Orient, vol. 135. Paris: École Française d'Extrême-Orient, 1984.

Sponberg, Alan, and Helen Hardacre, eds. *Maitreya, the Future Buddha.* Cambridge: Cambridge University Press, 1988.

Stein, Aurel. *Serindia: Detailed Report of Explorations in Central Asia and Westernmost China Carried out under the Orders of H. M. Indian Government.* 5 vols. London: Oxford University Press, 1921.

Strickmann, Michel. "On the Alchemy of T'ao Hung-ching." In *Facets of Taoism: Essays in Chinese Religion.* Ed. Holmes Welch and Anna Seidel. New Haven: Yale University Press, 1979. Pp. 123–92.

―――. "India in the Chinese Looking-Glass." In *The Silk Route and the Diamond Path.* Ed. D. E. Klimburg-Salter. Los Angeles: UCLA Art Council, 1982. Pp. 53–63.

―――. "Magical Medicine: Therapeutic Rituals in East Asian Tradition." Unpublished book manuscript, 1989.

―――. "The Mao Shan Revelations: Taoism and the Aristocracy." *TP* 63.1 (1977):1–64.

―――. *Le taoïsme du Mao chan: chronique d'une révélation.* Mémoires de l'Institut des Hautes Études Chinoises, vol. 17. Paris: Institut des Hautes Études Chinoises, 1981.

Su, Ying-hui 蘇瑩輝. *Tun-huang-hsüeh kai-yao* 敦煌學概要. Taipei: Chung-hua ts'ung-shu pien-pan wei-yüan-hui, 1964.

Sun, Hsiu-shen 孫修身. "Liu Sa-ho ho-shang shih-chi k'ao" 劉薩訶和尚事跡考. In *I-chiu-pa-san-nien ch'üan-kuo tun-huang hsüeh-shu t'ao-lun-hui wen-chi, shih-k'u, i-shu* 1983 年全國敦煌學術討論會文集,石窟藝術, vol. 1. Ed. Tun-huang wen-wu yen-chiu-so 敦煌文物研究所. Lan-chou: Kan-su jen-min ch'u-pan-she, 1987. Pp. 272–310.

―――. "Mo-kao-k'u te fo-chiao shih-chi ku-shih hua" 莫高窟的佛教史跡故事畫. In *Tun-huang mo-kao-k'u* 敦煌莫高窟. 5 vols. Ed. Tun-

huang wen-wu yen-chiu-so 敦煌文物研究所. Chung-kuo shih-k'u
中國石窟. Peking: Wen-wu ch'u-pan-she, 1982–1987. 4:204–13.

Sunayama, Minoru 砂山稔. "Don'yō to *jōdo sanmai kyō*" 曇曜と淨度
三昧經. *Nihon chūgoku gakkai hō* 日本中國學會報 no. 25 (1973):
41–591.

Suzuki, Kei 鈴木敬. *Chūgoku kaiga sōgō zuroku* 中國繪畫總合圖錄.
Comprehensive Illustrated Catalogue of Chinese Paintings. 5 vols. Tokyo:
Tokyo University Press, 1982–1983.

————. *Mindai kaiga shi kenkyū: seppa* 明代繪畫史研究:浙派. Tokyo:
Mokujisha, 1968.

Taishō shinshū daizōkyō sakuin 大正新修大藏經索引. 45 vols. to date.
Tokyo: Taishō shinshū daizōkyō kankōkai, 1940–.

Takao, Giken 高雄義堅. *Sōdai bukkyō shi no kenkyū* 宋代仏教史の研究.
Kyoto: Hyakkaen, 1975.

Tanaka, Hisao 田中久夫. *Bukkyō minzoku to sosen saishi* 仏教民俗と祖
先祭祀. Kyoto: Nagata bunshōdō, 1986.

————. *Sosen saishi no kenkyū* 祖先祭祀の研究. Nihon minzokugaku
kenkyū sōsho 日本民俗學研究叢書. Tokyo: Kōbundō, 1978.

Tanaka, Ichimatsu 田中一松. "Riku Shinchū jūō zu" 陸信忠十王圖.
Kokka 國華 no. 878 (May 1965):27–31.

T'ang, Keng-ou 唐耕耦 and T'ao Hung-chi 陶宏基, eds. *Tun-huang she-
hui ching-chi wen-hsien chen-chi shih-lu* 敦煌社會經濟文獻真蹟釋錄.
5 vols. Peking: Shu-mu wen-hsien ch'u-pan-she, 1986–1990.

Teiser, Stephen F. "Dreamer, Painter, and Guide: Tao-ming's Career in
Hell." Paper presented at the Annual Meeting of the Association for
Asian Studies, April 1988, San Francisco.

————. *The Ghost Festival in Medieval China.* Princeton: Princeton University Press, 1988.

————. "Ghosts and Ancestors in Medieval Chinese Religion: The Yü-
lan-p'en Festival as Mortuary Ritual." *History of Religions* 26.1 (August.
1986):47–67.

————. "The Growth of Purgatory." In *Religion and Society in T'ang and
Sung China.* Ed. Patricia B. Ebrey and Peter N. Gregory. Honolulu:
University of Hawaii Press, 1993.

————. " 'Having Once Died and Returned to Life': Representations of
Hell in Medieval China." *HJAS* 48.2 (December 1988): 433–64.

————. "Hymns for the Dead in the Age of the Mansucript." *Gest Library
Journal* 5.1 (Spring 1992):26–56.

Teng, Ssu-yü, trans. *Family Instructions for the Yen Clan by Yen Chih-t'ui.*
Leiden: E. J. Brill, 1968.

Terasaki, Keidō 寺崎敬道. "Konponsetsu issaiubu ni tsuite no ichi
kōsatsu: *Sankei mujō kyō* no shūkyōteki imi" 根本説一切有部につい
ての一考察:三啓無常經の宗教的意味. *IBK* 39.2 (March 1991):
61–63.

Thompson, Stith. *The Folktale*. 1946. Reprint ed. Berkeley: University of California Press, 1977.

Tohi, Yoshikazu 土肥義和. "Kigigun jidai" 歸義軍時代. In *Tonkō no rekishi* 敦煌の歴史. Ed. Enoki Kazuo 榎一雄. Kōza tonkō 講座敦煌, vol. 2. Tokyo: Daitō shuppansha, 1980. Pp. 233–308.

Tokiwa, Daijō 常盤大定. *Gokan yori sō sei ni itaru yakkyō sōroku* 後漢より宋齊に至る訳經總錄. Tokyo: Kokusho kankōkai, 1973.

Tokuno, Kyoko. "The Evaluation of Indigenous Scriptures in Chinese Buddhist Bibliographical Catalogues." In *Chinese Buddhist Apocrypha*. Ed. Robert E. Buswell, Jr. Honolulu: University of Hawaii Press, 1990. Pp. 31–74.

Tokushi, Yūshō 禿氏祐祥, and Ogawa Kan'ichi 小川貫式. "*Jūō shōshichi kyō* sanzuken no kōzō" 十王生七經讚圖卷の構造. In *Chūō ajia bukkyō to bijutsu* 中央アジア佛教と美術. Ed. Seiiki bunka kenkyūkai 西域文化研究會. Seiiki bunka kenkyū 西域文化研究, vol. 5. Kyoto: Hōzōkan, 1963. Pp. 255–96.

Tōyō bunko tonkō bunken kenkyū iinkai 東洋文庫敦煌文獻研究委員會, ed. *Seiiki shutsudo kanbun bunken bunrui mokuroku* 西域出土漢文文獻分類目錄. Vols. 1 and 2: *Sutain tonkō bunken ryobi kenkyū bunken ni in'yō shōkai seraretaru seiiki shutsudo kanbun bunrui mokuroku shokō, hi bukkyō bunken no bu, komonjorui* スタイン敦煌文獻及び研究文獻に引用紹介せられたる西域出土漢文文獻分類目錄初稿,非佛教文獻之部,古文書類. Tokyo: Tōyō bunko tonkō bunken kenkyū iinkai, 1964, 1967. Vol. 3: *Tonkō bunken bunrui mokuroku, dōkyō no bu* 敦煌文獻分類目錄,道教之部. Ed. Yoshioka Yoshitoyo 吉岡義豊. Tokyo: Tōyō bunko tonkō bunken kenkyū iinkai, 1969. Vol. 4: *Tonkō shutsudo bungaku bunken bunrui mokuroku fu kaisetsu: sutain bon perio bon* 敦煌出土文學文獻分類目錄附解説:スタインペリオ本. Ed. Kanaoka Shōkō 金冈照光. Tokyo: Tōyō bunko tonkō bunken kenkyū iinkai, 1971.

Ts'ai, Yün-ch'en 蔡運辰. *Erh-shih-wu-chung tsang-ching mu-lu tui-chao k'ao-shih* 二十五種藏經目錄對照考釋. Taipei: Hsin-wen-feng ch'u-pan kung-ssu, 1983.

Ts'ao, Shih-pang (Tso, Sze-bong) 曹仕邦. "Lun *shih-men cheng-t'ung* tui chi-chuan t'i-ts'ai te yün-yung" 論釋門正統對紀傳體裁的運用. *Hsin-ya hsüeh-pao* 新亞學報 11 (March 1976):149–222.

Tsuchihashi, Shūkō 土橋秀高. "Sutain shūshū no ju hossai kaigi ni tsuite" スタイン收集の受八齋戒儀について. *IBK* 9.1 (January 1961):217–20.

——. "Tonkō bon ju bosatsu kaigi kō" 敦煌本受菩薩戒儀考. *IBK* 8.1 (January 1960):33–42.

——. "Tonkō bon ni mirareru shuju no bosatsu kaigi: sutain bon o chūshin to shite" 敦煌本にみられる種種の菩薩戒儀—スタイン本を中心として. In *Rekishi to bijutsu no shomondai* 歴史と美術の

諸問題. Ed. Seiiki bunka kenkyūkai 西域文化研究會. Seiiki bunka kenkyū 西域文化研究, vol. 6. Kyoto: Hōzōkan, 1963. Pp. 93–178.

_____. "Tonkō no ritsuzō" 敦煌の律藏. In *Tonkō to chūgoku bukkyō* 敦煌と中國仏教. Ed. Makita Tairyō 牧田諦亮 and Fukui Fumimasa 福井文雅. Kōza tonkō 講座敦煌, vol. 7. Tokyo: Daitō shuppansha, 1984. Pp. 241–77.

_____. "Chūgoku ni okeru konma no hensen: sutain bon o chūshin to shite" 中國における羯磨の變遷:スタイン本を中心として. *TG* 35 (March 1964):439–522.

_____. "Tonkō shutsudo ritten no tokushoku: sutain bon o shu to shite" 敦煌出土律典の特色:スタイン本を主として. *IBK* 7.1 (December 1958):245–49.

Tsukamoto, Zenryū 塚本善隆. "Inro bosatsu shinkō ni tsuite" 引路菩薩信仰に就いて. *TG* 1 (March 1931):130–82.

_____. *Tō chūki no jōdo kyō: toku ni Hōshō zenji no kenkyū* 唐中期の淨土教:特に法照禪師の研究. 1932. Repr. Tsukamoto Zenryū. *Chūgoku jōdo kyō shi kenkyū* 中國淨土教史研究. *Tsukamoto Zenryū chosaku shū* 塚本善隆著作集, vol. 4. Tokyo: Daitō shuppansha, 1976.

Tu, Tou-ch'eng 杜斗城. *Tun-huang-pen fo-shuo shih-wang ching chiao-lu yen-chiu* 敦煌本佛説十王經校錄研究. Lan-chou: Kan-su chiao-yü ch'u-pan-she, 1989.

Tun-huang chüan-tzu, kuo-li chung-yang t'u-shu-kuan ts'ang (國立中央圖書館藏)敦煌卷子. 6 vols. Taipei: Shih-men t'u-shu, 1976.

Tun-huang-hsüeh 敦煌學. Ed. Hsiang-kang hsin-ya yen-chiu-so tun-huang hsüeh-hui 香港新亞研究所敦煌學會. Beg. 1974.

Tun-huang-hsüeh chi-k'an 敦煌學輯刊. Ed. Lan-chou ta-hsüeh tun-huang-hsüeh yen-chiu-tsu 蘭州大學敦煌學研究組. Beg. 1980.

Tun-huang wen-wu yen-chiu-so 敦煌文物研究所, ed. *Tun-huang mo-kao-k'u nei-jung tsung-lu* 敦煌莫高窟内容總錄. Peking: Wen-wu ch'u-pan-she, 1982.

_____, ed. *Tun-huang mo-kao-k'u* 敦煌莫高窟. 5 vols. Chung-kuo shih-k'u 中國石窟. Peking: Wen-wu ch'u-pan-she, 1982–1987.

Tun-huang yen-chiu 敦煌研究. Ed. Tun-huang yen-chiu-yüan 敦煌研究院. Beg. 1982.

Tun-huang yen-chiu-yüan 敦煌研究院, ed. *Tun-huang* 敦煌. Lan-chou: Chiang-su mei-shu ch'u-pan-she, Kan-su jen-min ch'u-pan-she, 1990.

_____, ed. *Tun-huang mo-kao-k'u kung-yang-jen t'i-chi* 敦煌莫高窟供養人題記. Peking: Wen-wu ch'u-pan-she, 1986.

Tung, Tso-pin 董作賓. *Chung-kuo nien-li tsung-p'u* 中國年歷總譜. Hong Kong: Hong Kong University Press, 1960.

_____. "Ta-t'ang t'ung-kuang ssu-nein chü-chu li ho-pi" 大唐同光四年具注曆合璧. *Chung-yang yen-chiu-yüan li-shih yü-yen yen-chiu-so chi-*

k'an 中央研究院歷史語言研究所集刊 30.2 (October 1959): 1043–62.

Twitchett, Denis C. *Financial Administration under the T'ang Dynasty.* 2d ed. Cambridge: Cambridge University Press, 1970.

———. "The Monasteries and China's Economy in Medieval Times." *BSOAS* 19.3 (1957):526–49.

———. "Monastic Estates in T'ang China." *AM*, n.s., 5.2 (1956):123–46.

Tz'u-i 慈怡, ed. *Fo-kuang ta-tz'u-tien* 佛光大辭典. 8 vols. Kao-hsiung: Fo-kuang ch'u-pan-she, 1989.

Uchida, Masao 内田正男. *Koyomi to toki no jiten: nihon no rekihō to jihō* 暦と時の事典：日本の暦法と時法. Tokyo: Yūzankaku, 1986.

Ueyama, Daishun 上山大峻. "Daibankoku daitoku sanzō hōshi shamon Hōjō no kenkyū" 大蕃國大德三藏法師沙門法成の研究. *TG* 38 (March 1967):133–98; 39 (March 1968):119–222.

———. "Donkō to tonkō no bukkyōgaku" 曇曠と敦煌の佛教學. *TG* 35 (March 1964):141–214.

Ui, Hakuju 宇井伯壽. *Yakkyō shi kenkyū* 譯經史研究. Tokyo: Iwanami shoten, 1971.

Van der Loon, Piet. *Taoist Books in the Libraries of the Sung Period: A Critical Study and Index.* Oxford Oriental Institute Monographs, no. 7. London: Ithaca Press, 1984.

Vandier-Nicolas, Nicole. *Bannières et peintures de Touen-houang conservés au Musée Guimet.* Mission Paul Pelliot, Documents Archéologiques Publiés sous les Auspices de l'Académie des Inscriptions et Belles-lettres, vols. 14, 15. Paris: Éditions de la Centre National pour Recherche Scientifique, 1974, 1976.

———. *Śāriputra et les six maîtres d'erreur: facsimile du manuscrit chinois 4524 de la Bibliothèque nationale.* Mission Pelliot en Asie Centrale, Série-In-Quarto. Paris: Imprimerie Nationale, 1954.

Verschuer, Charlotte von. "Le voyage de Jōjin au mont Tiantai." *TP* 77.1–3 (1991):1–48.

Vetch, Hélène. "Lieou Sa-ho et les grottes de Mo-kao." In *Nouvelles contributions aux études de Touen-houang.* Ed. Michel Soymié. Centre de Recherches d'Histoire et de Philologie de la IVᵉ Section de l'École pratique des Hautes Études, Hautes Études Orientales, 2:17. Geneva: Librairie Droz, 1981. Pp. 137–48.

———. "Liu Sahe: traditions et iconographie." In *Les peintures murales et les manuscrits de Dunhuang: colloque franco-chinois organisé par la Fondation Singer-Polignac à Paris, les 21, 22 et 23 février 1983.* Ed. Michel Soymié. Paris: Éditions de la Fondation Singer-Polignac, 1984. Pp. 61–78.

Visser, Marinus Willem de. *The Bodhisattva Ti-tsang (Jizo) in China and Japan.* Berlin: Oesterheld and Co., 1914.

Waley, Arthur. *Catalogue of Paintings Recovered from Tun-huang by Sir Aurel Stein.* London: The British Museum, 1931.

Wang, Chung-min 王重民. *Tun-huang i-shu tsung-mu so-yin* 敦煌遺書
總目索引. Peking: Shang-wu yin-shu-kuan, 1962.

_____. *Tun-huang ku-chi hsü-lu* 敦煌古籍敘錄. 1958. Repr. *Tun-
huang ku-chi hsü-lu hsin-pien* 敦煌古籍敘錄新編. 18 vols. Ed.
Huang Yung-wu 黃永武. Taipei: Hsin-wen-feng ch'u-pan kung-
ssu, 1986.

_____, et al, eds. *Tun-huang pien-wen chi* 敦煌變文集. 2 vols. Peking:
Jen-min wen-hsüeh ch'u-pan-she, 1957.

Wang, Hui-min 王惠民. "Tun-huang shui-yüeh kuan-yin hsiang" 敦
煌水月觀音像. *Tun-huang yen-chiu* 敦煌研究 1987.1 (cum. no.
10) (February 1987):31–38.

Wang, I 汪怡, et al. *Kuo-yü tz'u-tien* 國語辭典 (*Gwoyeu Tsyrdean*), 3d ed.
Rev. by Chao Yüan-jen 趙元任. 4 vols. Taipei: T'ai-wan shang-wu
yin-shu-kuan, 1978.

Wang, Jun-hua (Wong, Yoon-wah) 王潤華. *Ssu-k'ung T'u hsin-lun* 司空
圖新論. Taipei: Tung-ta t'u-shu kung-ssu, 1989.

Wang, Po-min 王伯敏. *Chou Fang* 周昉. Chung-kuo hua-chia
ts'ung-shu 中國畫家叢書. Shanghai: Shang-hai jen-min mei-shu
ch'u-pan-she, 1958.

Wang, Wen-yen 王文顏. *Fo-tien han-i chih yen-chiu* 佛典漢譯之研究.
T'ien-hua fo-hsüeh ts'ung-k'an 天華佛學叢刊, no. 21. Taipei:
T'ien-hua ch'u-pan kung-ssu, 1984.

Watanabe, Hajime 渡邊元. "Kanki aru sō gen butsuga" 款記ある宋
元佛畫. *Bijitsu kenkyū* 美術研究, no. 45 (September 1935):422–
28.

Watanabe, Masako. "An Iconographic Study of 'Ten Kings' Paintings."
M. A. thesis, University of British Columbia, 1984.

Weinstein, Stanley. *Buddhism under the T'ang.* Cambridge: Cambridge
University Press, 1987.

Whitaker, K. P. K. "Tsaur Jyr and the Introduction of *Fannbay* 梵唄
into China." *BSOAS* 20 (1957):585–97.

Whitfield, Roderick. *The Art of Central Asia: The Stein Collection in the British
Museum.* Photographs by Takahashi Bin. 3 vols. Tokyo: Kodansha,
1982–1985.

Wu, Ch'i-yü 吳其昱. "Daibankoku daitoku sanzō hōshi Hōjō den kō"
大蕃國大德三藏法師法成伝考. Trans. Fukui Fumimasa 福井文
雅 and Higuchi Masaru 樋口勝. In *Tonkō to chūgoku bukkyō* 敦煌
と中國仏教. Ed. Makita Tairyō 牧田諦亮 and Fukui Fumimasa
福井文雅. Kōza tonkō 講座敦煌, vol. 7. Tokyo: Daitō shuppansha, 1984. Pp. 383–414.

Wu, Hung. *The Wu Liang Shrine: The Ideology of Early Chinese Pictorial Art.*
Stanford: Stanford University Press, 1989.

Wu, Man-kung 吳曼公. "Tun-huang shih-k'u la-pa jan-teng fen-p'ei
k'u-k'an ming-shu" 敦煌石窟臘八燃燈分配窟龕名數. *WW* 1959.5
(cum. no. 105) (May 1959):49.

Yabuki, Keiki 矢吹慶輝, trans. "*Bussetsu jizō bosatsu hosshin innen jūō kyō*"
佛說地藏菩薩發心因緣十王經. In *Kokuyaku issaikyō, indo senjutsubu*
國譯一切經，印度撰述部, vol. 44. 152 vols. 1929–1936; repr. ed.
Tokyo: Daitō shuppansha, 1969–1979.

———. *Meisha yoin* 鳴沙餘韻. Tokyo: Iwanami shoten, 1930.

———. *Meisha yoin kaisetsu* 鳴沙餘韻解説. Two parts in one vol.
Tokyo: Iwanami shoten, 1933.

———. *Sangai kyō no kenkyū* 三階教の研究. Tokyo: Iwanami shoten,
1927.

Yamaguchi, Zuihō 山口瑞鳳. "Toban shihai jidai" 吐蕃支配時代.
In *Tonkō no rekishi* 敦煌の歴史. Ed. Enoki Kazuo 榎一雄. Kōza tonkō
講座敦煌, vol. 2. Tokyo: Daitō shuppansha, 1980. Pp. 195–232.

Yamazaki, Hiroshi 山崎宏. *Zui tō bukkyō shi no kenkyū* 隋唐佛教史の研究.
Kyoto: Hōzōkan, 1967.

Yao, Ming-ta 姚名達. *Chung-kuo mu-lu-hsüeh shih* 中國目錄學史. Taipei:
T'ai-wan shang-wu yin-shu-kuan, 1957.

Yoshioka, Yoshitoyo 吉岡義豐. "Chūgoku minkan no jigoku jūō shinkō
ni tsuite" 中國民間の地獄十王信仰について. In *Bukkyō bunka
ronshū* 佛教文化論集. Ed. Kawasaki daishi kyōgaku kenkyūjo 川崎
大師教學研究所. Tokyo: Kawasaki daishi heikanji, 1975.

———. *Dōkyō kyōten shi ron* 道教經典史論. Tokyo: Dōkyō kankōkai,
1955.

Zürcher, Erik. "Buddhism and Education in T'ang Times." In *Neo-Confu-
cian Education: The Formative Stage*. Ed. Wm. Theodore de Bary and
John W. Chaffee. Berkeley: University of Calfornia Press, 1989.
Pp. 19–56.

———. *The Buddhist Conquest of China: The Spread and Adaptation of Buddhism in Early Medieval China*, rev. ed. Leiden: E. J. Brill, 1972.

———. "Late Han Vernacular Elements in the Earliest Buddhist
Translations." *Journal of the Chinese Language Teachers Association* 12.3
(October 1977):177–203.

———. "A New Look at the Earliest Chinese Buddhist Texts." In *From
Benares to Beijing: Essays on Buddhism and Chinese Religion in Honour of
Prof. Jan Yün-hua*. Ed. Koichi Shinohara and Gregory Schopen.
Oakville, Ontario: Mosaic Press, 1991. Pp. 277–304.

Index

Index of Manuscripts and Cave Inscriptions

About the Author

STEPHEN F. TEISER currently teaches in the Department of
Religion at Princeton University. His 1988 book, *The Ghost
Festival in Medieval China,* was awarded the prize established
by the American Council of Learned Societies for the best
first book published that year in the field of the history of religions. His articles deal with issues in Chinese religions and
the history of Buddhism. He holds degrees from Oberlin College and Princeton University.